ARGONAUTS OF THE DESERT

Copenhagen International Seminar

General Editor: Thomas L. Thompson and Ingrid Hjelm, both at the University of Copenhagen
Editors: Niels Peter Lemche and Mogens Müller, both at the University of Copenhagen
Language Revision Editor: James West

Other volumes in the series include:

Origin Myths and Holy Places in the Old Testament
A Study of Aetiological Narratives
Łukasz Niesiołowski-Spanò

The Expression 'Son of Man' and the Development of Christology
A History of Interpretation
Mogens Müller

Japheth Ben Ali's Book of Jeremiah
A Critical Edition and Linguistic Analysis of the Judaeo-Arabic Translation
Joshua A. Sabih

Changing Perspectives I
Studies in the History, Literature and Religion of Biblical Israel
John Van Seters

ARGONAUTS OF THE DESERT

STRUCTURAL ANALYSIS OF THE HEBREW BIBLE

PHILIPPE WAJDENBAUM

SHEFFIELD OAKVILLE

Published by Equinox Publishing Ltd.

UK: Unit S3, Kelham House, 3 Lancaster Street, Sheffield, S3 8AF
USA: DBBC, 28 Main Street, Oakville, CT 06779

www.equinoxpub.com

First published 2011

Library of Congress Cataloguing-in-Publication Data
A catalogue record for this book is available from the Library of Congress

ISBN-13:   9781845539245   (hardback)

Typeset and copy-edited by Forthcoming Publications
www.forthpub.com

Printed and bound in the UK by the MPG Books Group

Contents

2.

Exodus 146

3.

Leviticus 172

Acknowledgments

This book is based upon a doctoral dissertation in Social Sciences–Anthropology, completed at the Université Libre de Bruxelles (ULB) in 2008, with the support of a doctoral fellowship granted by the Fonds National de la Recherche Scientifique (FRS-FNRS) of Belgium (2005–2009).

First, I wish warmly to thank my supervisor Professor Michèle Broze, for guiding me and supporting me throughout this research. Her precious advice has helped me to find my way into Greek literature. By being demanding, she pushed me always to search for more, and actually to find more. I thank her for trusting in this project, and I hope that this book is worthy of her trust. I also wish to thank my co-supervisor, Mr. Philippe Jespers, who first suggested that I write a Ph.D. thesis on the Bible using an anthropological approach, after having supervised my Master's thesis.

Professor Thomas L. Thompson kindly accepted an invitation to ask as the examiner of my thesis, and the present book is a result of our encounter. I wish to thank him, first, for the inspiration that his work has given to this research, and especially, along with Professor Niels Peter Lemche, for allowing me to publish these results in the Copenhagen International Seminar series, which is a great honour.

I owe to Professor Yaakov S. Kupitz from the Hebrew University of Jerusalem the knowledge of the deep similarities between Plato's *Laws* and biblical Israel. I am indebted to him for many ideas in the present work, and I wish to express how grateful I am for his precious help.

The first drafts of this book needed considerable revision and improvement, and I offer my sincere thanks to my friends Mr. Noah Maurer, who thoroughly reworked many passages, and Mr. Marc Appels, for patiently correcting my mistakes. I also thank Professor Jim West for his helpful revisions and comments, and Thomas L. Thompson for offering further advice. I wish to thank Dr Duncan Burns for the fine preparation of this book for publication. I also thank Ms. Val Hall of Equinox Publishing.

Professor Jacques Cazeaux has also been a great source of inspiration for this research, and I thank him for also acting as an examiner of my doctoral dissertation. Many teachers at the ULB have shown their interest and support; of these I wish to thank especially Professor Baudouin Decharneux, who was the president of the accompanying committee and member of my panel of examiners; Professor Pierre Petit, who presided at my dissertation's public defence; and Professor Pierre de Maret for his valuable support. All the researchers and professors of the Centre Interdisciplinaire d'Etude des Religions et de la Laïcité (CIERL) have given me precious comments and support. I have learned a lot as well from participating in the sessions of the SIRE (Séminaire Interdisciplinaire de Recherche et d'Etude) organised by Professor Ioanna Papadopoulou. I thank again Professors Michèle Broze and Philippe Talon, for giving me several occasions to present and teach my work to their students and at the Institut des Hautes Etudes de Belgique. I also thank Emanuel Pfoh from the University of La Plata. I thank Professor Françoise Héritier of the Collège de France for her interest in and support of my research. I wish to dedicate this book to the memory of Professor Claude Lévi-Strauss, who will remain my principal source of inspiration and methodology.

Finally, I wish to thank my brothers, my family, all my friends, and the Vismets. I especially wish to thank my parents, who have always supported and encouraged me throughout all my years of studies.

Introduction:
Hypothesis and Thesis

The first hypothesis that underlies this research is: 'Is a structural analysis of the Bible relevant?' The structural analysis developed by Claude Lévi-Strauss invites one to compare the variants of a myth so as to define the rules that led to their transformation. To do so, an anthropologist defines a cultural geographic area in which contacts between populations are proved, and considers that a myth is comprised of all of its variants—meaning that one version alone of a myth is not held to be unique and authentic (as opposed to others which would be considered corruptions). However, Lévi-Strauss shows that the nature of any myth is to reinvent itself through each new speaker who appropriates it. A structuralist will therefore examine all the variants of a myth found in a defined geographic area. For Lévi-Strauss, a comparative analysis of myths coming from populations that have not been in contact throughout history may be done, but is irrelevant, as opposed to a comparative analysis focused on a limited cultural area.[1]

Lévi-Strauss never tried to analyse the Bible with his method, except in a late article from 1988. In this he compared the strange utterance of Zipporah when she circumcised her son (Exod 4:25-26) to a rite of the Bororos from Brazil, but he admitted that the similarity found was only due to a mere coincidence; therefore this article was not meant to convince its audience. Yet, Lévi-Strauss seemed to suggest that a proper structural analysis of the Bible could be done.

If we consider the biblical narratives as mythical (even though they recall some historical events) we can examine all the similar narratives found in the literatures of the neighbouring countries, starting with the closest: Syria (notably, the texts from Ugarit that tell of the mythology and religion which the Bible calls 'Canaanite'[2]), Phoenicia, Egypt and Mesopotamia. Such comparative work has been the object of numerous

1. Claude Lévi-Strauss, 'Exode sur Exode', *L'Homme* 106–107 (1988): 13-23.
2. See André Caquot and Maurice Sznycer, *Ugaritic Religion*, Leiden: Brill, 1980.

studies and publications.[3] The main tendency since the end of the nineteenth century has been to think that the Hebrew Bible was born in an
essentially Semitic literary context, borrowing notably from mythical
themes in Mesopotamian literature. It is commonly agreed upon that the
narratives covering the first eleven chapters of Genesis were inspired by
Babylonian myths about the creation of the world and of humans, the
herb of immortality, the flood and the confusion of tongues—respectively—found in such texts as the *Enuma Elish*, the *Epic of Gilgamesh*
and the *Epic of Enmerkar*. On the other hand, the book of Kings contains
elements that have been confirmed by Assyrian discoveries: some of the
names of the kings of Israel and Judah from the ninth to the sixth century
B.C.E. have been found in Assyrian and Babylonian archives.[4] The
attacks on Samaria by Sargon II in 782 B.C.E. and on Jerusalem by
Nebuchadnezzar in 587 B.C.E. have been confirmed by Assyrian and
Babylonian sources. From this very brief overview it appears that the
connections between biblical and Assyro-Babylonian literatures are
centred both at the beginning of the Bible, in narratives that can be
viewed as myths, as well as at the end of the book of Kings, which tells
of the destruction of the kingdoms of Israel and Judah. From these facts,
it is suggested that the biblical authors had knowledge not only of
Mesopotamian mythology that harkens back to the third millennium
B.C.E., which they used as a source for the prologue of Genesis, but also
of royal archives proper to Judah and Israel that are the principal sources
for the book of Kings. Finally, some biblical laws share obvious similarities with the famous *Code of Hammurabi*.

Biblical books from Genesis to 2 Kings are continuous, and the
narrative chain they form is the object of the present analysis. If Assyro-
Babylonian literatures offer both mythical and historical parallels to the
beginning and end of the Bible, what about all the intermediary narratives (such as the stories of the Patriarchs; slavery in Egypt and the
Exodus; the biblical laws given to the people of Israel during their forty
years of wandering in the desert; the conquest of the land of Canaan and
the division of its territory into twelve tribes, including the period of
dissensions that followed its conquest as related in the book of Judges; as
well as the beginnings of the united monarchy of Saul, David and
Solomon until the division of Israel and Judah into two distinct kingdoms

3. For an anthology of parallels between biblical and Near Eastern texts, see
William Hallo, ed., *The Context of Scripture*. I. *Canonical Compositions from the
Biblical World*, Leiden/New York: Brill, 1997.

4. Israel Finkelstein and Neil Asher Silberman, *The Bible Unearthed*, New York:
Free Press, 2001.

that were eventually annihilated by Assyria and Babylon)? Are these traditions proper to Israel, or can we find similar narratives in the literature of another culture? This work tries to answer these questions through the literature of a country that is not so remote from Judea, a country that since the fourth century B.C.E. spread its culture over the Near East by conquest—Greece.

The second hypothesis, which grew rapidly from the initial observations of this research, is: 'Does Greek literature show narratives from mythical and historical types that would be similar to those found in the Bible, and if so, may we infer that the biblical authors had a direct knowledge of this literature?' From the most exhaustive comparison possible between biblical narratives and Greek mythology, numerous similarities have appeared that cover the vast majority of the narratives in the books of Genesis to 2 Kings, for which very similar equivalents can be found in the texts of the main Greek authors. These strong similarities constitute the main argument of the present work. Three sub-hypotheses result upon reflecting on these resemblances. (1) 'Did the Greeks and the Judeans, as well as neighbours such as the Phoenicians, share a common cultural background—one that would have been appropriated in a different way by each culture?' This would be a hypothesis guided by reservation, one that would only gather these similarities without pre-judging the extent of the diffusion; in considering that the path of this diffusion cannot be traced solely to the texts, and in presuming, rightfully or not, that it would have been an oral—and therefore lost—tradition that birthed these writings. (2) 'There may have been contacts and direct borrowings from one culture to the other, meaning that Greek literature may have appropriated stories from the Semitic world or from the Bible itself, or that the Bible may have taken myths from Greek literature.' If we infer that there has been borrowing, then we should ask if it was via oral transmission or if there are direct links between the texts. Even if the first sub-hypothesis is the easiest to defend, the present work is founded on the second. I have come to believe that the Bible borrows mythical, literary and philosophical themes from the major Greek authors. Therefore, it would have to have been written after the death of one of the most important of them in 350 B.C.E., Plato, and after Judea had become a Greek province after the conquest of Alexander the Great. Over the course of two centuries, Judea was colonised and Hellenised so much that Judeans progressively integrated Greek culture into theirs. Hence, the third sub-hypothesis: (3) 'As the Bible was authored by one or more Judean scholars educated in the Greek fashion—an education based on literature and philosophy—it is a collection of writings that would have appropriated the Greek tradition in order to make it a national epic of the people of Israel'. The Bible is a Hebrew narrative tainted with theological and political philosophy and inspired by the writings of Plato, one that is embellished with Greek myths and adapted to the characters and locations of the Near East.

According to the results of my analysis, the Bible's author(s) wanted to transpose—in the form of their own national epic—the Ideal State of Plato's *Laws*, a political and theological project initiated in the *Republic*. The biblical story, recalling the foundation of a twelve-tribe State that is endowed with divine laws which enable it to live ideally, seems to be inspired by Plato's *Laws*, probably the least known to moderns of the philosopher's dialogues. I will analyse all the similar laws between the two texts as well as their respective theologies, and will try to show that even biblical monotheism owes a debt to Plato. To enhance this platonic utopia with narrative, the biblical author(s) used Greek sources— Herodotus serves as a source for myths and stories in 'historical prose'.[5] Then come the great Greek mythological cycles: the Argonauts, the Heraclean cycle, the Theban cycle and the Trojan cycle by such authors as Homer, Pindar and the Tragedians, whom I believe were sources of inspiration for the Bible. Its author(s) borrowed myths, split them up and transformed them according to need, yet traces were left, perhaps intentionally, of these borrowings. In Genesis–Kings there exists an opposition between the twelve-tribe Ideal State—a State governed only by laws, for which the plan is given by God to Moses and which is founded by Joshua—and the monarchy. The monarchy of the nations in Genesis and Exodus, and that of Israel in the books of Samuel and Kings, is one whose excesses will first bring Israel to division, and then to its eventual downfall. The biblical story from Genesis to Kings is a coherent and unified literary work that can be analysed by itself—as Jacques Cazeaux does[6]—without referring to the alleged sources of the texts, regardless of whether they be 'Yahwist' or 'Elohist', as the documentary hypothesis posits, or even Greek, as in my view. Whatever its sources and dating may be, the Bible is first and foremost a collection of books—extremely well written, and too rarely read.

Whoever authored the Bible seems to have had access to reliable archives about the kings of Israel and Judah, which are regularly referred

5. See Jan-Wim Wesselius, *The Origin of the History of Israel: Herodotus' Histories as Blueprint for the First Books of the Bible*, London/New York: Sheffield Academic Press, 2002.

6. Jacques Cazeaux, *Le partage de minuit, essai sur la Genèse*, Lectio Divina 174, Paris: Cerf, 2006.

to in 1 and 2 Kings. Going back into the past, starting from these historical characters and events, from the fall of Jerusalem and the deportation
of the Judean elite to Babylon, the Bible's author(s) created a masterful
fiction, with the fictitious kings as the first causes of decadence: Saul the
disobedient possessed king, David the adulterous murderer, and Solomon
the apostate tyrant. Before that came the civil war of the tribes against
the smallest of them, Benjamin—which explains why Israel later committed the fatal mistake of asking the prophet Samuel for a king. The
period of the Judges is characterised by a lack of national unity against
external and sometimes internal enemies. Going further back to the
foundation of the twelve-tribe State and the distribution of land via
lottery, a form of immutable cadastre that was transmissible from father
to son, was directly inspired by Plato's *Laws*. Even before that was the
wandering in the desert and Moses receiving the Law. Many of these
laws can also be seen in the works of Plato. However, many biblical laws
do not relate to Greek literature, and can be found in the *Code of Hammurabi*. As we will see, the Exodus—the great departure from Egypt—
also derives from Greek sources. And in Genesis the Patriarchal narratives portray ideal characters faithful to God, who renounce any royal
pretension and even the possession of the Promised Land.[7] By following
the reverse stream of the Bible we are brought back to Babylon, Babel,
as the place of departure of Abram to Canaan in Genesis 11, as well as
the end of the journey for his Judean descendants in 2 Kings 24–25. This
'snake biting its own tail' construction can help us understand the
presence of Babylon at the beginning and the end of the Bible. However,
this does not necessarily mean that the Bible was born during the Exile.
Babylon in the biblical narrative is a character, in the same way as Moses
or Yahweh.

The thesis of a Bible born of the Hellenistic era, one that was inspired
freely but mainly by Greek literature, gives rise to doubtful reactions
because it seems innovative and goes against the dominant theories on
the origins of the Bible. Scholars such as Thomas L. Thompson,[8] Niels
Peter Lemche[9] and Philip R. Davies[10] have recently brought the idea of a
Hellenistic dating of the Bible. This was long deemed unthinkable. They
start from the fact that the Bible only appears in history in the Hellenistic

---

7. Ibid.

8. Thomas L. Thompson, *The Mythic Past*, New York: Basic Books, 1999.

9. Niels Peter Lemche, 'The Old Testament: A Hellenistic Book?', in *Did Moses
Speak Attic?*, ed. L.L. Grabbe, Sheffield: Sheffield Academic Press, 1998, 287-318.

10. Philip R. Davies, *In Search of 'Ancient Israel'*, Sheffield: Sheffield Academic
Press, 1992.

era with certainty, both in terms of manuscripts and of knowledge of the Jews and their religion by Greek and Roman authors. Nothing seems to indicate that the Bible may have existed prior to that period. I will give a detailed analysis of the arguments of the proponents of the different dates further on, and will show how I agree with the latest dating possible. As an anthropologist, I try to adopt Lévi-Strauss' position of the 'view from afar' (*'regard éloigné'*). This consists of looking at society from afar as if it seemed a strange and exotic culture that ethnology has brought to light. During the colonial era it was understood that the ethnologist studied external societies, thought to be primitive, whereas the sociologist studied his own 'evolved' society. Decolonisation has broken down the boundary between these two disciplines, so much so that they are now seen as two specialisations of the same science. I learned the method of structural analysis from Lévi-Strauss' *Mythologiques*. I try to apply this method to the Bible faithfully, being conscious of a necessary adaptation due to the differences of material, a difference that essentially is based on the mode of transmission.[11] I came into the field of biblical studies like an ethnographer would have—filled with preconceived ideas that were learnt from authors who thought they had known the people they studied. Like the ethnographer, I do not believe in the myths and deities of the subjects which I study.

In the nineteenth century, anthropology was guided by evolutionism and ethnocentrism. Westerners thought that the religions of 'exotic' peoples were vain superstition and comparable to pagan religions of antiquity, and that Christianity had overthrown them, revealed as being the religion of the only 'true' god. Anthropologists saw in 'primitive' societies a stage of religious evolution through which the Western world itself had passed—a mixture of animism and polytheism in which Judeo-Christian monotheism was seen as the perfect achievement of religion. As it grew more scientific, anthropology refrained from creating hierarchies between societies and began to praise a form of cultural relativism, along with the growth of atheism in the Western world. Upon this anthropological basis, I consider Judeo-Christian religion (the use of this term will be justified throughout the present work) as I would any other. This must be specified in the very first pages in order to distinguish myself from the 'believing' scholars often involved in biblical studies.

When the ethnologist compares narratives of different tribes of the Americas and concludes that the same myth spread from tribe to tribe

11. See Michèle Broze, Baudouin Decharneux, Philippe Jespers and Danielle Jonckers, *Oralité et Ecriture dans la Pratique du Mythe* (Civilisations 46.1-2; Brussels: Institut de Sociologie de l'Université Libre de Bruxelles, 1998).

with each new speaker transforming it in his own way, it is unlikely that he/she will offend the descendants of the American Natives, who often discover their ancestors' cultures through the works of ethnologists, as colonisation destroyed these cultures over five centuries. It is even more unlikely that he will offend his Western readers. No one will take offence to the 'bird nester' story of the *Mythologiques* being called a myth, variants of which Lévi-Strauss found from one distant end of the American continent to the other. In the same way, no one will be shocked to learn that the Germanic myth of Siegfried's death is a variant of the Greek myth of Achilles' death: both are lethally wounded in the only vulnerable spot of their bodies, the shoulder and heel, respectively. The difficulty of this work is in its confrontation with religious ideology, both Jewish and Christian, which still holds that the Bible is at the least very ancient, if not altogether of divine origin. As a social anthropologist it is my role to take into account the extremely strong resistance a comparative analysis of the Bible with Greek literature will provoke in some quarters; which may explain why a deep comparative analysis of the Bible with Plato's *Laws* has not been done before.

In the following chapters I will give a critical analysis of the theories of the emergence of the Bible. In this general introduction, I will only underline the religious bias that has kept biblical studies in a closed circle; most scholars working in this field are believers, and the most important paradigms still given credit today have been fabricated by theologians, mostly Protestant (Wellhausen, von Rad, etc.). Even though there has been an evolution in recognition of the mythical character of some biblical narratives (at least for the oldest ones in the biblical chronology), they are still thought of as coming from authentic traditions proper to Israel. The idea of a Bible having borrowed its main themes from the Greeks goes against the belief of a divinely revealed text, or of its authentic and original character; the belief that there is something unique in the Bible, something unprecedented, precisely unprecedented by the Greeks. It must be immediately qualified that the biblical text is original and unique, yet its originality and uniqueness derive from how the narratives, most of them coming from the Greek tradition, have been assembled to form a unified and coherent fiction.

Beyond the thesis of the Bible as a Hellenistic-era book—the positive aspect of the study—I will show how biblical criticism has become a new version of the biblical myth—its continuation, that has allowed it to remain almost untouchable until the present, even though biblical criticism took the form of scientific speech that shattered religious dogmas. 'Any myth consists of all of its variants' is a fundamental rule that I apply. To illustrate this rule, Lévi-Strauss used the case of the myth of Oedipus.[12] The version known from Homer's *Odyssey* is no more authentic than Sophocles' *Oedipus the King*, which has become 'canonical', nor is it more 'authentic' than Freud's psychological interpretation. For Lévi-Strauss, the 'Oedipus complex' is not an interpretation that has understood the hidden meaning of the myth; it is only a new version of it to be held among others on the same level. According to Lévi-Strauss, interpretation is neither true nor false; it is a systematically new version of a myth. Only structural analysis pretends to be able to break this infinite circle by explaining the relations between the variants yet always refusing to search for the 'sense' of the myth.[13] I will consider biblical criticism's hypotheses in the same way: the Yahwist and the Deuteronomist, objects of numerous publications, are mythical characters in the same sense as Moses and Josiah. Indeed, the former, although he existed, came to replace the latter in the modern version of the myth of the Bible's origins.

I propose to see the Bible as a 'total social fact', as Marcel Mauss conceived it.[14] A total social fact can never be reduced to one of its aspects, be it religious, economical or social. The Bible is a collection of books, but it is also a social fact beyond its content; for it at the basis of two religions. I will try to show that the relations between Judaism and Christianity are different than what the evolutionist vision of History indicates. If the Hebrew Bible is indeed a Hellenistic book, then Judaism and Christianity both developed in the Greco-Roman and Mediterranean worlds, and both share Hellenic and platonic roots. Neither of them recognise this common background, hidden by their shared belief in the divine inspiration of the Scriptures. The Bible is at the core of two religions, yet it appears that religion may not be a 'response to a need of spirituality' but a very efficient instrument of control of one social class over another. As per Pierre Bourdieu, the use of sacred texts and rituals confers legitimacy upon a dominant class over lower classes. This legitimacy hides a *symbolic violence*, meaning that it reproduces the vision of the dominant class from generation to generation by using 'pious lies', transmitted by a *pedagogic authority*.[15] This never-manifested symbolic violence is at its paroxysm in *the absolute denial of the Greek cultural*

---

12. Lévi-Strauss, 'La structure des mythes', in *Anthropologie structurale*, Paris: Plon, 1958, 235-65.

13. Lévi-Strauss, *Mythologiques*. IV. *L'homme nu*, Paris: Plon, 1971, 577.

14. Marcel Mauss, *Essai sur le don*, Paris: Quadrige P.U.F., 2007.

15. Pierre Bourdieu and Jean-Claude Passeron, *La reproduction, essai pour une théorie générale de l'enseignement*, Paris: Editions de minuit, 1970.

origins of the Judeo-Christian religion. The demonstration of that origin is quite easy, whereas the most difficult part was the conception of the very idea of a Bible inspired by the Greeks, since scholarship on every level—from schools to universities, both secular and religious—had excluded this possibility.

My skills as a social anthropologist then reside in my ability to describe the biblical phenomenon as a whole, not only in finding the literary sources of its theological and political project (the political dialogues of Plato) and in describing how these sources were adapted in the Bible itself, at the centre of the analysis, but also in analysing the conditions of its perpetuation. In the present introduction I will treat apologetic works from Jewish and Christian writers of antiquity, who held that the Bible had inspired Greek literature. This shows how old this question is. I understand fully how the present work may seem *a priori* simplistic. Every day of the four years that this research has lasted I have encountered reactions of doubt, hostility and resentment, but also (and fortunately) of benevolent curiosity. The present work may shatter the most deeply anchored belief in the Western mind, the belief in the Jewish origin of both the Old Testament and of Christianity—which is, according to the New Testament, a heterodox movement founded by Jesus inside Judaism that became an autonomous religion after his death. We will question the reality of this schism between the two religions, rather speaking of a symbiosis than a break. I wish to express in this introduction how I was personally struck, even mortified by these discoveries, not so much because it damages a belief that I do not have, but because of the simplicity of the solution. The thesis is not childish in its simplicity for it is based on the complexity of the biblical text and its many sources. Still, my astonishment that a complete and neutral comparative study of the Bible with Plato had not been done before never decreased. All of this—reactions of hostility to the thesis and its absence during two millennia—are objects of analysis for the anthropologist.

Doubt, hostility and resentment, sometimes expressed verbally and violently, come possibly from the disappointment of my readers and listeners. They can neither conceive that the solution may be that simple nor that none have been known to say it before. Therefore, according to them, I must be wrong and my methodology must be naïve or insufficient. This resistance, this rejection *a priori* of the thesis, coming both from believers and non-believers, is a testament to the total success of the biblical project and the deep attachment of Westerners to the sacredness of the text.

It must be specified in these first pages that no negative judgment is held against the Bible for its relatively late character and its having taken inspiration from the Greeks. On the contrary, I admire the masterpiece that it is, and believe that it may be even better understood in knowing its sources. The anteriority of the Greek sources is never thought to make them superior, nor vice-versa. Any myth consists of all of its variants, therefore *both Plato's Ideal State in the Laws and biblical Israel form one sole myth.* Indeed, the very occultation of the dependence of a text upon the other (the Bible being extremely widespread whereas Plato's *Laws* are read only by a few professional philosophers and some *amateurs* of Plato) is that which I call a myth. The pleasure felt when discovering the sources of a text is like a feeling of strangeness mixed with amusement, similar to encountering the *prototype* of a familiar object such as the bicycle or airplane. The disproportion of the first velocipede's wheels or the fragile aspect of the first plane's wings make us smile, yet we are conscious that both the inventor and the one who perfected the invention were equally necessary.

As we compare Greek classical texts with the Bible we find that they contained its seeds. However, no single verse of the Bible will have been modified after this analysis, meaning that the Bible, whatever may be said about it, remains a unique text with its own literary qualities that can never be reduced to its sources. Contrary to the documentary hypothesis, my demonstration of Greek sources as the Bible's origin aims to prove that it was a sole author who wrote the books from Genesis to Kings. Spinoza's hypothesis was that a single writer created the 'Enneateuch' based on previous 'documents',[16] one that has been reinforced recently by Wesselius and again by Cazeaux, the latter speaking of a final redactor whose weight is nearly as important as that of the author. Not only does my thesis contradict the documentary hypothesis, but it considers that the split between the so-called Pentateuch and the so-called Historical Books (Joshua, Judges, Samuel and Kings) is due merely to the religious tradition and does not reflect the primary intention of their single author.

The tradition that attributes the writing of the Pentateuch to Moses, of the book of Joshua to Joshua, and of most biblical books to biblical characters is somehow relayed by modern theology, as it places the writers later in the biblical chronology—but still within that chronology: King Josiah published Deuteronomy, Jeremiah wrote it, and Ezra published

---

16. Baruch Spinoza, *Traité des autorités théologique et politique*, Paris: Gallimard, 1954.

the Pentateuch in its final form.[17] Therein lies the great paradox of monotheism: the sacred book that reveals the only one God, the Bible, must have been written by multiple writers. To have a single writer for Genesis–Kings, and possibly for other biblical books, contradicts the idea of the transmission of the divine word, and of a tradition proper to a people. It is the brilliant work sprung from a single man's mind, based on the traditions of a foreign country. Of course, the creation of the Bible was not *ex-nihilo*; there were archives of the kings of Israel and Judah, the more or less exclusive cult of Yahweh, some feasts, some eating prohibitions, the weekly period of rest, circumcision, the Hebrew language itself—anything that could not be found in the Greek texts. But this research has led me to question everything that I used to hold as specifically Jewish in the Bible. First it was the narratives, then the laws, and eventually the conception of the divine.

My reasoning is hypothetical-deductive. If I do not deny that there indeed were Mesopotamian, 'Canaanite' and properly Judean influences in the Bible, I will show the Greek influence to be preponderant in terms of both quantity and quality, as the Bible is, in my analysis, a reflection of the political philosophy inspired by Plato's writings, thus making the Hellenistic dating most likely. It must be said that I had no idea about this Greek influence or Hellenistic dating when I started this work in 2004. It came to me after a few months of working on comparing texts. Before that, I held the documentary hypothesis as plausible. Starting with some basic similarities between the Bible and Greek mythology that could be thought as superficial and due to mere chance, I stated that these similarities hid a deeper Greek anchor, and that Greek sources could be found for biblical narratives and laws. This work will show the results obtained, in the order of the biblical narrative, sparing the reader the need to traverse the labyrinth of four years of research. Had the hypothesis of Greek influence been wrong, the findings of parallels would have stopped quickly and I would have had to admit that they were indeed due to chance. But it was not the case, to my great surprise, and to my greatest intellectual satisfaction. The hypothesis has been confirmed by experience, in ways I could never have imagined.

Scientific prudence requires that I avoid insisting on dating and on the sense of diffusion. This work could be presented as an anthology of similarities, many of them unpublished, between Greek and biblical literatures. The pertinence of these similarities is difficult to challenge, I believe. However, it seems hazardous for scholars to want to establish a

17. Richard Elliott Friedman, *Who Wrote the Bible?*, San Francisco: Harper One, 1997.

date in the absence of evidence that would be, according to them, more decisive. I should therefore restrain myself in only showing the similarities, and should conclude that they are due to a common background of the ancient people of the Mediterranean, with a rather consensual dating of the Bible to the Persian era, concomitant of the Classical era in Greece. I could not come to such a minimal conclusion because it would contradict the very grounds of my method of research. It is by rejecting a conservative date and considering the exposure of Judea to Greek culture during the Hellenistic era that these parallels were discovered. To deny the basic hypothesis while keeping the results that confirm it would be senseless. The borrowing from the Greeks and the Hellenistic dating are the only ways to explain the presence of these parallels. This work will attempt to justify how and why.

East of Eden

In the four volumes of the *Mythologiques* Lévi-Strauss goes from South to North America following the lead of the 'bird nester', a myth used as a reference for his survey. Found first among the Bororos of Brazil, Lévi-Strauss finds it all the way to north-western America. Oral transmission of myths of the Americas shows a surprising stability. Even through significant mutations they have maintained their basic structure across millennia of diffusion over the double continent. When I started this research I thought that the same process was at work between Greece and the Near East, and therefore any similarity that I would find would be due to a diffusion of myths based on oral transmission. But we do not know much about oral transmission in antiquity. In Greece the *rhapsodoi* and *aiodoi*, professional musicians and tellers, told myths. Should we believe the same holds for the Near East? Michael Astour has shown in *Hellenosemitica*[18] that Greeks and Phoenicians were in contact at least since the Mycenaean era. Some Phoenicians had settled in Cyprus and maybe also in Cadmea, a region in which the related myths contain characters with Semitic names such as Cadmos (coming from the Semitic root QDM, meaning East). The Theban cycle shows clearly some influence from the Near East. But scholars such as Astour, Cyrus Gordon[19] and Martin L. West[20] tend to think that this diffusion from the East to the

18. Michael Astour, *Hellenosemitica*, Leiden: E.J. Brill, 1965.
19. Cyrus Gordon, *Before the Bible: The Common Background of Greek and Hebrew Civilisations*, London: Collins, 1962.
20. Martin L. West, *The East Face of Helicon*, Oxford/New York: Clarendon Press, 1997.

West can explain both the Semitic elements in Greek mythology *and* Greek parallels with the Bible, the latter being exclusively Semitic according to them. This is a vicious circle in which comparative studies are stuck. These writings have been tremendous sources for finding parallels, but they rarely consider the possibility of a Greek influence on the East, as their titles imply. The Bible is thought of as an intermediary product between Mesopotamian and Greek texts, Judea being in the middle of them. I will show that a linear diffusion only from East to West is not tenable. Greece is surely the inheritor of the Near East regarding many cultural aspects, yet in the Hellenistic era after the conquest of Alexander the Great this heritage was brought back to Asia, its source. As the city-states of mainland Greece were ruined and Rome was emerging, the Hellenised Near East became the new centre of Greek culture. Being in contact with this immense culture, conquered peoples started to write down their own histories and mythologies in Greek; Berossus in Mesopotamia, Manetho in Egypt.

How to apply the structural method, developed for oral myths, to a written text like the Bible? Lévi-Strauss actually worked on written reports from missionaries and ethnologists. The problem does not come from the method, but from the idea that the Bible itself is a report of oral traditions, arranged by scribes. This supposition is not verifiable. We only have the Bible, which is a written and coherent text. Every biblical book from Genesis to 2 Kings is the continuation of the previous one. Since Martin Noth's work,[21] it is generally admitted that books from Deuteronomy to 2 Kings were of the same writer, called the Deuteronomic Historian. It is my opinion that every book from Genesis to 2 Kings is of the same author. His work should be seen as one of literature rather than history, in our modern understanding. The hypothesis of a single writer, already suggested by Spinoza, is rarely followed by biblical scholarship. Classical scholars recognise that Herodotus wrote the nine books of his *Historia* and that Plato wrote at least twenty-eight dialogues. Herodotus and Plato had assistants, surely, yet they were able to conceive of and supervise literary works of that size. Why would the same not hold true for the Bible?

Let us imagine that Judea has now been conquered for a century and its sacerdotal class is now fully Hellenised. A man, educated in the Greek fashion, perhaps in Alexandria, has grown up learning all the Greek 'classics'—Homer, Hesiod, Herodotus, the great Tragic playwrights, Plato—and that which he may have read in the Alexandrian canon,

---

21. Martin Noth, *The Deuteronomistic History*, 2nd ed., Sheffield: Sheffield Academic Press, 1991.

established by Aristophanes of Byzantium and Aristarchus of Samothrace. He wants to create a literary work that can compete with those he has read, one that will give birth to his political and religious utopia, Israel. On the one hand, theories about the origins of the Bible tend to admit that the same writer wrote some books; on the other hand, several books and articles compare Greek myths with the Bible. It is the absence of a synthesis of all these data that is questioned here.

Why Isn't It the Other Way Around?

Why can we not suppose that the Greeks took inspiration from the Bible, or from similar traditions arising in the Near East? The answer is a complicated one, and this entire work will explain why it is believed by the present writer that the Bible was inspired by the Greeks and not the other way around. Here are a few reasons. First, Greek literature is a world of *intertextuality*. All authors refer systematically to their predecessors and contemporaries, more or less openly. Greek authors would not need to draw on the Bible as they already had plenty of other references. Most of the Greek authors were not anonymous, and their existence is assured. While the exception to this is Homer (and perhaps Hesiod as well), whose *Iliad* and *Odyssey* were written at the latest in the sixth century B.C.E., all the other writers such as Pindar, Herodotus, Aeschylus, Sophocles, Euripides, Plato and Apollonius of Rhodes were real people. We do not have the same level of certainty concerning the alleged authors of the Bible in the religious tradition, that is, biblical characters such as Moses and Joshua.

None of these Greek authors had any knowledge of the Bible or of the Jews, not even Herodotus, who travelled through the region he called Palestine in the fifth century B.C.E. He seemed to have ignored Judea, and there is little chance that he plagiarised the Bible without ever admitting it in his work. There is even less chance that all of the Greek writers, separated by centuries, would have taken some stories or laws from the Bible. Yet it was this very idea which was defended by such Fathers of the Church as Clement of Alexandria and Origen, and later by Eusebius of Caesarea. Before them, Hellenised Jewish writers like Philo of Alexandria and Josephus Flavius wrote that Plato had taken inspiration from Moses' Law.

Must we still follow these ancient apologetic writers, or shall we admit that indeed there was a borrowing, though from the biblical writers towards the Greeks? As a structuralist I do not believe that speaking of 'plagiarism' is correct; to use another anachronistic term, the Bible could be seen as a *remake* of the main Greek epics, or even more simply an *homage* to Greek literature.

A second piece of evidence that Greeks did not borrow anything from the Bible is in Greek iconography. Myths were drawn, painted, sculpted and carved, and due to the influence of theatre there has been a parallel evolution in the fifth century B.C.E. of the texts and their visual representations. In contrast, the Bible forbids representation (Exod 20:4). No piece of art prior to the Hellenistic era confirms it as an ancient text. But an argument from silence is not sufficient. One could argue that the very absence of iconography tends to prove that the Bible existed at that time. But then one would have to ignore all the statues of 'Canaanite' deities that have been discovered by archaeologists, such as Asherah, Astarte, Anath and Baal, all the 'army of heaven' that the Bible despises (see King Manasseh's cult of theses gods, 2 Kgs 21:3).[22] The kingdoms of Israel and Judah, which supposedly knew the Pentateuch or its first drafts, were deeply polytheistic. The religion that the Bible calls 'Canaanite' was dominant and the biblical writer retrospectively interpreted that fact as chronic infidelity of Israel to Yahweh, which brought about the eventual destruction of Jerusalem. Again, even if little place is left for the Bible to have existed in this past, one could use the argument of Canaanite deities found in Israel as evidence that the Bible is right, since it condemns these cults!

Leaving archaeology to archaeologists, my work will focus on the apparent borrowing of the biblical writer(s) from Greek authors. A third example is the fact that almost every chapter of the Bible corresponds to a Greek myth, whereas the opposite is not true, Greek mythology being far more extensive than the Bible. The Bible combines too many elements found in the works of distinct Greek authors to think that each of them could have borrowed from the Bible, or that they could have had the same ideas by chance. Either we stand by the Church's Fathers' position, or we admit that the Bible was inspired by the Greeks. As we will see there is no place for another explanation—that of a random diffusion—which would be impossible to trace. The fourth piece of evidence is as long as the present work. Let me simply say for now that all the Greek myths are linked together. The heroes descend from the gods and a complex genealogy links all of them. The synthetic work of Apollodorus' *Library* allows us to find our way in this mythic labyrinth.

22. Raphaël Patai, *The Hebrew Goddess*, Detroit: Wayne State University Press, 1990.

Ariadne's Thread winds through Greek mythology from the birth of the Gods to the war of Troy, the end of the mythic age and the beginnings of the 'historical' era. The Argonauts of Apollonius of Rhodes are the fathers of Homer's heroes. This rich and complex intertextuality has allowed the 'biblical writer' to create an original epic on a fantastic level of sophistication. We will see how the Greek mythical genealogies have been dismantled and reconstructed through a specific filter.

This work will emphasise similar passages from Greek classical texts and the Bible, but the reader may want to consult their wider context as these passages constitute visible crossing points, showing what the biblical writer used directly. However, all that remained unused is still to be considered as a source for his inspiration, his style. I invite the reader to share the sense of vertigo I felt in realising that when reading Homer, Herodotus or Plato, even in translation, one is reading the same lines as 'the author' of the Bible once did.

Claude Lévi-Strauss' Structural Anthropology

To analyse myths I use the method of Claude Lévi-Strauss (developed from the 1950s to the 1990s and borrowing concepts from structural linguistics), which he first applied to kinship studies and later to myths. The four volumes of the *Mythologiques* are the basis of my methodology. The first principle of structural analysis is: 'Any myth consists of all of its variants', as Lévi-Strauss first explained in his article 'La structure des mythes'.[23] No variant is seen to be more genuine than another, and one must try to understand the mechanisms of transformation at play between the variants. Lévi-Strauss explains that myths are beyond language and that the linguistic model is not sufficient to comprehend them, hence he suggests using the musical model. A full score of music can be read in two senses: one reads the melody played by a given instrument from left to right—the diachronic dimension; and when reading from top to bottom, one sees all instruments playing at the same time—the synchronic dimension, harmony. Lévi-Strauss thinks that both dimensions must be taken into account in 'reading' a myth. A myth can be understood in its diachronic dimension but also in its synchronic, whereby one can identify 'packs of relations'. In the case of the Bible, it can be read from the creation of the world to the fall of Jerusalem, but we can also find relations within it that link different stories in a synchronic way. For example, we will see how Jacob and David appear as a single double-sided character.

23. See n. 12.

In comparing myths to language, Lévi-Strauss describes them as being as complex as crystals are in comparison to regular matter; crystals are composed of molecules of matter, but the structure of crystal is comparable to that of molecules. In the same way, myths are composed of language yet are far more complex than language. Lévi-Strauss sees them to be the ultimate manifestation of how the human mind thinks; myths are not a 'primitive' or 'pre-logical' discourse, rather the contrary. Therefore, by questioning the Greek roots of the Bible—the 'ethnologic' level of the problem—we have grounds for a more anthropological reflection about what is at stake in the human mind when creating such stories.

In *Anthropologie stucturale II*, Lévi-Strauss reiterates the fundamental rules of the structural analysis of myths: (1) a myth must never be interpreted on only one level—there is no privileged explanation; (2) a myth must never be interpreted alone, but in relation to other myths that altogether constitute a 'group of transformations' (a notion borrowed from mathematics); and (3) a group of myths must never be interpreted alone, but in relation to groups of myths and to the ethnography of the societies from which they come. Any historical data, political, economical, artistic and so on, must be taken into account.[24] I will remain faithful to these rules, so that in what follows: (1) the Bible will not be interpreted by itself, but will be analysed with regard to it variants, most of which are found in Greek literature; (2) the different variants of the Greek myths will be studied; (3) the data from the Hellenistic era will be taken into account in order to help us understand why and how the borrowing happened.

Along with the musical model, Lévi-Strauss applies the linguistic model to myths. For structural linguistics, language is made up of smaller units such as *phonemes* which alone have no meaning, only in relation to other phonemes. For Lévi-Strauss, '*mythemes*' (small narratives) constitute myths in the same manner. These mythemes have no universal or archetypal meaning, as that meaning can only be found in relation to other mythemes—or more precisely, in the mechanism that transforms these mythemes from one variant to the other. A mytheme has no specific definition but is identified as a recurrent element in myths. According to Lévi-Strauss, a myth tries to answer questions from day-to-day life yet never reaches an answer. Therefore, any new narrator of a myth will change small or large details, so much so that all logical possibilities will be explored until the myth reaches exhaustion. As an

---

24. Lévi-Strauss, *Anthropologie structurale*, 83.

initial biblical example let us take the binding of Isaac in Genesis 22. Abraham is about to sacrifice his son to Yahweh when a divine messenger stops him. Abraham sacrifices a ram, whose horns are embedded in a bush, instead of Isaac.

In the Greek variant, Athamas, King of Boeotia, is about to sacrifice his son Phrixos to Zeus because of a false oracle, when a winged ram sent by Zeus takes Phrixos on its back and brings him safely to Colchis (modern-day Georgia). There, to thank Zeus for saving his life, Phrixos sacrifices the ram and hangs the Golden Fleece on an oak. We can distinguish several mythemes in this narrative: a father is about to sacrifice his son to the supreme god, a divine messenger intervenes, the son is saved, and a ram is sacrificed in his stead. But there is an inversion of one detail: in the Greek version the ram's fleece is hung in a tree after the sacrifice, whereas in the biblical version the ram's horns are embedded in a bush before the sacrifice. This inversion is very typical of mythical transformations, and can be seen as the 'fingerprint' of the tradent. Lévi-Strauss explains these inversions—a myth or a sequence of myths cannot be understood if it were not opposable to other versions of the same myth, or even myths that seem to be the exact opposite.[25] It is the structuralist's task to demonstrate that myths whose resemblances seem superficial or accidental happen to be a part of the same group of transformations.[26] In the case of the Isaac–Phrixos parallel, we will question why biblical scholarship has not judged it relevant to investigate further, even though it is a well-known tale, as we will come to understand that this Greek myth is the prologue of the Argonautic epic—one of the main sources of the Bible.

The Linguistic Argument

I have worked mainly with translated texts, not focusing on linguistic aspects, which may raise doubts among philologists. Lévi-Strauss received the same criticism when writing the *Mythologiques*; because it was impossible for him to learn hundreds of languages, he used translations of Native American myths. What seemed to be a weakness in his method was revealed to be an advantage, as he realised that *a myth is always a translation.*[27] We can never find the original version of a myth since a myth is always a translation of a previous version that either

25.   Claude Lévi-Strauss, *La voie des Masques*, Paris: Plon, 1979, 58.

26.   Claude Lévi-Strauss, *Mythologiques*. I. *Le Cru et le Cuit*, Paris: Plon, 1964, 164.

27.   Lévi-Strauss, *L'homme nu*, 575.

comes from a foreign population or from within the same population—though even then every new teller will appropriate the myth and transform it somehow:

> From an empirical point of view, any myth is at the same time primitive towards itself and derived from other myths. It stands, not within a language or within a culture or sub-culture, but at the articulation point of these with other languages or other cultures. A myth is never from its own language, it is a perspective on another language.[28]

The substance of a myth is not to be found in the style, the narration or syntax, but in the story as it is told. Of course, a philological study would bring more details for interpretation, but it would not modify the semantic content. A myth reduced to its semantic reality shrugs off its linguistic support:

> A language bearing a myth loses pertinence regarding a meaning that is preserved when adapted to different linguistic supports. The signifying function of the myth works not within the language, but above it.[29]

Lévi-Strauss' observations of American myths are relevant in our understanding of the Bible, as we will see that the Bible is not an exception to these principles but is exactly derived from another culture and another language; a 'translation' and adaptation of Greek mythology into Hebrew. Furthermore, the structural analyst can produce a relevant work based on translations. However, though beyond my abilities, a linguistic analysis is necessary and could add an immense amount of information; I only wish to provide an impulse for the field of biblical studies, in order to make a Hellenistic dating of the text acceptable, which would perhaps inspire linguists to consider Greek etymologies for Biblical Hebrew. Though this work will focus on stories and mythical themes—leaving linguistic issues to linguists—a few Greek etymologies will be suggested, but not as determining arguments. Moreover, there is no contemporary biblical version that should be considered more genuine than another. The Masoretic text, the Septuagint, the Qumran Scrolls and so on, are to be held as valid versions of the Bible, and despite their differences they all speak of the birth of Israel from the Patriarchs to the Twelve Tribes up to the Judges and the Kings. The worst translation would not change the fact that the notion of the Twelve Tribes of Israel received lots of land by lottery, transmissible from father to son, and that this is similar to the cadastre of Plato's State in the *Laws*.

28. Ibid., 577, my translation.
29. Ibid., 580, my translation.

The Question of Diffusion and Borrowing
in Histoire de Lynx

When adapting the structural method to the Bible, the question of diffusion arises. Lévi-Strauss admits that similar myths may appear
throughout the world due to the finite cognitive capacities of humans,
though the surveys of Lévi-Strauss in *Mythologiques, La potière
jalouse*[30] and *Histoire de Lynx*[31] are about variants of myths that have
spread across the American continent. In the latter book, Lévi-Strauss is
faced with a puzzle in the chapter *Mythes indiens, contes français:*[32]
some North-American myths share striking similarities with European
tales. At first glance, one would think that themes were borrowed from
the French *coureurs des bois* who ran across Canada during the seventeenth to the nineteenth centuries C.E. and often told tales as an exchange
for hospitality. The stories of *Lynx, Coyote* and *Snanaz* resemble a
mixture of French tales such as *Jean le Teigneux* (a hero with an ugly
skin who then is revealed to be beautiful) and *Jean de l'Ours* (a hero
raised by an animal who ends up marrying the king's daughter), while
the story of twins in *Lodge Boy and Thrown-away* seems to be an exact
copy of the French novel *Valentin et Orson* (two twins separated at
birth—one raised in society [hence in culture], the other in nature—who
become heroes together when they met as adults). We will not go into
the details of these stories here. The issue is that Lévi-Strauss found
similar stories in both South and Central America (among the Bororos
and the Aztecs, respectively) that had been collected by missionaries in
the early sixteenth century C.E.—hence the influence of the *coureurs des
bois* was out of the question. This would mean that American myths
similar to European tales existed before the conquest, and thus that when
both populations came into contact, borrowings were made *because* of
these pre-existing similarities.

Moreover, Lévi-Strauss reminds us that European tales hearken back
to ancient mythology, their roots so extremely old that the Native American ancestors who came from Asia through the Bering Strait, may have
brought these stories with them. Lévi-Strauss asserts that diffusion
should be held plausible even when we are not able to trace it. Such an
extreme example is useful in adapting the method to the Bible and
comparing it with Greek myths and philosophy. As Judea and Greece are
very close, and Greece conquered and colonised Judea for two centuries,

---

30.   Claude Lévi-Strauss, *La potière jalouse*, Paris: Plon, 1985.
31.   Claude Lévi-Strauss, *Histoire de Lynx*, Paris: Plon, 1991.
32.   Ibid., 241-55.

diffusion can be held as almost certain. It is rational to believe that similarities between the Bible and Greek literature are due to exchange and not coincidence. We could easily imagine a common background shared by the people of the Mediterranean, but the fact is that we are dealing with written texts and not oral traditions, so it is more likely to presume that texts were borrowed directly from other texts rather than inventing a 'missing link'—an oral tradition for which we have absolutely no evidence. The myths studied by Lévi-Strauss do come from an oral tradition, as those societies had no written one; therefore he lacked crucial information to understand the path of diffusion. In the case of the Bible, we do have data that allow us to propose sound historical hypotheses. We may think that the biblical author used Greek material to embellish a pre-existing tradition or text, but we will see that there is little space for this tradition to have existed. One may also ask how the structural method is still relevant when speaking of a single author. Lévi-Strauss answers this in '*L'homme nu*': any myth starts from an individual's imagination, but in order to become a myth this individual creation must lose all the qualities that may be related to its author. Therefore, the difference between an individual creation and a myth recognised as such by a community is one of degree, not of kind. In this respect, structural analysis can apply both to collective traditions and works of a single author.[33] Any individual work is a potential myth, yet only its adoption into the collective mode actualises its '*mythism*'. Even if the Bible (from Genesis to Kings) were indeed written by a single author, it only later became the tradition of a people—not the other way around.

Finally comes the question of sense; to give an interpretation of a myth is to create a new variant of it. By refraining from interpretation, Lévi-Strauss adopts philosophical prudence, which allows him to avoid reducing a myth to something else. Even structural analysis is considered to be a new version of a given myth—this having an advantage over the other versions in that it makes explicit what they only implied, and integrates them on a new level where substance and form are definitively fused. Once revealed to itself, the structure of a myth is not capable of any new incarnation; the myth will cease to reproduce itself through infinite new versions.[34] I will remain faithful to these principles, only comparing biblical stories or laws to their Greek counterparts, and will refrain from trying to understand an alleged deeper meaning of the myths. We will then gain an understanding of how their author thought

33. Lévi-Strauss, *L'homme nu*, 560.
34. Ibid., 561.

and from where he took those ideas, but we will not uncover anything about the meaning of life, a deity or the soul. We will only have found the one who remained famous for theorizing these subjects—Plato.

Biblical Criticism and the Documentary Hypothesis

Both Jewish and Christian tradition hold that Moses wrote the five first books of the Bible (called the Torah, Law or Pentateuch) and that this collection is the word of God. But Deuteronomy ends with the death of Moses. In the seventeenth century C.E., in Spinoza's *Theological and Political Treatise*, Spinoza wonders how Moses could have written about his own death in Deuteronomy. According to Spinoza, the biblical author would have used previous documents that he may have compiled. Biblical scholarship sees Spinoza as one of its patrons; however, it seems that the details of Spinoza's arguments were often disregarded. Spinoza thought that the books from Genesis to Kings (including Ruth) were the continuation of one another and had all been written by one single 'historian' using previous 'documents'. The author, Spinoza supposed, was the scribe Ezra. The unity of these books is apparent in their style, language and purpose: to explain how Israel had received its laws and how it had disobeyed them, bringing upon itself the sentence of divine destruction.[35]

Biblical literary criticism was developed later based on the idea that the writers of the Bible 'edited' previous documents, compiled by a final 'redactor'. John Van Seters has recently shown how this idea was imported from the criticism of Homer's texts, and how this method has no scientific basis. Classical scholars abandoned the idea of a Hellenistic redactor of Homer's works; therefore Van Seters asks why biblical scholarship has not yet abandoned the 'documentary hypothesis'.[36] The documentary hypothesis is the theory which supposes that several literary strata, stemming from different sources, are identifiable in the Pentateuch. For example, two narratives of the creation seem to appear in Genesis 1 and 2, so they are thought to come from two different sources. In a series of articles Julius Wellhausen,[37] a Protestant theologian from the nineteenth century, summed up theories that were born in the seventeenth and eighteenth centuries. Wellhausen did not invent the

---

35. Spinoza, *Theological and Political Treatise*, Chapter 8.
36. John Van Seters, *The Edited Bible: The Curious History of the 'Editor' in Biblical Criticism*, Winona Lake, Ind.: Eisenbrauns, 2006.
37. Notably in *Die Composition des Hexateuchs und der historichen Bücher des Alter Testaments*, 4th ed., Berlin, 1963.

documentary hypothesis, but his name remains attached to it. Passages where the biblical god is named 'Yahweh' were said to belong to the 'J' or *Yahwist* source, and where 'Elohim' is used such passages show the influence of the 'E' or *Elohist* source—J and E being the oldest layers. As Deuteronomy is seemingly different from Leviticus in its theology, it may too stem from a different theologian, known as the author of the 'D' source.

The *Priestly* source, 'P', is believed to have written Leviticus and passages concerned with ritual. There would also have been a late final redactor, 'R', who would have compiled all these sources together. But as Van Seters argues, the interpretation of the role of that redactor, or editor, is imprecisely stated from one scholar to another. Most especially, Van Seters sees a contradiction in the role attributed to editors: either they preserve respectfully the works they edit, or they change it according to their own interpretations. G. von Rad[38] contributed to the project and gave a 'personality' to each source: J was born during Solomon's reign, justified David's dynasty, and would belong to Judah; E was born in the ninth or eighth century B.C.E. in the kingdom of Israel and promoted its theology focused on the 'fear of God'; D was born under Josiah in the late seventh century B.C.E., its theology revolving around the covenant with God and the centralisation of the cult in Jerusalem; finally, P was born during the exile and was concerned with the authority of the priests. This vague chronology of the Bible's sources supposed an evolution of Jewish theology that could still be seen in the text. In the nineteenth century evolutionism was the dominant theory, both in biology (as seen with Darwinism) and in religious anthropology (Frazer and Tylor created hierarchies in religions according to their tendency towards monotheism).

According to Thomas Römer, Wellhausen's subjectivity appears in his desire to make the sources composed during the monarchy seem more 'authentic' than the legalist sources, thought of as late and, therefore, more remote from the 'original' Jewish faith. For Römer, this shows a convergence between the results of biblical criticism and the theological options of liberal Protestantism, as, in both cases, the Law is considered to be something secondary.[39] Wellhausen was a man of his time, so naturally he believed monarchic Israel to be closer to the true divine message than the late clergy-governed and post-exilic Judea. For Römer, Wellhausen had been influenced by the unification of Germany by

---

38. G. von Rad, *Théologie de l'Ancien Testament*, Geneva: Labor et Fidès, 1972.

39. Thomas Römer, 'La formation du Pentateuque selon l'exégèse historico-critique', in *Introduction à l'Ancien Testament*, Geneva: Labor et Fidès, 2004, 67-84.

Bismarck in 1871; therefore he was eager to consider monarchy as the best form of government.[40] Wellhausen's aversion to legalist and religious aspects reflected his liberal Protestantism, and the idea that the 'decadence' of the 'true' Jewish religion had prepared for the advent of Jesus, prophet and reformer, who would reinstate the ethical principles of 'true Judaism'. Römer points out how the fundamentals of the documentary hypothesis imply a degeneration of Jewish religion that justifies its replacement by Christianity.

In the 1940s, Martin Noth, a German theologian and exegete, qualified the documentary hypothesis and spoke of a 'Deuteronomistic Historian' who wrote the books of Deuteronomy, Joshua, Judges, Samuel and Kings during the exile.[41] Therefore, there would have been a 'Tetrateuch'— Genesis, Exodus, Leviticus and Numbers—to which the 'Deuteronomistic History' would have been attached. Noth tried to understand how oral traditions, according to him born during the pre-monarchic period, came into their literary form—supposedly the works of the first writers, J and E. But in the absence of evidence, this reconstruction was quite arbitrary. F.M. Cross[42] and R.E. Friedman, adopting Noth, thought that this Deuteronomistic History would have been comprised of two strata, Dtr.1 and Dtr.2, the first dating from Josiah's reign and the second from the exilic period. Friedman believes that these two strata may have been written and revised by the same person, the prophet Jeremiah, initially when he lived at Josiah's court and again later in Egypt during the exile.[43] The 'final redactor', R, who would have combined the Tetrateuch with the Deuteronomistic History and harmonised them, must have been the scribe Ezra. This provides him with a theory that allows one to fall back on Spinoza's initial intuition. Römer sees each of these theories as reflecting their own epoch. Noth conceived of an exiled writer who meditated on the causes of his country's ruin, which was actually his own situation as he fled from Nazi Germany; a lonely historian writing in his office, hating the totalitarian regime that brought about the downfall of his nation.[44] In the same way, Römer sees a typical American optimism in Cross' theory of the first Deuteronomist, who knew the flourishing kingship of Josiah, whose idealised portrait recalled the

---

40.   Thomas Römer, 'L'exégèse et l'air du temps', *Théolib* 16 (2001): 26-39.
41.   Noth, *The Deuteronomistic History*.
42.   Frank Moore Cross, *The Themes of the Book of Kings and the Structure of the Deuteronomistic History*, Cambridge, Mass.: Harvard University Press, 1973.
43.   Friedman, *Who Wrote the Bible?*.
44.   Römer, 'La formation du Pentateuque', 75.

founding fathers of the USA. The second Deuteronomist would therefore have written only the pessimistic passages because he had to explain Jerusalem's fall theologically.

The Collapsing of the Consensus

The most conservative milieus—both Jewish and Christian—first contested the documentary hypothesis, denying that there were distinct sources of the biblical text, which denial thereby conferred more legitimacy upon it among liberal universities. Very little dispute arose among scholars, to the point that the documentary hypothesis slowly grew into a theological dogma that could not be questioned. But in the 1970s, serious criticism of this model appeared, notably from John Van Seters[45] and Thomas L. Thompson.[46] Thompson argued that the Patriarchal traditions could not be dated to as far back as the second millennium B.C.E., but were fictions invented in the sixth century B.C.E. at the earliest; Van Seters argued that biblical narratives should be compared to Greek and Roman historiographies, such as those of Herodotus and Titus Livius. The dissension among scholars grew more intense as none would agree on the exact attribution of biblical passages to the alleged sources of documentary hypothesis. Rolf Rendtorff suggested that the focus be on the final form of the text rather than on its sources, proposing to replace these non-existent 'sources' with the term 'fragments'—big narrative units—like Genesis 1–11, Genesis 12–50, and Exodus 1–15, and so on.[47] As Römer comments, the aforementioned authors precipitated a 'crisis of the Pentateuch' that led to a period of anarchy such that no new consensus has arisen even today. By demolishing the evolutionary model of the documentary hypothesis, biblical studies entered the post-modern era.[48] Römer divides the field into four main streams: the 'traditionalists', who still hold the documentary hypothesis as valid; the 'progressives', who also maintain the model but suggest later dates for the sources; the 'post-moderns', who admit the existence of divergent theologies in the Pentateuch but reject the evolutionist model; and the 'pragmatics', who think that the diachronic reconstitution of the sources is too uncertain,

---

45. John Van Seters, *Abraham in History and Tradition*, New Haven/London: Yale University Press, 1975.

46. Thomas L. Thompson, *The Historicity of Patriarchal Narratives*, BZAW 133, Berlin/New York: W. de Gruyter, 1974.

47. Rolf Rendtorff, 'The "Yahwist" as a Theologian? The Dilemma of Pentateuchal Criticism', *JSOT* 3 (1976): 2-9.

48. Römer, 'La formation du Pentateuque', 82.

and suggest focusing on the final form, taking their inspiration from structuralist methods. Pierre Bordreuil and Françoise Briquel-Chatonnet lament that today no one agrees, so that there are as many theories about the origins of the Bible as there are scholars.[49] Flemming A.J. Nielsen argues that since all the variants of the documentary hypothesis are mutually exclusive, none can be verifiable or scientific.[50]

Keith Whitelam even speaks of a 'collapsing of the consensus' in biblical studies since the 1980s.[51] According to him, biblical scholars have invented an ancient Israel by projecting their way of thinking onto the past; the Bible was the work of archivists of the State, who wrote only history. Biblical scholars tend to present themselves as their spiritual heirs, seen as being objective and pious. These scholars can be viewed almost as a new clergy, whose dogma is the documentary hypothesis. Whitelam bases his criticism on Edward Said's *Orientalism*,[52] one of the first works of post-colonial studies. Said demonstrated how the 'Orient' was a scholarly invention opposed to the Western world and serving a colonial agenda. But Said's work did not examine how oriental studies were used to recreate a past for ancient Israel. Whitelam shows that one does not need to study the Bedouins to understand Abraham's character, as he is fictitious. Israeli-Palestinian archaeology has long been used with the intent of legitimizing the modern State of Israel. For example, the pacific infiltration of the first Israelites in Canaan, as imagined by Albrecht Alt, reflected, according to Whitelam, the actual immigration of Jews during the 1920s in British-protected Palestine and not any event that took place in the second millennium B.C.E. Biblical studies are rarely free of ideology, and Whitelam calls for more neutrality. He calls 'biblical archaeology' the 'quest of the West for itself', since the authenticity of the Old Testament is the pre-condition of Jesus' divinity.

Many scholars thus agree that there is no more agreement, that all previous models have reached their limits. From this quick overview of the history of biblical scholarship we see that it has long remained closed to comparative studies with Greek literature. When we come to compare

49. Pierre Bordreuil and Françoise Briquel-Chatonnet, *Le temps de la Bible*, Paris: Gallimard, 2000, 15.

50. Flemming A.J. Nielsen, *The Tragedy in History, Herodotus and the Deuteronomistic History*, Sheffield: Sheffield Academic Press, 1997.

51. Keith Whitelam, *The Invention of Ancient Israel: The Silencing of Palestinian History*, Sheffield: Sheffield Academic Press, 1997.

52. Edward Said, *L'Orientalisme—L'Orient créé par l'Occident*, Paris: Seuil, 1997.

Plato's *Laws* and Herodotus' *Histories* with biblical laws and stories, these debates over which came first in the Bible—the laws or the stories—will appear quite futile. Römer pointed out the ideologies behind the most influential paradigms, but one could ask what 'ideology' has prevented biblical scholars from comparing the Bible with a text so obviously similar to it, Plato's *Laws*. We will understand that, prior to the Bible, there never were any sources identified as J, E, D or P. Yet, I believe Spinoza's intuition was right—the single author of Genesis–Kings did use 'documents'. But, most of these documents (except for the annals of the kings of Israel and Judah[53]) had never really been lost: they are the Greek classical texts. Even though my theory contradicts the documentary hypothesis, it does indicate that there were sources that preceded the Bible, so it could be called, quite ironically, the 'Hellenic documentary hypothesis'. The main difference with the traditional hypothesis is that with mine I am able to render these sources, which allows me to break the logical circle in which biblical scholarship has been held for centuries, which sought the Bible's sources only within the Bible itself. Moreover, the sources are not considered to be previous authentic sacred texts that would have been edited by redactors, but simply as *sources of inspiration* for an original literary work.

We have seen how the great paradigms of Wellhausen and Noth reflected their political situations unintentionally. By reading the Bible, we can see that it tells the story of political change. First the twelve-tribe Ideal State was founded, governed only by the law (Joshua), but because that organisation was not tenable (Judges) a monarchy was instituted (Samuel), which caused the country to split and eventually fall (Kings). None of these periods is held to be more representative of the 'true' Israel than another. The opposition between the 'nomocratic' State and the monarchic State stands at the core of the narration imagined by the biblical writer; which we will argue is based on Plato's political dialogues—the *Statesman* (criticism of tyranny), the *Republic* (foundation of an imaginary State, being the definition of justice), the *Laws* (foundation of a more concrete State, as opposed to the abstract *Republic*) and the *Critias* (or the *Atlantis*, the myth of an Ideal State destroyed by Zeus because its kings gave up the divine laws received by their ancestors).

---

53. References to the annals of the Kings of Israel and Judah in the book of Kings may reflect a literary technique, itself borrowed from Greek literature. See Katherine Stott, *Why Did They Write This Way? Reflections on References to Written Documents in the Hebrew Bible and Ancient Literature*, Library of Hebrew Bible/ Old Testament Studies 492; New York: T&T Clark International, 2008.

We will find very accurate parallels that make that hypothesis certain. Therefore one must ask why such a comparative study with Plato has not been done before. The Judeo-Christian religion, still present in modern society, is based on the Bible and even though movements of secularisation and laicisation have diminished its weight it still remains the major moral reference point. As the philosopher Michel Onfray stated, even if the practising of religion is in constant diminution there exists a Judeo-Christian *episteme* (as Michel Foucault would call it) that actually reinforces itself as religion becomes less visible.[54] As Onfray explains, the very fact that religion becomes more and more abstract and private—detached from ritual and mythology—is what makes it more powerful than ever. The weight of religion is most likely the prime explanation for understanding why biblical scholarship has long been focused on trying to prove the authenticity of the Bible. Indeed, most biblical scholars come into that field guided by faith.

Most faculties dealing with biblical scholarship are theology faculties; therefore they seek a rational version of the divine inspiration of the Bible. Even though the documentary hypothesis seemed to shatter the belief in the Bible being inspired by God and even though it was originally decried by the Jewish and Christian faiths, it slowly became acceptable to believers; in fact, Pope Pius XII explicitly promoted it in his encyclical of 1943.[55]

The *Letter of Aristeas* is a text from the second or first century B.C.E. that tells how the Bible was first translated into Greek in the third century B.C.E. at the request of King Ptolemy II Philadelphus, who was eager to know the wisdom of the Jews. Seventy-two scribes were installed in lodges and worked separately, but when their translations were compared they were all found to be the same. This miracle showed that divine inspiration was acknowledged in this translation, and thus that the Greek language was destined to receive the divine word, as it would eventually be the language of the Gospels. The documentary hypothesis is not so remote from that legend: several writers separated by time and space all worked on their own texts, and when their texts were assembled together, the Bible as we know it appeared miraculously. As we have seen from Lévi-Strauss—that any interpretation of a myth is a new variant of it—we may consider the *Letter of Aristeas* and the documentary hypothesis to be two variants of the myth of the divine inspiration of the Bible. Both of them are myths that have a clearly defined function; to hide the real

54. Michel Onfray, *Traité d'athéologie, physique de la métaphysique*, Paris: Grasset, 2005, 70-83.
55. Friedman, *Who Wrote the Bible?*, 25.

source of inspiration of the Bible—the Greek classical texts. What probably happened is the exact opposite of what the *Letter of Aristeas* tells us: some Jewish priests and scribes met some Alexandrian scholars and a 'translation' was made, but in the sense that the Greek classics were used as sources of inspiration to give birth to the original Hebrew Bible, which was eventually translated into Greek some time later. As an anthropologist, I will question how such legends and theories about the Bible have come to survive. The answer seems simple: they help maintain the Bible's sacred character. Most scholars still view the Bible from a theological perspective. We could even say that as long as modern society, which claims to be secular, has not recognised the Hellenic character of the Bible, that secularisation is not complete. Behind a so-called liberty, the biblical monument remains untouchable. Anything said about it must contribute to its mystique. 'To uncover its nakedness' would be the most terrible assault on Judeo-Christian decency.

This brief overview of the dominant theories about the origins of the Bible shows that my work does not ignore them. From the point of view of scientific epistemology we can try to understand why a systematic and profound comparison of the Bible with classical Greek literature has not been published until today. Again, the answer is simple: the Bible could not resist such an analysis as it demonstrates how almost every biblical narrative finds accurate parallels with Greek myths. If believers of Jewish and Christian faiths were aware of this, then the Bible could lose its credibility. Biblical scholarship has done all it could to maintain the Bible as a sacred text that is still relevant to modern society, as Hector Avalos argues. In his polemical book he calls for an end to modern biblical studies.[56] Sociologist Pierre Bourdieu has explained how university scholars use *symbolic violence* to ensure their authority in their field.[57] By presenting themselves as a legitimate institution, university scholars impose an arbitrary knowledge that is recognised by the masses as legitimate. But this intellectual domination is not completely passive; it comes from the demands of society. As both Avalos and Bourdieu (in their respective works) have put it, the media industry—the press, movies and television—plays an important role in the continuation of either the sacred character of the Bible or symbolic violence. The biblical field created theories that have allowed the Bible to survive only because masses of believers wanted it to. The Vatican finally admitted the validity of the documentary hypothesis, demonstrating that it never was a

---

56. Hector Avalos, *The End of Biblical Studies*, New York: Prometheus Books, 2007.

57. Bourdieu and Passeron, *La reproduction*.

serious scientific threat to the Bible. Since science has challenged the
Bible with the modern discoveries of evolution, genetics and many
others, it was important to protect and 'save' the Bible with a discourse
that took the form of science, giving it a new history different from that
proposed by religious tradition. However, I have tried to show how these
theories were only rationalised versions of the notion of divine inspiration. Biblical criticism did not make 'innocent mistakes'; it was a diver-
sion to prevent both scholars and non-scholars from knowing the true
origins of the Bible. However, no one person can be held directly responsible. The symbolic violence is a meta-phenomenon; those who engage
in it and those who suffer from it all share in the responsibility, none of
them being conscious of this mechanism. The majority of the divergent
conclusions of most biblical scholars are that the original sources of the
Bible have long been lost, and that only they, the scholars, can find them
within the biblical text. The initials of the sources (J, E, Dtr.1, etc.) sound
vaguely scientific, and the amateur will respect this seemingly solid
theory when reading an annotated Bible. These notes discourage one
from understanding the biblical narrative as being perfectly coherent, a
fine piece of literature. This is quite a paradox as these theories claim to
be 'theological', yet they undermine the beauty of the text by claiming it
to be full of blatant contradictions. These evolutionary theories want the
Bible to be seen as primitive and naïve, in essence an 'Old' Testament.
The Bible is dated from a period before the rise of classical culture in
Greece, prior to the fifth century B.C.E., so one would not consider a
comparison like the one presented here. The return of religion and the
weakening of atheism in the early twenty-first century can be explained
by, among other reasons, the fact that the Bible has not yet been the
object of a consistent and genuinely scientific analysis.

As the alleged J, E, D, and P sources can never be discovered (by hard
evidence such as scrolls in caves, etc.), biblical scholars used older
sources from the ancient Near East, that is, the Mesopotamian texts, to
try to prove how old the Bible was. So, for example, the *Enuma Elish*
became the indirect source for the creation narrative in Genesis, the *Epic
of Gilgamesh* became the indirect source for the deluge, and the *Code of
Hammurabi* the prototype for biblical laws. Consequently, even though
we already knew about similar stories and laws in the Greek tradition,
they are disregarded as being more recent than the Bible, not worthy of
comparison. These Mesopotamian parallels are widely accepted since
Babylon plays a major role in the biblical narrative, whereas apparently
Greece does not. Assyriological findings are employed to draw the Bible
back to a remote past, in order to make it essentially 'Semitic'. Any

possible Western influence is rejected, and in this particular case we see the 'Orient' is a scholarly invention, as Said stated. The Bible must remain Semitic, oriental, old and genuine for believers.

Biblical scholarship has betrayed Spinoza, as his single writer for Genesis–Kings has been mistaken for a 'final redactor'. Traces can be found that demonstrate that at the beginning of the modern era some thinkers were fully aware of the Hellenic origins of the Bible. Voltaire wrote several times in his *Dictionnaire philosophique*[58] (a serious parody of bishop Dom Calmet's *Dictionnaire biblique*[59]) that the Greeks and Romans had inspired biblical fables, surely not the other way around. The anonymous eighteenth-century author of *The Treatise of the Three Impostors* claimed in Chapter 9 that both the Old and the New Testaments had robbed Plato. These thinkers have not been heard, although they are still admired and commented upon.

Jacques Cazeaux

I will refer frequently in what follows to the works of Jacques Cazeaux,[60] a philologist specialising in Plato, Philo and the Bible. He thinks of the Bible as a coherent and well-written book, therefore his is close to what Römer calls the pragmatic approach. The question of the sources is secondary for Cazeaux, who considers the final form, which is an anti-royalist prophecy. From the genealogies of Genesis to Kings (or rather the other way around, as the text was probably conceived to begin from Kings) through the wandering in the desert and the troubled period of the Judges, everything is prepared for the reader to admit that Israel's truth is in the Law, and not in the possession of a land or in the ostentation of a monarchy. Cazeaux seems to be right, as he only *reads* the biblical text rather than dissecting it into a meaningless, primitive and naïve prose. Cazeaux emphasises the cadastre of the twelve tribes. He admits that the 'final chronicler', whose weight makes him comparable to an author, may have lived in the third century B.C.E. and was therefore aware of platonic philosophy.[61] According to him, the speech of Samuel decrying monarchy in 1 Samuel 8—when Israel asks the prophet to install a

---

58. Voltaire, *Dictionnaire philosophique*, Paris: Gallimard, 1994, see articles 'Abraham', 'Genèse' and 'Fables'.

59. Dom Calmet, 'Dictionnaire biblique', online: www.456-Bible.com.

60. Jacques Cazeaux, *Le refus de la guerre sainte—Josué, les Juges et Ruth*, Lectio Divina 174, Paris: Cerf, 1998; *Saül, David et Salomon*, Lectio Divina 174, Paris: Cerf, 2003; *Le partage de minuit, essai sur la Genèse*; *La contre-épopée du désert—L'Exode, le Lévitique, es Nombres*, Lectio Divina 174, Paris: Cerf, 2007.

61. Cazeaux, *Le partage de minuit*, 26, 79.

king—is the core of the biblical tale. God, through Samuel, explains how
the king will behave as a tyrant, appropriating both land and people. That
prophecy eventually became reality when the kings of Israel brought
about the fall of the country through their sins. Retrospectively, the
previous books from Genesis to Joshua can be read as participating in
this long 'prophecy' against kingship by proposing ideal portraits of the
Patriarchs—who resemble kings—and the founding of the twelve-tribe
State, governed by laws. I will show how the speech of Samuel is based
on Euripides' *Suppliants*, as well as the platonic origins of the political
philosophy of the Bible. Cazeaux's interpretation of the final form of the
Bible sheds light on the final intentions of the author, whereas my work
focuses on listing the Greek sources in accordance with Cazeaux's
political reading.

I will now review the positions of the three principal 'minimalists'
who hold the dating of the Bible to be from the late Persian era to the late
Hellenistic era: Philip R. Davies, Niels Peter Lemche and Thomas L.
Thompson, collectively known as the Sheffield–Copenhagen school.

Philip R. Davies

In his *In Search of 'Ancient Israel'*,[62] Davies distinguishes three forms of
'Ancient Israel': the first is the biblical Israel, a literary fiction that has
little to do with the second (and real one), a kingdom that existed from
the ninth to the eighth century B.C.E. that archaeology may study; the
third is the biblical scholars' Ancient Israel, a hybrid construction based
on the two others, between history and literature. The resemblance
between the biblical and historical Israel is superficial, not substantial.
Then who produced the Bible, if not 'Ancient Israel'? For Davies,
biblical criticism has always been in the hands of Christian theology.[63]
Literature is not the product of a society but of an intellectual, literate
elite. But even if the Bible was the production of the elite, Davies doubts
that the Bible reflects any particular religion that existed prior to it. The
Bible created the Jews, not the other way around. The Bible was first
created in the Judean establishment, then later was adopted by Judean
society as a national history with the aid of political power—that of the
Hasmonean kings.

Since biblical scholarship has always regarded biblical Israel as historical, what 'Ancient Israel' is searched for, if not that of the Bible?
This paradox and other contradictions led Davies to believe that the

---

62. See n. 10.
63. Ibid., 19 n. 4.

Bible was written during the Persian and Hellenistic eras, and it is that period which should be called 'biblical' rather than the 'pre-exilic' era during which the Bible did not exist. Most histories of Ancient Israel are rationalised paraphrases of the Bible that are neither historical nor biblical.[64] Ancient Israel was never a hypothesis—it was taken for granted. Davies points out how scholarship sets an arbitrary limit defining what is 'mythical' and what is 'historical'; by the time Davies was writing in 1992 that limit had moved from the time of the Patriarchs, once thought as historical figures, to the period of Judges, and more recently to 'Josiah's reformation'. If there are indeed some historical events in the Bible, then these are used to prove that everything in the Bible is historical, except for the miracles. Davies uses the example of Sennacherib's campaign; the Assyrian inscription for its account is as subjective as the biblical narrative (2 Kgs 19), and historians will paraphrase both in order to confirm that 2 Kings was written by the Deuteronomist living during Josiah's reign. For Davies, biblical scholarship is like 'a dog chasing its own tail' due to the belief that the authors of the Bible lived during the period described in the Bible—what Davies calls circular reasoning.[65] The Bible must be dated later than its contents, and it should be considered that narratives were not genuine traditions but inventions of the writers. The so-called reformation of Josiah, as conceived by Noth and his followers, is a perfect example of circular reasoning: the Bible tells how the Law of Moses was recovered in the temple, and that Josiah proclaimed it again in 2 Kings 22–23. Noth believed that this story, without any other evidence than the Bible itself, actually reflected the redaction of the Deuteronomistic History. Theologians do not look so much for the origins of Israel's faith, but of their own. The search for literary strata within the biblical text is also a form of circular reasoning, as these sources can never be verified. The same goes for the seventy-year 'exilic period'—thought of as a time of intense literary production when the D source was finished and the P source was written, yet about which the Bible remains almost silent. This version of the Exile is a scholarly invention, even less plausible than the biblical account. Ancient Israel is a theological construction in the same respects as biblical Israel is.[66] Ancient Israel has much more to do with theology than with history because most biblical scholars are theologians—some

64. Ibid., 24.
65. Ibid., 35.
66. This agrees with Lévi-Strauss' principle that any interpretation of a myth is a new version of it.

of them clergy—and, therefore, Ancient Israel appears as an embryonic Church. Some theologians are in search of themselves, not of historical truth.[67]

Niels Peter Lemche

With Thomas L. Thompson, Lemche is one of the first scholars to date the whole Bible from the Hellenistic era. In 'The Old Testament: A Hellenistic Book?',[68] he notes the main difference between the Septuagint and the Hebrew Bible: the latter does not contain books about the Hellenistic era, as 1 and 2 Maccabees or Ben Sira, even though they seem to be similarly inspired. The compilers of the Hebrew canon would have chosen not to include these books as their Bible as they had to finish their tale before the Hellenistic era. Yet the book of Daniel refers to it (Daniel supposedly living in the sixth century B.C.E.), albeit in the form of prophecy. Books such as Ecclesiastes and Song of Songs, which biblical criticism usually admits as being Hellenistic, were attributed to Solomon in order to fit in the canon. Lemche denounces circular reasoning in the dating of the Bible, as does Davies. The book of Samuel appears complete in Codex Vaticanus from 350 C.E.; this should be considered the *terminus ad quem* for it, or, more reasonably, the fragmented scrolls of Qumran. Scholars should track back in the past to the uncertain based upon that which is certain (the tangible texts), not the other way around, as most scholars do. As Davies does, Lemche points out how Josiah's reformation could not be held to be historical on the sole basis of a rationalised paraphrasing of the Bible.[69] To break this circle, Lemche suggests starting from the texts in their existing forms in order to seek a more distant past. The concept of biblical Israel seems to be a late one, born from a general movement towards monotheism that arose from India to Greece beginning around the fifth century B.C.E. Unlike Davies, Lemche thinks that the Persian era would not have seen the birth of the Bible, considering the Hellenistic era to be more likely since we know it was a period of cultural production and since biblical historiography shows similarities with Greek historiography. Nothing proves that the Bible is not a Hellenistic book since it appears materially in that time; those who believe it is older should produce evidence, but not based on the Bible itself. According to Lemche, the temporal distance between the

---

67. Ibid., 45.
68. See n. 9.
69. Recent attempts by archaeologist Israel Finkelstein to confirm it via a centralisation of cult in Jerusalem during the seventh century B.C.E. have failed to show direct evidence of the existence of the Bible at the time.

Old and the New Testaments is minimal; they both belong to a similar culture and show more continuity than what is usually assumed. In another contribution in the same book,[70] Lemche tries to recreate the 'mental matrix' of the biblical writers, and suggests that they may have been influenced by Greek philosophy. Lemche reviews the different paradigms from the controversy of 'Babel und Bibel' to the model of the amphictyony conceived by Noth, all of which were abandoned. For him, the Bible should be compared with Herodotus and Titus Livius, and not seen as a 'Primary History' but as a sophisticated piece of literature. Traces of Hellenism can be found; yet even if Mesopotamian influences are present, the text must be dated by its most recent elements and not by the oldest. Lemche states that the concept of a biblical Israel is contrary to any society that once existed in ancient Palestine. 'Biblical Israel' is an invented story based on a few historical events, one that sprung from the minds of the biblical writers and their modern paraphrasers, that is, the historical-critical scholars of the past two hundred years.[71]

Thomas L. Thompson
Thompson argues that 'biblical archaeology' has long tried to prove the historicity of biblical narratives, an attitude that he calls 'naïve realism'.[72] Most biblical narratives are first and foremost theological rather than historical. Biblical archaeology has been attempting to confirm biblical narratives since its inception, but recently it had to confront the fact that even the united monarchy of David and Solomon was mythical. The dichotomy between Canaanites and Israelites is probably artificial as well. The Bible is a theological book, and looking for history in it is a misunderstanding of its aim. The first monarchic State with a religious cult centred in Jerusalem appears with certainty in the second century B.C.E., as the Hasmonean State, which came to independence after the revolt of the Maccabees against the Greeks. The first manuscripts of the Bible are dated from that period, and nothing proves that the Bible could have existed before this. The people of Judea would have considered themselves to be the 'New Israel' as opposed to the 'Lost Israel' of the Bible. As found in annals, 'historical' kings would have been used to reflect present kings, for example, the reformer Josiah would represent

70. Niels Peter Lemche, 'How Does One Date an Expression of Mental History? The Old Testament and Hellenism', in Grabbe, ed., *Did Moses Speak Attic?*, 220-24.
71. Niels Peter Lemche, 'On the Problems of Reconstructing pre-Hellenistic Israelite (Palestinian) History', contribution to the symposium of Aarhus University 1999. Online: http://www.pphf.hu/kat/bib/cikkek/prehellen.pdf.
72. Thompson, *The Mythic Past*, p. 230

John Hyrcanus. Most biblical themes, from the expulsion from the
Garden of Eden to the Tower of Babel, revolve around the idea of a lost
paradise that represents both Babylon and Jerusalem itself. The destruction and fall of Jerusalem at the hands of Babylon (or Babel—Hebrew
uses the same word whereas translations do not) is augured by its
beginning.

The Bible was born only after Alexander's conquest of the East and
the division of his empire among his generals. This fact may have
inspired the division of biblical Israel, as it seems more and more likely
that the kingdoms of Judah and Israel were always distinct. For Thompson, the Bible does not reflect any historical past, nor even any religion
of the past, because the Bible is much more recent than has long been
believed. Biblical texts were the products of Hellenised Jews who took
inspiration from Socrates' and Plato's philosophies, and who thought
that the gods of Greek mythology were only metaphors for a divine
reality that could not be comprehended by men. The biblical god is not
the ultimate god, inaccessible to humankind, but rather a character. By
comparing platonic and biblical writings we will see how Thompson's
idea is correct.

Professors Davies, Lemche and Thompson all have suggested a late
dating of the Bible, and called for more objectivity in biblical studies. As
the Bible appears concretely in the Hellenistic era (in terms of manuscripts and of the knowledge of the Jews and their Bible that other
cultures had—especially the Greeks and the Romans) they state it is
more reasonable to believe that it was born during that period. Through a
comparative analysis of the Bible with Greek classical literature I will try
to show how these 'minimalist' theories are correct. In the conclusion we
will have to question more deeply why such a late dating and the theory
of Greek influence were not raised until very recently, using Freud's
psychoanalysis, Nietzsche's philosophy and Bourdieu's concept of symbolic violence.

Yaakov S. Kupitz
To conclude this brief overview of biblical scholarship, I would like to
mention the work of Yaakov S. Kupitz, professor of Mathematics at the
Hebrew University of Jerusalem. Kupitz wrote an article that compares
several Greek themes with the Bible, and states that it is a Hellenistic
book that borrowed directly from Greek literature.[73] Kupitz also suggests

---

73. Yaakov S. Kupitz, 'La Bible est-elle un plagiat?', *Sciences et Avenir*,
occasional paper, December 1997, 85-88.

some Greek etymologies for Biblical Hebrew words. For instance, Jacob buys a piece of land in Shechem for a hundred *kesita* (Gen 33:19), a word that Kupitz links to the Lydian currency *cistophorus*, or *kiste* for short, ultimately giving us the word *k'sita*. Therefore, biblical writers would have left a blatant anachronism, as Jacob was using a currency that was born in the late third century B.C.E. According to Kupitz, biblical writers knew Greek literature very well, which they admired and wanted to imitate when facing the flow of Hellenism. The Philistines in biblical narratives could easily represent the Greeks, being invaders who came from the sea. The Philistine pantheon and idols, which are mocked, would hide references to the Greek gods. Kupitz compares the duel between David and Goliath to that of Menelaus and Paris in the *Iliad*, and shows how a fable of Aesop, *The trees and the olive tree*, appears word for word in Jotham's speech in Judg 9:8-15. Samson is compared to Heracles, and the point is made that Greek iconography and literature are full of representations of Heracles; the Bible only speaks of Samson in four chapters, which leaves little doubt about who borrowed from whom. But the most important and original point of Kupitz's article is that the territorial organisation of biblical Israel, divided into lots of land and distributed by draw to the twelve tribes, is similar to that of Plato's *Laws* (745 b-c).

Four Possible Eras: Royal, Exilic, Persian and Hellenistic

I believe that the Bible was written in the Hellenistic era, but other periods may be considered as well. We will examine the reasons why the Hellenistic era is the most likely.

The Royal Era

Although most scholars admit that the Bible came after this period, some will maintain that it contains relevant information about history. William G. Dever[74] answers the minimalists in stating that the Merneptah Stele indicates that a people called Israel did live in the region in the thirteenth century B.C.E., a people that obviously gave birth to the kingdom of Israel in the ninth century B.C.E. Moreover, in Genesis the Bible describes the country of Canaan as being governed by small kings constantly at war, and that Egypt was dominant in the region; this description corresponds with the letters of Tell-Amarna in which we learn about the Apirus or Habirus, a nomadic people that caused troubles between Egypt and

---

74. William G. Dever, *Aux origines d'Israël*, Paris: Bayard, 2005.

Canaan and could be identified with the first Hebrews. The book of
Judges describes constant fights between the Canaanites and the Israelites, a context that archaeology seems to confirm. 'Proto-Israelites' can
be identified in the late second millennium B.C.E. as the kingdoms of
Judah and Israel appeared a few centuries later. Dever may be correct,
but none of these arguments are evidence of the existence of the Bible,
they only show that some aspects of the Bible offer a plausible historical
reconstruction of the past. These explanations do not, however, take into
account the parallels with Greek literature that we will present.

The Exilic Era

Little is known from this period. In fact, the elite of Judea were deported
to Babylon. It is still the sixth century B.C.E. though, before the rise of
classical culture in Greece and before the historiography invented by
Herodotus, to which the Bible owes a lot. Lists of kings existed that were
used by the biblical writers. Mesopotamian myths that are recycled in
Genesis do not prove that the exiled Judeans appropriated them; these
myths continued to live on in the Hellenistic era as Berossus has shown,
and even later. Even though the Exile did happen, we must understand it
as part of the biblical narrative.

The Persian Era

According to the books of Ezra and Nehemiah, the Persian rulers from
Cyrus to Artaxerxes allowed the Jews to return to Jerusalem, and helped
with the building of the second temple. Jean Soler believes that this era
saw the 'invention of monotheism'[75] as the influence of Persian religion
would have led the Jews to consider their regional god, Yahweh, as a
unique god who alone created the universe. Soler thinks this invention
was made after the writing of the Bible, when it became a national
tradition. I disagree with Soler's position as it still speaks from the perspective of religious evolutionism in that it fails to understand that the
Bible is not a primitive literary work; rather, it was written directly under
highly philosophical influences—mainly that of Plato. Moreover, this
evolution of religion towards monotheism is actually part of the biblical
narrative; in a world where polytheism and sin ruled, a pious people and
their ancestors came to discover the only god. Once again, interpretation
is a new version of the myth. Most scholars still paraphrase the divine
revelation, always later in chronology, but the Persian era is kept as the
ultimate end-point. Jan-Wim Wesselius[76] (whose work has been very

75. Jean Soler, *L'invention du monothéisme*, Paris: Fallois, 2002.
76. Wesselius, *The Origin of the History of Israel*.

inspirational for me as he was the first to state that Genesis–Kings was directly and mainly inspired by Herodotus' *Histories*) thinks that this emulation would have taken place in the late fifth century B.C.E., only a few decades after Herodotus' writing. Apparently, Wesselius wants to match the date of this writing with the biblical character of Ezra, whom Spinoza thought was the single author of the Bible. But why disregard other Greek authors as possible sources, such as Homer or Plato?

The Persian era is contemporaneous with the papyri of Elephantine, which describe an Egyptian city peopled by Judeans since the sixth century B.C.E., after the destruction of Jerusalem. The papyri give us considerable information about these Judeans, and about the fact that they neither followed nor even knew of the Bible.[77] None of these papyri, from the fifth century B.C.E. to the Hellenistic era, are extracts of the Bible. In them we come to know of a Judean woman named Mitbahyah who lived in the fifth century B.C.E. and who was married three times, first to a Judean and then to two Egyptians. In her letters she swears by the name of Yahweh, yet associates him with the Canaanite goddess Anat and the Egyptian gods Khnoum and Sati. In another letter we find a man who swears by 'Anat-Yaho', which shows that these deities were revered as a couple. All of this goes against the grain of the biblical religion. The Persian era was not the locale of the invention of monotheism, at least not in Elephantine. The mixed marriages of Mitbahyah and Egyptian men are contrary to the principles of Ezra, yet most especially so, a woman taking the initiative of divorce is in formal contradiction of Deut 24:1-4, as only a husband can repudiate his wife (a law that still prevails in modern Judaism).[78] There also was a temple of Yahweh in Elephantine, which speaks against the centralisation of the cult as described in Deuteronomy 12. Most scholars think that the Judeans of Elephantine had a religion that did not respect Deuteronomy, because supposedly it had only been written during Josiah's reign in the late seventh century B.C.E.; therefore it had not spread to the communities in Egypt. I do not think that the Judeans of Elephantine were heterodox. Neither Deuteronomy nor any other biblical book could have been disrespected, since these did not yet exist. These letters give us precious information about Judean religion before the birth of the Bible. Judeans revered Yahweh as their tutelary deity but accepted the existence of other gods and did not hesitate to swear by their names. Biblical writers commented upon that fact and interpreted it as a chronic infidelity

77. Joseph Mélèze-Modrezejewski, *Les Juifs d'Égypte, de Ramsès II à Hadrien*, Paris: Armand Collin, 1991.
78. Ibid., 34.

to Yahweh, seen to be the cause of the fall of Jerusalem. In these papyri we hear about troubles caused by the sacrificing of rams in the temple of Yahweh which offended the Egyptian worshipers of Khnoum, a ram-god. The temple was destroyed by Egyptians and rebuilt with Persian funds, but the Judeans had to desist from sacrificing any more rams and could only burn incense. We will see a possible reference to this very episode in analysing the Exodus story. Finally, there is a papyrus that also explains how Judean soldiers formed a contingent for the Persian King Darius. This gives us a clue that Judeans participated (as did all conquered peoples) in the wars launched by Darius and Xerxes upon Greece—something that is never referred to in the Bible, yet is the main subject of Herodotus' *Histories*.

The Hellenistic era (330–140 B.C.E.)

I will discuss here ideas discussed in a book by Claude Orrieux and Edouard Will,[79] who applied concepts of post-colonial anthropology to what happened in Judea when the Greeks colonized it. The interesting point is that these two scholars ignored the possibility of a Hellenistic Bible, though it is exactly what they were looking for yet could not find.

They wanted to understand the reactions of the Judeans of Judea (as opposed to Judeans in other countries, such as Egypt) facing acculturation, specifically concerning religion. As is seen in ethnologic and historical literatures, religious syncretism tends to appear when cultures meet. For instance, the Egyptian goddess Isis was adopted by the Greeks and the Romans and identified with Demeter. But in every such case of religious syncretism, one must ask why it happened—what need it filled. For the peoples who submitted to the Greeks, adopting Greek religion was a means of joining the ranks of their masters.[80] As political anthropologist George Balandier explained, four reactions appear when facing acculturation: (1) Active acceptance, which consists of collaborating with those in power. Acculturation touches different facets of life such as language, religion, clothing, and so on. Examples of such Hellenised Jews are described in 2 Maccabees and Josephus Flavius (*Antiquities* 12). (2) Passive acceptance by the masses, which allow themselves to be dominated. (3) Passive opposition—as in fleeing, striking, or in showing psychological symptoms such as anxiety. On the social level this creates utopian aspirations, messianic expectations and hopes of freedom through independence. (4) Active opposition, which can be political, economical

---

79. Claude Orrieux and Édouard Will, *Ioudaïsmos—Hellenismos; essai sur le judaïsme judéen à l'époque hellénistique*, Nancy: P.U., 1986.
80. Ibid., 20.

or socio-cultural. 'Counter-acculturation' is not simply a rejection of the dominant culture in favour of the indigenous culture, but it often consists of using some aspect of the masters' culture against them as a weapon of liberation.[81]

I believe that the writing of the Bible matches this fourth concept; Greek culture was used in order to make both a national history and a religion, as well as to resist Hellenisation and gain independence (which eventually happened). In the early second century B.C.E., according to 2 Maccabees, the Hellenised High Priests Jason and Menelaus tried to impose Hellenism upon Jerusalem. These Greek names are most probably Hellenised forms of Hebrew names, perhaps Joshua and Menahem. Orrieux and Will explain that Hellenism had reached the core of Jewish religion, unsurprisingly. They believe the sacerdotal milieu was the first to have had to become Hellenised, due to its administrative and political links with the Greek rulers. They also would have had to adopt the Greek language in order to maintain relations with the Egyptian communities of Judeans, who neither spoke Hebrew nor Aramaic any longer. The authors suppose that a Greek school existed in Jerusalem to educate bilingual priests and scribes. For the Temple, Hellenisation was a necessity in order to maintain Israel's coherence.[82]

Of course, Orrieux and Will thought that the Bible, by this time, had existed already for centuries, that it had been translated in Alexandria and other places, but their pertinent remarks may help us understand the profile of the biblical writers according to my hypothesis. It is more than likely that a sacerdotal authority acknowledged the Bible, if not published it; otherwise it would not have gained its sacred status. The possibility of there having been a Greek school in Jerusalem or that future priests and scribes would have had to study in Alexandria explains how the biblical writers, who may have been priests, came into contact with Greek literature. For it is certain that in order to learn Greek one has to read the Greek classics, which actually became 'classics' through the process of canonisation in the third century B.C.E. in Alexandria.

The Hellenistic era seems to me to be the most plausible for the birth of the Bible, as the reaction of 'counter-acculturation' reached a peak in the second century B.C.E. with the revolt of the Maccabees and the establishment of the Hasmonean State. When the Bible became the official history and source of religion, Hellenism was retrospectively seen as a threat and the Hellenised character of the Bible passed into shadow. Orrieux and Will explain how acculturation is doubly selective, as it only

81. Ibid., 30.
82. Ibid., 115.

touches some classes of the population and since indigenous cultural elements are selectively preserved. For instance, circumcision is not a Greek practise, though it has been preserved in the Bible as a primary commandment. In 1 Macc 1:15 it is explained how Hellenised Jews had their foreskins 'remade' in order to avoid mockery in the gymnasia. Orrieux and Will believe that Hellenisation was a privilege of the higher classes that aggravated social tensions, so much so that it caused the Maccabean revolt—initially a conflict between Jews that later became a war against the Seleucids. Both religious and social aspects must be taken into account.[83]

Orrieux and Will strive to identify the 'cultural focal zone' of Judean society—the social group that was most influential—which was, according to them, the priests and the first doctors of the Law, or rabbis. In 2 Maccabees 4 it is stated that the High Priest Jason instituted laws contrary to the Torah, and that under Menelaus the Torah was abandoned. Will and Orrieux believe that the Torah was an obstacle impeding Hellenisation, therefore Jews who were seduced by Hellenism had to give it up. However, I believe that this social conflict between 'Hellenism' and 'Judaism' actually gave birth to the Bible, for its authors used Greek literary sources and laws. There were probably many religious laws before the Bible, such as circumcision, weekly rest and others, but as these faced the threat of abandonment in the face of Hellenism's seductive power—which had reached even the priests—a new 'Law' was produced that digested and transformed Hellenism into the Hebrew Bible itself. Acculturation was achieved even as the Bible's Greek origins were denied. The use of Greek myths that had been transformed through the prism of monotheism was seen to be a compromise between the two cultures by the biblical writers. Of course, the problem with this reconstruction is that the biblical books of Maccabees (belonging in the Septuagint canon) cannot be considered to be reliable historical sources; they only give us an echo of what may have happened—one must avoid the trap of a rationalised paraphrase of biblical books because they are primarily theological and not historical. Because that is what Will and Orrieux did, they could not find what they were looking for, although they were very close. Indeed, at the end of their survey they conclude that the cultural focal zone (identified as the religious zone) does not work as it should, as it seems from the books of Maccabees that Hellenism, being 'defeated', brought no change at all. But according to anthropologists the cultural focal zone should be the most open to innovations from the dominant culture. So they ask themselves, 'Why is it that there

83. Ibid., 123.

are no traces of Greek influences in Judean culture if the religious milieu of the priesthood were indeed that focal zone?' Apparently, the Law remained the same while monotheism and priesthood were maintained. Either the focal zone of a society is not always open to innovations or Judean society was an exception, but these poor conclusions left Orrieux and Will disappointed and frustrated.[84] Was the anthropological theory wrong, or was Judea an exception? It is from their very lack of conclusions that we can understand that their analysis was fine, albeit based on too much trust in the biblical and para-biblical sources of Maccabees and Josephus. According to my hypothesis, the priestly milieu was indeed Hellenised up to the point when the Bible was created—a text that fully appropriates the highest aspects of Greek culture into a new form. The theory was right, and Judea was not an exception. As the two French scholars ignored the possibility of a Hellenistic Bible (though they cannot be blamed for this as the idea was almost unknown in the 1980s), they missed the mark. Interestingly, the Hebrew Bible does not contain 1 and 2 Maccabees, and their (alleged) original Hebrew forms have never been found; yet the Jewish tradition knows their content, and the feast of Hanukah still celebrates the victory of 'Jewish light against Greek darkness'.

The Great Mythical Greek Cycles

I will give here short summaries of the main epics of Greek mythology that I believe were used as sources for the Bible. As we will analyse the Bible in its chronological order, these summaries will help understanding how these epics were dismantled and re-arranged around the narrative structure of the life and death of the Platonic Ideal State.

The Argonauts

It all started with Ixion who, by killing his father-in-law, committed the first murder in the history of humankind. Shunned by others, Ixion was welcomed on Mount Olympus by Zeus, who forgave him. But Ixion tried to seduce his host's wife, Hera, and to punish him Zeus created Nephele—a cloud-goddess resembling Hera. From the union of Ixion and Nephele was born a bastard creature, Kentauros, ancestor of the Centaurs. Nephele later became the wife of Athamas, son of Aeolus king of Boeotia, and bore him a son, Phrixos, and a daughter, Helle. Athamas rejected Nephele and took another wife, Ino, daughter of Cadmus, who gave him two sons, Melicertes and Learchus. As Ino hated the first

84. Ibid., 124-25.

children of her husband, she orchestrated a fake oracle that swayed Athamas to sacrifice Phrixos to Zeus on Mount Laphystion. As Athamas was about to kill his son, Zeus sent a flying ram that spirited away both Phrixos and Helle on its back. Helle fell in the sea, however, which was then named after her—the Hellespont. Phrixos reached Colchis, sacrificed the ram there to thank Zeus for saving his life, and hung its Golden Fleece on an oak tree.

Salmoneus, brother of Athamas, had a daughter named Tyro. From her union with Poseidon she gave birth to Pelias and Neleus. She later married her uncle Cretheus, king of Thessaly, brother of Athamas and Salmoneus, and gave birth to Aeson. Pelias usurped the throne of Thessaly and placed Aeson, its legitimate inheritor, under arrest in the city of Iolchos. Aeson secretly begat a son Jason, raised away from the city by the Centaur Chiron. Twenty years later Jason, grown up, entered the court of Iolchos (having lost a single sandal on the way). Pelias recognised the sign that had been foretold to him: a man with only one shoe would cause his death. Jason claimed the throne of Iolchos as the legitimate inheritor of Cretheus. Pelias feigned acceptance on the condition that Jason bring back the Golden Fleece from Colchis. Meanwhile, Phrixos' ghost had haunted Pelias' dreams because he had not received a proper burial. As both Jason and Pelias were descendants of Aeolus they were related to Phrixos and thus obligated to appease his soul.

Jason accepted the challenge and embarked on a great expedition, calling upon all the heroes of Greece: Orpheus, Heracles, Castor and Pollux, Laertes (father of Ulysses), Peleus (father of Achilles), Argos and many others. Argos built a boat that was named after him, the Argo, and so the Argonauts set sail to Colchis in search of the Golden Fleece. Many adventures took place on their journey. Among the better-known tales are their union with the women of the island of Lemnos (who had killed their husbands and male children) and how they freed the blind seer Phineus from the food-thieving harpies. Facing the Bosporus and the Strait of Messina, they passed through the Symplegades clashing rocks and avoided the twin perils of the man-eating monster Scylla and the great whirlpool Charybdis. Jason and his ship reached Colchis, country of the terrible King Aetes. The king pretended that he would give the Golden Fleece to the Argonauts if one of them succeeded in yoking his two brazen oxen, ploughing the land and sowing it with the teeth of a dragon (which was to magically give rise to armed soldiers). Medea, daughter of Aetes, fell in love with Jason and betrayed her father by giving Jason a drug that made him invulnerable. Jason overcame Aetes' challenge and took the Golden Fleece from the sacred wood with the help of Medea. Aetes, who never intended to part with the Fleece, chased the escaping Argonauts with his fleet. Jason married Medea on the island of the Phaecians, and they escaped Aetes. After a storm the Argo ended up stranded on the coasts of Libya where Euphemos, an Argonaut, received a piece of soil from Triton with the promise that his descendants would own that land. The Argonauts sailed around Crete where the giant Talos threw rocks at them, eventually reaching Greece. There, Medea had Pelias killed by his own daughters. Jason left the throne of Iolchos to Acastus, Pelias' son, and went to Corinth. Ten years later, when Jason wanted to marry the king's daughter Glaucea, an enraged Medea decided to kill their two children. She fled to Athens on a winged chariot sent by her grandfather Helios, the Sun God. In Athens she had a son, Medos, with Aegeus, but was later forced to go back to Colchis after she tried to poison Theseus, Aegeus' son. Jason died alone in Iolchos, killed while sitting under the Argo's prow, which fell on his head. The Argonautic epic is known through many sources as far back as Homer, who was the first to refer to it. Pindar was the first poet to tell the epic in extended form in his fourth *Pythian Ode*. Aeschylus, Sophocles and Euripides wrote many plays about characters of this epic (most of which are lost)— Euripides' *Medea* being the most famous. We will examine fragments of his *Phrixos* and *Ino* later. Pindar, Herodotus and Apollonius of Rhodes all relate this epic explicitly to the foundation of the Greek colony of Cyrene in Libya, as Euphemos' stuttering descendant Battos guided his people there and ruled over them for forty years.

The Theban Cycle
The cycle of Thebes is linked to that of the Argonauts. Cadmus, son of Agenor king of Phoenicia, went in search of his sister Europa—abducted by Zeus in the form of a bull. Unto Zeus she gave birth to Minos and Rhadamanthis. Minos became king of Crete and was revered as the first lawgiver, inspired by his father Zeus. Eventually Cadmus renounced his search for his sister and founded the city of Thebes. An oracle had told him to follow a cow that had never been yoked until it stopped. So he did, and upon the spot where the cow died of exhaustion he sowed the teeth of a dragon he had killed; from these teeth armed men arose from the soil and then fought each other until all but five were slain. These five were the first inhabitants of Thebes—the *autochthons*, born from the earth. Cadmus had several daughters, notably Ino who married Athamas, and Semele. Semele asked Zeus, her lover, to appear to her in all his glory, which killed her. Zeus rescued her unborn child and sowed it into his thigh, where it matured; Zeus then later 'gave birth' to Dionysus.

Pentheus, grandson of Cadmus, refused to recognise Dionysus' godhood and the god caused him to be dismembered by his mother and aunts who had become *Bacchantes* (as portrayed in Euripides' play). Two brothers, Amphion and Zetos, built the walls of Thebes; Amphion moved the stones with the sound of his lyre. Laius, descendant of Cadmus, abandoned his son Oedipus because an oracle had foretold that his son would kill him and marry his wife, Jocasta. As foretold, Oedipus eventually killed Laius and married his own mother, not knowing they were his parents. When the truth was revealed (immortalized in Sophocles' *Oedipus the King*), Oedipus gouged out his eyes and Jocasta hanged herself. His sons Eteocles and Polynices killed each other for the throne of Thebes, seen in Aeschylus' *The Seven against Thebes*. One of these seven—Amphiraus—fell into the Earth that had opened up and was swallowed alive. For burying her dishonored brother Polynices, Oedipus' daughter Antigone was put to death by her uncle Creon (in Sophocles' *Antigone*). Before the Trojan War began, the sons of the Seven against Thebes—called the Epigones—launched another war and Thebes was destroyed. Alcmeon son of Amphiraus was exiled, for he had killed his own mother; he later founded a city that he named after his son, Acarnania. The myth that Cadmus came from Phoenicia may be the result of Semitic influences on archaic Greek culture. The name of his grandson Melicertes most likely derives from the Tyrian god Melkart, and the name of Belus (Agenor's brother) probably derives from Bel—known as Baal in the Bible. If the Greeks knew of mythical elements from the Near East these would not have been biblical, rather Phoenician, or what the Bible calls 'Canaanite'.

Heracles and his Ancestors

Acrisius and Proetus, Belus' descendants, fought each other since they were in their mother's womb. They fought for many years until they made peace and shared their father's land. Proetus once welcomed the hero Bellerophon into his home, and his wife fell in love with him. Bellerophon rejected her but she accused him of trying to ravish her. Not wanting to kill his guest, Proetus sent Bellerophon, carrying a sealed letter that instructed its receiver to kill its bearer, to his father-in-law Iobates. Iobates made Bellerophon fight the monster Chimera, yet the hero succeeded. An oracle had told Acrisius that his daughter Danae's son would kill him, so he locked her in a tower. However, Zeus came to her in the form of a golden rain and she later gave birth to Perseus; Acrisius cast out Danae and her baby into the sea, floating in a chest. When he was grown up, Perseus took vengeance upon his grandfather.

Perseus married Andromeda, with whom he had Sthenelus, Electryon and Alceus. Electryon's daughter Alcmene married Alceus' son Amphytrion. Amphytrion went to war, where he seduced his enemy's daughter, Comaetho; she acquiesced to cut the magic hair of her father Pterelas, which made him invulnerable. Meanwhile, Zeus came to Alcmene in the guise of her husband and she became pregnant—at the same time as Sthenelus' wife. Zeus, about to have a new son, claimed that the child to be born would have supremacy over his brothers and would reign on Argos and Mycenae. Hera, jealous of her husband's infidelity, made him swear to what he had just said; she then delayed Alcmene's delivery and hastened the birth of Sthenelus' son. Eurystheus, descended from Zeus through Perseus, was born before Heracles, and Alcmene, fearing Hera's wrath, abandoned her baby. Hera happened to find him and wanted him to suckle, but he bit her breast. Athena, his sister, suggested that he be returned to his mother so she could breastfeed. While growing up Heracles defeated the lion of Mount Cytheron and, as a reward, King Thespios offered him his fifty daughters. However, Heracles thought he had slept with the same woman every night. Heracles ended up marrying Megara, but Hera drove him crazy and he killed their children. According to some, as penitence he accepted the twelve labours ordered by Eurystheus. During these labours he joined the Argonauts, but later left them in order to reach the garden of the Hesperides (where, protected by a dragon, was kept a tree with golden apples). In Egypt, Heracles freed the seven daughters of Atlas from king Busiris. His second wife Deianira was duped into offering him a tunic that had been poisoned with the blood of a centaur, and he died by donning it. Heracles became a god after his death and married the goddess Hebe. His descendants, the Heraclids, were granted the conquest of the Peloponnesus, though they had to wait for three generations.

The Main Greek Authors

Homer

The debate about the origins of the *Iliad* and the *Odyssey* resembles the debate over the origins of the Bible, as scholars thought that several redactors and editors had changed the text.[85] Recently, most scholars have admitted that these texts are unified and coherent. The Greek tradition holds that in the sixth century B.C.E. the Athenian tyrant Pisistratus put songs to writing that were previously only part of the oral tradition,

85. For a discussion of how the criticism of Homer gave birth to biblical criticism, see Van Seters, *The Edited Bible*.

which can be seen as the *terminus a quo*. In the fifth century B.C.E. Herodotus quotes Homer, who had become the ultimate reference for Greek literature. The *Iliad* tells us of the last year of the war of the Greeks against Troy. Leading up to the war, Helen, Spartan queen and wife of Menelaus, was ravished and abducted by a Trojan prince, Paris. As all the numerous suitors of Helen had sworn to whomever she would marry that they would unite in need to defend her honour, the Greeks mounted a massive campaign against Troy. Trojan King Priam refused to surrender Helen, and Troy was besieged for ten years. The *Iliad* opens as Agamemnon, leader of the Greek forces, seizes the Trojan woman Briseis who was taken by Achilles as a spoil of war. Achilles, son of Peleus the Argonaut, is the best of the Greek warriors; he becomes furious at the insult and retreats from the fight with his men, the Myrmidons. From this point on the Greeks start to lose the war until Patroclus, Achilles' cousin, leads the Myrmidons back on the battlefield wearing Achilles' weapons and armour. Patroclus is killed by Hector, elder prince of Troy, and is avenged by Achilles. Achilles attaches Hector's body by the ankles to his chariot and drags him about the walls of Troy. At night, Priam sneaks into the Greek camp and begs Achilles to return his son's body for a proper funeral. Achilles accepts a ransom, and the Trojans are permitted to mourn their hero. The *Iliad* ends here but the Trojan epic, known through various sources, continues to tell of how Paris killed Achilles by shooting him through the ankle (his only vulnerable spot) with an arrow. Ulysses conceived of a giant wooden horse constructed in secret, inside of which Greek warriors hid. The Greeks pretended to retreat and the horse was 'abandoned' as a token of Trojan victory. Once taken inside the walls of Troy, the Greek soldiers sacked the city under cover of darkness and the city fell.

Ulysses was warned that he would not return for twenty years if he departed for the Trojan War. The *Odyssey* tells of the wanderings of Ulysses across the seas during his ten-year return home once the Trojan War was over. After defeating the cyclops Polyphemus, Ulysses reached the island of Circe. After trying in vain to convince Ulysses to stay with her, Circe told him how to invoke the ghost of the prophet Teiresias to find his way back home. Ulysses' crew shrinks in number throughout the story until his ship finally breaks. He eventually reached the island of the Phaecians where King Alkinoos and Queen Arete asked him to recall his stories. Upon his return to his home island of Ithaca, disguised as an old beggar by Athena, he encountered his son Telemachus and old servant Eumeus; together they plotted to kill those who would usurp that which was his—the suitors of his wife Penelope. At the conclusion of a contest Ulysses, revealing his identity, killed the suitors, winning his wife back.

Hesiod

Hesiod's *Theogony* describes the births of the Greek gods. Ouranos, the sky-god, was castrated by his son Cronos, whose brother was named Japet. Zeus, Cronos' son, defeated him and became the supreme god. To avoid that his own child would in turn overpower him, he devoured his pregnant wife Metis, thus gaining the knowledge of good and evil. In *Works and Days*, Hesiod told of the lost Golden Age, followed by a degeneration of humankind that lasts until Hesiod's time. There appears the theme of the first woman being the cause of all that is evil (recounted by Hesiod in both his *Theogony* and *Works and Days*), as a punishment for Prometheus having given fire to humankind. Plato widely commented upon Hesiod's poetry, and suggested that Ouranos' castration should either be told to a select few or it should be censored (*Rep.* 377e-78b).

Pindar

Pindar was a Boeotian poet born in the late sixth century B.C.E. who wrote four books of odes: the *Olympians*, the *Pythians*, the *Nemeans* and the *Isthmians*. His technique consisted of attaching the names of winners of athletic games to a mythical genealogy, by which he found a pretext for telling mythical stories. Pindar was the first known poet to write a long epic about the Argonauts (in the fourth *Pythian*).

Euripides

The three great tragic authors—Aeschylus, Sophocles and especially Euripides—were, in my estimation, also sources for the Bible. Many of their plays were lost, so to know them we must use the fragments that we have in addition to Roman era 'handbooks' such as Apollodorus' *Library* and Hyginus' *Fables* that summarised these lost plays. Euripides' plays have an important role as he wrote stories that took place both before and after the Argonautic epic. The fragmented play *Phrixos* is the prologue of the epic while *Medea*, almost intact, is the epilogue. It seems as though Apollonius of Rhodes implicitly referred to these plays so that his poem may be 'inserted' between them. In Apollonius' *Argonautica* Medea is portrayed as a pure virgin who loses her morality when she betrays her father for the love of Jason. At the end of the poem she displayed terrible fury by paralysing the brazen giant Talos with her gaze. All this foreshadows the tragic ending of Euripides' *Medea*, when she murders her own children. Later we will consider other plays of Euripides that have come to us, such as *Helen, The Bacchantes, Ion, The Suppliants* and *Hippolytus*.

Herodotus
The 'father of history' wrote a nine-volume book in prose relating the invasion of the Mediterranean by the Persians and how the Greeks stopped them. Throughout his survey (*Historia*), Herodotus of Halicarnassus (c. 484–425 B.C.E.) recounts the histories of the kingdoms of Lydia, Babylon (book I), Egypt (book II), Persia (book III), and of various Greek cities, mixing myth and history throughout. The nine books of the *Histories* are a fundamental and direct source for the nine books of the Bible from Genesis to Kings. These works, as they are written in prose, can be compared more easily than poetic writings. Jan-Wim Wesselius[86] has shown many similar themes between the two works, and more parallels that confirm his argument will be shown. We will analyse Herodotus' content in more detail when discussing the techniques of the biblical writer.

Apollonius of Rhodes
Apollonius of Rhodes (295–215 B.C.E.) was the head of the Library of Alexandria, after his master Callimachus. He wrote a four-book poem called the *Argonautica* that is the most familiar source for the epic of the Argonauts. For ages, his text was disregarded by classical scholarship as a sort of transition between Homer and Virgil's *Aeneid*. But several scholars have shown renewed interest in his work, such as Richard Hunter,[87] R. J. Clare,[88] Mary Margolies DeForest[89] and Virginia Knight.[90] Knight explains how Apollonius used Homer as his principal literary source and was influenced by him in terms of language, style and character portrayal, as the Argonauts are the fathers of Homer's heroes. The Alexandrian readership of Apollonius was able to recognise the many references to Homer and the geographical clues pointing towards Herodotus. Apollonius filled his text with allusions to previous authors— Homer, Herodotus and Euripides. I believe that the biblical writer learnt this technique as well (he may have studied in Alexandria in his youth and written in Jerusalem later), since we will see how the Bible,

---

86. Wesselius, *The Origin of the History of Israel*.

87. Richard Hunter, *The Argonautica of Apollonius: Literary Studies*, Cambridge: Cambridge University Press, 1993.

88. R.J. Clare, *The Path of the Argo*, Cambridge: Cambridge University Press, 2002.

89. Mary Margolies DeForest, *Apollonius' Argonautica: A Callimachean Epic*, Leiden: E.J. Brill, 1994.

90. Virginia Knight, *The Renewal of Epic—Responses to Homer in the Argonautica of Apollonios,* Leiden: E.J. Brill, 1995.

especially the book of Samuel, combines Homer and Apollonius as primary sources. The *Argonautica* ends with a promise to Euphemus that his descendants will inherit the land of Cyrene, a point that we will revisit.

Roman-Era Writers

As many Greek sources have been lost we will have to consider others from authors that wrote later than the Hellenistic era, such as Apollodorus' *Library*, Hyginus' *Fables*, Pausanias' *Description of Greece*, Strabo's *Geography*, Diodorus Siculus' *Library*, and Ovid's *Metamorphosis*. These authors are precious sources for understanding Greek and Roman mythologies, and most of them are very faithful to their original sources. The latter, whether lost or remaining, will be considered as possible sources for the Bible. Apollodorus' *Library* was a handbook for Roman students learning Greek mythology; the main advantage is that it relates all the mythical genealogies together, allowing us to understand how they were mixed in order to create the Bible. The *Library* will be our 'Ariadne's Thread' in crossing the maze of Greek mythology. There is little chance that all of these late authors borrowed anything from the Bible. However, Strabo and Ovid mentioned the Jews and their religion. Ovid's first book of *Metamorphosis* shows very striking similarities with Genesis 1–11, and two other of Ovid's stories are very similar to Genesis 18 and 19. Regarding these exceptional cases we may accept the idea of a common source for the Bible and Ovid, for it is certain that the Bible existed by his time. Still, we will see that Ovid's case is puzzling.

Plato

Plato lived in Athens from 427–350 B.C.E. He studied philosophy with Socrates, who was executed by Athenian authorities in the year 399. Plato wrote at least twenty-eight dialogues involving Socrates and Athenian notables; these dialogues concerned knowledge, the soul, the gods, the Ideas (of which our world is seen to be only a projection), and the utopian politics of cities modelled after divine virtues. In the *Republic*, or *Politeia*, Plato imagined a first ideal City that he defined through dialectics. Based on a reflection by Herodotus (III, 80-83), Plato examines three different forms of political rule: oligarchy, democracy and tyranny. Plato suggests the concepts of collective property and the dissolution of family. The *Republic* is about a utopia that seems impossible to realise in this world. Plato learnt this bitter lesson after he tried to found one in Sicily—when he was friend to Dion, brother-in-law of the tyrant

Dionysius, according to *Letter* VII. Plato was chased from Sicily, twice, and concluded his life in Athens where he wrote his last dialogue, the *Laws* (*Nomoi*). This long dialogue imagines another ideal City—a more realistic one governed by the laws enunciated by the Athenian Stranger in books IV–XII. No one who has ever read the Bible can avoid being struck by a most uncanny feeling of *déjà-vu* upon reading Plato's *Laws*, as it seems to be the prototype for biblical Israel. In modern philosophy the *Republic* has more prestige than the *Laws* (thought of as a late and unachieved dialogue that was poorly written and less philosophical, reflecting an old and disappointed Plato).

The *Laws* propose a program for the functioning of the State that covers every aspect of life: land property, marriage, agriculture, religion, homicide, and so on. The imaginary legislator whom the Athenian Stranger addresses becomes the central character, whose task is to adapt best to all the prescriptions of the Athenian. According to Létitia Mouze, the legislator must become a poet (and vice-versa) in order that the people obey the law willingly and not by force.[91]

The poet who had been chased in the *Republic* because he told lies about the gods (books II, III and X) had to come back to the new City to chant the virtues of the laws (*Laws* 817 a-d). Plato founded the first school of philosophy, the Academy,[92] in the garden of Academos in the suburbs of Athens. When residing in Sicily Plato let his disciple direct it, and it remained an institution for a millennium after his death until the Christian emperor Justinian had it closed. In the Hellenistic and Roman eras, the influence of the platonic Academy was immense throughout the Mediterranean. Among its most famous directors were Archesilas (who lived until 240 B.C.E.), Carneades (219–129 B.C.E.), Philo of Larissa (145–85 B.C.E.) and Antiochus of Ascalon (127–69 B.C.E.). The latter was Cicero's master, and his origins show us that a man from Palestine could study Plato's philosophy and reach the highest position in the Academy. We have seen how the writing of the Bible in the Hellenistic era can be seen as a reaction of counter-acculturation, in that the Judeans wanted to appropriate the Greeks' culture in order to free themselves from their domination. But we may just as well believe that some Greek scholars of the Academy were involved in the writing of the Bible. Antiochus lived in the time of the Hasmoneans. In fact, the City of the

91. Létitia Mouze, *Le législateur et le poète, une interprétation des Lois de Platon*, Lille: P.U. du Septentrion, 2005.

92. Jean Brun, *Platon et l'Académie*, Paris: P.U.F., 1960.

Laws is more than a utopia; it was meant to come to life, as stated in the last lines of the dialogue. For Mouze, the cities of the *Republic* and the *Laws* are not contradictory but complementary. As the *Republic* defines an ideal of justice, the *Laws* make it concrete. It is written in the *Laws* that the city that would consider women and goods as common property would be perfect and inhabited by gods, whereas the one proposed by the Athenian would be 'second best' (*Laws* 739 e). One can see the continuity between the two Cities. In *Republic* 368 e Socrates wants to define 'justice' both in man and in the soul, but he instead tried to define it in regard to the City, as it is a soul on a grander scale. The *Republic* ends with the myth of Er—a man who, having come back from the afterlife, perceived the destiny of the human soul. For Mouze the *Republic* is not about the foundation of an ideal City; rather, it is a dialogue about the soul. The only ideal City conceived by Plato is that of the *Laws*.

Many themes discussed in the *Laws* were already disputed in the *Republic*. In book IV Socrates speaks on subjects that should be the objects of legislation, such as contracts, workers, insults and aggressions, pressing charges, taxes and markets (*Rep.* 425 c-e), sacrifices and cults to the gods, temples and funerals (427 b). All these subjects are developed in detail in the *Laws*, showing that both texts are complementary and that Plato's interest for legislation was not only a question of old age. Book III of the *Laws* is concerned with the history of Troy, Persia and Greece, and how they came to adopt their legislations. For Mouze, this articulation between myth and history is new in Plato's dialogues; the role of the poet is used as a device to transmit the myth of the divine origins of the laws, thus enhancing the poet's importance. We will analyse how the myth of the Flood, the era of the Patriarchs and the gift of divine laws are all contained in book III, and how they served as a frame for the biblical narrative. When reading the *Laws* (especially book VII) it appears that the poet is needed by the City to promote the laws. The legislator himself must become a poet and therefore his laws should be preceded by preambles. The legislator and poet have the task of educating the people, whereas in the *Republic*, education was the privilege of only the philosopher-kings. The poet's speech is to be governed by law, yet he must associate the law with pleasure; as poetry is able to induce pleasure, it can have an educative function. In the *Republic* Plato had banned the poets, whereas in the *Laws* they are allowed (and even urged) to come back. Since both works are different, poetry fills a different role in each. This must be emphasised, as Plato is often known in modern philosophy for his positions in the *Republic*. Twentieth-century readers of Plato may have seen a precursor of modern dictatorships in this control of poetry,[93] and Mouze wants to distinguish between the *Republic* and the *Laws*—for poets have a greater emphasis in the latter. Plato's first concern is the soul: How can the poet touch it? Plato considers his City to be the 'truest tragedy' (*Laws* 817 b) as it obeys the canon of Greek tragedy: a just man is happy, rewarded by the laws and the gods, while an unjust man is unhappy and punished. In the *Laws*, Plato does not legislate about poetry but rather about music (*mousika* in Greek—meaning anything that is inspired by the Muses). In book IX of the *Republic* the mind of the tyrannical man is analysed, a man who is a tyrant over his people because he himself is lorded over by his own erotic impulses. The Athenian of the *Laws* imagines a temperate king who is able to promote the laws, or even to abdicate in deference to them. We will see the ways in which the biblical writer gave life to these anonymous portraits.

I believe that the biblical writer read the *Laws* and followed Plato's advice; he had to rewrite myths in order for the people to accept the laws as divine. The transformation of Greek myths into Hebrew myths around the pillar of the law is the ultimate key to understanding the Bible as a narrative that gives life to Plato's ideal City in the form of a national epic. Luc Brisson has shown the importance of preambles in the *Laws*.[94]

The Athenian explains how the laws should be proclaimed with an argument, often a mythical example, to persuade the people of the justice of each (*Laws* 718 d). Brisson counted fourteen preambles in the *Laws*. We will see how the biblical writer used this technique, as several biblical laws are illustrated by an example of how obedience is rewarded and how disobedience is punished by God. A good example of this is seen in the biblical story of the humble and pious daughters of Zelophehad (Num 27 and 36) who pleaded for more just inheritance laws because, as their father had no sons, they were not allowed to inherit the family land. The men of their tribe then appealed to the law again because when the daughters got married their lots of land would be given to their husbands (hence lost to the tribe); the law was revised to oblige daughters that inherited their father's land to marry men from their paternal clan—ensuring that that the lots of land would remain in the same tribes. All of these laws are found in Plato's plan of the Ideal State (Plato, *Laws* 924 d–25 c). The law of levirate, which forces a man to

93. Karl Popper, *La société ouverte et ses ennemis*. I. *L'ascendant de Platon*, Paris: Seuil, 1979.

94. Luc Brisson, *Platon, les mots et les mythes, comment et pourquoi Platon nomma le mythe*, Paris: La Découverte, 1994.

marry his brother's widow if she is childless (Deut 25:5-10), is illustrated by an example of fatal disobedience in the story of Tamar (Gen 38).

Why would such a literary project be born in Judea? Let us suppose that we are in the third or second century B.C.E. A Judean man wants to study Greek literature and philosophy. He has the choice between schools, such as the Library of Alexandria or the Athenian Academy. In the latter, decades after the master's death, what if the goal of giving life to the Ideal State were still alive among the followers? Plato's disciples might have regarded his last dialogue as *Plato's testament*. We will try to show that the biblical writer was a fine reader of Plato. Where he learned platonic philosophy remains impossible to tell, be it in Athens, Alexandria, Antioch or Jerusalem. Still, we know from the example of Antiochus of Ascalon that people from Judea and Palestine did travel to Greece to reach the core of the platonic Academy.[95] It seems that Judea was fertile ground for an attempt at the 'platonic experiment' of the *Laws*. Tyrants governed Sicily—they understood Plato's political ideas to be a threat to their sovereignty for which he was rebuked twice. Ptolemaic or Seleucid Judea, on the other hand, was a small province governed by a Hellenised elite. We could view the project of emulating Plato's Ideal State in the form of a national epic as being a reaction of a colonised elite appropriating the dominant culture, but it could also be that the project came to fruition with the direct help of disciples of the Academy. Since Judea was completely under the influence of the Greeks, an extreme hypothesis would be to consider that some Greek disciples of a platonic school themselves participated in the writing of the Bible, as a sort of 'platonic experiment'. What would happen if, as the Athenian character in the *Laws* suggests, the people were told that their ancestors received divine laws? In the same way that Plato tried to influence Sicilian tyrants to establish his Ideal State, what if some disciples of the Academy tried to influence either the Hellenised priests governing Judea or the Hasmonean kings themselves in order to make them accept the biblical project as a national history and theology?

The Bible tells of how the twelve-tribe State was founded by Joshua after the death of Moses and how this State was eventually destroyed because its kings had abandoned the divine laws given to their ancestors. This framework is found in Plato's *Critias*, the myth of Atlantis. We must understand the links between Plato's political dialogues, all of which contain elements that are found in the biblical narrative. In Plato's *Republic* and *Laws* the Ideal States are projects that were hopefully to

95. Strabo, in his *Geog.* XVI, 2, 29, specifies that Antiochus was a native of Ascalon (by that time a Judean city).

have been realized, whereas the *Critias* and the *Timaeus* both recall the story of the Ideal State Atlantis in a narrative form. Although the *Laws* are the main source of inspiration for the Bible, these other dialogues were used as well. Biblical Israel is a sort of Atlantis, a State that could have been perfect had it not degenerated by losing its divine essence. Israel's hubris is punished by a divine sentence, exactly as in the *Critias*. Themes from the *Republic* were used as well—in book X, Er has a vision of a column of souls going up and down; this is reflected in Jacob's dream of the ladder (Gen 28:11-19), and by a significant homonym appearing in his grandson, *Er*, the son of Judah (Gen 38:3). The biblical writer likes to leave 'fingerprints' by using names from his sources, as he wants the reader to understand his riddle. But there is more in the Bible from the *Republic*. The famous allegory of the Cave from book VII compares the work of the philosopher to that of a man freed from a cave in which he was imprisoned with others for his entire life, having been held in such a manner that all they could see were the shadows that outside objects cast on the rear cave wall through their small cave-fire. Once brought outside into the light, the man only then understands that what he had always seen were but shadows of a greater reality. The light of the sun is seen as the Idea of the Good, the ultimate manifestation of the unique God, the Demiurge who created all the cosmos. The philosopher is then compelled to go back into the cave to free his comrades, and guide them into the light—even though he resists, and even though his former comrades may not believe him and may even make an attempt on his life. In putting those words into Socrates' mouth Plato foreshadows his master's tragic fate, for the Athenians put him to death following the accusation of denying the existence of the gods (Aristophanes' parody of Socrates' ideas in the *Clouds* may have caused these accusations; cf. Plato, *The Apology of Socrates* 19 d). This allegory that has been studied by generations of philosophers is the framework of the Exodus story, as Professor Kupitz has found. Though the sons of Israel have become slaves in Egypt, one of them, Moses, is freed from this condition and raised in the royal family. When grown up, Moses flees from Egypt to the desert of Midian where he meets Yahweh in the burning bush. Yahweh reveals his sacred name and gives Moses a divine mission to go back to Egypt, free his people from slavery and guide them to the Promised Land of…Plato's *Laws*.

Plato gave up the *Republic* for the *Laws* because the former was too utopian (or maybe it was never meant to come to life). The biblical writer knew this and he based his Israel on the second Ideal State, though from the first one he retained the plot of the people who were freed from ignorance and brought to a higher spiritual plane by a philosopher who contemplated the divine truth. As Plato did not want to end up like his master Socrates—who was accused of denying the existence of the Greek gods and was put to death for it—he never denied the Greek gods, but in the *Republic* he explained how their representation by Homer and Hesiod were false, and in book X he speaks of the Demiurge—a nameless god that created the universe. This Demiurge appears in the *Timaeus* (a dialogue supposed to have taken place the day after the *Republic*, thus its continuation) as the creator of the traditional Greek gods. It is important to understand that Plato and Socrates were aware of 'monotheism', but Socrates lost his life for defending this idea out loud; Plato found a compromise in his dialogues, which proved how unjust Socrates' death was. In the Cave allegory, the prisoners revered the shadows on the wall as deities; these shadows were but a mockery of the gods, while the Idea of the Good represents the only God. Therefore, we can understand that biblical monotheism owes a lot to Plato, in the sense that Israel's slavery in Egypt is itself a metaphor of the slavery caused by the worship of false gods (a recurring theme in the biblical narrative).

In both Plato's works and the Bible, the Law is considered to be a way to access virtue and to cleanse the soul of its sins, most of which come from the body's appetites. By acknowledging that Genesis–Kings is a single unitary story based on platonic philosophy, we come to realise that the main character of that epic is the human soul. As Socrates proposes in the *Republic* to define the soul from the just City, the Bible transforms a man, Jacob—Israel, into the State of twelve tribes, born from his twelve sons. Israel is at the same time a man, the platonic City of the *Laws*, and the concept of the soul; here is the riddle that unfolds when understanding the platonic sources of the Bible. Jacob had a vision of divine messengers going up and down a huge ladder, a vision very similar to that of Er at the end of the *Republic* (one of the grandsons of Jacob is also named Er). The biblical Er died childless, and Judah gave two sons to his son's widow, Tamar. Notable among the descendants of Judah and Tamar is Boaz of Bethlehem, who marries Ruth the Moabitess. We will see how this love story was inspired by the union of Poros and Penia— Plenty and Poverty—who gave birth to Eros—Love—in Plato's *Symposium*. We will see that the same literary process is at stake: a platonic allegory is enacted by biblical characters. Ruth and Boaz are the great-grandparents of David, whom I call the red-haired 'literary twin' of Jacob, the second king of Israel, and a horrible tyrant. David—allied with the Philistines—seizes upon the opportunity of King Saul's death. With the help of mercenaries he ravishes the throne, allowing Saul's inheritors to kill one another off. David does not hesitate to order the death of a valiant soldier and to steal his wife, who will become the mother of the apostate Solomon, himself responsible for bringing Israel to schism under Rehoboam.

Far from the popular tradition that considers these kings to be heroes, a literal reading of Samuel and Kings, as Jacques Cazeaux suggests, shows that Israel's kings were its worst enemies, weakening it from the inside. For Cazeaux, Genesis reflects an inverted image of monarchic Israel and Judah through the idealised portraits of the Patriarchs.[96] A single, common message permeates Genesis–Kings: the Law is higher than the king. The Israel founded by Joshua—that of the twelve tribes without a government—should have prevailed eternally, but the violent period of the Judges led Israel to ask the prophet Samuel for a king. As Samuel foretold it, a king would bring the country to its downfall (1 Sam 8:10-18). The Patriarchs Abraham, Isaac and Jacob are the opposites of kings, as they abdicate their power and renounce the possession of the land promised to them. Abraham leaves the best part of the land to his nephew Lot, Isaac is satisfied with Beer-Sheba, and Jacob departs Canaan to end his life in Egypt. Even though each received a divine promise to possess the land, and all had the might to conquer it (we see Abraham fighting in Gen 14 and Jacob's sons as well in Gen 34), they all renounce their claim. Genesis' happy ending in Egypt can seem some-how disappointing to a reader who does not understand why Israel stayed out of its Promised Land, Canaan, since the famine that caused the exodus to Egypt was over. According to Cazeaux, this end perhaps reflects how Israel's truth lies in permanent Exile rather than in the Promised Land's corrupting tenure. The true Promised Land of Israel is the Law, writes Cazeaux, a guarantee of the fraternal unity of Jacob's twelve sons. But is that Law the one revealed on Mount Sinai as the Bible claims, is it the Law of the priests in exile as believed by modern, albeit obsolete, biblical criticism, or is it definitely derived from Plato's *Laws*, a mixture of Athenian and Dorian laws?

On the authenticity of Plato's Laws. How can one prove that the Bible borrowed from the *Laws* and not the other way around; that the resemblances are not due to mere chance? The reasoning here will be deductive. If it can be shown how Plato conjured his Ideal State based on Greek sources, then one may admit that the Bible took inspiration from him. Indeed, given that both texts put forth the same laws (sometimes in the same order) it would be an astonishing coincidence if the Bible had

96. Cazeaux, *Le partage de minuit*.

been written in phases over the centuries. Plato conceived of his State based upon existing Greek institutions and laws, and therefore borrowed nothing from the Bible. For instance, the *epiclerate* law, which allows a daughter to inherit her father's land if she marries a man from the family is not as universal as one may think at first glance. That law appears in Plato's *Laws* as a typical Athenian one, but it was not in use the same way in Sparta and Crete. We must delve into ancient Greek law to understand what Plato took from it. G.R. Morrow[97] has shown how Plato's State in the *Laws* is an idealised version of Athens; it is a cross between the Athens of the fourth century B.C.E. and that of Solon, the legendary legislator of the seventh century B.C.E. Plato introduced Solon as his ancestor in his cousin Critias' speech in the dialogue *Critias*.

The cities of Sparta and Crete (realised along the Dorian model) were also sources of inspiration for Plato's City of the *Laws*. This explains why the three protagonists of the dialogue are, in addition to the anonymous Athenian, a Cretan named Cleinias and a Spartan called Megillos. These three characters reflect what the Ideal State will be—a mixture of Athenian and Dorian institutions. The Athenian dominates the discussion while the other two mostly acknowledge his words; this shows how the Athenian model prevails in the constitution. According to Morrow, the Dorians were admired and respected by the Ionian Athenians for having preserved an ancient way of life. Crete and Sparta were praised for their customs, and were often described as having 'sister laws' (*adelphoi nomoi, Laws* 683 a). Crete is known for its mythical legislator Minos, who was his father Zeus' confidant and from whom he received his laws (*Laws* 624 a). Sparta had Lycurgus, whose laws were sanctioned by Apollo (as mentioned in Plutarch's *Life of Lycurgus* and in Herodotus I, 65). It is likely that Plato used Xenophon's *Republic of the Lacedemonians* as a source for Spartan law and education. Many parallels have been noticed by Morrow, such as the *syssitia*—the meals in common (Xenophon's *Republic of the Lacedemonians* V // *Laws* 842 b). Indeed, the whole seventh book of the *Laws* can be compared to Xenophon's text. One must take into account that both Xenophon and Plato were Socrates' students, thus their writings tend to reflect each other.

In his analysis, Morrow distinguishes the Cretan, Spartan and Athenian components of Plato's City. Plato's admiration for Sparta was long explained by his aristocratic descent and by his preference for aristocratic power to Athenian democracy. But Morrow believes that after the defeat of the Peloponnesian wars the Athenians generally tended to envy the

---

97. G.R. Morrow, *Plato's Cretan City*, Princeton: Princeton University Press, 1960.

Dorian States for having preserved an old stability, as Athens was thought to have been ruined in part by an excess of democracy (as the Athenian proclaims in *Laws* 698 b-702 e). For modern observers, Athens symbolises an evolution towards democracy whereas Dorian cities show a form of 'arrested development'. For the disillusioned Athenians of the fourth century B.C.E., even moderate conservatives were tempted to cite Crete and Sparta as models. It seems that Plato felt that way, as the *Republic* already showed. It says that Sparta is the best of the imperfect cities (*Republic* book VIII), and that the Dorian musical mode is preferred to the Ionian (*Rep.* 399 a). The City in *Laws* was to be made of Cretan colonists (*Laws* 708 a), realised somewhere in Crete. Cleinias the Cretan speaks of Gortyne, the most important Cretan city of the time that was famous for its laws (the Gortyne code of laws has actually been discovered by archaeologists).[98] The location of the ideal City in Crete shows how Plato wanted to distance it from Athens, so as to anchor his City in a kind of idealised Greek past. The division of the land in lots distributed by lottery is referred to as a typical Spartan custom (*Laws* 684 d-e). Morrow believes that the democratic Athenian model was contested at the time, and that the Spartan model was envied. There was likely a growing conservative movement in Athens, nostalgic for the times of Solon before Pericles. In 403 B.C.E. there was a revision of Athenian law in which Solon was brought as a reference. Demosthenes often quoted Solon in his civil addresses, and Solon also plays an important role in Plato's dialogues. The institution of the four classes in the *Laws* (698 b for Athens, 744 a-e for the colony) comes clearly from Solon's reformation, as we know it from Aristotle's *Constitution of Athens* (VII, 3). Finally, we must understand the role of 'ancient Athens' in Plato's dialogues. The *Menexenus* tells the myth of the foundation of Athens. In the *Timaeus* and the *Critias*, ancient Athens is shown defeating Atlantis—an allusion to the Athens of the fifth century B.C.E., victorious over Persia. For Morrow, all this shows that Plato was not anti-Athenian and pro-Spartan as many commentators thought. The ideal City was to follow a model that is mainly Athenian mixed with some old Dorian institutions. It seems that Plato wanted to reclaim the moderation and simplicity of the Dorians that the Athenians lacked. Plato's City is an idealised Hellenic City, and though we find a strong Dorian influence it is closer to Athens than to Sparta.

---

98. See Catherine Dobias-Lalou, ed., *Des dialectes grecs aux lois de Gortyne*, Nancy: A.D.R.A.; Paris: De Boccard, 1999.

Morrow's work can shed light on the production of the Bible. Indeed, the biblical State may appear to the reader as archaic, constructed of old institutions. But it does not mean that the Bible was written when these institutions were in existence, nor even that they once existed in Judea at all. If biblical Israel may appear 'Spartan', rude and austere, it is because it has borrowed Spartan aspects of Plato's City. The book of Judges (the most violent) is full of disguised Spartan heroes, as Gideon, Abimelech and Jephthah hide Spartan royalty—Leonidas, Cleomenes and Dorieus. On the other hand, it is noticeable that mention is made of neither the typical Spartan education and communal meals nor the Athenian classes in the Bible. There have been few studies on Plato's *Laws* compared to other dialogues, though in recent years French scholarship has shown a renewed interest in them.[99] All these studies are relevant for understanding Plato and ancient Greek law; however, none of them mentions any link between the *Laws* and the Bible, as if none of these fine scholars seemed aware even of the possibility. This mutual ignorance by classical and biblical scholars alike must be questioned.

A *reductio ad absurdum* could be useful in proving the nullity of the documentary hypothesis. We will see that chs. 20–23 of Exodus and chs. 12–26 of Deuteronomy describe laws similar to Plato's—several times in the same order. Critics referred to them as the 'Covenant Code' and the 'Deuteronomic Code', respectively, the latter coming from the D source. Certain passages in Leviticus (supposedly from the P source) about sexuality (ch. 18), priesthood (ch. 21) and the interdiction to sell the lots of land (ch. 25) are also close to some of Plato's laws. No classical scholar or historian of philosophy would likely imagine that Plato's *Laws* were a mixture of layers that were written in different eras. All agree that Plato was the original author of the dialogue, even though a rumour spread by Diogenes Laertus (III, 37) claimed that Plato's disciple, Philip of Opus, had to finish the dialogue himself because of his master's death (this rumour is now obsolete). The text of the *Laws* is coherent and well

99. See Léo Strauss, *Socrates and Aristophanes*, New York/London: Basic Books, 1966; *La Cité et l'homme*, Paris: Librairie générale française, (1963) 2005; Jean-François Pradeau, *Platon et la cité*, Paris: P.U.F., 1997; Jean-François Balaudé, *D'une cité possible: sur les Lois de Platon*, Nanterre: Université Paris X, 1995; Jean-Marie Bertrand, *De l'écriture à l'oralité: une lecture des Lois de Platon*, Paris: Publications de la Sorbonne, 1999; Christophe Rogue, *D'une cité l'autre—Essai sur la politique platonicienne, de la République aux Lois*, Paris: Armand Collin, 2005; Pierre Sineux, ed., *Le législateur et la loi dans l'Antiquité: hommage à Françoise Ruzé*, Cæn: Presses Universitaires de Cæn, 2005; or the new translation in French of Luc Brisson and Jean-François Pradeau, *Timée—Critias*, Paris: Flammarion, 2001.

written, as all recent studies agree. So I ask: Considering two texts that contain similar laws, sometimes given in the same order, why would one have been composed by pious priests based on the D and P sources, the other being a mixture of Athenian and Dorian institutions? How could both end up so similar? Should we posit a Dionysian Plato (call him 'Pl. D') living in the sixth century B.C.E. and a fifth century B.C.E. Apollonian Plato ('Pl. A'), the works of both which would have been compiled by Philip, the 'final redactor' ('Ph. R'), in the fourth century B.C.E.? Or, why not consider as well a Spartan Plato—the source of the Megillos character—a Cretan Plato—the source for Cleinias—and an Athenian Plato, all of which would have been compiled during the 'Exile' in Sicily?

The documentary hypothesis has no validity at all as it imposes sources upon the biblical text without ever being able to prove the existence of these sources outside of the Bible; a simple example of circular reasoning. Plato's *Laws* is an opus that is admitted as being genuine, dated by classical scholars who ignore biblical debates. Plato's *Laws* are one of the main sources of biblical legislation. Someone already thought of this concept, though the other way around.

Josephus Flavius: Against Apion

Josephus Flavius was a Hellenised Jewish writer from the first century C.E. that was close to the imperial Roman power. He wrote *Antiquities* in Greek—a long paraphrase of the Bible that included a history of the Jews from the Hellenistic era to his time. He also wrote *The War of the Jews* (relating the Jewish revolution against Roman occupation during the years 60–70 C.E.), as well as an apologetic treatise called *Against Apion* in which he defended Jewish religious practices from the accusations of several other writers. Josephus' aim was to present the Jewish faith to his Roman readers. The Fathers of the Church later used him (along with Philo of Alexandria) for apologetic purposes. *Against Apion* (*Contra Apionem*)—shows a point of contention about the antiquity of Judaism. In book I, 1-5, Josephus introduces his work as a response to these allegations, and says he will explain why so few Greek authors mentioned the Jews. Indeed, some of them ignored the Jews while others 'pretended' to ignore them. This argument over the silence of the main Greek authors concerning the Jews is still relevant today in our debate. The first book quotes Manetho, a Hellenised Egyptian writer who interpreted the Exodus story thusly: that the Jews were chased out of Egypt because they were lepers. Josephus also quotes Berossus, a Hellenised Babylonian writer who recalled the story of the creation, the deluge, and the generations of kings who lived for millennia. For Josephus these tales were a testimony to the Bible's authenticity, although he admits that Berossus did not mention the Jews (Gmirkin discusses that Berossus may have been the source for the Mesopotamian myths in the Bible).[100] Josephus also quotes Greek authors. Herodotus mentioned Syrians of Palestine that practised circumcision (Herodotus II, 104), though Josephus thinks Herodotus actually meant the Jews (*C.A.* I, 168-71). Josephus believed as well that the *Solymians* mentioned in Xerxes' army were the inhabitants of Jerusalem. Aristotle would have met a very wise Jewish philosopher (*C.A.* I, 177-82). It is noteworthy that Eusebius' *Preaparatio Evangelica* (book IX) uses all these quotations in the same order.[101] Josephus admits that none of these Greek authors mentioned the Jews by name except for Hecateus of Abdera. In the second book Josephus answers the harsh criticisms of Apion, who was clearly an anti-Semite, almost in the modern sense of the term. The debate starts in the second part of book II, when Apollonius Molon accused Moses of being an impostor (II, 145). Josephus tries to show that Moses was older than all the famous Greek legislators, such as Solon and Lycurgus:

> And this is the character of our legislator, he was no impostor, no deceiver, as his revilers say, thought unjustly, but such a one as they brag Minos to have been among the Greeks, and other legislators after him; for some of them believe that they had their laws from Zeus, others from Apollo and his oracle at Delphi. (*C.A.* II, 161-62)[102]

These lines of Josephus recall the very first lines of Plato's *Laws*:

> —The Athenian Stranger: 'Tell me, Strangers, is a God supposed to be the author of your laws, or some man?'—Cleinias: 'A God, Stranger, in very truth a God. Among us Cretans is he said to have been Zeus, but in Lacedemon, whence our friend here comes, I believe they would say that Apollo is their lawgiver. Would they not, Megillus?'—Megillus: 'Certainly'. (Plato, *Laws* 624 a)[103]

Josephus' reference to Plato is the start of a relatively explicit comparison between Plato and Moses; Moses has shown that God is eternal and immutable, knowable through his power but unknowable in essence. According to Josephus, the Greek philosophers (such as Pythagoras,

---

100.   Russell E. Gmirkin, *Berossus and Genesis, Manetho and Exodus: Hellenistic Histories and the Date of the Pentateuch*, Library of Hebrew Bible/Old Testament Studies, 433; Copenhagen International Series, 15; New York/London: T&T Clark International, 2006.

101.   See Sabrina Inowlocki, *Eusebius and the Jewish Authors—His Citation Technique in an Apologetic Context*, Leiden/Boston: Brill, 2006.

102.   Translated by William Whitson.

103.   All citations of Plato follow the translations by Benjamin Jowett.

Anaxagoras and Plato) all had the same conception of the divine (*C.A.* II, 167-68). As Josephus wanted to impress his ideas upon a Greco-Roman audience, he used what could be considered 'coincidences' between the biblical and Greek laws and philosophies. Josephus wrote that Moses' law had produced the (implicitly platonic) four virtues of Justice, Temperance, Strength and Concord (*polytos*), replacing the usual Wisdom (*phronesis*) (*C.A.* II, 170). He states that God revealed his laws to Moses (as Zeus allegedly revealed his laws to Minos) because '*There is only one temple for one God, since the fellow always loves the fellow, the temple is common for all, as God is common for all*' (*C.A.* II, 195). The phrase '*the fellow always loves the fellow*' is found in both Plato's *Lysis* (214 a) and *Symposium* (195 b), used as a quotation from Homer (*Od.* XVII, 218). Josephus says that prayers must be addressed to God for the salvation of the community, rather than to ask for material things (*C.A.* II, 196-97). This never appears in the Bible but it does in Plato's *Laws* (687 e)—that people must not pray to the gods for goods, but for wisdom. Josephus continues with his apology of the Jewish law, adding laws that are not found in the Bible, but that are found in the Talmud. Josephus mentions the prohibition against luxurious funerals (*C.A.* II, 205), which does appear in the Babylonian Talmud of the sixth century C.E. (*Moed Katan* 27a); such a law is also seen in Plato (*Laws* 958 d-59 a). We see the same confusion from Josephus a few lines further in *Contra Apionem* II, which says that if a judge accepts a present then he will be put to death (*C.A.* II, 207). That a judge cannot accept presents is indeed found in the Bible (Exod 23:8 as well as Deut 16:19 and 27:25), but nothing is said about the penalty. In *Laws* 955 c-d, however, it is written that a judge that accepts presents is to be put to death. It seems that, in his account of biblical laws, Josephus sometimes gets confused and quotes either laws from a hypothetical early version of the Mishna, or rather, he quotes Plato's *Laws*. He writes:

> …and this while those that have attempted to write somewhat of the same kind for politic government, and for laws, are accused as composing monstrous things, and are said to have undertaken an impossible task upon them. And here I will say nothing of those other philosophers who have undertaken any thing of this nature in their writings. But even Plato himself, who is so admired by the Greeks on account of that gravity in his manners, and force in his words, and that ability he had to persuade men beyond all other philosophers, is little better than laughed at and exposed to ridicule on that account, by those that pretend to sagacity in political affairs; although he that shall diligently peruse his writings will find his precepts to be somewhat gentle, and pretty near to the customs of the generality of mankind. (*C.A.* II, 222-24)

Josephus confesses here that he knows the similarities between Plato's *Laws* and the Bible. However, as he did not find the many religious precepts of Leviticus and Numbers in the works of Plato, Josephus concludes that Plato's *Laws* are easier to achieve. Furthermore, Josephus criticises the Greek religion and the scandalous behaviour of its gods, demonstrating that he has read carefully Plato's criticism of them (*C.A.* II, 236-59).

Josephus wants to show that the Bible conforms to Plato's description of the divine:

> Nay, Plato principally imitated our legislator in this point, that he enjoined his citizens to have the main regard to this precept, 'That every one of them should learn their laws accurately'. He also ordained, that they should not admit of foreigners intermixing with their own people at random; and provided that the commonwealth should keep itself pure, and consist of such only as persevered in their own laws. (*C.A.* II, 257)

According to Josephus, Plato imitated the Bible regarding both the conception of the divine, which should not be represented as Homer did, and the conception of the law:

> We have already demonstrated that our laws have been such as have always inspired admiration and imitation into all other men; nay, the earliest Grecian philosophers, though in appearance they observed the laws of their own countries, yet did they, in their actions, and their philosophic doctrines, follow our legislator, and instructed men to live sparingly, and to have friendly communication one with another. (*C.A.* II, 280-81)

Josephus might not have been successful among those of the Jewish tradition, but the Fathers of the Church took his argument of the 'theft of the Greeks' and developed it; Eusebius literally quotes *Against Apion* in book IX of his *Praeparatio Evangelica*. In comparing Plato and the Bible, Josephus demonstrates—albeit unconsciously—the very platonic origins of the Bible; but he inverts this by claiming that it was the Greek philosophers, Plato especially, that imitated Moses. The previous quotations from Josephus were offered in order to show that these similarities were discussed in antiquity—hence, the constant refusal of biblical scholars to follow this simple lead must be questioned.

Origen

It is likely that the Fathers of the Church dealt with what they may have considered a serious threat that could have jeopardized the future of Christianity; the platonic Academy of Athens, which continued to be very influential until the sixth century C.E., when Justinian (the Christian emperor of the Eastern Roman Empire) had it closed. It is probable that platonic philosophers did notice similarities to the Bible, and they may have claimed that biblical laws were copied from those of their 'divine Plato'. In fact, we do have the indirect testimony of Celsus, a platonic philosopher from the second century C.E. whose lost book, *The True Word*, remains known through quotations and summaries in Origen's *Contra Celsum*. In book V, according to Origen, Celsus compared the Old Testament with Plato and concluded that Plato was the original source, appearing more sophisticated in language than the relatively simple Bible. Origen argued against this, claiming that the Bible merely addresses a wider audience (*C.C.* V, 65). I believe that Celsus' argument is relevant, as the Bible turns the dialectic platonic philosophy into the form of an epic that can be read by the layman. Origen admired Plato, but condemned him for not abandoning idolatry (*C.C.* V, 43; VI, 17). This is also a relevant argument because the Bible rewrites Greek mythology through a monotheistic prism that was inspired by Plato, who risked his life defending the idea of a single god. For Origen, Moses is both anterior and superior to Plato, and even to Homer. Origen asks: '*For how was it possible that they should have heard one who was not yet born?*'[104] (*C.C.* VI, 7), as the Greek alphabet did not exist by the alleged time of the writing of the Torah. Even though Celsus' text has been lost, we understand his main argument to be the platonic inspiration of both the Old and the New Testament. As the chronological argument does not hold up for the New Testament, Origen said that the Gospellers—who were not cultivated men and could not have read Plato's elitist writings—wrote the words of Jesus directly:

> It is not our purpose at present, however, to speak of those who acknowledge another god than the one worshipped by the Jews, but to defend ourselves, and to show that it was impossible for the prophets of the Jews, whose writings are reckoned among ours, to have borrowed anything from Plato, because they were older than he. (*C.C.* VI, 19)

Furthermore, regarding the concept of the Promised Land having been inspired by Plato's celestial earth:

> For our part, our purpose has been simply to say that what we affirm of that sacred land has not been taken from Plato or any of the Greeks, but that they rather—living as they did not only after Moses, who was the oldest, but even after most of the prophets—borrowed from them. (*C.C.* VII, 30).

Origen admired the Jews for their superior wisdom, but wrote:

104. Translated by Frederick Crombie.

> And would that they had not sinned, and transgressed the law, and slain
> the prophets in former times, and in these latter days conspired against
> Jesus, that we might be in possession of a pattern of a heavenly city which
> even Plato would have sought to describe; although I doubt whether he
> could have accomplished as much as was done by Moses and those who
> followed him, who nourished a 'chosen generation', and 'a holy nation',
> dedicated to God, with words free from all superstition. (*C.C.* V, 43)

Origen implicitly admits how Plato's ideal City is similar to that of
biblical Israel. For Origen, Plato only imagined such a City, but Moses
gave it life. I believe that biblical Israel was actually modelled on Plato's
City of the *Laws*. The debate between Celsus and Origen is essentially
the same as the one discussed in the present work. Both original texts
from Apion and Celsus have been lost to time; all that remains are the
answers to these texts by Jewish and Christian apologists, because
Christianity won its battle against paganism and original Platonism.

Eusebius

Eusebius of Caesarea, bishop in the fourth century, influenced Constantine, the first Roman emperor who converted to Christianity. Eusebius
seems to have been inspired by both Josephus' *Against Apion* and
Origen's *Against Celsus*, and in his *Preaparatio Evangelica* he continued
along these lines of reasoning toward an accurate comparison of the texts
of Plato and the Bible. For S. Inowlocki, the transition from a Jewish
apologetic to a Christian apologetic was possible because Josephus had
already addressed a Greco-Roman audience.[105] Eusebius' work shows us
that the debate was still not concluded three centuries after Josephus:
either Plato or Moses borrowed from the other, but who from whom?
Eusebius did not believe that the same 'divine' laws could have appeared
by chance; as Moses lived long before Plato, it must have been Plato
who copied Moses. The main goal of the *Apodeixis* (Eusebius' master-
work, comprising the *Preaparatio Evangelica* and the *Demonstratio
Evangelica*) is for pagans to convert to Christianity, the spiritual inheritor
of Judaism. Books XI–XIII of the *Preaparatio Evangelica* explain how
Plato took inspiration from the Bible:

> Our twelfth Book of the Preparation for the Gospel will now from this
> point supply what was lacking in the preceding Book in proof of Plato's
> accordance with the Hebrew Oracles, like the harmony of a well-tuned
> lyre. We shall begin with a defence of our Faith, that is reviled among the
> multitude. (*P.E.* XII, 1:1)[106]

---

105. Inowlocki, *Eusebius and the Jewish Authors*, 272.
106. Translated by E.H. Gifford.

Eusebius quotes Aristobulus, a Jewish philosopher:

> It is evident that Plato closely followed our legislation, and has carefully
> studied the several precepts contained in it. For others before Demetrius
> Phalereus, and prior to the supremacy of Alexander and the Persians,
> have translated both the narrative of the exodus of the Hebrews our
> fellow countrymen from Egypt, and the fame of all that had happened to
> them, and the conquest of the land, and the exposition of the whole Law;
> so that it is manifest that many things have been borrowed by the afore-
> said philosopher, for he is very learned: as also Pythagoras transferred
> many of our precepts and inserted them in his own system of doctrines.
> (*P.E.* XIII, 12:1)

We see from these examples that the parallels were known and debated.
Did all of these writers take advantage of mere coincidences? In book
XII Eusebius compares many laws from both texts, such as: one should
fear and honour one's parents (Exod 20:12; Lev 19:3 // *Laws* 931 e);
Hebrews shall not have Hebrew slaves for more than seven years (Exod
21:2; Deut 15:12 // *Rep.* 469 c—where Greeks shall not have Greek
slaves); landmarks should not be moved, as they are sacred (Deut 19:14
// *Laws* 842 e); if one were to cause damage to another's land, said
damage must be repaid (Exod 22:5 // *Laws* 843 c); a son may not be
judged for his father's crimes (Deut 24:16 // *Laws* 856 c); a thief must
repay double the amount stolen (Exod 22:2-3 // *Laws* 857 a); a thief
breaking in at night may be killed (Exod 22:4 // *Laws* 874 b); if a bull or
another beast kills a man, then its owner may be prosecuted for murder
and the animal will be put to death (Exod 21:28-29 // *Laws* 873 d); and
the City will be divided into twelve lots given to twelve tribes (Num 26 //
Laws 704 d, 745 b, 760 d). God tells Ezekiel how the people of Israel are
like a mixture of copper, tin, iron, lead and silver (Ezek 22:18); similarly,
Socrates explained how the Guardians of the City will be told they were
made of gold, silver, iron and copper (*Rep.* 416 a). Eusebius quotes the
Republic and the *Laws* and, as Josephus had done previously, explains
how the idea of God in Plato's dialogues is close to that of the Bible. As
discussed in the *Republic*, the censorship of Homer's poems was supposed to have resulted from the biblical conception of a God that neither
lies nor deceives humans:

> When Moses had laid down a plan of legislating for men, he thought that
> he must have in his preface an account of ancient times: and he makes
> mention of the Flood, and of the subsequent life of mankind, and then he
> describes the social life of the men of old among the Hebrews who were
> friends of God, and also of those who were proved otherwise in offences,
> because he considered that the narration of these things would be a paral-
> lel to his legislation. And in like manner Plato also, when he proceeds to

write down laws, affects the same method with Moses. In the preface, for instance, of the Laws, he has made use of his account of ancient times, making mention of a flood, and of the mode of life after the flood. Listen at least to what he says at the beginning of the third Book of the Laws. (*P.E.* XII, 15)

This point is of great importance, as Eusebius indicates how the very structures of both the Bible and Plato's *Laws* are alike; indeed *Laws* book III speaks of a flood followed by a patriarchal life prior to the issuing of the laws, as is also found in Genesis and the subsequent legislative books. Eusebius concludes book XII by writing:

Also all the other passages expressed like these in the words of the Hebrews anticipated the interpretation put forth at length by Plato. And so you will find, by carefully examining each of them point by point, that it agrees with the Hebrew writings. And by doctrines of the Hebrews I mean not only the oracles of Moses, but also those of all the other godly men after Moses, whether prophets or apostles of our Saviour, whose consent in doctrines must fairly render them worthy of one and the same title. (*P.E.* XII, 52:35)

Eusebius advises the reader that his demonstration is not exhaustive, and suggests that one read more. I cannot help but be extremely surprised at the fact that neither biblical nor classical scholarship have explored this very clear clue left by Eusebius. This denial embodies the core of my thesis. The platonic roots of biblical religion were known in antiquity, but have been repressed since Christianity triumphed in the fourth century C.E., shortly after Eusebius wrote his *Preaparatio Evangelica* and Constantine embraced the Christian faith. Henceforth, it became impossible even to *consider* that the Bible perhaps borrowed from Plato. The demonstration of my thesis will be very similar to that of Eusebius, except that my conclusions are the exact opposite. This work will use the same method as Eusebius, which entails offering quotations which are punctuated by commentary, letting the texts speak for themselves.

In book X of the *Preaparatio Evangelica*, Eusebius establishes a chronology of the Greek and biblical authors to understand who borrowed from whom (*P.E.* X, 8). He notices that the most important Greek philosophers—Thales, Socrates and Plato—were all born during the time of the Persian domination of Judea '*when the prophecies had ceased among the Hebrews*'—therefore, Plato learned his philosophy from the 'Hebrews' (*P.E.* X, 14). This point is also relevant as Eusebius only relays the intention of the biblical writer; the Hebrew Bible indeed ends with the stories of Ezra and Nehemiah in the Persian era, somewhere in the fifth century B.C.E., thus before Plato's works. The biblical writer intended this chronological argument—the story of Israel must end before the rise of platonic philosophy and the Hellenisation of Judea.

To this day, a substantial and systematic comparison of Plato and the Bible has not been done—that very fact alone being a sign of the intellectual repression that both Judaism and Christianity have exerted. The conversion of the Emperor Constantine to Christianity, followed by the conversion of the Roman Empire under Theodosius I in 380 C.E., has locked the debate for centuries. The victory of 'Judeo-Christian' Platonism over the original (which was widespread across the empire) is a focal point in the history of Western civilisation. As Plato's philosophy was held to be divine in the Roman Empire, Christian apologists succeeded in convincing emperors (who had their own political agendas) that the Bible was older than and superior to Plato's writings. Indeed, my work on the origins of the Bible may concern Christian religion even before it concerns Jewish religion since it is Christian philosophy that became dominant in Europe. This was probably because both the Old and the New Testaments shared a common platonic background that was familiar to apparent neophytes. Who knows how many texts by 'pagan' philosophers that attacked Christian faith based on the accusation of plagiarism (such as those of Apion and Celsus) have been 'lost'? The works of Origen and Eusebius (as well as Clement of Alexandria) effectively have neutralised the threat of the Greek classical texts by arguing that the biblical books were all older. This mentality has prevailed in modern scholarship to the extent that theologians and philosophers study the Bible and Plato separately. Eusebius refers to Plato's doctrine of the noble lie—that myths and fables should be used to educate the youth (*Rep.* 414 c; *Laws* 663 d)—as something that Moses too would have used (*P.E.* XII, 31). Perhaps, as he had studied both works so carefully, Eusebius may have been aware that Plato's *Laws* inspired the Old Testament. However, wanting to promote Christian faith he may have chosen to reverse that story, admitting that a lie is noble when done for the good of the people. What is certain is that the conversion of Roman emperors to Christianity led to the closing of the platonic Academy in the sixth century C.E., and consequently of the comparative debate altogether.

Biblical scholarship has failed to analyse the Bible in the light of Plato since its beginning: even though it was possible for anyone to follow Eusebius' work and, as he suggested, to compare more of Plato's texts with the Bible. It was possible to consider that the parallels raised by Eusebius were not due to mere coincidence, nor to the biblical inspiration of Plato.

The Techniques of the Biblical Writer

Dismantling and Refitting of the Greek Sources

The books from Genesis to Kings, often called the Primary History, tell a continuous story from the creation of the world to the fall of Jerusalem. This narrative was inspired by Plato's *Laws* and Herodotus' *Histories*, as well as the mythic cycles of Heracles, the Argonauts, Thebes, and Troy. In order to make the borrowing seem less blatant, the biblical writer dismantled these stories/texts entirely and re-composed them according to a specific pattern. One can say that to do so he used 'mythemes' (minimal mythic units)—as per Lévi-Strauss' meaning of the word. The case of Herodotus is clear, as Wesselius has shown. Second Kings ends at a period of time a little before the opening of the first book of the *Histories*—in the sixth century B.C.E. with the birth of Cyrus, who will conquer Babylon. For Wesselius this is not due to chance, but is rather the biblical writer's deliberate homage to his main source of inspiration.[107] The first book of Herodotus could be read almost as the continuation of 2 Kings: Nebuchadnezzar destroys Jerusalem in 587 B.C.E. (as in 2 Kgs 24), and Herodotus tells how Cyrus will cause the fall of Babylon under Nabonides in 538 B.C.E. We will see that Croesus, the main hero of Herodotus' first book, was used to create the character of Solomon in 1 Kings. Thus, Herodotus' first book was used as a source for the Bible's last book (referring to Genesis–Kings). Herodotus' second book, about Egypt, is a source for three biblical books: Genesis and Exodus (as part of the stories of Abram, Joseph and Moses occur in Egypt) as well as 2 Kings. In 2 Kings the writer quotes a source—the annals of the kings of Israel and Judah—that contains historical events confirmed by archaeology. However, the writer blended this document with legendary tales about the kings of Egypt that he found in Herodotus' second book. Moreover, and not without some irony, he took advantage of overlapping historical information found in both sources. Thus, he fused the accounts of the Assyrian King Sennacherib's campaign westward into one story (2 Kgs 18–19 // Herodotus II, 141), and did the same with the campaign of Pharaoh Neco into Syria (2 Kgs 23:29 // Herodotus II, 158-59). These two stories, where the Bible and Herodotus obviously meet, are but the proverbial tip of the iceberg. They compel us to dig more deeply through the works of Herodotus, and we will see that many kings of Israel and Judah were modelled after his characters. Only one who reads both texts is able to understand the irony of the biblical writer, who, in comparing the kings of Israel to the Pharaohs of Egypt, delivered his message: by

---

107. Wesselius, *The Origin of the History of Israel*, 72.

electing kings, Israel fell back into slavery from which it had been freed by God in Egypt. Behind this reflection lies the platonic idea that the law prevails over any form of government.

Herodotus' third book tells about the kings of Persia—their customs, day-to-day life at the court, and the conspiracy of a false king that led Darius to power. This third book appears to be the source of the biblical book of Esther. Esther takes place in the royal court of Susa, and appears to come from the same author as a sort of epilogue. Possible proof of this is that there is no double use of themes (see Chapter 9). The fourth book describes the world of the Scythians, and Herodotus gives various geographical descriptions (IV, 36-45) that have some connections with the 'Table of Nations' in Genesis 10. At the end of the fourth book, Herodotus describes the foundation of the Greek colony of Cyrene in Libya, which shares many similarities with the story of Moses. Battus appears as the prototype of Moses—a man with a stutter who received the divine mission of guiding his people to a land promised to their ancestor Euphemus the Argonaut, who corresponds to Abraham. This narrative is important in linking the epic of the Argonauts to the foundation of the platonic State. Pindar (*Pythians* IV and V), Herodotus (IV, 154-55) and Apollonius of Rhodes (*Argonautica* IV, 1730-65) all relate the Argonauts to the foundation of Cyrene.[108] As Plato's State in the *Laws* was to be a colony conquered by force (*Laws* 702 b-d), the biblical writer mixed Greek mythical traditions about Cyrene with the platonic utopia. This kind of reasoning tends to prove that the Bible is dependent upon these sources of inspiration, as it combines various diverse elements found among them all. Books V to IX of Herodotus supply elements for the Bible in a more random way, while many narratives from Judges come from stories of Greek kings. Finally, the fall of Jerusalem depicted in 2 Kings 24 was directly inspired by the fall of Sestos in the last book of Herodotus (IX, 115-20). Both texts end with a similar story; Wesselius believes it to be an ultimate reference intended to lead the reader back to Herodotus.[109]

The biblical author worked the same way with platonic sources, dismantling the order of Plato's *Laws* and recreating it in the books of Exodus, Leviticus, Numbers and Deuteronomy. Of course, the main difference between the two is in the telling; Plato's *Laws* is a project discussed by three old men, whereas the Bible is a story of a people that receive these laws from God as they wander in the desert. This author put

108. See Claude Calame, *Mythe et histoire dans l'Antiquité grecque: la création symbolique d'une colonie*, Lausanne: Payot, 1996.
109. Wesselius, *The Origin of the History of Israel*, 45.

a platonic introduction (compiled from such dialogues as *Timaeus*, *Gorgias*, *Phaedo*, *Protagoras*, the *Statesman* and the *Symposium*) in the first chapters of Genesis, combining several myths about the origins of the world and of humankind. These parallels are difficult to admit when reading the Bible from the beginning, as in the past biblical scholars have tied these first chapters to Mesopotamian myths. It is through the comparison of the laws in the legislative books that, in retrospect, we can understand the platonic touch in the first chapters of Genesis. The biblical writer made a continuous story out of narratives that are found separated across the platonic dialogues. In his borrowing of Herodotus and of Plato, the biblical writer traced a linear chronology (though we can still read his work in both diachronic and synchronic ways). Surprisingly, we will find the myth of the birth of Eros (*Sym.* 203 b-c) adapted in the book of Ruth, which is probably from the same author as well. As previously mentioned, the *Critias* (or the *Atlantis*) was used as a general framework for the whole biblical narrative, as it tells how an Ideal State degenerated and brought the sentence of divine destruction upon itself— all because the kings gave up the sacred laws that their ancestors had sworn to respect eternally (*Crit.* 121 c). We will see how the oath of Israel in accepting the laws (Exod 24:1-11) is quite similar to that of the first kings of Atlantis (*Crit.* 119 d-20 c).

Platonic laws are found in books IV to XII of the *Laws*. Book V lays out the territorial organisation of the City, with the twelve tribes subdivided into plots that are distributed by lottery and paternally inherited. We find that in Numbers (chs. 1; 26; 27; 36) God submits an identical cadastre to Moses in the form of a project, and Joshua gives it life (Josh 14–19). Book VI tells of the various functions of the City, notably priesthood (*Laws* 759 a-60 a)—which is very close to Leviticus 21. Book VII speaks of education. It was not used as a textual source, however it explains (as illustrated above) how the poet must tell myths that support the laws—an idea that is at the core of the biblical writing. Book VIII establishes rules for sexuality, which can be compared to Leviticus 18 and 20; it also prescribes laws for agriculture that are found in Deuteronomy. Book IX includes many parallels with the Bible in its discussion of crime: violence, theft and murder. In it are laws that appear in Exodus, several times in the same order, which leaves little doubt about which text was dependent upon which. Even though some of these laws are ancient and appear in the *Code of Hammurabi*, we will show how *Laws* was a direct source for the Bible. Plato's reasoning about murder is logical. He starts with involuntary homicide, then proceeds to voluntary homicide, whether premeditated or not; this progression is interrupted in the Bible, as the laws are laid out across Exodus, Numbers and Deuteronomy. Book X of the *Laws* is about cults, and in Deuteronomy one can find the same calls for the denouncement of heretics and the prohibition of private altars, magic, spells and enchantments. Book XI is about property and transactions—again, the same laws appear in Deuteronomy. Legislation on women's right of inheritance is found in Numbers, which is linked to the matter of the cadastre. Book XII gives laws concerning war and funerals. The biblical author used the same process for Herodotus and Plato, the two major sources; the narratives and laws were taken from their original orders and re-arranged differently in the Bible so as to make the borrowing less visible. Yet, here and there, the order remains the same. I believe that these cases are deliberate 'fingerprints' left by the author for the erudite reader, to point subtly to his sources. The same technique was used for the Bible's other sources: the Greek epics of Heracles, Thebes, Troy and the Argonauts. We will see for instance that some elements of the Heraclean cycle have been used in Genesis in the telling of the youth of Jacob, as well as for a story in Exodus about Moses. The rest of the cycle was used to create the character of Samson in Judges. Again, I reiterate that there is no double use of 'mythemes'— one Greek mytheme translates to one biblical mytheme. This perfect balance would not have been the case if the parallels were due to chance or oral diffusion. On the contrary, this economy of mythical themes is the evidence of a constructed and conscious work. Parts of the epic of the Argonauts are found in Genesis (the binding of Isaac) and in Samuel and Kings (David's troubles with Mephibosheth, Saul's legitimate heir). The Trojan War and predominantly the *Iliad* were used as sources for the battle scenes in Samuel. It is already noticeable that each biblical book seems to have a privileged source that gives it a distinctive 'colour'; Samuel seems mainly Homeric, Judges and Kings depend mostly upon Herodotus; Joshua and the legislative books owe a lot to Plato's *Laws*; and Joseph's story seems to be inspired by Ulysses' return in the *Odyssey*. Genesis mixes all the sources in such a way that all further books can be related to it.

Fusion of Several Greek Characters into One Biblical Character
No biblical character is the incarnation of just one single Greek character; each is a composite of various Greek characters. The only exception is Samson, who follows his model Heracles closely. However, we just saw that some parts of the Heraclean cycle were applied to the characters of Jacob and Moses, and Aristeus (the first beekeeper, closely tied to Heracles in Pindar's *Ninth Pythian*) was an inspiration for Samson's

character. There is always logic to how the characters are combined. Abraham was based on founders of great lineage such as King Anaxandrides of Sparta and Euphemos the Argonaut; he thus encounters the fate of Athamas, who had to sacrifice his son to Zeus (in the prologue of the Argonautic epic). Moses is made of many different characters, and David as well. Solomon was based on Croesus (who appears in the first book of Herodotus), but also on Pharaoh Cheops in book II—as he relegated his own people to build temples and palaces for him.[110]

Keeping of Homonyms and Homophones

Several names appear in common between Greek and biblical texts. The best example is the character of *Japhet*, son of Noah (Gen 9 and 10). *Japhet* is a homonym of *Japet* or *Japetos*, the Titan who appeared most notably in Hesiod's *Theogony*. This has been long noticed by scholars and is thought to result from Semitic influences on Hesiod's work. The biblical Japhet is the son of Noah, while in the oldest account of the Deluge in Greek literature, Pindar's *Ninth Olympian Ode* (40-56), Japet is the father of Prometheus and Epimetheus—respectively, the fathers of Deucalion and Pyrrha who play the biblical parts of Noah and his wife— or Mesopotamian Ut-Napishtim. The biblical writer had knowledge of the Mesopotamian account of the Deluge, as seen in the detail of Noah sending birds to find land (as in the *Epic of Gilgamesh* and Berossus), but as the name Japhet persists he also must have had knowledge of the Greek version. In Gen 10:2-5, Japhet is the father of Ion, ancestor of the Greeks (though pronounced 'Yavan' by the Masoretes and 'Yovan' by the Septuagint, the Hebrew consonants *yod-waw-nun* spell 'ION'). Ion appears in the Greek tradition as a direct descendant of Deucalion (and hence of Japhet too; see Herodotus I, 146; V, 66; Euripides' *Ion*), and as the eponymous ancestor of the Ionian Greeks. The traditional Greek genealogy is compressed in Genesis, making Japhet Ion's father. *Whenever Genesis was written, these verses demonstrate that the author possessed knowledge not only of the Greeks but also of their mythical genealogies.*

Names from the Greek tradition are retained and replaced on the genealogic scale, a process that occurs several times. Japhet went from being grandfather of Deucalion to Noah's son. *Caineus*, king of the Lapiths, was the descendant of Ixion, humankind's first murderer (as in the works of Homer, Pindar, Apollonius and Apollodorus); an association that gives rise to the character of *Cain*. These homonyms may

---

110. Jacques Cazeaux (*Saül, David et Salomon*) has developed an analysis of Solomon that shows how the biblical writer compared him implicitly to a Pharaoh.

create a sort of confusion for a reader who knows both literatures. We will also find that the name of *Er* the Pamphylian (the hero of Plato's eschatological myth of *Rep.* X) is homophonous with Judah's son *Er* (Gen 38). Although the biblical Er seems to be an insignificant character, he is a clue to the platonic riddle that is the genealogy of David. All these subtle allusions are 'fingerprints' left by the biblical writer that lead back to his sources, hints that only one who has read both the Greek and biblical literature can understand. In this respect, Greek classical literature must be seen as the *hypotext* of the Bible, meaning the texts that surround and inspire it as a *hypertext*.[111] The technique of leaving homonyms that are displaced on the genealogic scale corresponds to the first technique of dismantling and re-arranging the order of the sources; in both cases, clues are left for the reader as deliberate references. The Bible is far from a plagiarism, as it recognises its sources of inspiration through these cryptic allusions.

Ex eventu *Prophecies: The Hellenistic Era as a* Blind Spot

The use of prophecies concerning the Hellenistic era (which for a non-believer are anachronistic) is yet another example of open references in the Bible. The book of Daniel tells how the prophet, living in Babylon during the sixth century B.C.E., had a vision of times to come, referred to as 'the end of times'—the Hellenistic era (Dan 8:17). As Daniel does not understand the cryptic prophecy, the angel Gabriel explains: the king of the Greeks will conquer the East (Dan 8:21) and his generals will share his empire after his death (Dan 8:22) until such a time when another king (generally identified with Antiochus IV Epiphanes) will persecute the Jews (8:23-25). On these grounds, biblical criticism unanimously considers the book of Daniel, or at least that part of it, to have been written after the fact in the second century B.C.E. If one does not believe that humans can foresee the future, then one must admit that biblical prophecies were written after that which they announce—*ex eventu*. On the other hand, some participants in the Jewish and Christian faiths may consider Daniel as evidence that prophecies are true, and that the book was written in Babylon by Daniel himself.

The same goes for any biblical book supposedly older than the book of Daniel, for they too contain prophecies of future events. But the further in the past the story was supposed to have taken place, the more vague is the prophecy. Noah predicts that his son Japhet will expand and dwell in

---

111.   See Gérard Genette, *Palimpseste, la littérature au second degré*, Paris: Seuil, 1982. As an example, Genette writes that Homer's *Odyssey* is the hypotext for Virgil's *Aeneid*, as well as for Joyce's *Ulysses*.

the tents of Sem' (Gen 9:27), meaning that the descendants of Japhet will come to live among the descendants of Sem—the 'Semites'. The allusion can concern either Madai—one of Japhet's sons, as the Medes, allied with the Persians, who defeated Babylon in 538 B.C.E.—or the Greeks through Ion and his descendants who conquered the Persian empire between 330 and 320 B.C.E. under Alexander the Great. Furthermore, in Numbers, the prophet Balaam foresees that fleets sent from Kittim (a son of Ion in Gen 10:5) will subdue Assur (Assyria) and Eber (the 'Hebrews'—Eber being a descendant of Sem, Gen 10:21, 26): 'But ships shall come from the coast of Kittim, and they shall afflict Asshur, and shall afflict Eber, and he also shall come to destruction' (Num 24:24).

Both prophecies of Noah and Balaam, when read together, point with precision to the coming of Alexander and his fleets—which did set sail from Cyprus, named Kittim in the Bible after its capital Kittion. Twice in the Pentateuch—but I would rather speak of *Enneateuch*—clear references are made to the Greek's invasion of the Near East, and even to their fall; it would be rather easy to argue that these are late additions. On the contrary, it all makes sense once one is familiar with the tone and technique of the biblical writer, who hides neither the period in which he wrote nor his sources of inspiration.

There seems to be no logical reason to treat the 'Pentateuch' or any other biblical book differently than the book of Daniel. Only tradition tells us of the alleged biblical authors and times of writing. The three other great biblical prophets (Isaiah, Jeremiah and Ezekiel) also allude to the Hellenistic era, even though supposedly these characters lived in the eighth, seventh and sixth centuries B.C.E., respectively. Biblical criticism had to invent a 'Deutero-Isaiah' said to have written onward from ch. 40 where the prophecies about the Persian conquest seem to be too accurate; for example, Cyrus is named and considered to be the instrument of God's revenge against Babylon. For biblical scholarship, only a contemporary of the facts could have written these chapters. The first thirty-nine chapters would still have come from the hand of the first Isaiah, even though these very chapters also predict future events! The book of Isaiah seems very coherent to me, and in the last chapter the Greeks are mentioned as the descendants of Ion (Isa 66:19).

Jeremiah, who knew the last reigning King Zedekiah, predicted the fall of Babylon (Jer 41). But Jeremiah also prophesied the fall of Elam, an archaic term for Persia (Jer 49:34-39): 'And I will bring against Elam the four winds from the four quarters of heaven, and will scatter them toward all those winds; and there shall be no nation whither the dispersed of Elam shall not come' (Jer 49:36). These four winds are easily recognised as the four kings contemplated by Daniel in his vision, who are the four generals of Alexander: 'And the he-goat magnified himself exceedingly; and when he was strong, the great horn was broken; and instead of it there came up the appearance of four horns toward the four winds of heaven' (Dan 8:8). In both cases, the Diadochi are compared to four winds. When Daniel had this vision he was transported to Susa in Elam: 'And I saw in the vision; now it was so, that when I saw, I was in Shushan the castle, which is in the province of Elam; and I saw in the vision, and I was by the stream Ulai' (Dan 8:2). Jeremiah is supposed to have lived in the early sixth century B.C.E., but his prophecies about the fall of Persia do not take place until the late fourth century B.C.E.

These anachronisms are fundamental in dating *all* of the biblical books to the Hellenistic era. All these prophecies seem to indicate that they were contemporaneous, written by people that knew each other and worked together, likely under a supervisor, whom I believe was the main author of Genesis–Kings. The whole biblical history ends at the time of the Persian domination, right before the coming of Alexander. The prophets Haggai, Zechariah and Malachi, are supposed to have lived in the fifth century B.C.E. The Hellenistic era appears as the *blind spot* of the Bible. The Hellenistic era is present in many places throughout the Bible, but we do not see it for what it is. I call it the blind spot of the Bible for this is the point at which the Bible, a text opened to the past, attaches itself to the author's present in the same way the retina is attached to the brain via the optic nerve. This linkage creates a little blindness for which our brain compensates by reconstructing reality through habit.

The Hellenistic era does appear in the books of Maccabees, which relate this period in terms of narratives and not in terms of prophecies. Perhaps, as Lemche stated, this is the reason why they were not accepted in the Hebrew canon.[112] Whether the books of Maccabees were part of the original plan or whether they were from a second generation of biblical books, one cannot tell; however, their function seems to be to hide the very birth of the Bible in this era, portraying the Jews as fighting to preserve their ancestral traditions in the face of Greek acculturation.

Doubled Narratives and 'Linear Literary Dossier'
Wesselius found another explanation for the presence of seemingly redundant narratives in the Bible. These duplicated stories were used by biblical critics as a primary argument in claiming that the biblical text is made of several strata (for instance, the two versions of the creation of humans in Gen 1 and 2, or the two versions of the death of Saul in

112.   Lemche, 'The Old Testament: A Hellenistic Book?'

1 Sam 31 and 2 Sam 1). For Wesselius, they can be explained as being in imitation of Herodotus, as he often gives two accounts of the same story depending upon the information collected. The foundation of Cyrene is told twice: first the version of the Thereans from the metropolis, and second the version of the Cyreneans from the colony (Herodotus IV, 154). The foundation of Thera is also told with the version of the Thereans, as well as with that of the Lacedemonians (Herodotus IV, 150). Herodotus justifies these doubled stories as being a result of his survey, and he lets his reader judge which version seems more plausible. In imitating Herodotus, the biblical writer used the same technique, but he remained an anonymous narrator and did not comment upon such doubled stories in his text.

For Wesselius, this allows three ways of reading the Bible. The first reading is a 'religious' one that seeks to harmonise the different stories into one continuous narrative. Second, one may believe that these stories reflect the fact that several genuine and contradictory traditions are compiled in the biblical text; Wesselius thus understands the documentary hypothesis as resulting from the intentions of the biblical writer. As this writer took stories from a foreign tradition, he may have wanted to give his text the appearance of authenticity—what appears to the reader to be editorial mistakes may be a source of comfort, as the text seems to be based on ancient traditions. This is what Wesselius calls a 'literary linear dossier'—a compilation of traditions in chronological order, with deliberate disharmonies. Finally, the third possible reading uncovers the Greek sources behind the text and understands the many allusions that point to them. These three levels of reading coexist, making the Bible a very sophisticated piece of literature. Sometimes, doubled narratives appear following each other, as in the case of Saul's death on the battlefield. Other times, similar stories appear separated by several tomes, as in the story of Lot in Sodom (Gen 19) and the Levite in Gibeah (Judg 19). I will try to show how the story of David in Samuel is a repetition of the story of Jacob in Genesis. Jacob and David are the Bible's 'literary twins'; both of them are the incarnation of Israel, which is at the same time a man, a State and the soul—as in the platonic conception of the *Republic* (434 e-35 a). I will also show how the stories of Tamar (Gen 38) and Rahab (Josh 2 and 6) use the same dialectic of doubling; they tell of a Canaanite woman who, pregnant with twins, is likened to the walls surrounding the Canaanite city of Jericho and the 'delivery' of the two spies sent by Joshua. I call this technique the use of diptychs: two-folded scenes that explain one another. Among these biblical diptychs is one that permeates the whole work—the implicit

comparison between Babylon and Jerusalem.[113] The fall of Babel in
Genesis 11 is reflected in the fall of Jerusalem to Babel in 2 Kings 24.
The beginning of the Bible foretells the end, and vice-versa. Although
the fall of Jerusalem is a historical event, it is interpreted philosophically
as the loss of paradise. The expulsion of Adam and Eve from the Garden
of Eden is a metaphor for God's exiling of Israel from its Promised Land
for disobeying the divine laws. According to the platonic pattern, all the
characters of the Bible are one—the soul.

'Intertextuality' and 'Extratextuality'

Intertextuality is a concept first introduced by post-structuralist Julia
Kristeva; it was enhanced by Gérard Genette.[114] As we just saw, the Bible
uses internal references but it also employs many references to external
texts. The author left clues, his 'fingerprints', that point to his sources.
This technique has always been used in Greek literature. For instance,
the *Iliad* and the *Odyssey* reflect each other; there appears to be some
sort of dialogue between them in the use of language and themes that
suggest that the same person (or team) wrote them both.[115] In the third
century B.C.E. Apollonius of Rhodes wrote his *Argonautica* in response
to Homer, leaving myriad references to his primary source—either
literary (as in the formulations or vocabulary) or literal (such as characters common to both epics, like Circe, Alkinoos, Nausicaa, etc.).[116]
According to V. Knight, scholars of the third century B.C.E. re-dis-
covered Homer's poetry and learned it by heart; Apollonius' work was
somehow meant to flatter their erudition, as if recognising that the
numerous references played some sort of intellectual game. I believe the
biblical author was raised in such a milieu and may have been familiar
with Apollonius' work, since he was the chief of the Library. The biblical writer pushed the technique to a third level, as his text combines the
Argonautica and Homer (especially in the book of Samuel). As Michèle
Broze and Françoise Labrique explain regarding Apuleus' *Metamorphosis*: 'It is clear that the ancients elaborate an extremely sophisticated
construction that cumulates intertextuality as external reference and
mirror games as inner reference'.[117] The biblical writer also knew of links

113.   Thompson, *The Mythic Past*, 24-26, 42, 88-89.
114.   Genette, *Palimpseste*.
115.   Pietro Pucci, *Ulysse Polutropos, lectures intertextuelles de l'Iliade et
l'Odyssée*, Lille: Presses Universitaires du Septentrion, 1995.
116.   See Knight, *The Renewal of Epic*.
117.   Michèle Broze and Françoise Labrique, 'Hélène, le cheval de bois et la
peau de l'âne', in *Le mythe d'Hélène*, ed. Michèle Broze et al., Brussels: Ousia,
2003, 133-87 (186).

between works of Herodotus and Plato. Pierre Vidal-Naquet has shown how Plato's *Critias* could be read as a pastiche of Herodotus.[118] Plato wanted to prove the authenticity of his narrative as well by referring to the sources that first told it (the Egyptian priests—as in Herodotus' second book).

For Luc Brisson, Plato uses the same vocabulary and style as Herodotus and Thucydides. It is obvious to Brisson that Plato took inspiration from Herodotus' second book, imitating him with both respect and irony.[119] For instance, the kings of Atlantis that share the land (*Crit.* 120 c-d) are inspired by the twelve kings of Egypt (Herodotus II, 147). We have already mentioned that Herodotus' second book is a source for Egyptian narratives in Genesis and Exodus, as well as for the decadence of the kings of Israel in the book of Kings. Herein lies the genius of the biblical writer: as Plato himself took inspiration from Herodotus to create his myth of the Ideal State and its decadence, the biblical writer mixed both Plato and Herodotus as sources for his own epic. The influence of Plato is everywhere in Genesis–Kings, visible when platonic myths are re-told or platonic laws are proclaimed, but also as a philosophical framework for the criticism of monarchy in Samuel and Kings. As Plato himself read and commented upon Homer, Herodotus and Euripides, the biblical writer took advantage of all the pre-existing links within Greek literature and recreated them in his work. This argument is central in the demonstration of the borrowing: the probability is miniscule that an independent author could have produced a text containing so many similarities with Greek literature without heeding it, and that by pure chance this work would have reproduced the links of intertextuality between the Greek texts. The similarities are far too accurate to consider that they could result from 'general themes shared by all humanity' or from 'archetypes from a collective unconscious'. We must notice that most of the Greek sources used by the biblical writer have been passed down to us. Except for some lost tragedies, most major Greek authors have been preserved through the process of canonisation that took place in Alexandria (under the supervision of Aristarchus of Samothrace and Aristophanes of Byzantium, both of whom were disciples of Apollonius of Rhodes). The biblical writer may have used the Alexandrian canon, which would point to the second century B.C.E. as the time of the writing of the Bible.

---

118.   Pierre Vidal-Naquet, 'Athènes et l'Atlantide', in *Le chasseur noir*, Paris: Maspero, 1981, 335-60.

119.   Brisson and Pradeau, *Timée—Critias*, 321.

Anonymity and Apocryphal Sources

As the writer of the Bible remained anonymous, he can be confused with the anonymous narrator—so much so that religious tradition has dismantled his work and assigned several authors to it. It is still believed that the 'Pentateuch' was written earlier than the 'Prophets'. Nowhere is it stated that the law written by Moses is the actual Pentateuch. On the contrary, we are told that Moses wrote the law, but it is never explained how this law came to be a part of the narrative of the Bible. This Law of Moses appears in the time of King Josiah as a distinct book (or scroll) that was found in the temple, after it had been forgotten for centuries (2 Kgs 22). This literary technique of alluding to a book within a book may also be interpreted in three ways. The first is the identification of Moses' book with the Pentateuch, as seen in Judeo-Christian tradition. The second interpretation searches for an ancient Jewish text that may be identified with Moses' law, like the D source (written supposedly at Josiah's court) or the P source (written during the Exile). The third is in understanding that Moses' law is an apocryphal text that hides the very source of biblical legislation—Plato's *Laws*. As with other sources invoked by the Bible, such as the Book of the Wars of Yahweh (Num 21:14) or the Book of the Just (Josh 10:13), Moses' law is apocryphal.[120] Having never existed, it serves to distract the reader from the Greek sources, contrary to the other techniques that lead the reader to them. The source of the annals of the kings of Judah and Israel appears to be genuine, since archaeology has confirmed events and names from 1 and 2 Kings.[121] Many laws of the Bible do not appear in the works of Plato; therefore we can infer that some religious laws already existed in Judea, though I would not dare to say that prior to the writing of the Bible they were yet compiled in a sacred code that was attributed to Moses.

The single narrator of Genesis–Kings appears to have witnessed the fall of Jerusalem. However, this 'extradiegetic' narrator[122] is not the author, who points to his sources with great irony. Behind Homeric texts may be found a single author (or several anonymous ones), and it is not surprising to see the same debate about their origins as is seen in biblical scholarship. Indeed, John Van Seters believes that Homeric scholarship itself gave birth to the documentary hypothesis.[123] Pietro Pucci has shown

120.　For a discussion of books cited in the biblical narrative, see Stott, *Why Did They Write This Way?*

121.　See Finkelstein and Silberman, *The Bible Unearthed.*

122.　As per Genette's definition of an omniscient and anonymous narrator; see Gérard Genette, *Figures II*, Paris: Seuil, 1969.

123.　Van Seters, *The Edited Bible.*

how the narrators of the *Iliad* and the *Odyssey* feign ignorance of one another, when their authors are obviously the same.[124] Similarly, the narrator of the Bible should know nothing of Plato and Herodotus, as he supposedly lived before them. But the author behaves like the infant Hermes, swearing he is too young to have stolen Apollo's cattle (see the *Homeric Hymn to Hermes*).

Plato himself used anonymity, not naming himself in the dialogues. It is his master Socrates who speaks—with the exception of in the *Laws*, where Socrates is replaced by the anonymous Athenian Stranger. As Plato hid himself behind Socrates, we may never have known who wrote the dialogues were it not for the works of Aristotle and the *Letters*, written by Plato's disciples. Plato does appear as a silent disciple of Socrates in the *Apology* and *Phaedo*, but in his dialogues he never says anything. André Laks considers Plato as a dramaturge who does not put himself on stage, like his fellow Xenophon in the *Memorabilia*.[125] Laks points out the paradox of Plato's anonymity: in book III of the *Republic*, the *mimesis* is criticised as a trick that allows the imitating artist to hide behind his work, which is precisely what Plato does. But then who speaks in Plato's dialogues? Is it Socrates or Plato himself? Laks believes that Plato can be seen in Socrates' questioners, as in the *Republic*, where Plato's elder brothers Glaucus and Adimantus take on that role. Scholars generally believe that Plato's early dialogues reflect an agreement with his master's teachings, whereas in later dialogues more independence is shown. This culminates in his last one, the *Laws*, where Socrates is absent and is replaced by the Athenian Stranger—who may be closer to Plato himself. Regarding this progressive disappearance of Socrates in Plato's dialogues, one can refer to Sylvain Delcominette's idea that the dialogues stage the myth of inverted time found in the *Statesman*—that men are born old, rejuvenate, become children, and then eventually disappear. Similarly, so does Socrates in the dialogues: he lives out his last hours in the *Apology*, *Crito* and *Phaedo*, in the *Statesman* he is a young man, while in the *Laws* he is gone altogether.[126] As Plato humbly erases himself for Socrates to see, the biblical writer did the same with Moses, who has been viewed, unsurprisingly, as the author of the Pentateuch. Biblical Israel's Socrates is not Moses, however, but another...

124. Pucci, *Ulysse Polutropos*, 37.
125. André Laks, 'Qu'importe qui parle: l'anonymat platonicien et ses antécédents', in *Identités d'auteur dans l'Antiquité et la tradition européenne*, ed. Claude Calame and Roger Chartier, Grenoble: Jérôme Millon, 2004, 99-119.
126. Sylvain Delcominette, *L'inventivité dialectique dans le Politique de Platon*, Brussels: Ousia, 2000, 203.

Platonic anonymity has given birth to apocryphal platonic dialogues, the authenticity of which was already questioned by Diogenes Laertus in his catalogue of the dialogues. Most of them, like the *Epinomis* or the *Minos*, are still considered to be apocryphal (or dubious at best); even the *Laws* were considered as possibly not being Plato's, though now they are acknowledged as genuine. I believe that this long-standing discrediting of the *Laws* may have something to do with the persistent unconscious denial of both biblical and philosophical scholars in seeing it as the possible source of the Bible. Apocryphal platonic dialogues were written in the centuries after Plato's death, thus in the Hellenistic period, which shows that emulation of Plato was common in the Greek world and even beyond. In the first century B.C.E. the Roman statesman Cicero, a disciple of Antiochus of Ascalon (head of the platonic Academy of Athens) wrote his own versions of the *Republic* and *Laws* in Latin. In these two dialogues Cicero himself appears, discussing Plato with his friends. Attempts to emulate or comment upon Plato's philosophy were not unusual, and the writing of the Bible may be included in this movement that reached both Rome and Jerusalem. By erasing himself from his work, the biblical writer conferred a sense of timelessness upon it. He figuratively let himself die in his texts, thus reaching immortality through teaching—an idea found in Plato's *Symposium*.

Adaptation into Hebrew

The biblical writer transposed Greek myths into another geographic and historical frame, in Hebrew. Still, this Biblical Hebrew is full of Greek loan words, specifically the vocabulary concerning rituals. It is difficult, if not impossible, to distinguish what may be the biblical author's neologisms from Greek words that had already permeated the Hebrew language. But it is not unusual for writers to evolve a language through the use of loan words from another, as Shakespeare did in bringing Latin loan words into English usage. Modern Hebrew is practically the lone work of Eliezer Ben-Yehuda, who filled in Biblical Hebrew's missing vocabulary with Arabic loan words. The papyri of Elephantine show that after the Greek conquest the Jews rapidly adopted the Greek language instead of Aramaic, and even took on Greek names.[127] On the other hand, the Greeks inherited and enhanced the Phoenician alphabet, in turn necessarily bringing Semitic loan words into Greek. The linguistic issue is the same as the mythical one: early Semitic influence on archaic Greece does not preclude a later Greek influence on the Near East. As mentioned previously, I leave the linguistic matter to linguists. Biblical

127.   Mélèze-Modrezejewski, *Les Juifs d'Égypte*.

Hebrew is prose that resembles that of Herodotus. Regardless of the use of more poetic sources such as Homer, Apollonius or Herodotus, the same prose is maintained throughout most of Genesis–Kings for uniformity.[128] Yet some passages are poetical, such as the Song of the Red Sea (Exod 15:1-21) or the Song of Deborah (Judg 5)—often thought to reflect an 'older' stage of Hebrew. As in Greek (or any other) literature, the author may feel free to use language for poetic purposes that will seem more archaic. These songs in the Bible can be compared to certain chanted parts of Greek tragedies. Biblical Hebrew is full of alliterations and plays on words, insuring that the Hebrew text is the original version (again, let me repeat that I never imply that the Septuagint came first). The author often gives fancy etymologies of his characters' names, a feature that is also found in Herodotus.

'Monotheism'

'The Bible is the book of the revelation of the one God', yet to me this appears simply to be one of the techniques the biblical writer utilized—meaning that he re-wrote Greek myths according to the principle which holds that no other god than Yahweh truly exists. Yahweh is also called Elohim, the plural of El (meaning 'lord')—the name of a Canaanite god, father of Baal. Yahweh's name is found in ancient sources as being the tutelary god of Judah and Israel. But Yahweh also appears revered with other gods from the 'Canaanite' or Phoenician pantheon, there known as Asherah.[129] The biblical writer considered the gods Baal, Astarte and Moloch to be false idols that were worshipped by the indigenous Canaanites, whose customs were adopted by the sons of Israel, and which subsequently led them to the dispossession of their land. Archaeologist Israel Finkelstein has shown that the foreign origin of the Israelites is part of the biblical myth, and that the so-called Canaanites could well be the same people as the Israelites. The main difference between both peoples would be their religious practices. If this theory is right, one should question from which period did this difference arise, and if the biblical writer invented it (as Thomas L. Thompson thinks).[130] I suppose that the 'Canaanite' religion was still influential in the Hellenistic era, as proven by Phoenicia. There, the cult of these Semitic deities persisted until the Roman Empire's adoption of Christianity. It seems clear that if

---

128. For a discussion of the uniformity of Biblical Hebrew, see Ian Young, Robert Rezetko and Martin Ehrensvärd, *Linguistic Dating of Biblical Texts*, 2 vols., London: Equinox, 2008.

129. Patai, *The Hebrew Goddess*.

130. Thompson, *The Mythic Past*, 81, 91.

the biblical writer condemns these cults repeatedly as being abomina-
tions and the ultimate source of Israel's exile, it is because these cults
were a threat to the exclusive cult of Yahweh that his book aimed to
achieve. In fact, this Canaanite religion may have been the only one that
the kings of Judah and Israel worshipped—the Bible being the first
testimony to it! Yahweh was Judah's patron-god, but his cult was not yet
exclusive. The biblical author judged every king according to whether he
was faithful or not to Yahweh and to Moses' law. This judgment is
anachronistic, as this law was written by the same author who wrote the
book of Kings.

The rhetoric against the worship of these Semitic gods is one of the
main recurrent ideas of the Bible, the aim of which was to lead its
readers to conversion. Of course, during the Hellenistic era the polytheistic threat was enhanced with the coming of the Greek religion; this
gave rise to a form of syncretism—as witnessed in Phoenicia, where the
Tyrian god Melkart was renamed Heracles. The condemnation of these
'fake' gods designated the actual local gods, as well as the new Greek
ones as demons: 'They sacrificed unto demons, no-gods, gods that they
knew not, new gods that came up of late, which your fathers dreaded not'
(Deut 32:17). Even though the conception of a single god is the major
innovation of the Bible, the biblical author did not invent it. The pre-
Socratic philosophers already thought that the plurality of the gods hid a
unity: 'Single and almighty, sovereign of the mightiest, God neither
resembles us in spirit nor body. Humans, by making the gods in their
image, give them their thought, their voices and their faces' (Xenophanes, quoted by Clement of Alexandria, Stromata V). Xenophanes was
the master of Parmenides, who was the master of Socrates—the master
of Plato. In Plato's philosophy there is a transcendental god who existed
before the world and who created the gods of mythology—the Demiurge
of the *Republic* and *Timaeus*. As we saw, Plato could not deny the existence of the traditional gods lest he risk the death penalty like Socrates.
Thus, he tried to demonstrate that behind these gods was a nameless
superior entity. There also seems to have been a tendency in the Indo-
Iranian world toward the same philosophical concept, as Zoroastrianism
sees Ahura Mazda as being the great god, divided into several smaller
deities. It is interesting to note how the two branches of the ancient
Aryas, the Indians and the Iranians, had two classes of gods—the
Ashuras and the Devis (or Devas), though the nature of these characters
is inverted.[131] In the Indian *Rig Veda* epic, the benevolent Devis, guided
by Indra, the god of thunder, fight against the evil Ashuras; in the Persian

---

131.   George Dumézil, *Mythe et épopée, I, II et III*, Paris: Gallimard, 1995.

Aveshta, it is Ahura Mazda, the Great Ashura, who fights against the evil Devis. Two rival neighbouring branches of the Aryas demonised the gods of the other. This example can help us understand the situation of the West-Semitic gods, treated in the Bible either as demons or non-existent gods. The Devis were still considered to be benevolent deities in Persia until the Zoroastrian (or Mazdean) religion become the State religion of the Achaemenid Kings. The cult of the Devis was eventually prohibited under Xerxes.[132] In the same manner, in Christian tradition the word 'demon' acquired an opposite sense of what it meant in ancient Greece (notably in works of Hesiod and Plato), where a demon was a minor benevolent and protective deity; in Christianity this role was given to the angels, and demons were seen as evil. This inversion was due to the opposition of Christianity to the traditional religions of Greece and Rome. Those deities formerly revered were now seen to be evil (see Eusebius, *P.E.*, books III to VI). The biblical writer used the same technique to create his own religion; he thus demonised Semitic gods by associating them with the worst atrocities: ritual prostitution, human sacrifices, orgies, and so on. When reading the Ugaritic texts, however, one cannot help but see how the Bible differs, as Baal and the other gods do not seem evil at all, and Baal even resembles the biblical Yahweh.[133]

The biblical god is not alone. Yahweh has sons, who had children with human women (Gen 6:1-2). God speaks with what appears to be a celestial court, both when humans are created in the divine image (Gen 1:26) and upon descending to Earth to see the tower of Babel (Gen 11:7). In 1 Kgs 22:19, God is described as seated with a court of spirits, called the Army of Heaven. In Job 9:13, Yahweh is said to have defeated Rahab, a chaotic monster; this reminds us of how Baal defeated Yam, or how Marduk, the Babylonian god, defeated Tiamat. In Job 1 God discusses with Satan. Angels appear in the Bible, which correspond to both the platonic and Zoroastrian conception of a superior deity above others. Still, the sources of the Bible are more Greek than Persian, and we will see how Genesis can be seen as a pastiche of Hesiod's *Theogony*.

The Platonic Framework
The notion of *mimesis* found in Plato is a central one in the biblical writing. In book X of the *Republic*, Socrates discusses the work of a craftsman who imitates a divine model of furniture. God not only imagined all pieces of furniture, but the very model of the world that was

132.   Pierre Lecoq, *Les inscriptions de la Perse achéménide*, Paris: Gallimard, 1997, 105.
133.   Caquot and Sznycer, *Ugaritic Religion*.

created. We will see a literal echo of this discussion in Exodus, where, based upon the model given by God to Moses, Bezalel the craftsman fashions the furniture of the sanctuary.[134] Philo interpreted these chapters as being a metaphoric cosmogony (*De Vita Moses* II, 15-16), and indeed he was close to the author's intentions. In the following books of the Bible, the biblical State is founded with the same fidelity. The plan of the State is given to Moses in the legislative books, which Joshua will execute after the conquest. In the book of Joshua, the City of the *Laws* comes to life. This is the peak of biblical Israel, whose chronic infidelity will lead to its fall. The criticism of kingship that is found in the books of Judges (see the story of Abimelech), Samuel and Kings is also inspired by platonic reflections, as seen in the *Republic* and the *Statesman*. Plato is the main philosophical source that unites the books from Genesis– Kings. In the *Republic*, Socrates wants to define justice in the soul. But, as the soul cannot be studied, he proposes to study justice on the level of the City, which is a soul on a larger scale:

> …the quantity of justice is likely to be larger and more easily discernible. I propose therefore that we enquire into the nature of justice and injustice, first as they appear in the State, and secondly in the individual, proceeding from the greater to the lesser and comparing them. (Plato, *Rep.* 368 e-69 a)

As we have seen, the *Laws* seems to be less utopian than the *Republic*, but that difference comes from the fact that the latter only wants to define an ideal of justice, whereas the former plans a concrete State. The biblical writer understood this difference, and chose to show us the birth and death of the State of the *Laws*. Yet, he took ideas from the *Republic*. In Genesis, Jacob received the name of Israel after he fought with God's angel (Gen 32). Two chapters earlier, Jacob fathered twelve sons by his two wives and their two servants and they became the ancestors of the twelve tribes of Israel. In Numbers, Moses counts them twice (Num 1 and 26) and they move ordered in a sort of 'mystical square' (Num 2), with each tribal prince giving an identical offering to God (Num 7). In Joshua, they divide the land by lottery. In Judges, the tribes' unity is endangered several times, until the civil war that almost annihilates Benjamin. In books from Joshua to Kings, Israel is a State made of twelve tribes, yet in Genesis, Israel is a man with twelve sons. I believe that the source of this dialectic that compares the State to a man and vice-versa can be found in Plato's *Republic*. Throughout the biblical narrative there is only one character—the soul as well as the man—making the Bible primarily a philosophical book rather than a historical one.

---

134.   I owe this brilliant idea to Professor Kupitz. See also Eusebius, *P.E.* XII, 19.

An even more subtle platonic thread crosses the biblical books—the genealogy of King David. David is the new Jacob, his red-haired literary twin brother. As the king of Israel, he is Israel in and of himself. Furthermore, David is also the 'erotic tyrant' of the *Republic*, a man whose erotic instincts force him to tyrannise his people, as in the story of Uriah, 2 Samuel 11, where David has a faithful soldier killed so as to appropriate his wife. By analysing David's genealogy, we find that the meeting of his great-grandparents Ruth and Boaz was inspired by the myth of the birth of Eros (*Sym.* 203 b-c)—whose parents are Penia (Poverty) and Poros (Plenty). Combined with the clue of Er, the son of Judah, being a homonym of Er, the son of Armenios from the *Republic*, this leads us to interpret David's genealogy as a platonic riddle about Eros—Love—the soul's principle of motion.

Finally, the allegory of the Cave in the *Republic* is enacted in the story of the Exodus by biblical characters, as Moses frees the Israelites from their Egyptian 'prison'. Ultimately, the biblical writer gives us either extracts of or interpretations of platonic works. My work should not be misunderstood as being a mere accusation of the Bible's late plagiarism of Plato. On the contrary, the Bible's literary and philosophical value appears greater when one admits that it is much more than a clumsy assemblage of old legends held together by theology. Rather, the Bible is an interpretation of Greek literature through a platonic filter, in Hebrew, that deserves our admiration. Even though the biblical writer did not invent any of the stories in the Bible he deserves the title of author, as he created a unique work, the book *par excellence*, the Bible.

The Platonic Filter

At last, we come to a fundamental difference between Greek mythology and the Bible: the latter seems 'less mythical', as there is neither mention of Centaurs, Sirens, Pegasus nor Chimera. The Bible describes a world that would seem more rational and likely than the world of Greek mythology, if it weren't for God's miracles and interventions. We know that Plato had banned from his *Republic* mythical representations of the Gods that were found in the works of Homer and Hesiod. I believe that the biblical writer tried to model his work after Plato's advice. Hesiod told of how Cronos castrated his father Ouranos. For Plato, such a scandalous story should be forbidden, or told only to a closed circle. Another example is how Hera threw her son Hephaestus from Mount Olympus, causing his limp (Plato, *Rep.* 377 b-78 d). The biblical writer took the very stories that Plato wished to be censored and then re-wrote them in a more suitable way; Greek gods were played by human actors, while the biblical god is described as being incapable of lying. The biblical god is just, never the cause of evil; people bring bad things upon themselves by doing wrong:

> Let this then be one of our rules and principles concerning the gods, to which our poets and reciters will be expected to conform—that God is not the author of all things, but of good only. (Plato, *Rep.* 380 c)

To tell of how the gods can change appearance becomes forbidden (*Rep.* 381 c-e), still, we will see how the biblical god can take on human appearance (Gen 18 and 19; Judg 13). Plato's character of Socrates admits that a lie is sometimes necessary. The gods, however, cannot lie:

> —Then the superhuman and divine is absolutely incapable of false-hood?—Yes.—Then is God perfectly simple and true both in word and deed; he changes not; he deceives not, either by sign or word, by dream or waking vision.—Your thoughts, he said, are the reflection of my own.—You agree with me then, I said, that this is the second type or form in which we should write and speak about divine things. The gods are not magicians who transform themselves, neither do they deceive mankind in any way.—I grant that.—Then, although we are admirers of Homer, we do not admire the lying dream which Zeus sends to Agamemnon. (*Rep.* 382 e-83 a)

The biblical god does not lie either, and it will be seen how the Homeric story of Zeus sending a lying dream to King Agamemnon (*Iliad* II) has been 'corrected' through that platonic rule, changed into the story of a lying spirit that was sent by God to King Ahab. There the lie is revealed, and then annulled by God's prophet Micaiah (1 Kgs 22). In book III of the *Republic*, Plato gives examples of Homeric passages that he wishes to censor. A suitable narrator should imitate only irreproachable heroes:

> Then he will adopt a mode of narration such as we have illustrated out of Homer, that is to say, his style will be both imitative and narrative; but there will be very little of the former, and a great deal of the latter. (*Rep.* 396 e)

After banning the traditional poet from the City, Plato says:

> For we mean to employ for our souls' health the rougher and severer poet or story-teller, who will imitate the style of the virtuous only, and will follow those models which we prescribed at first when we began the education of our soldiers (*Rep.* 398 a-b).

As the transition from one City to the other is made by the legislator becoming a poet, the biblical writer acts both as the poet of the *Republic* and the legislator of the *Laws*. The Bible thus tells stories found in Homer and other Greek sources, but applies a platonic filter to them. Yet, some exceptions do appear, like Balaam's donkey that speaks to him (as Achilles' horses do as well), or Lot's wife who is transformed into a salt statue—the only *metamorphosis* in the Bible.

Foreword to the Chapters

I will now analyse the books of the Bible from Genesis to Kings, each chapter corresponding to one book. The book of Ruth is to be analysed in the chapter devoted to Judges, and the book of Esther is analysed in the chapter on Kings, before the conclusions. As I have already explained, the order of the Bible does not correspond to the order of the Greek myths, which is why I gave brief summaries of them in this first part. Additionally, Genesis–Kings was most likely conceived of backwards, the author using the annals of the kings of Israel and Judah where he found traces of people who existed and events that occurred; from there he went back into a mythical past that he created based on Greek sources of inspiration. Therefore, the reader may even choose to read these chapters backwards. Genesis is the book that blends all these sources together, while the other books often depend on one predominant source (Samuel is closer to the *Iliad*, whereas Judges and Kings are closer to Herodotus). As all later stories can be linked to it, Genesis combines so many various sources that its analysis is the most complex, perhaps resulting in an appearance of confusion that may leave the reader dubious. Upon first glance, the parallels between Greek sources and Genesis can be thought of as due to mere chance. But as we proceed, the riddle will unfold and these parallels will become more and more convincing. As the reading of the Bible requires patience and memory on the part of the reader, so too does this demonstration. I will quote biblical and Greek passages, so the reader can see the parallels without having to consult the many works involved. However, it is impossible to quote everything, as this book would then be several thousands of pages in length. Choices had to be made; some passages are quoted, while others are only referred to. The analysis of the first eleven chapters of Genesis will emphasise their Greek aspect, considering the Mesopotamian influence on them has been discussed thoroughly enough. That Mesopotamian influence is fully acknowledged, but my aim is to show that the Greek influence is dominant throughout the whole biblical narrative—it should thus be dated accordingly.

1.

Genesis

In the Beginning was Timaeus

In *Timaeus* Plato gives his vision of the creation of the world, one that seems close to that of Genesis yet at the same time far more sophisticated. The biblical creation happens in six days, plus one day of rest. On the first day light and darkness are created. Light is good. On the second day waters from below and from above are separated. On the third day the earth, the sea and vegetation are created. On the fourth day the stars and other heavenly objects are brought into being. On the fifth day come creatures of the sea and birds, and on the sixth land animals and humans. The seventh day was one of godly rest. The human, Adam, was created in God's image:

> So God created humankind in his image, in the image of God he created them, male and female he created them... God saw everything he had done, and indeed, it was very good. (Gen 1:27, 31)[1]

In *Timaeus* Plato asks himself whether the world has always existed or whether it was created. He opines that it was created, but according to which pattern? (Plato, *Tim.* 28d).

Note *Tim.* 29 a-b, which reads:

> If the world be indeed fair and the artificer good, it is manifest that he must have looked to that which is eternal; but if what cannot be said without blasphemy is true, then to the created pattern. Every one will see that he must have looked to, the eternal; for the world is the fairest of creations and he is the best of causes. And having been created in this way, the world has been framed in the likeness of that which is apprehended by reason and mind and is unchangeable, and must therefore of necessity, if this is admitted, be a copy of something.

---

1. All biblical citations follow the New Revised Standard Version of the Bible.

This being supposed, let us proceed to the next stage: In the likeness of what animal did the Creator make the world? It would be an unworthy thing to liken it to any nature which exists as a part only; for nothing can be beautiful which is like any imperfect thing; but let us suppose the world to be the very image of that whole of which all other animals both individually and in their tribes are portions. For the original of the universe contains in itself all intelligible beings, just as this world comprehends us and all other visible creatures. For the Deity, intending to make this world like the fairest and most perfect of intelligible beings, framed one visible animal comprehending within itself all other animals of a kindred nature. Are we right in saying that there is one world, or that they are many and infinite? There must be one only, if the created copy is to accord with the original. For that which includes all other intelligible creatures cannot have a second or companion; in that case there would be need of another living being which would include both, and of which they would be parts, and the likeness would be more truly said to resemble not them, but that other which included them. In order then that the world might be solitary, like the perfect animal, the creator made not two worlds or an infinite number of them; but there is and ever will be one only-begotten and created heaven. (*Tim.* 29 e-30 d)

For Plato, God did not create the human in his image, but rather the world itself—the entirety of which is a soul. The world according to Plato is a spherical self-sufficient being that is animated with the seventh movement but not with the six others. This reminds us of the six days of the biblical creation and one day of rest:

The movement suited to his spherical form was assigned to him, being of all the seven that which is most appropriate to mind and intelligence; and he was made to move in the same manner and on the same spot, within his own limits revolving in a circle. All the other six motions were taken away from him, and he was made not to partake of their deviations... When the father creator saw the creature which he had made moving and living, the created image of the eternal gods, he rejoiced, and in his joy determined to make the copy still more like the original; and as this was eternal, he sought to make the universe eternal, so far as might be. (*Tim.* 34a, 37 c)

We see both similarities and differences. For Plato, the world was created in the platonic god's image and then the god rejoiced—like the biblical god. The human is at the centre of biblical creation, which can be explained by examining Plato's *Timaeus*, where the traditional gods of mythology appear as intermediaries. These gods were suppressed in the Bible, leaving the human as God's perfect creature. The platonic god then decides to create a 'mobile imitation of eternity'—time—and thus creates the asters that will measure it:

The sun and moon and five other stars, which are called the planets, were created by him in order to distinguish and preserve the numbers of time; and when he had made their several bodies, he placed them in the orbits in which the circle of the other was revolving in seven orbits seven stars. (*Tim.* 38 c)

God lighted a fire, which we now call the sun, in the second from the earth of these orbits, that it might give light to the whole of heaven, and that the animals, as many as nature intended, might participate in number, learning arithmetic from the revolution of the same and the like. Thus then, and for this reason the night and the day were created, being the period of the one most intelligent revolution. And the month is accomplished when the moon has completed her orbit and overtaken the sun, and the year when the sun has completed his own orbit. (*Tim.* 39 b-c)

And God said, 'Let there be lights in the dome of the sky to separate the day from the night; and let them be for signs and for seasons and for days and years, and let them be lights in the dome of the sky to give light upon the earth'. And it was so. God made the two great lights—the greater light to rule the day and the lesser light to rule the night—and the stars. God set them in the dome of the sky to give light upon the earth, to rule over the day and over the night, and to separate the light from the darkness. (Gen 1:14-18)

Thus far and until the birth of time the created universe was made in the likeness of the original, but inasmuch as all animals were not yet comprehended therein, it was still unlike. What remained, the creator then proceeded to fashion after the nature of the pattern. Now as in the ideal animal the mind perceives ideas or species of a certain nature and number, he thought that this created animal ought to have species of a like nature and number. There are four such; one of them is the heavenly race of the gods; another, the race of birds whose way is in the air; the third, the watery species; and the fourth, the pedestrian and land creatures. (*Tim.* 39 e-40 a)

We can see how accurate the parallels are—the sun was created both to separate day from night, and to mark the months, seasons and years. The main difference that does not appear clearly in Genesis is the creation of the species of the gods. Yet, the biblical god does have 'sons' (Gen 6:1). The three other species mentioned in Plato's account do appear in Genesis as well, but not in the same order: first, on the fifth day, came the aquatic animals and then the birds; the land creatures (including humans) were made on the sixth day. Plato's supreme god addresses the gods and asks them to create these three species—for if God were to create them directly then they would be equal to the gods and thus immortal (*Tim.* 41 b-d). This same concern is found further on in Genesis (3:22-23), after Adam and Eve ate from the tree of the knowledge of good and evil. The species of the gods is described as celestial bodies, the asters. It is said that the heavens and earth were realized along with all their armies (Gen 2:1), though these armies of the heavens do not appear until far later when, in a vision of the prophet Micaiah, they are seen as a celestial court of minor deities assisting Yahweh (1 Kgs 22:19). Hence, the equivalents of the gods of *Timaeus* do appear in Genesis as the army of heaven, and likely as Yahweh's sons as well. The platonic supreme god instructs the gods how to create living beings. These will be subject to their passions. Those who can dominate their passions will return to their original star after their death, whereas the weaker ones will reincarnate several times in animals until they reach a human form again—which permits them the possibility of escaping the cycle. This conception is similar to the metempsychosis of Hinduism and Buddhism. The platonic god gives laws to the gods, and will not be held responsible for any evil in the creatures. The platonic god thus says unto the gods:

> And do ye then interweave the mortal with the immortal, and make and beget living creatures, and give them food, and make them to grow, and receive them again in death. (*Tim.* 41 d)

> God blessed them, and God said to them, 'Be fruitful and multiply, and fill the earth and subdue it; and have dominion over the fish of the sea and over the birds of the air and over every living thing that moves upon the earth. (Gen 1:28)

Plato was not allowed to deny the existence of the traditional Greek gods; he expresses it ironically—since some people pretend to be their descendants, how can family issues be doubted (*Tim.* 40 d-e)? Insofar as the gods were masters of creation in Plato's account, the biblical author had the freedom to replace them with the human; hence humanity's dominion over the three other species. As Plato's supreme god was resting, the gods took the elements of fire, earth, water and air, and with them created bodies (*Tim.* 42 e).

This is rather like the biblical account of how the human is made of dust, and how God gives him breath (Gen 2:6-7). Other platonic dialogues may be linked to the first chapters of Genesis. In the *Phaedo*, Socrates describes the world of death; four rivers are said to cross through it, the Acheron, Pyriphlegeton, Styx and Cocytus (*Phaedo* 113 a-c), which may be linked to the four rivers of the biblical Eden—the Pishon, Gihon, Tigris and Euphrates (Gen 2:10-14). The Pishon can be identified with the Phasis from Greek literature, running through Colchis (Georgia) and thought to have been the eastern boundary of the world (Plato, *Phaedo* 109 c; Herodotus, IV, 37, 45, 86).

The Splitting of the Androgyne

A parallel that is known since antiquity (noticed in Eusebius, *P.E.* XII, 12) is that of the separation of the androgyne in Plato's *Symposium* and the biblical story of the creation of Eve from Adam's 'side' (see Gen 2:18-25). In Plato's *Symposium*, each participant in turn gives his definition of love. Aristophanes, a comic playwright that parodied Socrates in his *Clouds*, is portrayed as being good friends with Socrates, and both their speeches are the best ones of the evening. When Aristophanes' turn comes, he says that humankind used to be divided into three genders: the double males, the double females, and a gender with both sexes—the androgynes. They all were very mighty, and once tried to ascend to heaven by piling up mountains, as Homer related about the giants Ephialtes and Ottos (Plato, *Sym.* 190 b; see also Homer, *Il.* V, 385 and *Od.* XI, 305).

Note Plato, *Sym.* 190 c-e, which reads:

> At last, after a good deal of reflection, Zeus discovered a way. He said: 'Methinks I have a plan which will humble their pride and improve their manners; men shall continue to exist, but I will cut them in two and then they will be diminished in strength and increased in numbers; this will have the advantage of making them more profitable to us. They shall walk upright on two legs, and if they continue insolent and will not be quiet, I will split them again and they shall hop about on a single leg'. He spoke and cut men in two, like a sorb-apple which is halved for pickling, or as you might divide an egg with a hair; and as he cut them one after another, he bade Apollo give the face and the half of the neck a turn in order that the man might contemplate the section of himself: he would thus learn a lesson of humility. Apollo was also bidden to heal their wounds and compose their forms.

The double men that were halved became male homosexual couples, the double women were split into female homosexual couples, while the halved androgynes gave rise to heterosexual couples. These bisected humans began to pine for their other halves, and eventually wasted away of sadness.

Zeus then decided to move their reproductive organs to the front (as opposed to before, when they were vaguely somewhere else) so that reproduction could result from the union of man and woman. The idea can be found in Plato that the difference between the sexes is due to divine surgery. The usual Hebrew translation of the word 'rib' is *tsela*, which, as per rabbinic tradition (see Rashi's comment on these verses), can also mean 'side'—thus confirming the link with the androgyne of Plato. Yet we see more in Aristophanes' speech, when the first humans tried to ascend to heaven and the great god decided to punish them. This theme is found as well in the Tower of Babel story (Gen 11). Both stories end in an explanation of the origin of love: the union of a man and a woman recreates lost unity, through the birth of a child. Of course, Aristophanes' apology for male homosexuality is contrary to the Bible, yet we will see later that Plato too forbids it in his *Laws*. A sentence from the *Laws* is similar to the well-known passage of Genesis:

> Wherefore a man and his wife shall leave to his and her father and mother their own dwelling-places, and themselves go as to a colony and dwell there, and visit and be visited by their parents; and they shall beget and bring up children, handing on the torch of life from one generation to another, and worshipping the Gods according to law for ever. (*Laws* 776 a-b)

> So ancient is the desire of one another which is implanted in us, reuniting our original nature, making one of two, and healing the state of man. (*Sym.* 191 d)

> Therefore a man leaves his father and his mother and clings to his wife, and they become one flesh. (Gen 2:24)

The Golden Age

> In those days God himself was their shepherd, and ruled over them, just as man, over them, who is by comparison a divine being, still rules over the lower animals. Under him there were no forms of government or separate possession of women and children; for all men rose again from the earth, having no memory, of the past. And although they had nothing of this sort, the earth gave them fruits in abundance, which grew on trees and shrubs unbidden, and were not planted by the hand of man. And they dwelt naked, and mostly in the open air, for the temperature of their seasons, was mild; and they had no beds, but lay on soft couches of grass, which grew plentifully out of the earth. Such was the life of man in the days of Cronos, Socrates; the character of our present life which is said to be under Zeus, you know from your own experience. (Plato, *Statesman* 271 e-72 b)

> Suppose that the nurslings of Cronos, having this boundless leisure, and the power of holding intercourse, not only with men, but with the brute creation, had used all these advantages with a view to philosophy, conversing with the brutes as well as with one another, and learning of every nature which was gifted with any special power, and was able to contribute some special experience to the store of wisdom there would be no difficulty in deciding that they would be a thousand times happier than the men of our own day. Or, again, if they had merely eaten and drunk until they were full, and told stories to one another and to the animals—such stories as are now attributed to them—in this case also, as I should imagine, the answer would be easy. (*Statesman* 272 b-d)

These lines strongly echo Gen 3:1-5, as Eve discusses with the talking snake about the tree of knowledge of good and evil. One can see how the biblical author coarticulated the *Symposium*, as seen above, with the *Statesman*. In Genesis 2, we read of the birth of the first woman, inspired at the same time by both Plato and the myth of Pandora. Next, Adam and Eve are chased from Eden, which they tended and where they lived naked, for having eaten the forbidden fruit after discussing sacred knowledge with an animal. This parallel seems even more likely regarding Plato's myth of the *Protagoras*. When the gods created living beings, Prometheus and Epimetheus were given the task of providing animals with distinct attributes. However, Epimetheus forgot to give any qualities to the naked human, who had neither fur nor weapons—nor means of protection.

> The appointed hour was approaching when man in his turn was to go forth into the light of day; and Prometheus, not knowing how he could devise his salvation, stole the mechanical arts of Hephaestus and Athena, and fire with them (they could neither have been acquired nor used without fire), and gave them to man. Thus man had the wisdom necessary to the support of life, but political wisdom he had not; for that was in the keeping of Zeus, and the power of Prometheus did not extend to entering into the citadel of heaven, where Zeus dwelt, who moreover had terrible sentinels; but he did enter by stealth into the common workshop of Athena and Hephaestus, in which they used to practise their favourite arts, and carried off Hephaestus' art of working by fire, and also the art of Athena, and gave them to man. And in this way man was supplied with the means of life. But Prometheus is said to have been afterwards prosecuted for theft, owing to the blunder of Epimetheus. (Plato, *Protagoras* 321 b-e)

Here, as he did with the Golden Age, Plato recycles a myth from Hesiod. Prometheus offering fire to man and being punished by the supreme god Zeus is the source of the myth of the biblical serpent that compelled Eve to eat the fruit of the tree of knowledge. Afterward, the *Protagoras* tells of how the humans first lived apart, and then created cities. They lacked political knowledge, however, so Zeus had Hermes give them reverence and justice. Note that the *Protagoras* gives details about how Prometheus and Epimetheus created the living beings, since *Timaeus* does not mention the names of the gods who helped. As the gods cannot appear explicitly in Genesis, the character of Prometheus is replaced with that of a serpent; this concept is based upon the idea of discussion with animals found in the *Statesman*. Moreover, the *Protagoras* mentions the beginnings of religion and the founding of the first cities, as in Genesis 4:

> Now man, having a share of the divine attributes, was at first the only one of the animals who had any gods, because he alone was of their kindred; and he would raise altars and images of them… After a while the desire of self-preservation gathered them into cities; but when they were gathered together, having no art of government, they evil intreated one another, and were again in process of dispersion and destruction. (*Protagoras* 322 a-b)

> Cain knew his wife, and she conceived and bore Enoch; and he built a city, and named it Enoch after his son Enoch… Adam knew his wife again, and she bore a son and named him Seth, for she said, 'God has appointed for me another child instead of Abel, because Cain killed him'. To Seth also a son was born, and he named him Enosh. At that time people began to invoke the name of the Lord. (Gen 4:17, 25-26)

It seems like the biblical writer carefully wove all the platonic myths about primitive humanity into a single, continuous story. All these myths tend to explain the actual human situation, where cities and States are corrupt and filled with injustice; in Plato's philosophy they justify the elaboration of Ideal States such as in the *Republic* and the *Laws*. The myth of the flood is also present in the *Laws*, which we will momentarily analyse. These parallels will seem more acceptable as we see that biblical Israel was indeed inspired by the State of the *Laws*. Also worth mentioning is a platonic myth in the *Gorgias* (523 a-34 a) where Plato explains how men lost the knowledge of when they would die. By not respecting the only law given to them, Adam and Eve were expelled from the Garden of Eden; this can be seen to be a miniature of the whole biblical narrative, as Israel is exiled from its land for disobeying God's (or rather Plato's) laws. Thus the first four chapters of the Bible contain a dense platonic introduction, mixing myths from *Timaeus*, *Symposium*, *Statesman* and *Protagoras*, and probably also from the *Phaedo* and *Gorgias*. Biblical scholarship has emphasised the apparent Mesopotamian aspect of these chapters, yet we see that the Bible is closer to the platonic dialogues than to any other tradition.

Eve / Pandora

The platonic version of the theft of fire by Prometheus is a myth that was first told by Hesiod in his *Theogony* and *Works and Days*. Zeus not only decides to punish the thief Prometheus but humans as well for receiving it, so he sends them a terrible gift—the first woman. Hephaestus fashioned her body by mixing water and earth, Athena taught her the arts of women, Aphrodite inspired violent desires within her, and Hermes filled her spirit with treachery. She was called Pandora, meaning that all the

gods had given her gifts. Hermes brought her to Epimetheus, who had
been warned by Prometheus not to accept any gifts from the gods.

> For before this the tribes of men lived on earth remote and free from ills
> and hard toil and heavy sickness which bring the Fates upon men; for in
> misery men grow old quickly. But the woman took off the great lid of the
> jar with her hands and scattered all these and her thought caused sorrow
> and mischief to men. Only Hope remained there in an unbreakable home
> within under the rim of the great jar, and did not fly out at the door; for
> before that, the lid of the jar stopped her, by the will of Aegis—holding
> Zeus who gathers the clouds. But the rest, countless plagues, wander
> amongst men; for earth is full of evils and the sea is full. Of themselves
> diseases come upon men continually by day and by night, bringing mis-
> chief to mortals silently; for wise Zeus took away speech from them. So
> is there no way to escape the will of Zeus. (Hesiod, *Works and Days*
> 90-105)[2]

> And to the man he said 'Because you have listened to the voice of your
> wife, and have eaten of the tree about which I commanded you, "You
> shall not eat of it", cursed is the ground because of you; in toil you shall
> eat of it all the days of your life; thorns and thistles it shall bring forth for
> you; and you shall eat the plants of the field. By the sweat of your
> face you shall eat bread until you return to the ground, for out of it you
> were taken; you are dust, and to dust you shall return.' (Gen 3:17-19)

In both stories, the first woman is the cause of all evils, of humankind's
passing out of the Golden Age, the necessity to till the earth and ultimately human mortality. We see an inversion of the sequence of events
in each myth: in the Greek version Prometheus has stolen fire for humankind, whom Zeus punishes with the first woman, the cause of all things
evil; the biblical version inverts this sequence, resulting in a story slightly
less misogynistic whereby the woman is offered to the man as a helper,
after which she passes him the forbidden fruit (in this version the man
and the woman are equally responsible). The *Argonautica* relates a story
of a sacred tree, guarded by a dragon; found in the garden of the Hesperides (daughters of Atlas), the tree bore precious golden apples that
were stolen by Heracles (Apollonius of Rhodes, *Argonautica* IV, 1397-
1405). In combining this story of the golden apples stolen by Heracles
with Prometheus stealing fire by hiding it in the stem of a fennel, the
biblical author created the story of the tree of the knowledge of good and
evil. It is no coincidence, as both Prometheus and Atlas are brothers,
sons of the Titan Japet. Since the equivalent name of Japhet appears in
Genesis, we could try to find other etymologies: though inspired by

---

2.   Translated by Hugh G. Evelyn-White.

Pandora, Eve's Hebrew name *Hava* (Gen 3:20) may be linked to the goddess *Hebe* (Hesiod, *Theog.* 950-55) who married Heracles after he became a god. Moreover, a few verses after Hesiod tells the myth of Pandora in the *Theogony*, the poet tells of how Zeus ate the goddess Metis, who gave him the supreme knowledge of good and evil; which can be related to the biblical motif of the knowledge of good and evil (Gen 2:17).

Note Hesiod, *Theog.* 885-900, which reads:

> Now Zeus, king of the gods, made Metis his wife first, and she was wisest among gods and mortal men. But when she was about to bring forth the goddess bright-eyed Athena, Zeus craftily deceived her with cunning words and put her in his own belly, as Earth and starry Heaven advised. For they advised him so, to the end that no other should hold royal sway over the eternal gods in place of Zeus; for very wise children were destined to be born of her, first the maiden bright-eyed Tritogeneia, equal to her father in strength and in wise understanding; but afterwards she was to bear a son of overbearing spirit king of gods and men. *But Zeus put her into his own belly first, that the goddess might devise for him both good and evil.*

The First Murderer and the Demi-gods

The prologue of the epic of the Argonauts relates the first murder in humankind's history. The details of this story are initially known via Pindar (*Pythian* II, 20-48). Ixion had married Dia, daughter of Hesioneus, but Ixion refused to give his father-in-law the customary dowry, and killed him. All the humans shunned Ixion, but Zeus welcomed him on Mount Olympus. Once there, however, Ixion tried to seduce Hera, his host's wife, who reported the transgression. To see if she was telling the truth Zeus created a cloud-goddess, Nephele (meaning 'cloud'), in the image of Hera and offered it to Ixion. Ixion impregnated Nephele, and she spawned a bastard creature that was called Kentauros. Kentauros ran off into the wilderness and lay with a mare, giving rise to the race of the Centaurs—half men and half horses. Nephele was later engaged to Athamas, king of Boeotia, to whom she gave two children, Phrixos and Helle. Athamas rejected Nephele and took a second wife, Ino, daughter of Cadmus, who plotted against Phrixos and Helle. She bribed messengers to fake an oracle, ordering Athamas to sacrifice Phrixos to Zeus on Mount Laphystion. As he was about to do it, Zeus, who refused human sacrifices, sent a golden ram that took Phrixos on its back and brought him safely to Colchis. Once there, Phrixos sacrificed the ram and hung its Golden Fleece upon an oak (Apollodorus, *Library* I, 7, 9).

We recognise here the story of Abraham and Isaac, and we will analyse it in due time. But the story of Ixion also shows a parallel with the character of Cain, humankind's first murderer in the Bible, who killed his own brother Abel (Gen 4). God punishes Cain by exiling him, but when Cain confesses his crime God promises to protect him against anyone who would try to avenge Abel (Gen 4:13-16). This blood-reprisal is found as well in similar terms in Plato's *Laws*:

> 'Today you have driven me away from the soil, and I shall be hidden from your face; I shall be a fugitive and a wanderer on the earth, and anyone who meets me may kill me.' (Gen 4:14)

> But if (a murderer) fly and will not stand his trial, let him fly for ever; or, if he set foot anywhere on any part of the murdered man's country, let any relation of the deceased, or any other citizen who may first happen to meet with him, kill him with impunity, or bind and deliver him to those among the judges of the case who are magistrates, that they may put him to death. (Plato, *Laws* 871 d-e)

Ixion not only spawned the race of Centaurs through Nephele, but also the Lapiths through his human wife, Dia. The war between the Centaurs and the Lapiths is a famous episode of Greek mythology. Among the Lapiths was their king, Caineus, whom Nestor mentions in the beginning of the *Iliad*; and seen also in Apollonius of Rhodes' catalogue of the Argonauts:

> Never again can I behold such men as Pirithous and Dryas shepherd of his people, or as *Caineus*, Exadius, godlike Polyphemus, and Theseus son of Aegeus, peer of the immortals. These were the mightiest men ever born upon this earth: mightiest were they, and when they fought the fiercest tribes of mountain savages they utterly overthrew them. (Homer, *Il.* I, 265-270; see also II, 743)[3]

> There came too Koronos, son of *Kaineus*, leaving behind rich Gyrton; he was a good warrior, but did not surpass his father. For poets tell that, though destroyed by the centaurs, Kaineus was still alive. Alone and cut off from the other heroes he drove the centaurs off; they charged back, but as they advanced they had not the strength to push him back or to kill him. Unwounded and unbending he passed beneath the earth, knocked down by a storm of heavy fir-trees. (*Argonautica* I, 60-65)[4]

This Caineus is a direct descendant of Ixion, the first murderer, whose name sounds quite like Cain. At the end of Hesiod's *Theogony* we are told how mortal women gave birth to heroes like Jason, Achilles and

---

3. Translated by Samuel Butler.
4. Translated by Richard Hunter.

Heracles through their union with male gods. In Genesis, it is said that the sons of God loved the daughters of men, and they fathered a generation of heroes called the *Nephilim* (Gen 6:1-4). This word, usually not translated from Hebrew, can be linked to the Hebrew *naphal* (meaning 'to fall')—hence the Nephilim may be considered 'fallen angels'. I believe *Nephilim* can be directly linked to the cloud goddess *Nephele*. Ixion and Nephele gave rise to the Centaurs, and the Lapiths, whose king is named Caineus, came from Ixion and Dia; it seems as though the biblical writer took inspiration from this story—known through several Greek sources such as Homer, Pindar, Apollonius and others—and kept the names that were derived from these sources. This is a process that we will encounter several times: names are kept but displaced on the genealogic scale. The biblical writer used Hesiod's *Works and Days* as a framework for these chapters. Since the end of the Golden Age caused by the first woman Pandora (Eve), humanity degenerated into violence. After the Golden Age came the Silver Age and the Bronze Age, followed by the Age of Heroes:

> But when earth had covered this generation also, Zeus the son of Cronos made yet another, the fourth, upon the fruitful earth, which was nobler and more righteous, a god-like race of hero-men who are called demi-gods, the race before our own, throughout the boundless earth. (Hesiod, *Works and Days* 156)

> When people began to multiply on the face of the ground, and daughters were born to them, the sons of God saw that they were fair; and they took wives for themselves of all that they chose. Then the Lord said, 'My spirit shall not abide in mortals for ever, for they are flesh; their days shall be one hundred and twenty years'. The Nephilim were on the earth in those days—and also afterwards—when the sons of God went in to the daughters of humans, who bore children to them. These were the heroes that were of old, warriors of renown. (Gen 6:1-4)

Cain / Alcmæon

Cain said to his brother Abel, 'Let us go out to the field'. And when they were in the field, Cain rose up against his brother Abel and killed him. Then the Lord said to Cain, 'Where is your brother Abel?' He said, 'I do not know; am I my brother's keeper?' And the Lord said, 'What have you done? Listen; your brother's blood is crying out to me from the ground! And now you are cursed from the ground, which has opened its mouth to receive your brother's blood from your hand. When you till the ground, it will no longer yield to you its strength; you will be a fugitive and a wanderer on the earth'. Cain said to the Lord, 'My punishment is greater than I can bear! Today you have driven me away from the soil, and I shall be hidden from your face; I shall be a fugitive and a wanderer on the earth, and anyone who meets me may kill me'. Then the Lord said to him, 'Not so! Whoever kills Cain will suffer a sevenfold vengeance'. And the Lord put a mark on Cain, so that no one who came upon him would kill him. Then Cain went away from the presence of the Lord, and settled in the land of Nod, east of Eden. Cain knew his wife, and she conceived and bore Enoch; and he built a city, and named it Enoch after his son Enoch. (Gen 4:8-17)

It is reported that Apollo by his oracle did assign this place for an habitation to Alcmæon the son of Amphiareus, at such time as he wandered up and down for the killing of his mother; telling him, 'that he should never be free from the terrors that haunted him, till he had found out and seated himself in such a land, as when he slew his mother, the sun had never seen nor was then land, because all other lands were polluted by him'. Hereupon being at a nonplus, as they say, with much ado he observed this ground congested by the River Achelöus, and thought there was enough cast up to serve his turn, already, since the time of the slaughter of his mother, after which it was now a long time that he had been a wanderer. Therefore seating himself in the places about the Œniades, he reigned there, and named the country after the name of his son Acarnas. Thus goes the report, as we have heard it concerning Alcmæon. (Thucydides, II, 102)[5]

Professor Yaakov S. Kupitz was the first to elucidate this very accurate parallel. We see how both Cain and Alcmeon become wanderers because they murdered a relative, causing the Earth to be impure, and how each finally settles and names the new city or country after his son.

The Flood

It is well known that the Mesopotamian account of the flood found in the *Epic of Gilgamesh* is similar to the biblical account (compare Gen 8:6-12 and the *Epic of Gilgamesh*, Tablet XI). There are several Greek and Roman versions of the flood as well, but none of them contain the detail of sending out birds, common to the Mesopotamian and the biblical accounts. For many years this parallel has been used as evidence of the Bible's antiquity. I cannot deny such a strong resemblance, but I prefer to use Professor Lemche's methodology: the biblical text must be dated according to its most recent parts, not the oldest. Even if the biblical writer knew the Mesopotamian version of the flood story, there is evidence that he knew the Greek version as well.

5. Translated by Richard Crowley.

Berossus, a Hellenised Babylonian priest, transmitted the Mesopotamian myths in Greek form in the third century B.C.E. Both Berossus and the *Epic of Gilgamesh* recall the flood according to its oldest version, that of Atrahasis.[6] It is likely that if the biblical writer did indeed live in the Hellenistic era and read Greek literature, he would have come to know the Mesopotamian myths in their Greek form via Berossus.[7] But the text of Berossus is only known from quotations from late Jewish and Christian authors like Josephus and Eusebius, thus I will refrain from interpreting them. The oldest Greek version of the flood is found in Pindar:

> Of such things talk thou not; leave war of immortals and all strife aside; and bring thy words to the city of Protogeneia, where by decree of Zeus of the bickering lightning-flash Pyrrha and Deukalion coming down from Parnassos first fixed their home, and without bed of marriage made out of stones a race to be one folk: and hence cometh the name of peoples. Awake for them the clear-toned gale of song, and if old wine be best, yet among songs prefer the newer flowers. Truly men say that once a mighty water swept over the dark earth, but by the craft of Zeus an ebb suddenly drew off the flood. From these first men came anciently your ancestors of the brazen shields, sons of the women of the stock of *Iapetos* and of the mighty Kronidai, Kings that dwelt in the land continually. (Pindar, *Olympian* IX, 40-56)[8]

Deucalion and Pyrrha (corresponding to the biblical characters of Noah and his wife) are the children of Prometheus and Epimetheus, respectively, and the grandchildren of Iapetos, or Japet—a homonym for one of Noah's sons, Japhet. This is the same process as found in the example of Caineus whereby a name is kept but displaced on the genealogic scale. Japet is the grandfather of the survivors of the flood in the Greek version, yet in the biblical account he becomes the survivors' son. The name Japet is neither found in the Atrahasis and Gilgamesh epics nor in Berossus; it comes from the Greek tradition. Moreover, after coming out of the ark Noah blesses Shem and Japhet, and foretells how Japhet will expand and dwell in the tents of Shem (Gen 9:27). As discussed in the Introduction, this is a prophecy deliberately pointing to the period of the Greek conquest of the Near East. Both the prophecy and the Greek etymology of the name Japhet indicate the time of writing of Genesis in the very

6. Jean Bottéro and Samuel Noah Kramer, *Lorsque les Dieux faisaient l'homme*, Paris: Gallimard, 1989, 576-601.

7. For a discussion on the dependence of the Bible upon Berossus, see Gmirkin, *Berossus and Genesis*.

8. Translated by T.K. Hubbard.

first chapters. As Eusebius notes, Plato mentions the deluge in the *Laws*
(*P.E.* XII, 15:1-6). For Eusebius, Plato followed the same pattern as the
Pentateuch, describing how for many generations after the deluge humanity lived a pastoral life, and that the necessity to make laws for the first
cities came only later:

> Do you believe that there is any truth in ancient traditions? CLEINIAS:
> What traditions? ATHENIAN: The traditions about the many destructions
> of mankind which have been occasioned by deluges and pestilences, and
> in many other ways, and of the survival of a remnant? CLEINIAS: Every
> one is disposed to believe them. ATHENIAN: Let us consider one of
> them, that which was caused by the famous deluge. CLEINIAS: What are
> we to observe about it? ATHENIAN: I mean to say that those who then
> escaped would only be hill shepherds,—small sparks of the human race
> preserved on the tops of mountains. CLEINIAS: Clearly. ATHENIAN:
> Such survivors would necessarily be unacquainted with the arts and the
> various devices which are suggested to the dwellers in cities by interest or
> ambition, and with all the wrongs which they contrive against one
> another. (Plato, *Laws* 677 a-b)

> And were not such states composed of men who had been dispersed in
> single habitations and families by the poverty which attended the devasta-
> tions; and did not the eldest then rule among them, because with them
> government originated in the authority of a father and a mother, whom,
> like a flock of birds, they followed, forming one troop under the patriar-
> chal rule and sovereignty of their parents, which of all sovereignties is the
> most just? (*Laws* 680 d-e)

Plato describes how humanity lived according to a patriarchal system,
the elders exercising authority. This is the exact framework of Genesis,
as demonstrated by the fact that the cycles of the 'Patriarchs', Abraham,
Isaac and Jacob start after the stories of the flood and the tower of Babel.
After the discussion of patriarchal life in the *Laws* comes the building of
Troy and other cities such as Sparta, Athens, and the establishment of the
Persian State. Plato's historical reconstruction allows him to introduce
his speech concerning the Ideal State; as an excess of democracy was
thought to have ruined Athens and Persia was ruled by too much despot-
ism, Plato's State tried to achieve a balance between the two regimes.
We see just such a political framework in Genesis in the story of Babel,
the first great city, and later with Egypt and its kings. These organisa-
tions are described as unjust, completely beholden to the power of a
single king. Contrastingly, Israel came out of Egypt to conquer Canaan
and there founded a kingless State governed by divine laws. Eusebius
noticed this similarity between the texts and thought that Plato had
copied Moses. Although I believe the contrary, I find Eusebius' point to

be very relevant. Even if the most ancient version of the deluge comes from the Sumerian tradition, and even if the biblical writer knew of this tradition, he inserted it into a platonic framework—that of a political discussion about the ideal form of the State. The first eleven chapters of Genesis are indeed inspired by Mesopotamian myths, but there is a more recent Greek layer that is just as obvious. The evolution of humankind in the Bible—from the ideal life in Eden to the degeneration that led up to the deluge, and from the discussion of patriarchal life to the gift of laws—is all found in Plato's dialogues.

The Castration of Ouranos / The Drunkenness of Noah

Noah, a man of the soil, was the first to plant a vineyard. He drank some of the wine and became drunk, and he lay uncovered in his tent. And Ham, the father of Canaan, saw the nakedness of his father, and told his two brothers outside. Then Shem and Japheth took a garment, laid it on both their shoulders, and walked backwards and covered the nakedness of their father; their faces were turned away, and they did not see their father's nakedness. When Noah awoke from his wine and knew what his youngest son had done to him, he said, 'Cursed be Canaan; lowest of slaves shall he be to his brothers'. He also said, 'Blessed by the Lord my God be Shem; and let Canaan be his slave. May God make space for Japheth, and let him live in the tents of Shem; and let Canaan be his slave'. (Gen 9:20-27)

I have asserted that this prophecy about Japhet, being the ancestor of the Greeks, reflects the arrival of the Greeks in the Near East during the Hellenistic era. But we should also note the similarity of this story to the castration of Ouranos in Hesiod's *Theogony*. It is said that Ouranos, god of the sky and heavens, would make love to Gaia, the earth-goddess, yet he refused to let the children created from this union be born from their mother's body. As Gaia was in great pain, Cronos, her youngest son, accepted his mother's mission to attack his father. Gaia gave Cronos a sickle (made of the *adamas* metal) and with it he severed Ouranos' genitalia, throwing them into the Ocean. The goddess Aphrodite was born from the foam that came out of the severed member:

But afterwards she lay with Heaven and bare deep-swirling Oceanus, Coeus and Crius and Hyperion and *Iapetus*, Theia and Rhea, Themis and Mnemosyne and gold-crowned Phoebe and lovely Tethys. After them was born Cronos the wily, youngest and most terrible of her children, and he hated his lusty sire. (Hesiod, *Theog.* 130-40)

And Heaven came, bringing on night and longing for love, and he lay about Earth spreading himself full upon her. Then the son from his

> ambush stretched forth his left hand and in his right took the great long sickle with jagged teeth, and swiftly lopped off his own father's members and cast them away to fall behind him. (Hesiod, *Theog.* 175-80)

> But these sons whom he begot himself great Heaven used to call Titans (Strainers) in reproach, for he said that they strained and did presumptuously a fearful deed, and that vengeance for it would come afterwards. (Hesiod, *Theog.* 207-10)

As mentioned in the Introduction, Plato thought that such a scandalous story should be censored, or at least told to a limited group of initiates (Plato, *Rep.* 377 b). It seems likely that the biblical writer recycled that story but modified the detail of Cronos castrating his father into Ham seeing his father naked; it is most noteworthy that some Jewish midrashim interpret Ham's deed as an actual castration (see *Midrash Rabba* and Rashi on these verses). Regarding the similarity of Adam and Eve resembling Plato's androgyne, rabbinic exegesis linked that biblical story with the Greek version. The biblical writer used a myth from Hesiod but transformed it according to Plato's rules in the *Republic*—this story is not about gods, but about humans (albeit humans that lived for centuries, being somehow in-between gods and men). Canaan is cursed, for Israel, descended from Shem, is to possess his land. The proof that the biblical story is indeed inspired by Hesiod lies in the retention of the name Japhet, homonym of the Titan Iapetos. In both texts, the youngest son commits a shameless act against his father, and has a brother called Japhet. This deliberate 'fingerprint' is furthermore the heralding of the coming of the Greeks. One should also mention how the *Sibylline Oracles*, a text of the Roman era, strangely confused the Japhet of the Bible with that of the Greek tradition (*Sib. Or.* III, 105-13). This text considers the Greek gods to have been in fact famous humans, a tendency that had become widespread since the work of philosopher Euhemerus, who seemed to have produced a rationalised version of Greek mythology. The Bible itself takes the same road, as humans replaced the gods of Greek mythology. This process of 'demythologising' is already present in the Bible, and was interpreted accordingly by the author of the *Sibylline Oracles*. Euhemerism was not only used in antiquity, for as we have seen the documentary hypothesis is but a rationalised version of the divine inspiration of the Bible.

The Table of Nations

In Genesis 10, we are told how the descendants of the three sons of Noah populated the earth. Herodotus mentions the division of the earth into three continents, each with a woman's name: Europe, Asia and Libya; Europe was Cadmus' sister, Asia was Prometheus' wife, and Libya was an African woman (Herodotus, IV, 45). Let us focus on the descendants of Japheth:

> The descendants of Japheth: Gomer, Magog, Madai, Javan, Tubal, Meshech, and Tiras. The descendants of Gomer: Ashkenaz, Riphath, and Togarmah. The descendants of Javan: Elishah, Tarshish, Kittim, and Rodanim. (Gen 10:2-4)

We can identify most of them through the works of Herodotus. Of course, the biblical writer may have known of these people without knowledge of Herodotus, but my intention is to highlight their presence in the Greek sources. *Gomer* stands for the Cimmerians, living on the North coast of the Black Sea—today's Ukraine (the name of the region, *Crimea*, retains the original root). *Magog* could possibly be derived from the name *Gyges*; *Guges* was Iapetus' giant brother in Hesiod. Another Gyges was the king of Lydia who fought the Cimmerians (Herodotus I, 1-17). Madai is the Medes. *Javan*, spelled ION in Hebrew, is the eponymous ancestor of the Ionian Greeks (Herodotus I, 146 and V, 66); in the Greek tradition Ion is the descendant of Iapetus through Prometheus and Deucalion, whereas in Genesis Ion is the direct son of Japhet. *Tubal* and *Meshech* can be identified with the Tibarenians and the Moschians (Herodotus III, 94 and VII, 78 and Apollonius, *Argonautica* II, 1010-15). *Tiras* seems to refer to the Thracians, and *Ashkenaz* to the Scythians. Apollonius mentions a people called the Ripheans that lived between the Scythians and the Thracians (*Argonautica* IV, 285-290) that are probably linked with biblical *Riphath*. The Sarmatians (Herodotus IV, 21; 100-117) can be identified with *Togarmah*. Considering the sons of Javan: *Elishah* most likely corresponds to the Greek city of Elis, *Tarshish* to Tarsus, *Kittim* to Kittion (capital of Cyprus), while *Dodanim* is probably a misspelling of *Rodanim*, meaning Rhodes as we read in 1 Chr 1:7. This misspelling can be easily explained, for in the copying of Hebrew manuscripts, mistaking the very similar letters *dalet* and *resh* is common. The biblical writer had a relatively good knowledge of the Greeks, their mythical ancestry and geography. Among the sons of Canaan are mentioned the *Girgashim* (Gen 10:17), whom I believe can be linked to the *Colchians*; the proof of this may be that today *Colchis* is called *Georgia*, showing the same transformation of the root. But why would the biblical writer claim this people as being descended from Canaan and Ham if they were geographically closer to the Scythians and other descendants of Japhet? An answer is found in Herodotus:

For the Colchians manifestly are Egyptians and I speak having myself perceived it before I heard it from others. And, when it had come to my attention, I asked both groups and the Colchians remembered the Egyptians more than the Egyptians the Colchians. But the Egyptians asserted they considered the Colchians to be descended from Sesostris' host. I myself guessed it not only because of this, that they are black-skinned and woolly-haired (that alone in fact amounts to nothing, because there are also others like that), but even more because of this fact, that the Colchians, the Egyptians and the Ethiopians are the only ones of all human beings to have circumcised themselves their pudenda from the beginning. The Phoenicians and the Syrians in Palaestina themselves agree they have learned that from the Egyptians, while the Syrians round the Thermodon river and the Parthenius and the Macronians who are their neighbours assert they have learned it recently from the Colchians; the above are the only ones of human beings to circumcise themselves and they manifestly do after the same fashion as the Egyptians. But among the Egyptians themselves and the Ethiopians I am not able to say which learned the practice thoroughly from the other, since indeed it manifestly is something ancient. Yet that men learned it thoroughly through their intercourse with Egypt, the following in fact comes to be a great proof for me: however many of the Phoenicians have had intercourse with Greece, no longer imitate the Egyptians, but rather do not circumcise the pudenda of those born later. (Herodotus II, 104)[9]

According to Wesselius, the Syrians of Palestine in Herodotus could be identified to the Israelites of the Bible.[10] Many Egyptian rituals described by Herodotus appear similar to those of the Bible, such as circumcision. It is worth noting that Herodotus believed that Colchians were of Egyptian or African origin due to the similarity of their looks and cus-toms to the Egyptians. The biblical writer thus seems to have used Herodotus as a source in making the Girgashim descendants of Canaan and Ham.

The Tower of Babel

The confusion of tongues, in Gen 11:7, is a mythical theme found as well in the Sumerian epic of *Enmerkar*. As we saw previously in analysing the androgyne story in Plato's *Symposium*, the motif of humans aspiring to reach heaven to defy the gods is also found in Greek mythology in the story of the giants Ephialtes and Ottos, who piled up mountains trying to ascend to the heavens. This tradition is known from Homer, Plato, and the Roman author Ovid. One must note that the structure of the first book

9. Translated by George Rawlinson.
10. Wesselius, *The Origin of the History of Israel*, 98-99.

of Ovid's *Metamorphosis* (the creation of the world and then of human-kind, the episode of the giants, followed by the deluge) is extremely close to that of Genesis 1–11. In the Bible though, the story of the tower of Babel (Gen 11:1-10) takes place after the deluge.

Note Ovid, *Metam.* I, 150-70, which reads:

> Rendering the heights of heaven no safer than the earth, they say the giants attempted to take the Celestial kingdom, piling mountains up to the distant stars. Then the all-powerful father of the gods hurled his bolt of lightning, fractured Olympus and threw Mount Pelion down from Ossa below. Her sons' dreadful bodies, buried by that mass, drenched Earth with streams of blood, and they say she warmed it to new life, so that a trace of her children might remain, transforming it into the shape of human beings. But these progeny also despising the gods were savage, violent, and eager for slaughter, so that you might know they were born from blood. When Saturn's son, the father of the gods, saw this from his highest citadel, he groaned, and recalling the vile feast at Lycaon's table, so recent it was still unknown, his mind filled with a great anger fitting for Jupiter, and he called the gods to council, a summons that brooked no delay.[11]

Again, the biblical writer may have mixed a Mesopotamian source—likely Berossus—with a Greek story. Genesis 11:3 describes how the builders used 'bricks for stones and bitumen for mortar'. This fits with Herodotus' description of the actual tower of Babylon:

> At the same time as they dug the ditch, they made bricks of the earth that came from the excavation and, on moulding sufficient bricks, baked them in ovens; afterwards, *having hot asphalt as mortar and every thirty courses of brick* stuffing mats of reeds in between, they built first the ditch's lips and second the wall itself in the same manner… And in the middle of the shrine a solid tower is built, a stade in both its length and its breadth, and on top of that tower another tower stands, and one again on top of that, up to eight towers. Moreover, an ascent to them that extends round all the towers on the outside in a circle has been made, and for one somewhere at the middle of the ascent is a resting-place and chairs for reposing, on which the ascending sit down and repose. And in the last tower a large temple is in place and in the temple a large couch is placed, well smoothed, and by it a golden table is placed. (Herodotus I, 179, 181)

The realistic details of the asphalt used as mortar and the baked bricks are not found in both Herodotus and the Bible by chance; rather, they are deliberate 'fingerprints' that were left, as we will see, in every chapter of the Bible. The temple of Bel-Marduk described by Herodotus was called the *Etemenanki*; it was the real tower of Babylon, still visible in the fifth

---

11. Translated by Samuel Garth.

century B.C.E. Solomon fortified Jerusalem and built its temple (1 Kgs 5–9). Jerusalem was destroyed by Babylon (2 Kgs 24), and Babylon was taken in turn by Cyrus (Herodotus I, 188-91). Though Babylon is Jerusalem's enemy, Genesis' Babel represents Jerusalem itself at the same time.[12] It is Jerusalem's hubris that is criticised in Genesis 11, decrying the ambition of Solomon and those kings of Israel that disobeyed God's law. These first chapters of Genesis that show Mesopotamian influences intend to compare Babylon with Jerusalem implicitly. The loss of Eden and the tower of Babel are both metaphors for Israel's future demise. Such a literary construction is actually found in Plato's *Critias*. Indeed, while Atlantis is the barbaric enemy of ancient Athens, it simultaneously represents the Athens of Plato's time ruined by the hubris of its rulers. The fall of Atlantis, ordered by Zeus in mythical times, reflects the actual decline of Athens in the early fourth century B.C.E., after the Peloponnesian wars.[13] What makes this even more interesting is that Plato himself took inspiration from the first three books of Herodotus in formulating his Ideal State.[14] The temple of Atlantis itself as described by Plato (*Critias* 116 c-17 a) seems inspired by the tower of Babylon as described by Herodotus. As explained in the Introduction, the biblical writer takes advantage of existing links between the Greek authors—another example of which we will see in Exodus 24—with the oath of Israel accepting the laws. One must note (as Jacques Cazeaux does[15]) that there is no distinction in Hebrew, as there is in modern translations, between the words 'Babel' in Genesis and 'Babylon' in Kings; the same word, Babel, is used in both books, making the circular reference very clear for the Hebrew reader.

Abraham / Euphemos: The Promised Land

Herodotus tells the story of how Jason and the Argonauts were stranded in Libya in the Lake Triton; Jason offered a tripod to the god Triton and in return received a promise that, were that tripod to be taken away, the descendants of the Argonauts would give rise to a hundred Greek cities (Herodotus IV, 179). Apollonius of Rhodes also gives details of this story: Euphemos dreamed that a clod of land offered by Triton had transformed into a young woman, to whom he made love. She explained to him that she symbolised his descendants, and he told his dream to

---

12. Thompson, *The Mythic Past*, 24-26.
13. Brisson and Pradeau, 'Introduction', 324-26.
14. Ibid., 322.
15. Cazeaux, *Le partage de minuit*.

Jason. Jason told him to throw the clod into the sea, from which the island of Calliste was born:

> Ah! Most glorious is the fate which awaits you. If you throw the clod into the sea, the gods will fashion from it an island, where the future sons of your sons will dwell, since Triton presented you this piece of the Libyan land as a gift. (Apollonius of Rhodes, *Argonautica* IV, 1749-53)

> From it arose the island of Calliste, the holy nurse of the sons of Euphemos. Once upon a time they lived in Sintian Lemnos, but were driven out of Lemnos by the Tyrrhenians and went to Sparta to settle in the land. When they left Sparta, Theras, the noble son of Autesion, led them to the island of Calliste, and you, Theras, gave the island your name. But these things happened long after Euphemos. (*Argonautica* IV, 1757-64)

The *Argonautica* ends a few verses later. For a reader unaware of this tale, this ending may seem out of place, as Euphemos played a minor role in the epic. But for those who are familiar with Herodotus it is obvious that Apollonius is referring to the foundation of Thera and Cyrene. Indeed, Herodotus tells how the descendants of Euphemos, living in Lemnos, were chased to Sparta, and how Theras brought them to the island of Calliste and changed its name. Later, a descendant of Euphemos, Battos, had to guide his people to found the colony of Cyrene, though he protested because he had a stutter (Herodotus IV, 145-59). We can link the character of Euphemos to Abram, who several times received the promise that those descended from him would possess the land of Canaan after spending four hundred years in Egypt in slavery (Gen 15:13-16). The Exodus story is foretold to Abram, in which Moses appears as the equivalent of Battos, as both received a divine mission to guide their people to a land that had been promised to their ancestors. The same framework appears in the Argonautic epic and in the Bible. As Plato's City must be a colony, the author recycled the myth of the foundation of Cyrene. The problem is that, since his wife Sarai is barren, Abram has no heir.

Abraham / Anaxandrides

In Genesis 16, we are told how Sarai, who was barren, suggested Abram to father a child to her servant Hagar. That child was Ishmael. But Hagar then despised her mistress, and God allowed Sarai to have a son in Genesis 21. Many scholars have linked this story to a law that appears in the *Code of Hammurabi* (144-46): if a man is married to a priestess, who is not allowed to have children, then he may take a servant as a second wife so as to sire offspring, but the first wife will have no right to sell the servant if a rivalry were to arise between them. Such a case is indeed similar to the story of Abram, with the exception that Sarai is not a priestess, she is barren. We see a more accurate parallel of this situation in Herodotus:

> For to Anaxandrides, while he had as wife his own sister's daughter and that woman was satisfactory to him, children were not born and, that being like that, the ephors said after they had called for him, 'If, mind you, you provide not for yourself, well by us that must not be overlooked, for the family of Eurysthenes to become extinct. Now, you the wife that you have, since she brings forth not, send away for yourself and another marry, and by doing that you will please the Spartiates.' Then he replied by asserting that he would do neither of those things and they were counselling and advising not beautifully that that wife that he had, although she was without fault to him, he should let go away and another bring back home and that he would not obey them. Thereupon the ephors and the elders, having taken counsel, brought forward for Anaxandrides this: 'Since then we see that you are holding yourself to the wife that you have, you then keep doing that and refuse to take a step against that, that not any counsel of another kind concerning you the Spartiates may take. Of the wife that you have we ask not from you the sending away, but you to that one all that now you are furnishing keep furnishing and another in addition to that one bring in as a wife for producing children.' They saying that in some way, Anaxandrides went along and afterwards with two wives he was settled at two hearths and doing in no way Spartan things. Then, no long time having gone by, the wife who had gone afterwards at a later moment brought forth that very Cleomenes. Indeed that one was bringing out to light a king sitting by for the Spartiates and the previous wife, the previous time being without offspring, then somehow became pregnant and enjoyed that as chance. So that she was bearing by a true account the relatives of the wife who had gone after learned by inquiry and bothered her and they asserted for themselves that she was merely boasting, because she wanted to bring in another's child. And, they performing terrible acts, when the time was becoming short, through lack of belief's agency the ephors, sitting around, guarded over the woman while she was bringing forth. Then she, when she had brought forth Dorieus, immediately conceived Leonidas and after that one immediately conceived Cleombrotus and some indeed say that as twins Cleombrotus and Leonidas were born. And she who had brought forth Cleomenes and had gone after in the second place, who was the daughter of Prinetades, the son of Demarmenus, no longer was bringing forth the second time. (Herodotus V, 39-41)

The resemblance is pronounced—as the king or hero has a beloved wife that is barren, he is forced to take a second wife so that he may have an inheritor, but after that, miraculously, the first wife becomes pregnant. Moreover, we will see how all of the Spartan princes and kings born in that story will be used as models for the Judges: Dorieus for Jephthah, Leonidas for Gideon and Cleomenes for Abimelech. The author combined this story with another miraculous birth—that of Orion in Ovid's *Fasti*.

Abraham and Isaac / Hyrieus and Orion

Jupiter, and his brother who rules the deep ocean, were journeying together, with Mercury. It was the hour when yoked oxen drag back the plough, and the lamb kneels down to drink the full ewe's milk. By chance, an old man, Hyrieus, farmer of a tiny plot, saw them, as he stood in front of his meagre dwelling: And spoke to them: 'The way's long, little of day is left, and my threshold's welcoming to strangers'. He stressed his words with a look, inviting them again: They accepted his offer, hiding their divinity. They entered the old man's cottage, black with smoke: There was still a flicker of fire in yesterday's log. He knelt and blew the flames higher with his breath, and drew out broken brands, and chopped them up. Two pots stood there: the smaller contained beans, the other vegetables: each boiling beneath its lid. While they waited, he poured red wine with a trembling hand: The god of the sea accepted the first cup, and when he'd drained it, he said: 'Let Jupiter drink next'. Hearing the name of Jupiter the old man grew pale. Recovering his wits, he sacrificed the ox that ploughed his meagre land, and roasted it in a great fire: And he brought out wine, in smoke-streaked jars, that he'd once stored away as a young boy. Promptly they reclined on couches made of rushes, and covered with linen, but still not high enough. Now the table was bright with food, bright with wine: The bowl was red earthenware, with cups of beech wood. Jupiter's word was: 'If you've a wish, ask it: All will be yours'. The old man said calmly: 'I had a dear wife, whom I knew in the flower of my first youth. Where is she now, you ask? An urn contains her. I swore to her, calling on you gods, 'You'll be the only wife I'll take'. I spoke, and kept the oath. I ask for something else: I wish to be a father, and not a husband'. The gods agreed: All took their stand beside the ox-hide—I'm ashamed to describe the rest—Then they covered the soaking hide with earth: Ten months went past and a boy was born. Hyrieus called him Urion, because of his conception: The first letter has now lost its ancient sound. (Ovid, *Fasti* V, 495-545)

The Lord appeared to Abraham by the oaks of Mamre, as he sat at the entrance of his tent in the heat of the day. He looked up and saw three men standing near him. When he saw them, he ran from the tent entrance to meet them, and bowed down to the ground. He said, 'My lord, if I find favour with you, do not pass by your servant. Let a little water be brought, and wash your feet, and rest yourselves under the tree. Let me bring a little bread, that you may refresh yourselves, and after that you may pass on—since you have come to your servant.' So they said, 'Do as you have said'. And Abraham hastened into the tent to Sarah, and said, 'Make ready quickly three measures of choice flour, knead it, and make cakes'. Abraham ran to the herd, and took a calf, tender and good, and gave it to the servant, who hastened to prepare it. Then he took curds and milk and the calf that he had prepared, and set it before them; and he stood by them under the tree while they ate. They said to him, 'Where is your wife Sarah?' And he said, 'There, in the tent'. Then one said, 'I will surely return to you in due season, and your wife Sarah shall have a son'. And Sarah was listening at the tent entrance behind him. Now Abraham and Sarah were old, advanced in age; it had ceased to be with Sarah after the manner of women. So Sarah laughed to herself, saying, 'After I have grown old, and my husband is old, shall I have pleasure?' The Lord said to Abraham, 'Why did Sarah laugh, and say, "Shall I indeed bear a child, now that I am old?" Is anything too wonderful for the Lord? At the set time I will return to you, in due season, and Sarah shall have a son.' But Sarah denied, saying, 'I did not laugh'; for she was afraid. He said, 'Oh yes, you did laugh'. (Gen 18:1-15)

In Ovid's account three gods, Jupiter, Neptune and Mercury, visit the aged Hyrieus, while in Genesis they are three 'men' sent by God.[16] In both stories, the old man offers his hospitality and prepares a meal for his hosts, and they reward his piety with the promise of the birth of a son in the year to come. The three gods drained their essence, or rather ejaculated, onto the hide of the calf that had been sacrificed for the meal, and then buried it—thus Orion was born of an ox-hide that was triply fertilized by divine semen. Orion's name is derived from Urion, a name that Ovid relates to the root 'urine'. This action that Ovid finds shameful is absent from the Bible, instead we read of Abram's aged wife, barren her whole life; the biblical miracle is more 'moral' than the Roman version. I have dubbed this phenomenon the 'platonic filter'—a kind of censorship applied by the biblical writer to the representation of God. God may appear in a multiple and humanoid form, but he must not be portrayed ejaculating on an ox-hide in the presence of mortals. It is likely that Ovid used an older source of which we have no record that the biblical author may have known as well. The following parallels, however, make Ovid's case more puzzling. As 'any myth consists of all of its variants', I will make fairly extensive quotations of these texts, so that the reader may see how close they are.

---

16.   Bishop Dom Calmet had noticed this similarity in the eighteenth century, and Voltaire even made a parody of it; for Voltaire, the Romans could not have learnt anything from the minor province of Judea. See 'Ange', in Voltaire, *Dictionnaire philosophique*.

Lot, Philemon and Baucis,
Orpheus and Eurydice, Cyniras and Myrrha

There is a swamp not far from there, once habitable land but now the haunt of diving-birds and marsh-loving coots. Jupiter went there, disguised as a mortal, and Mercury, the descendant of Atlas, setting aside his wings, went with his father, carrying the caduceus. A thousand houses they approached, looking for a place to rest: a thousand houses were locked and bolted. But one received them: it was humble it is true, roofed with reeds and stems from the marsh, but godly Baucis and the equally aged Philemon, had been wedded in that cottage in their younger years, and there had grown old together. They made light of poverty by acknowledging it, and bearing it without discontent of mind. It was no matter if you asked for owner or servant there: those two were the whole household: they gave orders and carried them out equally. So when the gods from heaven met the humble household gods, and stooping down, passed the low doorway, the old man pulled out a bench, and requested them to rest their limbs, while over the bench Baucis threw a rough blanket... They had a goose, the guard for their tiny cottage: as hosts they prepared to sacrifice it for their divine guests. But, quick-winged, it wore the old people out and, for a long time, escaped them, at last appearing to take refuge with the gods themselves. Then the heaven-born ones told them not to kill it. 'We are gods', they said, 'and this neighbourhood will receive just punishment for its impiety, but to you we grant exemption from that evil. Just leave your house, and accompany our steps, as we climb that steep mountainside together. (Ovid, *Metam.* VIII, 620-725)

The two angels came to Sodom in the evening, and Lot was sitting in the gateway of Sodom. When Lot saw them, he rose to meet them, and bowed down with his face to the ground. He said, 'Please, my lords, turn aside to your servant's house and spend the night, and wash your feet; then you can rise early and go on your way'. They said, 'No; we will spend the night in the square'. But he urged them strongly; so they turned aside to him and entered his house; and he made them a feast, and baked unleavened bread, and they ate... Then the men said to Lot, 'Have you anyone else here? Sons-in-law, sons, daughters, or anyone you have in the city—bring them out of the place. For we are about to destroy this place, because the outcry against its people has become great before the Lord, and the Lord has sent us to destroy it.' So Lot went out and said to his sons-in-law, who were to marry his daughters, 'Up, get out of this place; for the Lord is about to destroy the city'. But he seemed to his sons-in-law to be jesting. When morning dawned, the angels urged Lot, saying, 'Get up, take your wife and your two daughters who are here, or else you will be consumed in the punishment of the city'. But he lingered; so the men seized him and his wife and his two daughters by the hand, the Lord being merciful to him, and they brought him out and left him outside the city. When they had brought them outside, they said, 'Flee for your life; do not look back or stop anywhere in the Plain; flee to the hills, or else you will be consumed'. (Gen 19:1-3, 12-17)

The stories are again extremely close: two angels or two gods (the two were three in both previous stories) come to visit a city in the guise of humans, and a pious man offers them hospitality. In Ovid's version, the details of the meal are described. The angels/gods reveal themselves and explain how, due to its inhabitants, the city will be destroyed, but that the pious couple will be spared and allowed to flee with them. In Genesis, the inhabitants of Sodom act perversely—they want to 'know' the guests of Lot, meaning to rape them. Here, the descendants of Canaan are accused of inhospitality; Lot is ready to give them his own virgin daughters. We must keep in mind these details of Genesis 19, for they appear again in the story of Gibeah in Judges 19. Lot negotiates with the angels to allow him to find refuge in Zoar. His sons-in-law from Sodom refuse to follow him. God destroys the city with fire, whereas the Roman story speaks of a flood. Philemon and Baucis will become the keepers of a temple, and eventually end their lives by merging together into a tree. The rest of Genesis 19 shows more parallels with Ovid; for example, Lot and his family are ordered to refrain from looking back at Sodom as they flee—also seen in the well-known story of Orpheus and Eurydice:

> They took the upward path, through the still silence, steep and dark, shadowy with dense fog, drawing near to the threshold of the upper world. Afraid she was no longer there, and eager to see her, the lover turned his eyes. In an instant she dropped back, and he, unhappy man, stretching out his arms to hold her and be held, clutched at nothing but the receding air. Dying a second time, now, there was no complaint to her husband (what, then, could she complain of, except that she had been loved?). She spoke a last 'farewell' that, now, scarcely reached his ears, and turned again towards that same place. (Ovid, *Metamorphosis* X, 45-50; see also Virgil, *Georgics* IV, 475-500)

> Then the Lord rained on Sodom and Gomorrah sulphur and fire from the Lord out of heaven; and he overthrew those cities, and all the Plain, and all the inhabitants of the cities, and what grew on the ground. But Lot's wife, behind him, looked back, and she became a pillar of salt. (Gen 19:24-26)

The motif of a woman who is lost because either she or her companion looked back is found in both the Bible and Ovid. The last episode of Lot's story is his act of incest with his two daughters. They made him drunk and slept with him alternately. The first daughter gave birth to Moab, ancestor of the Moabites, the second daughter gave birth to

Ben-Ammi, ancestor of the Ammonites (Gen 19:30-38). A very similar story is again found in Ovid's *Metamorphosis*. Myrrha, daughter of King Cinyras of Cyprus, had fallen in love with her father. As she could not repress these feelings she confessed them to her nurse, and the two of them plotted to inebriate him to the extent that he would not recognise the woman with whom he was going to lie. Myrrha slept with her father twelve nights in a row, yet on the last night he discovered her identity and wanted to kill her. She fled and transformed into a myrrh tree, later giving birth to the god Adonis (Ovid, *Metam.* X, 430-75).

It is noticeable that both Orpheus' and Myrrha's stories are found in *Metamorphosis* book X in the same order as their biblical equivalents, except that they are separated by other unrelated stories. When reading Genesis 18 and 19 one may ask what happens to the third angel, as only two went to Sodom. This corresponds accurately with Ovid's stories, as of the three gods present at the birth of Orion, Jupiter, Neptune and Mercury, only Jupiter and Mercury appear in the city of Philemon and Baucis. Lot's story mirrors that of Philemon and Baucis until the moment when they leave the city, when it diverges. Philemon and Baucis both end up safe, but Lot's wife is taken out of the picture because she disobeyed, looking back as in Eurydice's story; Lot's daughters are thus given a reason to sleep with their drunken father, as Myrrha did. So we find two consecutive chapters from Genesis that contain four stories similar to those found in Ovid. It is likely that both Ovid and the biblical writer shared a common source, probably from the Hellenistic era. It is supposed that Ovid was strongly influenced by Nicander of Colophon, whose texts have been lost.[17] It is unlikely that Ovid took inspiration from the Bible because of its demythologising process; the three gods impregnating the hide is a theme that has disappeared from the biblical version. There is very little chance that the opposite, a sort of re-enchanting of the biblical narratives, would have taken place.[18] It seems rather that the biblical writer re-wrote Greek stories, censoring them to fit with the principles elaborated in Plato's *Republic*. Let us notice that this 'censorship' only applies to the representation of the divine, whereas violent and shocking stories involving humans do appear in Genesis and the rest of the Bible.

17. Joseph Chamonard, 'Introduction', in *Ovide les Métamorphoses*, Paris: GF-Flammarion, 1966, 11-12.

18. For a discussion of these parallels, see 'Genèse' and 'Abraham', in Voltaire, *Dictionnaire philosophique*.

Isaac / Phrixos

In Genesis 22, God decides to test Abraham's faith. He orders him to sacrifice his beloved son Isaac on Mount Moriah. As Abraham accepts this, an angel sent by God stops his hand and blesses him with the promise that his descendants will be numerous:

> And Abraham looked up and saw a ram, caught in a thicket by its horns. Abraham went and took the ram and offered it up as a burnt-offering instead of his son. (Gen 22:13)

> Of the sons of Aeolus, Athamas ruled over Boeotia and begat a son Phrixus and a daughter Helle by Nephele. And he married a second wife, Ino, by whom he had Learchus and Melicertes. But Ino plotted against the children of Nephele and persuaded the women to parch the wheat; and having got the wheat they did so without the knowledge of the men. But the earth, being sown with parched wheat, did not yield its annual crops; so Athamas sent to Delphi to inquire how he might be delivered from the dearth. Now Ino persuaded the messengers to say it was foretold that the infertility would cease if Phrixus were sacrificed to Zeus. When Athamas heard that, he was forced by the inhabitants of the land to bring Phrixus to the altar. But Nephele caught him and her daughter up and gave them a ram with a Golden Fleece, which she had received from Hermes, and borne through the sky by the ram they crossed land and sea. But when they were over the sea which lies betwixt Sigeum and the Chersonese, Helle slipped into the deep and was drowned, and the sea was called Hellespont after her. But Phrixus came to the Colchians, whose king was Aeetes, son of the Sun and of Perseis, and brother of Circe and Pasiphae, whom Minos married. He received Phrixus and gave him one of his daughters, Chalciope. And Phrixus sacrificed the ram with the Golden Fleece to Zeus the god of Escape, and the fleece he gave to Aeetes, who nailed it to an oak in a grove of Ares. And Phrixus had children by Chalciope, to wit, Argus, Melas, Phrontis, and Cytisorus. (Apollodorus, *Library* I, 9, 1)[19]

Pseudo-Apollodorus is a source from the Roman era that tells us the story of Phrixos in its full form though many previous Greek authors knew of it. Notably so did Herodotus, who mentioned how Xerxes visited the place were the descendants of Athamas lived (Herodotus VII, 197). Apollonius also mentions this episode in his *Argonautica* as it is the origin of the Golden Fleece—which Jason and his comrades must discover and bring back to Greece. The sons of Phrixos tell this story when they meet the Argonauts, who were going from Colchis to Greece when their ship wrecked:

19. Apollodorus, *The Library* (trans. James George Frazer, Cambridge, Mass.: Harvard University Press, 1939).

> That a descendant from Aiolos called Phrixos travelled to Aia from Hellas
> I have no doubt you yourselves are already aware. Phrixos reached the city
> of Aietes mounted on a ram, which Hermes made golden, and even to this
> day you can see its fleece spread out on the thickly leaved branches of an
> oak. Then on its own instructions, Phrixos sacrificed the ram to the son
> of Cronos, Zeus Phyxios—this chosen from all his titles—and Aietes
> received him in the palace and, as a gesture of kindly intentions, gave him
> in marriage his daughter Calciope, and asked no bride-price for her. These
> two are our parents. (Apollonius of Rhodes, *Argonautica* II, 1140-60)

Jason explains to them that they are all cousins, descendants of Aeolus,
and that their encounter was by divine providence:

> But come, we wish to bring the Golden Fleece to Hellas. Help us and
> guide our voyage, since my expedition is to atone for the attempted
> sacrifice of Phrixos, which has brought Zeus' anger on the descendants of
> Aiolos. (*Argonautica* II, 1190-95)

The very reason for the Argonauts' journey is explained when Jason's
cousins meet: Zeus's anger was caused by the attempted sacrifice of
Phrixos. Zeus refuses human sacrifice, and Athamas, in believing and
acting upon Ino's false oracle, has committed a sin. In the Bible this
theme is transformed into a test, one that Abraham passes. Readers of the
Bible may raise the question of why God wants Isaac to be sacrificed. In
passing God's test Abraham receives a blessing for generations of his
offspring, whereas Athamas invokes a curse upon all the descendants of
Aeolus. This inversion of consequences accompanies an inversion of
sequence: according to Apollonius, Phrixos sacrifices the ram, on its own
instructions, and hangs its fleece on an oak; when Abraham sees a ram
with its thorns stuck in a thicket, he untangles it and then sacrifices it. As
the Greek version condemns the blind credulity of Athamas, the Bible
praises Abraham's abnegation. Euripides is probably counted among the
biblical writer's sources, as he wrote two divergent plays entitled *Phrixos*
(A and B) that are known to us only through fragments. It is likely that
Apollonius considered *Phrixos* to be a prologue to the Argonautic epic,
that his readers would have known this and that Euripides' tragedy
Medea was its epilogue. In the fragments of Phrixos it says:

> I am pious. If I suffer the same fate as that of the most impious, how could
> that be good? Or does Zeus, the best of all beings, have no sense of
> equity?[20]

---

20. Euripides, *Tragédies*. VIII. Deuxième partie: *Fragments de Bellérophon à
Protésilas, Paris: Les Belles Lettres, 2000, 369, my translation from the French.

Euripides questioned why Zeus would ask such for a horrible sacrifice, but this has disappeared from the Bible. It seems that in the other version of *Phrixos* by Euripides it was mentioned that Phrixos accepted the sacrifice, believing that it would cure the land (found in the summary of Pseudo-Hyginus, *Fables*, II). There, it is said that when the messenger who had brought Ino's false oracle saw Phrixos about to let himself be killed, he stopped Athamas and told him the truth—a version in which no golden ram appeared. It seems that Isaac accepts his sacrifice implicitly in Genesis, since when he asks his father where the victim was, he may have understood Abraham's prophetic answer—that God will provide it—as pointed to him. Still, in the Bible, Isaac does not flee from his father after the attempted sacrifice, nor does he marry the daughter of the king of his new country; absent as well is the notion of an attempted murder that must be atoned. Yet, all of this will appear further on in Genesis, in the story of Joseph.

Let us step back for a moment. We saw how Cain seemed to have been inspired by Ixion (who had fathered the Centaurs with Nephele, the cloud goddess) and his descendant Caineus. Now Nephele is encountered again as the first wife of Athamas and the mother of Phrixos. Both stories are linked, appearing as a thread in the biblical narrative. Moreover, we saw how Abraham corresponds to Euphemos (one of the Argonauts who received a divine promise from Triton that his descendants would own the land of Cyrene, symbolised by a clod). All of this follows a very definite purpose—the foundation of the biblical State, which shall be a colony, after its platonic model. The Argonautic epic starts with the stories of Ixion and Athamas and ends with the foundation of the Greek colony of Cyrene; in it the biblical author found a privileged source for his own foundation story. If we sum up the parallels appearing in the story of Abraham, it all makes sense: they all concern the uncertainty of whether or not the hero is going to be able to have descendants, as God promised him. His wife is barren so he takes a second wife, but then his first wife becomes pregnant (a miracle that is a censored version of the birth of Orion). The ultimate test is when at last Abraham is allowed an heir, God urges him to kill him, creating dramatic tension. The biblical writer did not assemble these stories randomly. He chose them carefully to create a new epic, the main concern of which is the royal lineage. Indeed, even the story of Lot (which explains how the Moabites and the Ammonites were born of incest) has something to do with King David's ancestry, as his great-grandmother Ruth was a Moabitess.

Jacob and Esau, Acrisios and Proetos, Heracles and Eurystheus

Isaac prayed to the Lord for his wife, because she was barren; and the Lord granted his prayer, and his wife Rebekah conceived. The children struggled together within her; and she said, 'If it is to be this way, why do I live?' So she went to inquire of the Lord. And the Lord said to her, 'Two nations are in your womb, and two peoples born of you shall be divided; one shall be stronger than the other, the elder shall serve the younger'. (Gen 25:21-23)

Lynceus reigned over Argos after Danaus and begat a son Abas by Hypermnestra; and Abas had twin sons Acrisius and Proetus by Aglaia, daughter of Mantineus. These two quarrelled with each other while they were still in the womb, and when they were grown up they waged war for the kingdom, and in the course of the war they were the first to invent shields. And Acrisius gained the mastery and drove Proetus from Argos; and Proetus went to Lycia to the court of Iobates or, as some say, of Amphianax, and married his daughter, whom Homer calls Antia, but the tragic poets call her Stheneboea. His father-in-law restored him to his own land with an army of Lycians, and he occupied Tiryns, which the Cyclopes had fortified for him. They divided the whole of the Argive territory between them and settled in it, Acrisius reigning over Argos and Proetus over Tiryns. (Apollodorus, *Library* 2, 2, 1)

This parallel has been long known, and James George Frazer noted it in his translation of Apollodorus' *Library*. Like the twins Acrisius and Proeteus, Jacob and Esau fought in their mother's womb, and after being enemies they were eventually to meet again to share the land that was promised to their father Isaac (Gen 33). Esau will be the ancestor of Edom and Jacob the ancestor of Israel (Gen 36). Proetus is a character that appears in book VI of Homer's *Iliad*, as mentioned by Apollodorus. Homer tells of how Proetus first welcomed the hero Bellerophon, but then sent him to his father-in-law bearing a sealed letter instructing the recipient to kill its bearer. Martin L. West noticed another parallel between the dispossession of Esau and the blessing of Jacob by Isaac on the one hand, and on the other hand the birth of Heracles and Eurystheus (*Il.* XIX).[21] In Genesis 27, the aged and blind Isaac wants to give his elder son Esau his blessing, so he sends Esau off to hunt some game, and promises to bless him upon his return. But Rebecca, who prefers Jacob, overhears and suggests that Jacob appear to his father in his brother's guise. Jacob points out that he has smooth skin yet Esau is hairy, so Rebecca tells him to kill two goats. She covers Jacob's arms with their

21. West, *The East Face of Helicon*, 441 n. 7.

hairs and cooks the meat for Isaac. Jacob then enters Isaac's tent wearing Esau's clothes, bearing the meal cooked by Rebecca. Though Isaac hears Jacob's voice, he thinks that he feels Esau's arms and, believing Jacob is Esau, blesses him. He says that he will become a large nation and will be lord over his brothers (Gen 27:29).

Only later does Esau appear with the game for Isaac, whereupon they both understand that Jacob arrived first. Esau cries and begs his father to bless him, but Isaac cannot undo his word; thus he gives Esau another blessing, inferior to that bestowed upon Jacob, and repeats that Jacob's brothers will be his servants (Gen 27:37). This is reminiscent of Noah blessing Shem and Japhet, and proclaiming that Canaan will be their servant (Gen 9:26). Here, Isaac prophesies the future of the kingdoms of Israel and Edom, as we will see in the books of Samuel and Kings. Esau wants to kill Jacob after this episode, so Jacob's mother suggests that he flee to her brother Laban, and to marry one of his daughters. M.L. West links this story of Esau, cheated out of his father's blessing by the treachery of Rebecca and Jacob, to the birth of Heracles and Eurystheus in the *Iliad*:

> Zeus, and Fate, and Erinys that walks in darkness struck me mad when we were assembled on the day that I took from Achilles the meed that had been awarded to him. What could I do? All things are in the hand of heaven, and Folly, eldest of Zeus' daughters, shuts men's eyes to their destruction. She walks delicately, not on the solid earth, but hovers over the heads of men to make them stumble or to ensnare them. 'Time was when she fooled Zeus himself, who they say is greatest whether of gods or men; for Hera, woman though she was, beguiled him on the day when Alcmena was to bring forth mighty Heracles in the fair city of Thebes. He told it out among the gods saying, 'Hear me all gods and goddesses, that I may speak even as I am minded; this day shall an Ilithuia, helper of women who are in labour, bring a man child into the world who shall be lord over all that dwell about him who are of my blood and lineage'. Then said Hera all crafty and full of guile, 'You will play false, and will not hold to your word. Swear me, O Olympian, swear me a great oath, that he who shall this day fall between the feet of a woman, shall be lord over all that dwell about him who are of your blood and lineage'. 'Thus she spoke, and Zeus suspected her not, but swore the great oath, to his much ruing thereafter. For Hera darted down from the high summit of Olympus, and went in haste to Achaean Argos where she knew that the noble wife of Sthenelus son of Perseus then was. She being with child and in her seventh month, Hera brought the child to birth though there was a month still wanting, but she stayed the offspring of Alcmena, and kept back the Ilithuiae. Then she went to tell Zeus the son of Cronos, and said, 'Father Zeus, lord of the lightning—I have a word for your ear.

> There is a fine child born this day, Eurystheus, son to Sthenelus the son of
> Perseus; he is of your lineage; it is well, therefore, that he should reign
> over the Argives'. 'On this Zeus was stung to the very quick, and in his
> rage he caught Folly by the hair, and swore a great oath that never should
> she again invade starry heaven and Olympus, for she was the bane of all.
> Then he whirled her round with a twist of his hand, and flung her down
> from heaven so that she fell on to the fields of mortal men; and he was
> ever angry with her when he saw his son groaning under the cruel labours
> that Eurystheus laid upon him. (Homer, *Il.* XIX, 90-125)

As West argues, we see how a father is about to give his favourite son
dominion over his brothers when his wife deceives him, so that the son
she favoured may benefit instead. Thus all because of Hera's jealousy,
Heracles was made to submit to Eurystheus and perform his famous
twelve labours—a story that is indeed similar to Rebecca's plan for
Jacob to manipulate Isaac into bestowing upon him the blessing of Esau.
West did not notice that both the story of Acrisius and Proetus and the
story of Heracles and Eurystheus are actually one and the same, for he
thinks that these resemblances are due to an oral diffusion from the East
to the West. By reading Apollodorus' *Library*, we understand that
Acrisius was none other than the grandfather of Perseus. Perseus married
Andromeda and had Sthenelus, Electryon and Alceus, while Sthenelus
married Nicipea:

> …and he had afterwards a son Eurystheus, who reigned also over
> Mycenae. For when Hercules was about to be born, Zeus declared among
> the gods that the descendant of Perseus then about to be born would reign
> over Mycenae, and Hera out of jealousy persuaded the Ilithyias to retard
> Alcmena's delivery, and contrived that Eurystheus, son of Sthenelus,
> should be born a seven-month child. (Apollodorus, *Library* 2, 4, 5)

Both Heracles and Eurystheus are descendants of Perseus, hence of
Acrisius as well. As we see in Pseudo-Apollodorus, the theme of the
twins that fought in the womb and the one of the father that was manipulated by his wife into unknowingly blessing another son than he expected
actually are both parts of the same story—that of Heracles and his
ancestors. This explains how the biblical writer used that mythical cycle
to give life to the antagonism between Jacob and Esau, and between
Israel and Edom. Even if these parallels have been noticed before, they
were thought to be the result of random diffusion. Here, we see that that
which is at stake is a rather simple logic. As Abraham and Isaac were
inspired by episodes from the Argonauts, Jacob is inspired by episodes of
the Heraclean cycle. Homer mentions these stories almost as anecdotes,
but Apollodorus' *Library* puts them in chronological order. Furthermore,

we will see how Jacob and David are a single, twofold character. They experience the same problems: the treacheries of a father-in-law (Laban and Saul), the idolatry of a wife (Rachel and Michal) that worships the *teraphim*, the rape of a daughter that was in turn avenged by their kin (Dinah by Simeon and Levi, and Thamar by Absalom), and the incest of a son in raping their concubines (Reuben and Absalom). David will commit murder by sending Uriah the Hittite to Joab bearing a sealed letter instructing Joab to have him killed on the battlefield (2 Sam 11). This theme is found as well in the story of Proetus (*Il.* VI, 150-60). This is one of the first pieces of evidence that both stories of Jacob and David, being parallel, were modelled after the same sources and written by the same, single author.

As explained in the Introduction, the order of these Greek sources is dismantled and re-arranged according to the author's will, but here we find that the fighting twins and the dispossessed elder still appear in the same order in the Greek epic as in Genesis 25–27. Jacob plays the role of Eurystheus and Esau plays Heracles. Perhaps, then, it is no coincidence that Esau is described as a rough hunter, who gives up his birthright for a lentil stew (Gen 25:29-34). Of course, Pseudo-Apollodorus was not a source for the Bible because it was written later, but Homer is considered to have been a textual source. The *Iliad* appears to be the primary source of inspiration for the cycle of David in the book of Samuel, and the cycle of Jacob is somehow its prologue. Apollodorus is used in the analysis to fill in the gaps left by lost sources. The cycle of Heracles is best known through Apollodorus and Diodorus Siculus. Let us not forget that, in this seemingly confusing use of various mythical Greek sources, the thread of the Bible is a criticism of the excesses of monarchy, opposed to the platonic Ideal State. Being the father of the twelve tribes, Jacob represents the first incarnation of Israel, and David appears as his literary 'reincarnation'. However, in abusing his power David will cause the Ideal State to fracture. As we explore Jacob's cycle further, we find more parallels with the cycle of Heracles.

Jacob and Laban / Heracles and Thespios

Jacob fled from the wrath of his brother and went to meet his maternal uncle Laban. Wishing to marry Laban's younger daughter Rachel, Jacob promises to work seven years for her hand. However, on the night of the wedding Laban sends Leah to Jacob's bed. Jacob lies with her, and only in the morning realises that she was Leah and not Rachel. Laban explains that his elder daughter was to be married before her younger sister, thus he proposes that Jacob marry Rachel the next week and work seven more years for her (Gen 29). Laban took advantage of Jacob, tricking him into marrying his two daughters by having them switch places:

> Now this Thespius was king of Thespiae, and Hercules went to him when he wished to catch the lion. The king entertained him for fifty days, and each night, as Hercules went forth to the hunt, Thespius bedded one of his daughters with him (fifty daughters having been borne to him by Megamede, daughter of Arneus); for he was anxious that all of them should have children by Hercules. Thus Hercules, though he thought that his bed-fellow was always the same, had intercourse with them all. And having vanquished the lion, he dressed himself in the skin and wore the scalp as a helmet/ (Apollodorus, *Library* 2, 4, 10)

Thespius wants to have grandchildren by Heracles, as he has no sons. Therefore, Thespius coerces him into sleeping with his fifty daughters (one by one), but Heracles thinks it is always the same woman; the same theme as Jacob sleeping with Leah, thinking she is Rachel. Jacob begat twelve sons, and Heracles' descendants went on to conquer Sardinia (Diodorus Sicilus, *Library* IV, 29, 4). Laban's cheating of Jacob and always refusing to give him what he worked for reminds us also of Laomedon, first king of Troy. Laomedon refused to pay Apollo and Poseidon, who had helped him build the walls of Troy. As recompense, the gods wanted his daughter Hesione to be sacrificed to a monster, but Laomedon asked Heracles to free her for the price of several horses. However, after Laomedon refused to pay again, Heracles then destroyed the city. His son Tlepolomus tells this story when facing Sarpedon on the Trojan battlefield, right before being killed:

> Far other was Heracles, my own brave and lion-hearted father, who came here for the horses of Laomedon, and though he had six ships only, and few men to follow him, sacked the city of Ilius and made a wilderness of her highways. You are a coward, and your people are falling from you. For all your strength, and all your coming from Lycia, you will be no help to the Trojans but will pass the gates of Hades vanquished by my hand (Homer, *Il.* V, 650-55; see also Ovid, *Metam.* XI, 210-15; Apollodorus, *Library* 2, 5, 9; 2, 6, 4; 3, 12; Hyginus, *Fables* 31 and 89; Diodorus Sicilus, *Library* IV, 42).

Thus, we have another story involving Heracles and a man who honoured neither his promises nor his payments.

Jacob and Laban / Sisyphus and Autolycus

Then Jacob took fresh rods of poplar and almond and plane, and peeled white streaks in them, exposing the white of the rods. He set the rods that he had peeled in front of the flocks in the troughs, that is, the watering-places, where the flocks came to drink. And since they bred when they came to drink, the flocks bred in front of the rods, and so the flocks produced young that were striped, speckled, and spotted. Jacob separated the lambs, and set the faces of the flocks toward the striped and the completely black animals in the flock of Laban; and he put his own droves apart, and did not put them with Laban's flock. Whenever the stronger of the flock were breeding, Jacob laid the rods in the troughs before the eyes of the flock, that they might breed among the rods, but for the feebler of the flock he did not lay them there; so the feebler were Laban's, and the stronger Jacob's. Thus the man grew exceedingly rich, and had large flocks, and male and female slaves, and camels and donkeys. (Gen 30:37-43)

Mercury gave to Autolycus, who he begat by Chione, the gift of being such a skilful thief that he could not be caught, making him able to change whatever he stole into some other form—from white to black, or from black to white, from a hornless animal to a horned one, or from horned one to a hornless. When he kept continually stealing from the herds of Sisyphus and couldn't be caught, Sisyphus was convinced he was stealing because Autolycus' number was increasing while his was growing smaller. In order to catch him, he put a mark on the hooves of his cattle. When autolycus had stolen in his usual way, Sisyphus came to him and identified the cattle he had stolen by their hooves, and took them away. While he was delaying there, he seduced Anticlia, the daughter of Autolycus. She was later given in marriage to Laertes, and bore Ulysses. Some writers accordingly call him Sisyphean; because of this parentage he was shrewd. (Hyginus, *Fable* 201)[22]

Like Apollodorus' *Library*, the *Fables* of Hyginus were a handbook for young Romans to learn the basics of Greek mythology, and they preserved summaries of lost myths and tragedies (such as Euripides' *Phrixos*). Jacob grew his cattle through a magical process, which decreased Laban's cattle, quite like Autolycus did with the cattle of Sisyphus. That Greek myth was itself inspired by the Homeric *Hymn to Hermes*, in which the poet tells of how infant Hermes stole the cattle of Apollo (Hermes being the father of Autolycus). The biblical writer used several Greek sources that involved a treacherous father-in-law, such as Thespios (who made Heracles sleep with different sisters), Laomedon (who refused to pay Heracles for his work) and Autolycus (who stole the

---

22. Translated by Mary Grant.

cattle of Sisyphus). Though Laban is a deceiver, Jacob will retaliate and prove that he is an even greater trickster than his father-in-law.

After twenty years of being exploited by Laban, Jacob will decide to leave with his wives, children and cattle. Rachel steals the *teraphim*—a word that seems to refer to small domestic idols. Laban chases Jacob, and asks for the return of his gods. Jacob, not knowing that Rachel has the *teraphim*, swears to put to death whomsoever is found with them. Laban inspects each tent, but Rachel hides the *teraphim* under her camel's saddle and sits on them. She pretends that she has her period and declines to get up in front of her father, and Laban gives up his search (Gen 31). This is an important detail in linking this story to the cycle of David. David's father-in-law Saul wants to kill him, but Michal, Saul's daughter tells her husband David to run away. She arranges the *teraphim* in her bed with a pillow of goat hair to create the illusion that David is lying sick (1 Sam 19:11-17). Just as the Bible requires that its readers exercise both memory and patience, we must wait until our analysis of the book of Samuel to understand all these details. After leaving Laban, Jacob will encounter Esau, whom he has not seen for twenty years. Jacob fears his brother's anger, and he stays awake at night. An angel comes to fight Jacob but is defeated by him, though Jacob's hip is broken and he walks thereafter with a limp. The next day he meets Esau, and they reconcile and share their father's land. Jacob walking with a limp and Esau having red hair are also details that will reappear in the story of David.

Dinah / Helen

In Genesis 34, Jacob's daughter Dinah is raped by Prince Shechem, from the city of the same name. Jacob accepts to marry Dinah to Shechem and to make an alliance with the Shechemites, under the condition that they circumcise themselves. Simeon and Levi, Dinah's brothers, decide to avenge their sister's honour and massacre all the Shechemites as they were recovering from the circumcision. This can be linked to Helen's abduction by King Theseus:

> And when Helen grew into a lovely woman, Theseus carried her off and brought her to Aphidnae. But when Theseus was in Hades, Pollux and Castor marched against Aphidnae, took the city, got possession of Helen, and led Aethra, the mother of Theseus, away captive. (Apollodorus, *Library* 3, 10, 7)

> Having made a compact with Pirithous that they would marry daughters
> of Zeus, Theseus, with the help of Pirithous, carried off Helen from
> Sparta for himself, when she was twelve years old, and in the endeavour
> to win Persephone as a bride for Pirithous he went down to Hades. And
> the Dioscuri, with the Lacedaemonians and Arcadians, captured Athens
> and carried away Helen, and with her Aethra, daughter of Pittheus, into
> captivity; but Demophon and Acamas fled. And the Dioscuri also brought
> back Menestheus from exile, and gave him the sovereignty of Athens.
> (Apollodorus, *Epitome* 1, 23)

Pirithous was the king of the Lapiths, whom Ixion begot to his human
wife, mother of Caineus. Now we have a very accurate parallel between
the stories of Helen and Dinah.[23] Both were ravished by a prince and then
taken back by two of their brothers, who devastated the city. The Greek
version explains the enmity between Sparta and Athens. The biblical
version tells of the first war between the sons of Israel and the sons of
Canaan; it foretells the conquest of Joshua, and also the bloodbath of the
first kingship of Abimelech that takes place in Shechem (Judg 9–10).
This is one of the only occurrences of the cycle of Theseus appearing in
the Bible, along with the story of Reuben's fault in the next section; the
biblical writer did not use the Minotaur and the Labyrinth.

Kupitz noticed that Jacob bought a piece of land in Sechem for a
hundred *kesitah* (Gen 33:19).[24] He links this word with the Lydian
currency *cistophorus*—in short *kiste*—that would have given the Hebrew
kesitah. This would be an obvious anachronism, since that currency did
not appear before the late third century B.C.E. Kupitz also notices how
Simeon and Levi used a weapon—in Hebrew called *makera* (Gen
49:5)—that sounds exactly like the Homeric Greek *machaira*, both meaning a sword (and so did Rashi notice this similarity). In my analysis, a
textual parallel appears with Homer's *Odyssey*:

> And the other sons of Jacob came upon the slain, and plundered the city,
> because their sister had been defiled. They took their flocks and their
> herds, their donkeys, and whatever was in the city and in the field. All
> their wealth, all their little ones and their wives, all that was in the houses,
> they captured and made their prey. (Gen 34:27-29)

> There I stationed my ships in the river, bidding my men stay by them and
> keep guard over them while I sent out scouts to reconnoitre from every
> point of vantage. But the men disobeyed my orders, took to their own
> devices, and ravaged the land of the Egyptians, killing the men, and
> taking their wives and children captive. (*Od.* XIV, 262-66)

23. Noticed by Gordon, *Before the Bible*, 285.
24. Kupitz, 'La Bible est-elle un plagiat?', 85.

Like Ulysses, Jacob did not want his men/sons to go and attack the people, but they did—killing all the men and taking the women and the children captive. We will find out much more about Ulysses' speech to Eumeus in book XIV of the *Odyssey* in comparison with the story of Joseph. Jacob's favourite wife Rachel will die giving birth to Benjamin, and Reuben—the elder son—soon after ends up sleeping with Leah's servant (Jacob's concubine).

Reuben / Hippolytus

> While Israel lived in that land, Reuben went and lay with Bilhah his father's concubine; and Israel heard of it. (Gen 35:22)

Only on his deathbed does Jacob punish Reuben, depriving him of his birthright:

> Reuben, you are my firstborn, my might and the first fruits of my vigour, excelling in rank and excelling in power. Unstable as water, you shall no longer excel because you went up on to your father's bed; then you defiled it—you went up on to my couch! (Gen 49:3-4)

In Euripides' *Hippolytus*, Phaedra accuses Theseus' son of ravishing her. Theseus believes it to be true, as Phaedra hanged herself and left a suicide note, though the truth is that she was in love with Hippolytus and could not bear the impossible situation. Theseus prayed unto his father Poseidon to have Hipollytus killed:

> I cannot close the door of my mouth on this mortal crime that I am ashamed to name. Hippolytus dared to lay his brutal hand on my bed, without respect for Zeus' sacred eye. Poseidon, my father, who once granted me three wishes, fulfil one now and destroy my son. (Euripides, *Hippolytus* 885-90)

Even though Hippolytus is innocent, Reuben is not. The accusations in Euripides and in the Bible are alike: a son 'went into his father's bed', meaning that he slept with his father's wife. Hippolytus will die in a chariot accident, a scene that is similar to the story of Absalom—after having raped the ten concubines of his father David (2 Sam 16), Absalom had a chariot accident, his hair caught in the branches of a tree; and was then murdered by Joab (2 Sam 18). Absalom had avenged his sister Tamar, who had been raped by Amnon—another of David's sons (2 Sam 13). The same stories take place in the cycles of Jacob and David: a daughter is raped; she is avenged by her brother(s); and a son commits incest with his father's concubine(s). In Jacob's blessing at the end of Genesis, the elder son Reuben loses his birthright because of his incestuous deed. Simeon and Levi, Jacob's second and third sons, are also disqualified because they slew the men of Shechem. Finally, Jacob prophesied on his deathbed that Judah was to inherit the kingship of Israel (Gen 49:8-12). David is to be the result of Jacob's promise, and ironically, lives out the same episodes as his ancestor. All of this shows us that the same author conceived of the biblical narratives and that they can be read, as Lévi-Strauss proposed, in both diachronic and synchronic order. Genesis is concerned with the events of the future, the kingship of Israel. The next chapter of Genesis tells of the genealogy of the descendants of Edom through its kings. 'These are the kings who reigned in the land of Edom, before any king reigned over the Israelites' (Gen 36:31). This is evidence that Genesis is oriented toward future events.

Judah and Tamar

Before analysing the story of Joseph, let us examine the story of Judah in Genesis 38. Judah had three sons by a Canaanite woman: Er, Onan and Shela. He married Er to Tamar, but Er died. According to the law of the levirate (Gen 38:8; Deut 25:5-10) Judah ordered Onan to marry Tamar. But Onan refused to have children with Tamar and used *coitus interruptus*, so God smote him. Judah wanted to spare his last son from marrying her; she resolved to dress up as a prostitute and to sleep with Judah. Tamar became pregnant, and since she had taken objects that implicated Judah, he was recognised as the father. These objects were his signet, his cord and his staff (Gen 38:18). Judah had twin sons with his daughter-in-law. This type of union is prohibited in Lev 18:15. Soon after the aforementioned description of the tower of Babylon, Herodotus tells us about the ritual prostitution of the Babylonian women. He also describes the traditional clothing of Babylonian men:

> Their boats, then, are like that and they wear clothing like this, a linen tunic that reaches the foot; then over it another tunic of wool one puts on, a white small cloak wraps round and wears native sandals pretty near to Boeotian slippers. Moreover, since they grow their hair long, they bind up their heads with turbans, and they're anointed over their whole body; *each has a signet ring and a handmade staff* and on top of each staff is fashioned either an apple or a rose or a lily or an eagle or something else, because their law is not to have a staff without a device… Quite the most shameful of the Babylonians' laws is this: every native woman must sit in the shrine of Aphrodite once in her life and have intercourse with a foreign man. Many, thinking unbefitting themselves to be mixed with all the others, inasmuch as they are high minded because of wealth, on

chariots in covered carriages drive to the shrine and stand and a large retinue follows them behind, while the greater number act this way: in Aphrodite's precinct many women sit down with a wreath of string round their heads; some go forward and some go back. And straight as a line ways that go through to the women extend every direction along the roads, through which the foreigners go and make their selection. Whenever a woman sits there, she departs to her house not before one of the foreigners should throw silver onto her knees and have intercourse with her outside the shrine. And with this throwing it on her he has to say this much: 'I invoke over you the goddess Mylitta' (The Assyrians call Aphrodite Mylitta). (Herodotus I, 195, 199)

At the very end of the *Histories* Herodotus describes how Xerxes seduced his daughter-in-law, and how he was caught because she possessed an object that belonged to him:

That time indeed, while he was in Sardis, he was in love with the woman of Masistes, and that while she was there. So, when, in respect to him, while he kept sending messages forth, she had the power not to be worked on utterly, and he would not bring violence forth out of respect for his brother Masistes, and the same thing was holding for his woman also—for she well knew that she would not obtain violence, thereupon indeed Xerxes, keeping himself from all else, was bringing about that following marriage for his son Darius, of the daughter of that woman and Masistes, because he thought that he would take hold of her more, if he did that. So, having betrothed and performed the deeds that were used according to law, he was driving off to Susa. Then, when he had come thither and brought for himself into his own place for Darius, thus indeed, as he ceased for himself from the woman of Masistes, so he, after having changed himself, was in love and obtaining the woman of Darius, Masistes' daughter, and that woman's name was Artaynte. So, time going forth, it become thoroughly known by inquiry in a manner like this: Amestris, Xerxes' woman, completely wove a robe, large and embroidered as well as worth beholding, and gave it to Xerxes, and he, having taken pleasure in, cast it round himself and went to Artaynte's side. Then, having taken pleasure in that one also, he bade her ask for whatever she wanted to became hers in return for services rendered him; for she would obtain, if she asked. So, because for it had to come out badly for her with her whole house, thereupon she said to Xerxes, 'Will you give me whatever I ask from you?', and he, thinking that she would ask for herself anything rather, promised and swore. Then she, when he had sworn without fear, asked for the robe, and Xerxes was coming to be of every kind, because he wanted not to make the gift in accordance with nothing else, but out of fear of Amestris, lest by her who even previously was guessing what was being done he be found out to be doing thus, and rather he was offering cities and abundant gold as well as an army, which no one was to rule other than that that one—and the army's a very Persian gift. Yet, since he could not produce persuasion, he gave the robe, and she, who was greatly rejoicing at the gift, was wearing and glorying in it. (Herodotus IX, 108-10)

Here we find the theme of the man who chooses a wife for his son but ends up sleeping with her—an affair that is revealed when she produces a token of his. In Genesis, the signet and the staff of Judah (from Herodotus' chapter about Babylonian customs) replace the robe of Xerxes. It seems that the biblical writer mixed the two stories of the Babylonian ritual prostitution and Xerxes being in love with his daughter-in-law.

Er, Son of Judah, and Er, Son of Armenios

Well, I said, I will tell you a tale; not one of the tales which Odysseus tells to the hero Alcinous, yet this too is a tale of a hero, Er the son of Armenius, a Pamphylian by birth. He was slain in battle, and ten days afterwards, when the bodies of the dead were taken up already in a state of corruption, his body was found unaffected by decay, and carried away home to be buried. And on the twelfth day, as he was lying on the funeral pile, he returned to life and told them what he had seen in the other world. He said that when his soul left the body he went on a journey with a great company, and that they came to a mysterious place at which there were two openings in the earth; they were near together, and over against them were two other openings in the heaven above. In the intermediate space there were judges seated, who commanded the just, after they had given judgment on them and had bound their sentences in front of them, to ascend by the heavenly way on the right hand; and in like manner the unjust were bidden by them to descend by the lower way on the left hand; these also bore the symbols of their deeds, but fastened on their backs. He drew near, and they told him that he was to be the messenger who would carry the report of the other world to men, and they bade him hear and see all that was to be heard and seen in that place. Then he beheld and saw on one side the souls departing at either opening of heaven and earth when sentence had been given on them; and at the two other openings other souls, some ascending out of the earth dusty and worn with travel, some descending out of heaven clean and bright. (Plato, *Rep.* X, 614 b-d)

Judah took a wife for Er his firstborn; her name was Tamar. But Er, Judah's firstborn, was wicked in the sight of the Lord, and the Lord put him to death. (Gen 38:6-7)

Here we find another example of how the biblical writer retains names from his Greek sources as 'fingerprints', displacing them on the genealogic scale. A few chapters earlier, Jacob has a vision of a ladder reaching up from the earth to heaven, upon which messengers go back and forth (Gen 28:10-17). The difference of course is that Jacob is dreaming, not dead like Plato's hero. Still, further on in Genesis we find the son of Judah, Jacob's grandson, bearing curiously the same name, Er. All we are told about him is that he died after marrying Tamar. Even though the visions do not serve the same purpose in each text, the appearance of that exact name, Er, is a clue that points to the platonic source. The coitus of Judah and Tamar results in the birth of the twins Perez and Zerah, in some manner replacing Er and Onan, Judah's two dead sons. David will be born of the offspring of Perez, as we are told specifically in the book of Ruth. The book of Ruth, set in the period of Judges, tells a story similar to that of Genesis 38. Ruth, a foreign widow of one of Perez's descendants, plots to bear a child by Boaz, a relative of her late husband; they become David's great-grandparents. It is only upon analysis of this story that the platonic riddle of David's genealogy will unfold. We will meet Tamar and her twin sons again in the story of Rahab (Josh 2 and 6). The death of Onan can be linked to a law of Plato and also to one story in Herodotus:

> But since Onan knew that the offspring would not be his, he spilled his semen on the ground whenever he went in to his brother's wife, so that he would not give offspring to his brother. What he did was displeasing in the sight of the Lord, and he put him to death also. (Gen 38:9-10)

> A good objection; but was I not just now saying that I had a way to make men use natural love and abstain from unnatural male love, not inten-tionally destroying the seeds of human increase, or sowing them in stony places, in which they will take no root; and that I would command them to abstain too from any female field of increase in which that which is sown is not likely to grow? (Plato, *Laws* 838 e)

> Therefore not desiring that children should be born to him from his newly-married wife, he had commerce with her not in the accustomed manner. (Herodotus I, 61)

Plato himself suggested that stories or preambles be used in order to show how God punishes disobedience. He who has intercourse with a woman without desiring children commits a mortal sin. The passage above from *Laws* can be shown to be the source of the biblical rules gov-erning sexuality in Leviticus. The issue of incest is important in the Bible; Lot gave birth to the Moabites and the Ammonites as a result of incest with his two daughters, yet Ruth, a Moabite woman, ends up being David's ancestor. As all the sexual transgressions in Genesis become forbidden in the next books by the law given to Israel, these stories appear as examples of what should not be done.

Joseph / Ulysses

Ulysses' return to his island of Ithaca dressed up as a beggar, his taking revenge on the suitors of his wife and revealing himself to his relatives, can be likened almost in the same order to the story of Joseph, who was sold by his brothers to slave merchants and taken to Egypt, and who many years later reappears to his brothers who thought he was dead. In book XIV of the *Odyssey* when Ulysses arrives in Ithaca, he meets his servant Eumeus, who does not recognise him, and invents a story about his origins, pretending to be the illegitimate son of a wealthy Cretan man that was excluded from his father's inheritance because of the legitimate sons. This very passage seems to be the source of the story of Jephthah (Judg 11:1-3), to be discussed later. 'Pseudo-Ulysses' went off to fight in the Trojan War and passed through Egypt when he returned. His men attacked the people there, killing the men and taking their wives and children captive; a few chapters earlier that same line was used to describe the attack on Shechem by the sons of Jacob. Ulysses then explains how the Egyptians fought back and encircled his people (this passage has an accurate echo in Exod 14, as we will see). Ulysses decides to beg the king:

> Zeus, however, put it in my mind to do thus—and I wish I had died then and there in Egypt instead, for there was much sorrow in store for me—I took off my helmet and shield and dropped my spear from my hand; then I went straight up to the king's chariot, clasped his knees and kissed them, whereon he spared my life, bade me get into his chariot, and took me weeping to his own home. Many made at me with their ashen spears and tried to kill me in their fury, but the king protected me, for he feared the wrath of Zeus the protector of strangers, who punishes those who do evil. I stayed there for seven years and got together much money among the Egyptians, for they all gave me something. (Homer, *Od.* XIV, 277-87)

> There will come seven years of great plenty throughout all the land of Egypt. After them there will arise seven years of famine, and all the plenty will be forgotten in the land of Egypt; the famine will consume the land. The plenty will no longer be known in the land because of the famine that will follow, for it will be very grievous. (Gen 41:29-31)

> He had him ride in the chariot of his second-in-command; and they cried out in front of him, 'Bow the knee!' Thus he set him over all the land of Egypt. (Gen 41:43)

> During the seven plenteous years the earth produced abundantly. He gathered up all the food of the seven years when there was plenty in the land of Egypt, and stored up food in the cities; he stored up in every city the food from the fields around it. (Gen 41:47-48)

Akin to 'Pseudo-Ulysses', Joseph becomes the friend of the Pharaoh, is paraded behind him on a chariot as a mark of honour, and the people are told to pay respect to him. Over a period of seven years, both Joseph and Ulysses receive either presents or food from the Egyptians. Joseph succeeded in interpreting the double dream of the Pharaoh, the reason for which he receives such honour. Ulysses interpreted a very similar dream upon confronting his wife Penelope, although she was unaware that the beggar was actually her long-lost husband:

> After two whole years, Pharaoh dreamed that he was standing by the Nile, and there came up out of the Nile seven sleek and fat cows, and they grazed in the reed grass. Then seven other cows, ugly and thin, came up out of the Nile after them, and stood by the other cows on the bank of the Nile. The ugly and thin cows ate up the seven sleek and fat cows. And Pharaoh awoke. Then he fell asleep and dreamed a second time; seven ears of grain, plump and good, were growing on one stalk. Then seven ears, thin and blighted by the east wind, sprouted after them. The thin ears swallowed up the seven plump and full ears. Pharaoh awoke, and it was a dream. In the morning his spirit was troubled; so he sent and called for all the magicians of Egypt and all its wise men. Pharaoh told them his dreams, but there was no one who could interpret them to Pharaoh. (Gen 41:1-7)

> Listen, then, to a dream that I have had and interpret it for me if you can. I have twenty geese about the house that eat mash out of a trough, and of which I am exceedingly fond. I have dreamed that a great eagle came swooping down from a mountain, and dug his curved beak into the neck of each of them till he had killed them all. Presently he soared off into the sky, and left them lying dead about the yard; whereon I wept in my room till all my maids gathered round me, so piteously was I grieving because the eagle had killed my geese. Then he came back again, and perching on a projecting rafter spoke to me with human voice, and told me to leave off crying. 'Be of good courage', he said, 'daughter of Icarius; this is no dream, but a vision of good omen that shall surely come to pass. The geese are the suitors, and I am no longer an eagle, but your own husband, who am come back to you, and who will bring these suitors to a disgraceful end'. On this I woke, and when I looked out I saw my geese at the trough eating their mash as usual'. 'This dream, Madam', replied Ulysses, 'can admit but of one interpretation, for had not Ulysses himself told you how it shall be fulfilled? The death of the suitors is portended, and not one single one of them will escape.' (*Od.* XIX, 535-65)

The resemblance is acute, as both dreamers see animals coming out of a river or eating at a trough that are killed by another animal. Pharaoh's dream is interpreted as representing the fourteen following years, seven of which are to be good, though seven will be bad; in Penelope's dream the twenty geese correspond to her twenty suitors, and actually reflect Ulysses' twenty years of absence (ten years fighting at Troy and ten years wandering home on the seas). If we read the continuation of the 'made-up' story of Ulysses, he claims that after his seven years in Egypt a Phoenician merchant took him in order to sell him as a slave. He escaped, but was later captured by Thesprotians, who also tried to sell him as a slave:

> So when Joseph came to his brothers, *they stripped him of his robe*, the long robe with sleeves that he wore; and they took him and threw him into a pit. The pit was empty; there was no water in it. *Then they sat down to eat*; and looking up they saw a caravan of Ishmaelites coming from Gilead, with their camels carrying gum, balm, and resin, on their way to carry it down to Egypt. Then Judah said to his brothers, 'What profit is there if we kill our brother and conceal his blood? Come, let us sell him to the Ishmaelites, and not lay our hands on him, for he is our brother, our own flesh.' And his brothers agreed. When some Midianite traders passed by, they drew Joseph up, lifting him out of the pit, and *sold him to the Ishmaelites for twenty pieces of silver*. And they took Joseph to Egypt. (Gen 37:23-28)

> These men hatched a plot against me that would have reduced me to the very extreme of misery, for when the ship had got some way out from land *they resolved on selling me as a slave. They stripped me of the shirt and cloak that I was wearing*, and gave me instead the tattered old clothes in which you now see me; then, towards nightfall, they reached the tilled lands of Ithaca, and there they bound me with a strong rope fast in the ship, while *they went on shore to get supper by the sea side*. But the gods soon undid my bonds for me, and having drawn my rags over my head I slid down the rudder into the sea, where I struck out and swam till I was well clear of them, and came ashore near a thick wood in which I lay concealed. They were very angry at my having escaped and went searching about for me, till at last they thought it was no further use and went back to their ship. The gods, having hidden me thus easily, then took me to a good man's door—for it seems that I am not to die yet awhile. (*Od.* XIV, 340-45)

We see that the hero is stripped of his clothes, and that the enemies later sit down to have a meal. Ulysses' 'made-up' story tells how he went to Egypt, became the friend of Pharaoh for seven years, and then was almost sold as a slave. The order of the story of Joseph is inverted: first his brothers sell him as a slave, he becomes the attendant of Potiphar but ends up in jail, later interprets the dreams of the servants of Pharaoh, and eventually interprets the dreams of Pharaoh himself, thus becoming the 'attendant' of all Egypt. This is a perfect example of the technique of dismantling the Greek sources and rearranging them in a different order.

Due to the famine that plagued Egypt and Canaan, Joseph had the chance to meet his brothers again when they were sent by Jacob to buy wheat. Joseph recognises his brothers, though they don't recognise him as he is dressed in the Egyptian fashion and because they believe he his dead. This is similar to Ulysses, who returns to Ithaca dressed as a beggar and bides his time before revealing his true identity. Let us analyse the details of how both characters have to hide their emotions in front of their loved ones, concealed until the moving moment of revelation.

Already by the seventeenth century C.E., Oxford scholar Zacharias Bogan had compared some of these details in his book *Homerus Hebraizon: sive comparatio Homeri cum scriptoribus sacris quoad normam loquendi*.[25] Bogan noticed how both Jacob and King Priam of Troy mourn the death of their favourite sons, Joseph and Hector (respectively):

> Many a son of mine has he slain in the flower of his youth, and yet, grieve for these as I may, I do so for one—Hector—more than for them all, and the bitterness of my sorrow will bring me down to the house of Hades. (*Il.* XXII, 423-26)

> But he said, 'My son shall not go down with you, for his brother is dead, and he alone is left. If harm should come to him on the journey that you are to make, you would bring down my grey hairs with sorrow to Sheol.' (Gen 42:38)

Joseph asked his brothers to go return to Canaan and to bring back Benjamin, the youngest son, to prove that they were not spies (the source of the accusation will be discussed later). Benjamin is brought, and Joseph had him accused of stealing a precious cup that was hidden in his luggage—which is also a Greek story. Let us now focus on the details of how the protagonists try to hide their emotions when seeing loved ones again, concealed until the time of revelation:

> As soon as (the dog) saw Ulysses standing there, he dropped his ears and wagged his tail, but he could not get close up to his master. When Ulysses saw the dog on the other side of the yard, dashed a tear from his eyes without Eumaeus seeing it. (*Od.* XVII 300-305)

> They did not know that Joseph understood them, since he spoke with them through an interpreter. He turned away from them and wept; then he returned and spoke to them. And he picked out Simeon and had him bound before their eyes. (Gen 42:23-24)

---

25. Quoted by West, *The East Face of Helicon*.

> Then he looked up and saw his brother Benjamin, his mother's son, and said, 'Is this your youngest brother, of whom you spoke to me? God be gracious to you, my son!' With that, Joseph hurried out, because he was overcome with affection for his brother, and he was about to weep. So he went into a private room and wept there. Then he washed his face and came out; and controlling himself he said, 'Serve the meal'. (Gen 43:29-31)

Penelope cries in her room, then decides to face the suitors. Her servant Eurynome tells her:

> 'My dear child', answered Eurynome, 'all that you have said is true, go and tell your son about it, but first wash yourself and anoint your face. Do not go about with your cheeks all covered with tears; it is not right that you should grieve so incessantly. (*Od.* XVIII, 170-75)

> It is I, Ulysses, who am here. I have suffered much, but at last, in the twentieth year, I am come back to my own country... As he spoke he drew his rags aside from the great scar, and when they had examined it thoroughly, they both of them wept about Ulysses, threw their arms round him and kissed his head and shoulders, while Ulysses kissed their hands and faces in return. (*Od.* XXI, 200-210)

> And he wept so loudly that the Egyptians heard it, and the household of Pharaoh heard it. Joseph said to his brothers, 'I am Joseph. Is my father still alive?' But his brothers could not answer him, so dismayed were they at his presence. (Gen 45:2-3)

> Then he fell upon his brother Benjamin's neck and wept, while Benjamin wept upon his neck. And he kissed all his brothers and wept upon them; and after that his brothers talked with him. (Gen 45:14-15)

The details are similar: the hero reveals his identity, his friends/brothers jump at his neck, and they embrace and kiss, weeping. After slaying the suitors Ulysses encounters his wife, though she does not believe him at first. We find no echo in Genesis of this part, since Joseph married an Egyptian woman. However, Ulysses does meet his aged father who, like Jacob, first doubts that his son could still be alive, but then is revitalized after seeing the evidence:

> So they went up out of Egypt and came to their father Jacob in the land of Canaan. And they told him, 'Joseph is still alive! He is even ruler over all the land of Egypt'. He was stunned; he could not believe them. But when they told him all the words of Joseph that he had said to them, and when he saw the wagons that Joseph had sent to carry him, *the spirit of their father Jacob revived.* (Gen 45:25-27)

> Joseph made ready his chariot and went up to meet his father Israel in Goshen. *He presented himself to him, fell on his neck, and wept on his neck a good while.* (Gen 46:29)

A dark cloud of sorrow fell upon Laertes as he listened. He filled both hands with the dust from off the ground and poured it over his grey head, groaning heavily as he did so. The heart of Ulysses was touched, and his nostrils quivered as he looked upon his father; *then he sprang towards him, flung his arms about him and kissed him*, saying, 'I am he, father, about whom you are asking—I have returned after having been away for twenty years. But cease your sighing and lamentation—we have no time to lose, for I should tell you that I have been killing the suitors in my house, to punish them for their insolence and crimes.' 'If you really are my son Ulysses', replied Laertes, 'and have come back again, you must give me such manifest proof of your identity as shall convince me'... Laertes' strength failed him when he heard the convincing proofs which his son had given him. He threw his arms about him, and Ulysses had to support him, or he would have gone off into a swoon; but as soon as he came to, *and was beginning to recover his senses*, he said... (*Od.* XXIV, 315-50)

The story of Joseph in Egypt finds its ultimate source in the story of Ulysses told to Eumeus, and the revelation of Joseph's identity is taken from the last chapters of the *Odyssey*. The main difference, of course, is that Joseph does not exact violent revenge upon his brothers who tried to kill him. He scares them by accusing them of being spies, hides money in their bags and confronts them with theft, then does the same with Benjamin and a cup. All of this has the effect of Judah imploring Joseph to have him killed instead of Benjamin, for Judah does not want his father Jacob to lose his favourite son a second time. Judah and the other brothers show sincere regret for what they had done to Joseph many years before, and it is only at that moment that Joseph decides to reveal himself, explaining that it was all God's plan. Genesis is punctuated with multiple accounts of sibling rivalry. First, Cain slew Abel, and God protected Cain against anyone who would want to avenge Abel. Later, Isaac and Ishmael were rivals, and Ishmael was rejected because of Sarah. Then, we saw how Jacob and Esau fought for their birthright and the blessings of their father. Next, the twelve sons of Jacob were born—they who represent the future tribes of Israel. The lesson taught by the biblical writer is that Israel's truth is the fraternal unity of the tribes—no brother can be missing, neither Joseph nor Benjamin.[26] Joseph proves to be more merciful than his model Ulysses, who kills the suitors and will have to atone for his crime, as explained in the last verses of the *Odyssey*. Yet, the biblical writer definitely left a 'fingerprint' that reveals how Joseph is modelled after Ulysses:

26. See Cazeaux, *Le partage de minuit*.

Joseph is a fruitful bough, a fruitful bough by a spring; his branches run over the wall. The archers fiercely attacked him; they shot at him and pressed him hard. Yet his bow remained taut, and his arms were made agile by the hands of the Mighty One of Jacob. (Gen 49:22-24)

To your defence, my friends! For respite none will he to his victorious hands afford, but, armed with bow and quiver, will dispatch shafts from the door till he have slain us all. Let us then show fight; draw your swords, and hold up the tables to shield you from his arrows. Let us have at him with a rush, to drive him from the pavement and doorway: we can then get through into the town, and raise such an alarm as shall soon stay his shooting. (*Od.* XXII, 70-72)

Ulysses begins to kill the suitors with his bow in book XXII, and, although they fight back at him, Ulysses will slay them all. Jacob's blessing of Joseph compares him to an archer that was attacked by others yet held out firmly against them. Since nothing in the story of Joseph hints that he may have been an archer, these verses can be read as a deliberate reference to the *Odyssey*.

Other Greek Parallels in the Joseph Story

The Spies

Other points of Joseph's story can be linked to other Greek sources. The part when Joseph pretends to accuse his brothers of being spies (Gen 42:9-15) is similar to the story of the king of the Ethiopians who accused the men sent by the Persian King Cambyses of being spies. The gifts brought by the 'Fish-eaters' resemble the gifts offered by Jacob as his sons go to Egypt for the second time (Gen 43:11):

When the Fish-eaters had come to Cambyses from Elephantine, he sent them to the Ethiopians, when he had given the injunction about what they had to say and they were bringing as gifts a purple garment, a torque for round the neck and bangles of gold, an alabaster vase of perfume and a jar of palm wine. Those Ethiopians then, to whom Cambyses sent off are said to be the tallest and most beautiful of all human beings and as to laws they assert that they use both others that are separate from those of all other human beings and, particularly, concerning the kingship one like this: whomever of the townsmen they judge to be tallest and in proportion to his height to have strength, they think that one worthy to be king. When indeed to those men then the Fish-eaters had come, they, offering the gifts to their king, said this: 'The king of the Persians, Cambyses, since he wants to become both your friend and foreign tie, sent us off on bidding us to come to speeches with you and offers you as gifts those things that even he himself takes most pleasure in using'. Then the

> Ethiopian, because he had learned that they had come as watchers, spoke
> them like this: 'Neither the king of the Persians sent you as bearers of
> gifts, since he preferred at much cost to become my foreign tie nor do you
> speak truths, as you are watchers of my rule, nor is he a just man; for, if
> he were just, he would neither have conceived a desire for a country other
> than his own nor be leading to slavery human beings, by whom he has
> been done no injustice' (Herodotus III, 20-21).

The difference is that these men were actual spies. One must keep the
future of Israel in mind though, for in Numbers 13 Moses will send
twelve spies (one per tribe) to explore the land of Canaan. In pretending
to accuse his brothers, Joseph is actually foretelling the conquest of
Canaan, when the tribes of Israel will leave Egypt.

The Cup Hidden in the Luggage
Joseph tricks his brothers yet again by hiding a precious cup in Benjamin's luggage. Benjamin and his brothers leave Joseph, then they are
arrested, and Benjamin is accused of having stolen Joseph's sacred cup
(Gen 44:1-13). Greek tradition relates how Aesop the fable teller was
unjustly killed by the Delphians (first told in Herodotus II, 134):

> It is said that Aesop had come to Delphi and made a fool of the people for
> having no land to cultivate and for living of the sacrifices offered to the
> god. The Delphians were angry and secretly hid a sacred cup in his lug-
> gage. Aesop, not knowing it, headed to Phocis, but the Delphians caught
> him up, discovered the cup, and accused him of sacrilege. (Scholiast of
> Aristophanes, *Wasps* 1446; see also Plutarch, Moralia, *On the Delays of
> Divine Vengeance* 556-57)

Even though the details of Aesop's death are known through late sources,
the first reference to it in Herodotus seems sufficient to think that the
biblical writer may have known the story of the cup, using it as a source
for the Joseph narrative. Joseph does not really believe his brothers to be
spies, nor does he really want to have Benjamin killed. The now-familiar
process of recycling Greek sources appears again. Unlike Ulysses and
the Delphians, Joseph had already forgiven his brothers for trying to kill
him, and only wanted to teach them a lesson.

The Friendly Pharaoh
Jacob journeys to Egypt after these events, and Pharaoh offers him some
land. This detail can be related to the Pharaoh Amasis, who was a great
friend to the Greeks:

> Then, because he had become a philhellene, Amasis showed forth other acts to several of the Greeks and in particular to those who came to Egypt gave the city of Naucratis to settle in and to those of them who wanted not to settle in it and voyaged thither gave places to set up altars and precincts for the gods in. (Herodotus II, 178)

> Then Pharaoh said to Joseph, 'Your father and your brothers have come to you. The land of Egypt is before you; settle your father and your brothers in the best part of the land; let them live in the land of Goshen; and if you know that there are capable men among them, put them in charge of my livestock.' (Gen 47:5-6)

This portrait of a friendly Pharaoh will be balanced in Exodus by the evil Pharaoh who reduces Israel to slavery (and who also draws inspiration from Herodotus). It seems that one can even identify the land of *Goshen* given to Israel with the mountain Herodotus calls *Casion* (Herodotus II, 6, 158), said to separate Egypt from Syria. The transformation of the Greek letter *kappa* into the Hebrew letter *gimel* is recurrent, the Colchians becoming the Girgashim.

Jacob / Cyrus

About to die, Jacob blesses his twelve sons and he foretells the future of Israel. As we saw previously, his three elder sons Reuben, Simeon and Levi were disqualified because of their sins, Judah is blessed and Jacob claims that kingship will be his inheritance (Gen 49:8-12). Jacob then blesses all his sons, asks to be buried with his fathers in Canaan, and breathes his last. As suggested by Professor Kupitz, this passage reminds us of Xenophon's *Cyropaedia*—the life of King Cyrus. Xenophon was, like Plato, a disciple of Socrates, and had written about the life of Cyrus in order to show that a good king could benefit his people.

I believe that Jacob is an inverted reflection of his descendant David. On his deathbed, Jacob prophesies the coming of the first king of Judah, David, who is modelled after the tyrannical man in Plato's *Republic* (book IX). At the end of the *Cyropaedia*, Cyrus senses the nearing of his own demise and gathers his sons around him. He chooses Cambyses to be his successor, and gives him advice on how to rule with justice (Xenophon, *Cyropaedia* VIII, 7). Of course, any reader of Herodotus knows that Cambyses becomes a mad tyrant. In the same manner, Jacob too on his deathbed reflects upon David's granting of kingship to his own son Solomon (1 Kgs 2)—who ends up murdering his brother Adonijah in order to be the sole inheritor of David's throne. The original sin of kingship—the will of transferring power from father to son—is heavily criticised in the books of Samuel and Kings. Genesis therefore represents a counterpoint in which the Patriarchs appear as benevolent rulers:

'And now', he added, 'now it seems to me that my life begins to ebb; I feel my spirit slipping away from those parts she leaves the first. If you would take my hand once more, or look into my eyes while life is there, draw near me now; but when I have covered my face, let no man look on me again, not even you, my sons. But you shall bid the Persians come, and all our allies, to my sepulchre; and you shall rejoice with me and congratulate me that I am safe at last, free from suffering or sorrow, whether I am with God or whether I have ceased to be. Give all who come the entertainment that is fitting in honour of a man whose life on earth was happy, and so send them away. Remember my last saying: show kindness to your friends, and then shall you have it in your power to chastise your enemies. Good-bye, my dear sons, bid your mother good-bye for me. And all my friends, who are here or far away, good-bye.' And with these words he gave his hand to them, and then he covered his face and died. (Xenophon, *Cyropaedia* VIII, 7)

Then he charged them, saying to them, 'I am about to be gathered to my people. Bury me with my ancestors—in the cave in the field of Ephron the Hittite, in the cave in the field at Machpelah, near Mamre, in the land of Canaan, in the field that Abraham bought from Ephron the Hittite as a burial site. There Abraham and his wife Sarah were buried; there Isaac and his wife Rebekah were buried; and there I buried Leah—the field and the cave that is in it were purchased from the Hittites.' When Jacob ended his charge to his sons, he drew up his feet into the bed, breathed his last, and was gathered to his people. (Gen 49:28-33)

2.

Exodus

The Pharaoh / Cheops

In Exodus, a new Pharaoh arises who hates the sons of Israel and decides to enslave them. The Israelites were to build the cities of Pithom and Rameses (Exod 1:7-14). Herodotus speaks of Pharaoh Cheops, who forced the Egyptians to build a pyramid for him:

> Now, until King Rhampsinitus all good laws were in Egypt, they said, and Egypt flourished greatly, but after him Cheops became their king and drove them to all kinds of wickedness; for he first shut down all the shrines and kept them from sacrificing and afterward bade all Egyptians work for him; to some, indeed, it was shown forth that from the stone-quarries in the Arabian mountain, from those places, they should drag stones up to the Nile and, when the stones had been ferried across the river by boats, he appointed others to receive them and to the so-called Libyan mountain, to that place, to drag them—they worked in a group of ten myriads of human beings on each and every occasion, each party three months—and time passed for the population who were being worn down, ten years on the way along which they dragged the stones, which they had built and is a work not a great deal smaller than the pyramid, so far as it seems to me—its length is five stades, its breadth ten fathoms, its height, where it itself is its highest, eight fathoms and its stone is hewn and with carved on figures; both on that very road the ten years went by and on what's on the crest on which the pyramids stand, the buildings underground, that he had built as burial-places for himself on an island by introducing a channel from the Nile, while, in the pyramid itself's case, twenty years' time went by in the making of it, whose each side in every direction is eight plethra, it being quadrangular, and equal in height and which is of stone hewn and fitted together in the highest degree. None of its stones are less than thirty feet. (Herodotus II, 124)

The difference between these two stories is that Cheops made slaves of his own people. But we do find such a character as well in the Bible—King Solomon. He forced the people of Israel to build his palace, that of his wife (an Egyptian princess), as well as the temple of Yahweh. The whole project lasted twenty years (1 Kgs 9:10), the labour being divided into rotating three-month shifts for gangs of ten thousand men (1 Kgs 5:13)—exactly as we see in Herodotus. It is important to keep in mind the synchronic reading of the Bible. As Jacques Cazeaux showed in his analysis, Solomon behaves like a pharaoh.[1] Israel became the slave of a foreign king in Exodus, while in Genesis (47:23) the Egyptians had become the slaves because of Pharaoh's debt—thanks to Joseph. In the story of Solomon, Israel becomes the slave of its own king, exactly as Samuel prophesied (1 Sam 8:8-18). The second book of Herodotus was used as a source for the stories that took place in Egypt, those at the end of Genesis and the beginning of Exodus, as well as for 1 and 2 Kings.

Moses / Sargon / Heracles

> My mother was a high priestess, my father I knew not. The brothers of my father loved the hills. My city is Azupiranu, which is situated on the banks of the Euphrates. My high priestess mother conceived me, in secret she bore me. She set me in a basket of rushes, with bitumen she sealed my lid. She cast me into the river which rose over me. The river bore me up and carried me to Akki, the drawer of water. Akki, the drawer of water, took me as his son and reared me. Akki, the drawer of water, appointed me as his gardener. While I was a gardener, Ishtar granted me her love, and for four and...years I exercised kingship. (*The Legend of Sargon of Akkad*)

This story is similar to the birth of Moses (Exod 2:1-3). But the parallel concerns only three verses from the story of Moses, while the rest of that tale can be likened to Greek stories. As with Genesis, the text should not be dated by its oldest aspects, but by its most recent ones.

> His sister stood at a distance, to see what would happen to him. The daughter of Pharaoh came down to bathe at the river, while her attendants walked beside the river. She saw the basket among the reeds and sent her maid to bring it. When she opened it, she saw the child. He was crying, and she took pity on him. 'This must be one of the Hebrews' children', she said. Then his sister said to Pharaoh's daughter, 'Shall I go and get you a nurse from the Hebrew women to nurse the child for you?' Pharaoh's daughter said to her, 'Yes'. So the girl went and called the child's mother. Pharaoh's daughter said to her, 'Take this child and nurse

---

1. Cazeaux, *Saül, David et Salomon.*

it for me, and I will give you your wages'. So the woman took the child and nursed it. When the child grew up, she brought him to Pharaoh's daughter, and she took him as her son. She named him Moses, 'because', she said, 'I drew him out of the water'. (Exod 2:5-10)

After Alcmenê had brought forth the babe, fearful of Hera's jealousy she exposed it at a place which to this time is called after him the Field of Heracles. Now at this very time Athena, approaching the spot in the company of Hera and being amazed at the natural vigour of the child, persuaded Hera to offer it the breast. But when the boy tugged upon her breast with greater violence than would be expected at his age, Hera was unable to endure the pain and cast the babe from her, whereupon Athena took it to its mother and urged her to rear it. And anyone may well be surprised at the unexpected turn of the affair; for the mother whose duty it was to love her own offspring was trying to destroy it, while she who cherished towards it a stepmother's hatred, in ignorance saved the life of one who was her natural enemy. (Diodorus Siculus, *Library* IV, 9, 6-7)[2]

Athena is Heracles' sister, as she is also a child of Zeus. She aided in the return of her infant brother so that his true mother might nurse him—a detail that does not appear in the story of Sargon. On the other hand, this story does take place in Diodorus' *Library*, right after Hera fooled Zeus into promising that Eurystheus would have dominion over Heracles. We saw the role of that story in Genesis, as being a source of the rivalry between Jacob and Esau. Now, the story of Heracles appears as a source for Moses—the rest of it is found in the story of Samson. Let us note that the story of Heracles' descendants may have been used as well. Several generations have passed since Jacob and his sons came to Egypt and now their descendants are about to leave, eventually to conquer Canaan, as it had been foretold to Abraham by God in Gen 15:13-16 (mentioning four generations).

There is a story of Heracles' descendants that echoes this delay of several generations. After Heracles died, his sons wished to conquer the Peloponnesus, which they thought belonged to their father, but they were told by an oracle to wait for three generations. The full account of the story is told in late sources (see Pseudo-Apollodorus, *Library* 2, 8, 9; Diodorus Siculus, *Library* IV, 58), yet it was also known in classical times (see Herodotus IX, 26; Euripides, *The Heraclids*; Plato, *Laws* 683 d). As Eurystheus and Heracles were inspirational sources for Jacob and Esau, it seems only logical to find a similar link in the story of their descendants.

---

2.   Translated by C.H. Oldfather.

Moses and the Daughters of Jethro /
Heracles and the Daughters of Atlas

The priest of Midian had seven daughters. They came to draw water, and filled the troughs to water their father's flock. But some shepherds came and drove them away. Moses got up and came to their defence and watered their flock. When they returned to their father Reuel, he said, 'How is it that you have come back so soon today?' They said, 'An Egyptian helped us against the shepherds; he even drew water for us and watered the flock'. He said to his daughters, 'Where is he? Why did you leave the man? Invite him to break bread.' Moses agreed to stay with the man, and he gave Moses his daughter Zipporah in marriage. (Exod 2:16-21)

The Pelasgians were settled down under Hymessus and, setting off thence, they were doing this injustice: namely, indeed, their daughters went constantly for water to Enneacrounus, because there were not during that time yet for them and not for all the other Greeks household servants, and, whenever they went, the Pelasgians through the agency of insolence and belittling were doing violence to them. (Herodotus VI, 134)

In the country known as Hesperitis there were two brothers whose fame was known abroad, Hesperus and Atlas. These brothers possessed flocks of sheep which excelled in beauty and were in colour of a golden yellow, this being the reason why the poets, in speaking of these sheep as mela, called them golden mela. Now Hesperus begat a daughter named Hesperis, whom he gave in marriage to his brother and after whom the land was given the name Hesperitis; and Atlas begat by her seven daughters, who were named after their father Atlantides, and after their mother, Hesperides. And since these Atlantides excelled in beauty and chastity, Busiris the king of the Egyptians, the account says, was seized with the desire to get the maidens into his power; and consequently he dispatched pirates by sea with orders to seize the girls and deliver them into his hands... Meanwhile the pirates had seized the girls while they were playing in a certain garden and carried them off, and fleeing swiftly to their ships had sailed away with them. Heracles came upon the pirates as they were taking their meal on a certain strand, and learning from the maidens what had taken place he slew the pirates to a man and brought the girls back to Atlas their father; and in return Atlas was so grateful to Heracles for his kindly deed that he not only gladly gave him such assistance as his Labour called for, but he also instructed him quite freely in the knowledge of astrology. (Diodorus Siculus, *Library* IV, 27)

In the second chapter of Exodus we find two themes from the cycle of Heracles: that of his birth, and his rescue of a prominent man's seven daughters. It seems as though the author mixed the plot of the maidens drawing water from a fountain with that of the seven daughters of Atlas.

Moses / Hesiod

M.L. West reports how the beginning of the *Theogony* and the vocation of Moses are similar: a shepherd tending his flocks on a mountain encounters a deity, receives a speech of divine inspiration, and a staff:[3]

> And one day they taught Hesiod glorious songs while he was shepherding his lambs under holy Helicon, and this word first the goddesses said to me—the Muses of Olympus, daughters of Zeus who holds the aegis: 'Shepherds of the wilderness, wretched things of shame, mere bellies, we know how to speak many false things as though they were true; but we know, when we will, to utter true things. So said the ready-voiced daughters of great Zeus, and they plucked and gave me a rod, a shoot of sturdy laurel, a marvellous thing, and breathed into me a divine voice to celebrate things that shall be and things there were aforetime; and they bade me sing of the race of the blessed gods that are eternally, but ever to sing of themselves both first and last. (Hesiod, *Theog.* 24-35)

> Moses was keeping the flock of his father-in-law Jethro, the priest of Midian; he led his flock beyond the wilderness, and came to Horeb, the mountain of God. There the angel of the Lord appeared to him in a flame of fire out of a bush; he looked, and the bush was blazing, yet it was not consumed. (Exod 3:1-2)

In Exod 4:1-5, Moses' staff is transformed into a snake, as a sign to show to the Israelites. Moses' mission is not poetic (at least, apparently), as he must guide his people to the land promised to their ancestors Abraham, Isaac and Jacob—which as we have already seen—comes from the end of the epic of the Argonauts.

Moses / Battus

We saw that Abraham received a promise that his descendants would dwell in the land of Canaan. I have linked Abraham's story with that of the Argonauts, as the episode of Isaac's binding seems to derive from the story of Phrixus and the Golden Fleece. Euphemus, one of the Argonauts, had also been promised that his descendants would first possess the island of Thera and then found the colony of Cyrene in Libya. Apollonius of Rhodes' *Argonautica* ends on that promise as a reference to Herodotus, who mentions that story in two different versions—that of the Thereans and the Cyreneans. According to Wesselius, this technique led the biblical writer to use doubled stories (see the Introduction):

---

3. West, *The East Face of Helicon*, 287.

Now, up to that account the Lacedaemonians give an account after the same fashion as the Theraeans, but from that point on only the Theraeans give an account that it happened thus: Grinnus, the son of Aesanius, being a descendent of that Theras and being king of Thera the island, came to Delphi and brought from his city a hecatomb. And there followed him both others of his fellow-citizens and, in particular, Battus, the son of Polymnestus, being in birth a Euphemid of the Minyae. Then to Grinnus the king of the Theraeans who was consulting the oracle about other matters Pythia proclaimed that he should found a city in Libya. And he replied by saying, 'I for my part, O lord, am too old by now and heavy to raise myself; bid you then one of these younger men do that'. At the same time he said that and pointed to Battus. Then so much, but afterwards having gone away, they maintained a lack of taking account of the oracle, because they neither knew Libya, where on earth it was, nor dared to an obscure matter to dispatch off a colony. (Herodotus IV, 150)

So thereafter, having taken up Phronime, Polymnestus, being an esteemed man among the Theraeans, kept her as a concubine. Then, time going round, there was born out to him a son hesitant in speech and lisping, to whom as a name was given Battus... For when that one had become a man, he went to Delphi about his voice and to him, when he was speaking his question, Pythia proclaimed this: *Battus, you came for voice; Lord Phoebus Apollo to sheep-rearing Libya sends you a founder.* Just as if she should say with the use of the Greek tongue, 'O basileu (king), you came for voice'. And he replied with this: *'O lord, I came to you to consult the oracle about my voice and you make me other proclamations of impossible things, as you bid colonize Libya. With what power? With what kind of band?'* Although he said that, he could not persuade him to make him other proclamations and, when she was prophesying after the same fashion as previously, Battus left her behind in the midst and was gone to Thera. (Herodotus IV, 155)

But Moses said to the Lord, 'O my Lord, I have never been eloquent, neither in the past nor even now that you have spoken to your servant; but I am slow of speech and slow of tongue'. (Exod 4:10)

These two stories of Herodotus are merged into one in Exodus. A man is chosen by a god to found a colony, following a promise made to his ancestor. In one version the man refuses because he feels too old, and asks that the deity send another (as does Grinnus), while in the other the man invokes the fact that he has a speech impediment (as does Battus), claiming that he does not feel strong enough. The 'fingerprint' that makes the reference quite certain is that Battus ruled over his people for forty years (Herodotus IV, 159), like Moses (Deut 1:3). From that point on the Israelites will wander in the desert as the Argonauts wandered on the seas, in search of a divine treasure—but in Israel's case it is not the Golden Fleece, but God's Law that they seek. The Israelites' journey is inspired by that famous epic, but re-written through a platonic filter; this is why I call them 'Argonauts of the Desert'. Indeed, the Israelites will not found a 'simple' colony as the descendants of Euphemus did; rather, they will found the Ideal State of Plato as imagined in the *Laws*—the plan for which will be given to Moses during the period of wandering. It must be noted that Phronime, the mother of Battos (Herodotus IV, 154), was hated by her stepmother, who convinced her father to have her killed by a man who ended up taking mercy on her and letting her live. This is the source of what eventually becomes the well-known European tale of Snow White. It appears from his literary genealogy that, quite ironically, Moses is the son of Snow White.

The Exodus / Euripides' Helen

Herodotus (II, 113-20) tells a story that negates Helen's adultery by asserting that she was never abducted by Paris to Troy, but was actually entrusted to King Proteus of Egypt. Upon returning from Troy, her husband Menelaus found her and brought her back to Sparta (as her honour was still intact). This story may remind us of Sarai and Abram in Egypt. The officials of Pharaoh brought Sarai to him; but plagues hit Egypt. Sarai was returned to her husband, and they were expelled out of Egypt (Gen 12:10-20).

Note Herodotus II, 119, which reads:

> And Menelaus having come to Egypt and having sailed up to Memphis, told the truth of these matters, and not only found great entertainment, but also received Helen unhurt, and all his own wealth besides. Then, however, after he had been thus dealt with, Menelaus showed himself ungrateful to the Egyptians; for when he set forth to sail away, contrary winds detained him, and as this condition of things lasted long, he devised an impious deed; for he took two children of natives and made sacrifice of them. After this, when it was known that he had done so, he became abhorred, and being pursued he escaped and got away in his ships to Libya; but whither he went besides after this, the Egyptians were not able to tell. Of these things they said that they found out part by inquiries, and the rest, namely that which happened in their own land, they related from sure and certain knowledge.

According to Jacques Cazeaux, Abram and Sarai's story in Egypt is a downsized version of the Exodus story.[4] Abram journeys to Egypt, quarrels with the Pharaoh, Egypt is beset by plagues, and Abram is sent back to whence he came. This foretells the events that will happen to his

---

4. Cazeaux, *Le partage de minuit*, 218.

descendants in chs. 1–15 of Exodus, and is a 'biblical insider' reference. We may, however, see some connections with the story of Helen and Menelaus, as the wife is kept by the Pharaoh and her husband (in her honour) is well treated and receives gifts. Missing, though, is the detail of the Pharaoh's threatening the wife's honour, and the husband who fears for his life. On the other hand, Menelaus sacrificed Egyptian children, reminiscent of the slaying of the first-born in Exod 12:29. Utilizing the same tradition as Herodotus, Euripides added details to his play *Helen*. Helen's care had been entrusted to King Proteus, but after he died his son Theoclymenus fell in love with Helen and wanted to marry her. She refused, as she was already married, and she decided to remain at Proteus' tomb as a suppliant:

> Helen: Now as long as Proteus gazed upon yon glorious sun, I was safe from marriage; but when o'er him the dark grave closed, the dead man's son was eager for my hand. But I, from regard to my former husband, am throwing myself down in suppliant wise before this tomb of Proteus, praying him to guard my husband's honour, that, though through Hellas I bear a name dishonoured, at least my body here may not incur disgrace (Euripides, *Helen* 55-68).[5]

Upon returning from Troy, Menelaus is stranded on the coast of Egypt. He is told that his wife is there, then finds her and gains her back. They plot to flee from Egypt, while trying to avoid the danger that the king will kill Menelaus for her love:

> Helen: Escape and fly with all thy speed from this land. Thou wilt be slain by him whose house this is. Menelaus: What have I done to merit such a fate? H: Thou hast arrived unexpectedly to thwart my marriage. M: What! Is some man bent on wedding my wife? H: Aye, and on heaping those insults on me, which I have hitherto endured. M: Is he some private prince, or a ruler of this land? H: The son of Proteus, king of the country… Of course thou knowest, then, all about my marriage. M: I do. But whether thou hast escaped thy lover, I know not. H: Be well assured I have kept my body chaste. (*Helen* 780-95)

Helen and Menelaus devise a strategy to escape from Egypt. Menelaus presents himself to the Pharaoh as a Greek soldier, pretending that their ship sank and that 'Menelaus' drowned. Theoclymenus then believes that he can marry Helen, as she is now a widow. Menelaus and Helen ask to offer a sacrifice to the dead in the sea, as Greek custom demands. Theoclymenus accepts quickly, overjoyed finally to be able to marry Helen. Here the play turns into a comedy; we see the Pharaoh's eagerness

5. Translated by E.P. Coleridge.

to respect the Greek customs, though the audience understands that his only thoughts are about marrying Helen. In a comical scene, Menelaus negotiates with the Pharaoh for everything that he will need for the sacrifice: a calf, a bed for the deceased, a Phoenician ship with sailors, and bronze weapons, for Menelaus was a valiant warrior. Theoclymenus worries a little:

> Theoclymenus: How far from the shore does the ship put out? Menelaus: So far that the foam in her wake can scarce be seen from the strand. Th: Why so? Wherefore doth Hellas observe this custom? M: That the billow may not cast up again our expiatory offerings. Th: Phoenician rowers will soon cover the distance. M: 'Twill be well done, and gratifying to Menelaus, too. Th: Canst thou not perform these rites well enough without Helen? M: This task belongs to mother, wife, or children. Th: 'Tis her task then, according to thee, to bury her husband. M: To be sure; piety demands that the dead be not robbed of their due. (*Helen* 1265-80)

Once aboard the ship, Menelaus and his men kill the rowers and flee Egypt. A messenger brings the news to Theoclymenus, who wants to chase Menelaus and Helen, but Castor and Pollux (Helen's brothers) appear. They tell Theoclymenus that a divine will has allowed Menelaus and Helen to escape, preventing him from committing an unjust act. Thus, in Euripides' *Helen* we find a true 'Exodus' out of Egypt. The theme of the Pharaoh in love with a married woman who is finally returned to her husband is similar to both the story of Abram and Sarai in Egypt and to the second version of that story about the Philistine king Abimelech (Gen 20).

Another textual echo in that chapter is the appearance of Castor and Pollux who explain to Theoclymenus that the gods prevented him from committing the sin of taking a married woman; which is similar to God explaining to Abimelech that Sarah is a married woman (Gen 20:3-7):

> DIOSCURI: Restrain those bursts of rage that hurry thee to undue lengths, Theoclymenus, king of this country. We are the twin sons of Zeus that call to thee by name, whom Leda bore one day, with Helen too who hath fled from thy palace. For thou art wroth for a marriage never destined for thee... Long, long ago had we our sister saved, seeing that Zeus has made us gods, but we were too weak for destiny as well as the deities, who willed these things to be. (*Helen* 1650-60)

We do not find the theme of Abraham pretending that his wife is his sister in the Greek sources, but the story of Menelaus and Helen fleeing from Egypt does show a striking similarity to the Exodus story. Indeed, Moses tricks Pharaoh by asking that Israel be allowed to offer a sacrifice during a three-day journey (as God orders him in Exod 3:18). Moses and

Aaron first confront Pharaoh and ask to leave for three days, but Pharaoh ignores them (Exod 5:1-4). Four plagues will strike Egypt initially. First, there is water that turns to blood; then, the coming of frogs. These two signs do not impress Pharaoh, for his magicians can do the same (Exod 7–8). Then come the gnats, and the magicians urge Pharaoh to let the Hebrews go for they believe it to be a sign from God, but Pharaoh refuses. Next come the flies, and for the first time Pharaoh concedes to let them go. Pharaoh asks the Israelites not to go too far, but Moses replies that they have to go far away. Then, Pharaoh changes his mind (Exod 8:25-32). This brings about the next three plagues: the death of the Egyptian flocks, festering boils, and hail. Again, Pharaoh pretends to accept, but as soon as the hail stops he changes his mind. The Egyptian people, however, begin to fear Israel's god (Exod 9:20). Pharaoh's counsellors advise him to call Moses and Aaron back. Pharaoh acquiesces conditionally, refusing to let the Israelite children accompany the adults (Exod 10:8-11). The plagues of locusts and darkness arrive next, and once more Pharaoh almost concedes. He allows the people to go, but wants their flocks to remain in Egypt. As Moses insists that the flocks must follow, Pharaoh refuses once more to let them go (Exod 10:24-29).

After this comes the final plague—the death of every Egyptian first-born—and finally, Pharaoh lets Israel go. In these chapters of negotiation, Moses behaves likes Menelaus in Euripides' *Helen*. First he asks to offer a sacrifice at a location three days away, and Pharaoh justifiably suspects that they want to escape. Pharaoh pretends to accept several times, yet always changes his mind. In ch. 8, he accepts after the first four plagues but asks that they not go too far. In ch. 10, Pharaoh only allows the men to go—the women, children and flocks are to stay in Egypt. All of these details appear in *Helen*. Menelaus maintains that he wants to offer a sacrifice at a certain distance, but he actually wants to escape. Theoclymenus asks why they must go so far, and Menelaus responds that the waves may carry some elements of the sacrifice back to shore. Contrastively, when Pharaoh prefers that the Israelites offer their sacrifice in Egypt, Moses invokes the difference between their customs. Theoclymenus wants Helen to stay behind, but Menelaus insists that she must come. Similarly, Pharaoh wants the women and children to remain, but Moses asserts that everyone be allowed to come. Theoclymenus offers up a bull from his own flocks for the sacrifice, while Moses demands that Pharaoh himself provide the cattle for the sacrifice (Exod 10:25). Some humour is found in these chapters, as the stubborn Pharaoh becomes ridiculous—his own counsellors and subjects begging him to let Israel go.

The Quarrel at Elephantine

One particular utterance of Moses in these chapters demands closer scrutiny:

> Then Pharaoh summoned Moses and Aaron, and said, 'Go, sacrifice to your God within the land'. But Moses said, 'It would not be right to do so; for the sacrifices that we offer to the Lord our God are offensive to the Egyptians. If we offer in the sight of the Egyptians sacrifices that are offensive to them, will they not stone us? (Exod 8:25-26)

There does in fact exist a source external to the Bible that confirms that the sacrifices offered by Judeans made the Egyptians quite angry—the papyri of Elephantine. In the fifth century B.C.E. the Judeans offered rams in sacrifice, which horrified the Egyptian worshippers of Khnoum, the ram-god. The Egyptian priests, who benefited from the support of the Persian rulers, had the temple of Yahweh burnt. This episode is known from a letter that was sent by the Judeans to the Persian authority requesting financial aid to rebuild the temple:

> Your servant Yedonyah son of Gamaryah, the named Mauzi son of Nathan, the named Shamayah son of Haggay, the named Hoshea son of Yatom and the named Hoshea son of Yatun—five men from Syena who reside in Elephantine the Fortress, speak so: If our lord wishes it, the sanctuary of Yahweh our god will be built in Elephantine the Fortress as it was before, and neither slaughter of rams, oxen, nor he-goats will be offered, only incense and oblation will be offered. May the lord look into this.[6]

In the Introduction we saw that the building of a temple to Yahweh outside of Jerusalem is contrary to Deuteronomy 12, which speaks of the future temple to be built by Solomon. The Judeans of Elephantine did not seem to respect the laws of the Bible, although they did worship Yahweh, and even prepared the feast of Passover (which was probably not yet related to its biblical aetiology). This conflict with the Egyptian worshippers of Khnoum seems to be echoed in Moses' explanation of how the Israelites' practices would be an abomination to the Egyptians, who would stone them. A quarrel that took place in the late fifth century B.C.E. is transposed to a remote era as a deliberate allusion to a fact that Hellenistic readers might still have been aware of.

---

6.   Mélèze-Modrezejewski, *Les Juifs d'Égypte*, my translation from French.

The Parting of the Red Sea

We saw above how the story of Joseph seemed to have been inspired by Ulysses' invented story about being in Egypt (*Od.* XIV). Ulysses describes how he went to Egypt after the Trojan War, and though he told his men not to attack the people they disobeyed, they massacred the men and took the women and children captive. Naturally the Egyptians fought back:

> The alarm was soon carried to the city, and when they heard the war cry, the people came out at daybreak till the plain was filled with horsemen and foot soldiers and with the gleam of armour. Then Zeus spread panic among my men, and they would no longer face the enemy, for they found themselves surrounded. The Egyptians killed many of us, and took the rest alive to do forced labour for them. (*Od.* XIV, 267-72)

> So he had his chariot made ready, and took his army with him; *he took six hundred picked chariots and all the other chariots of Egypt with officers over all of them.* The Lord hardened the heart of Pharaoh king of Egypt and he pursued the Israelites, who were going out boldly. The Egyptians pursued them, all Pharaoh's horses and chariots, his chariot drivers and his army; they overtook them camped by the sea, by Pi-hahiroth, in front of Baal-zephon. As Pharaoh drew near, the *Israelites looked back, and there were the Egyptians advancing on them. In great fear the Israelites cried out to the Lord.* (Exod 14:6-10)

Moses then stretched his hand and the Red Sea was opened. The Israelites came across it, is if the two parts of the sea were walls. When the Egyptians engaged in pursuing them, Moses stretched his hand again, and the waters covered the Egyptians, who drowned (Exod 14:21-29). A rather similar story is found in Herodotus:

> ...when three months had gone by while Artabazos was besieging the town, there came to be a great ebb of the sea backwards, which lasted for a long time; and the Barbarians, seeing that shallow water had been produced, endeavoured to get by into the peninsula of Pallene, but when they had passed through two fifth-parts of the distance, and yet three-fifths remained, which they must pass through before they were within Pallene, then there came upon them a great flood-tide of the sea, higher than ever before, as the natives of the place say, though high tides come often. So those of them who could not swim perished, and those who could were slain by the men of Potidaia who put out to them in boats. The cause of the high tide and flood and of that which befell the Persians was this, as the Potidaians say, namely that these same Persians who perished by means of the sea had committed impiety towards the temple of

> Poseidon and his image in the suburb of their town; and in saying that this
> was the cause, in my opinion they say well. The survivors of his army
> Artabazos led away to Thessaly to join Mardonios. (Herodotus VIII, 129)

The biblical writer conflated the story of Ulysses in Egypt with Herodotus' idea of the temporarily retreating waters, all in continuation of the
Exodus story inspired by Euripides' *Helen*. But these literary sources are
superimposed upon a more philosophical source—Plato.

The Exodus / The Allegory of the Cave

In book VII of the *Republic*, Plato, through the voice of Socrates,
describes a group of people that have lived all their life chained in a dark
cave. They were only able to see the inner wall of that cave, on which
shadows of objects passing by outside were projected. Socrates imagines
that one of these prisoners is freed from his chains and forced to climb to
the surface. Once he sees the outside light, his eyes cannot take it at first.
As he gets used to daylight, he understands that what he considered to be
realities within the cave were only shadows of more real objects. He then
comes to understand that the light of the sun is the Idea of the Good. He
will therefore pity his comrades, who held the shadows in the cave for
deities. Socrates wants this man to be forced to go back inside the cave,
although he will protest, to free his comrades and bring them to the outside light. Yet, they would probably not believe him, hold him for a fool,
and even want to kill him (Plato, *Rep.* VII, 514 b-17 b). This allegory
illustrates Plato's theory of ideas: our world is itself a projection of a
greater reality that we cannot apprehend for our senses are limited. Only
the philosopher may contemplate the original Idea of the Good (*Rep.* 508
c-509 a), which is a metaphor for the only god; the same who created the
world in Plato's *Timaeus*.

The platonic Allegory of the Cave can be seen as the framework of the
Exodus story. The Israelites have become a numerous people in Egypt,
and the new Pharaoh makes them slaves (Exod 1). Moses escapes this
fate and flees to the land of Midian (Exod 2). There, God appears to
Moses in the burning bush and tells him to go back to free the Israelites
from slavery so as to lead them to the land promised to Abraham, Isaac
and Jacob (Exod 3–4). But the colony that God tells Moses to found is
the State of Plato's *Laws*, a State divided into twelve tribes and governed
by excellent laws, as we will now see. The biblical writer's astuteness
lies in freeing the prisoners of the Cave to bring them to the Ideal State,
an idea that is already implicit in the *Republic*. In the *Republic*, the City
is surveyed because it represents soul on a greater scale. In my opinion,
biblical Israel as well is at the same time the Ideal State and a soul. Here

in Exodus this soul is freed from the illusions of an oppressive royal regime (that of Pharaoh) and brought to the desert to meet the true God, who will be revealed through divine laws.

That the prisoners would not want to leave their prison, and that they even think of killing their liberator, is found in Exodus when Pharaoh chases Israel. First, the Israelites complain because they preferred to serve the Egyptians rather than dying in the wilderness (Exod 14:11-12). Further, they complained about the bitterness of the waters of Mara, and Moses feared that they would stone him (Exod 17:2-4). In Plato's dialogues these considerations foretell Socrates' tragic fate, for he was put on trial for impiety and executed by the Athenians. Plato implicitly compared them to the inhabitants of the Cave, worshipping 'shadow gods' and unable to understand Socrates' divine philosophy. A platonic framework crosses the biblical narrative, one that will be more apparent when analysing the legislative books. The introduction of Genesis was made up of several platonic dialogues such as the *Timaeus*, *Phaedo*, *Symposium* and *Statesman*. Disposing of the whole platonic corpus, the biblical writer will favour the *Laws* over the *Republic*. His great idea was in spreading the reception of these laws along a journey of initiation that is a transposition of the journey of the Argonauts (where the Golden Fleece is replaced by divine laws). Let us examine the first of these laws.

First Laws

Chapters 20 to 23 of Exodus detail the first laws given to Israel (not counting the institution of Passover in ch. 12). These chapters have been called the 'Covenant Code' by biblical scholars and are supposed to be older than the 'Deuteronomic Code'—chs. 12 to 26 of Deuteronomy. We will see that both of these 'codes' have laws similar to those found in the *Laws* of Plato, which have been simply dispatched in a different order (though sometimes the order remains the same).

Children of Slaves

> If his master gives him a wife and she bears him sons or daughters, the wife and her children shall be her master's and he shall go out alone. (Exod 21:4)

> When a child is admitted to be the offspring of certain parents and is acknowledged by them, but there is need of a decision as to which parent the child is to follow—in case a female slave have intercourse with a male slave, or with a freeman or freedman, the offspring shall always belong to the master of the female slave. (Plato, *Laws* 930 d-e)

Murder and Outrage to Parents

Whoever strikes a person mortally shall be put to death. If it was not premeditated, but came about by an act of God, then I will appoint for you a place to which the killer may flee. But if someone wilfully attacks and kills another by treachery, you shall take the killer from my altar for execution. Whoever strikes father or mother shall be put to death. Whoever kidnaps a person, whether that person has been sold or is still held in possession, shall be put to death. Whoever curses father or mother shall be put to death. (Exod 21:12-17)

For the myth, or saying, or whatever we ought to call it, has been plainly set forth by priests of old; they have pronounced that the justice which guards and avenges the blood of kindred, follows the law of retaliation, and ordains that he who has done any murderous act should of necessity suffer that which he has done. He who has slain a father shall himself be slain at some time or other by his children—if a mother, he shall of necessity take a woman's nature, and lose his life at the hands of his offspring in after ages; for where the blood of a family has been polluted there is no other purification, nor can the pollution be washed out until the homicidal soul which did the deed has given life for life, and has propitiated and laid to sleep the wrath of the whole family. These are the retributions of Heaven, and by such punishments men should be deterred. (*Laws* 872 d-e)

But in his case, if he be convicted, the servants of the judges and the magistrates shall slay him at an appointed place without the city where three ways meet, and there expose his body naked, and each of the magistrates on behalf of the whole city shall take a stone and cast it upon the head of the dead man, and so deliver the city from pollution; after that, they shall bear him to the borders of the land, and cast him forth unburied, according to law. (*Laws* 873b)

Collective stoning is echoed in Lev 24:13-14.

Wounds

Whoever curses father or mother shall be put to death. When individuals quarrel and one strikes the other with a stone or fist so that the injured party, though not dead, is confined to bed, but recovers and walks around outside with the help of a staff, then the assailant shall be free of liability, except to pay for the loss of time, and to arrange for full recovery. When a slave-owner strikes a male or female slave with a rod and the slave dies immediately, the owner shall be punished. But if the slave survives for a day or two, there is no punishment; for the slave is the owner's property. (Exod 21:17-21)

If any one has a purpose and intention to slay another who is not his enemy, and whom the law does not permit him to slay, and he wounds him, but is unable to kill him, he who had the intent and has wounded him is not to be pitied—he deserves no consideration, but should be regarded as a murderer and be tried for murder. Still having respect to the fortune which has in a manner favoured him, and to the providence which in pity to him and to the wounded man saved the one from a fatal blow, and the other from an accursed fate and calamity—as a thank-offering to this deity, and in order not to oppose his will—in such a case the law will remit the punishment of death, and only compel the offender to emigrate to a neighbouring city for the rest of his life, where he shall remain in the enjoyment of all his possessions. But if he have injured the wounded man, he shall make such compensation for the injury as the court deciding the cause shall assess, and the same judges shall decide who would have decided if the man had died of his wounds. And if a child intentionally wound his parents, or a servant his master, death shall be the penalty. (*Laws* 876 e-77 b)

If he kill the slave of another in the belief that he is his own, he shall bear the master of the dead man harmless from loss, or shall pay a penalty of twice the value of the dead man, which the judges shall assess; but purifications must be used greater and more numerous than for those who committed homicide at the games—what they are to be, the interpreters whom the God appoints shall be authorised to declare. And if a man kills his own slave, when he has been purified according to law, he shall be quit of the homicide. (*Laws* 865 c-d)

The progression of the laws is almost identical in both cases. Biblical laws distinguish between voluntary and involuntary homicide; those convicted of involuntary homicide are exiled to certain cities of refuge (the list of which will be given in Num 35 and Deut 19, appearing to be the equivalent to the sentence of exile in Plato). Plato distinguishes between those assaults that result in death, or only in injury. In the latter case, the offender pays indemnities if the victim is incapacitated, exactly as in Exod 21:18-19. In both texts, those who strike their parents shall be put to death. Both texts also specify that slave owners can kill their own slaves, though only in a specific context. The next law in Plato (*Laws* 877e) is about a juridical fiction, posited in order that there may be a male inheritor for a house if the owner were to die childless. Plato touches on the issue of suicide after speaking about the laws governing patricide and matricide, and then discusses an animal or an object that may cause death.

The Murderous Animal[7]

> When an ox gores a man or a woman to death, the ox shall be stoned, and its flesh shall not be eaten; but the owner of the ox shall not be liable. If the ox has been accustomed to gore in the past, and its owner has been warned but has not restrained it, and it kills a man or a woman, the ox shall be stoned, and its owner also shall be put to death. If a ransom is imposed on the owner, then the owner shall pay whatever is imposed for the redemption of the victim's life. If it gores a boy or a girl, the owner shall be dealt with according to this same rule. If the ox gores a male or female slave, the owner shall pay to the slave-owner thirty shekels of silver, and the ox shall be stoned. (Exod 21:28-32)

> And if a beast of burden or other animal cause the death of any one, except in the case of anything of that kind happening to a competitor in the public contests, the kinsmen of the deceased shall prosecute the slayer for murder, and the wardens of the country, such, and so many as the kinsmen appoint, shall try the cause, and let the beast when condemned be slain by them, and let them cast it beyond the borders. (*Laws* 873 e)

Plato then speaks of a case where a body was found without a known murderer, a law that we will see in Deuteronomy. Plato then proceeds to homicides that are considered guiltless.

The Nocturnal Thief[8]

> When someone steals an ox or a sheep, and slaughters it or sells it, the thief shall pay five oxen for an ox, and four sheep for a sheep. If a thief is found breaking in, and is beaten to death, no blood-guilt is incurred; but if it happens after sunrise, blood-guilt is incurred. The thief shall make restitution, but if unable to do so, shall be sold for the theft. When the animal, whether ox or donkey or sheep, is found alive in the thief's possession, the thief shall pay double. (Exod 21:37–22:3)

> And now let us say in what cases and under what circumstances the murderer is rightly free from guilt: If a man catch a thief coming into his house by night to steal, and he take and kill him, or if he slay a footpad in self-defence, he shall be guiltless. (*Laws* 874 c)

These laws on the murderous animal and on the nocturnal thief are the same, and appear in the same order in both platonic and biblical texts. Earlier in *Laws*, Plato describes how the thief must pay double if caught:[9]

---

7. Noted by Eusebius, *P.E.* XII, 42
8. Eusebius, *P.E.* XII, 41
9. Eusebius, *P.E.* XII, 40.

> For a thief, whether he steal much or little, let there be one law, and one punishment for all alike: in the first place, let him pay double the amount of the theft if he be convicted, and if he have so much over and above the allotment—if he have not, he shall be bound until he pay the penalty, or persuade him who has obtained the sentence against him to forgive him. (*Laws* 857a)

These laws that Plato uses were part of the Athenian legislation, as recorded in the texts of Demosthenes: a thief must repay double the value of what was stolen (*Against Timocrates* 105), and one may kill a thief that breaks in at night (*Against Timocrates* 113-15). Let us see another example, noted by Professor Kupitz.

Damages to One's Field

> When someone causes a field or vineyard to be grazed over, or lets livestock loose to graze in someone else's field, restitution shall be made from the best in the owner's field or vineyard. When fire breaks out and catches in thorns so that the stacked grain or the standing grain or the field is consumed, the one who started the fire shall make full restitution. (Exod 22:5-6)

> If any one pastures his cattle on his neighbour's land, they shall see the injury, and adjudge the penalty. And if any one, by decoying the bees, gets possession of another's swarms, and draws them to himself by making noises, he shall pay the damage; or if any one sets fire to his own wood and takes no care of his neighbour's property, he shall be fined at the discretion of the magistrates. (*Laws* 843 d-e)

Again, we find the same laws in the same order. Just a few lines before, Plato says that boundary stones cannot be removed for they are sacred (*Laws* 842e)—the same law which is found in Deut 19:14. A little further on in the text, Plato allows strangers and old men to take a small amount of fruit from someone's field (*Laws* 844 d-45 c), as set forth in Deut 23:24-25. Even though some of these laws (such as those about the goring ox, nocturnal thief, or damages to one's field) are found in the very ancient *Code of Hammurabi,* they do not appear as closely spaced as nor are they in the same specific order as the laws found in *Laws* and Exodus 21–22. The biblical writer may have known the *Code of Hammurabi,* or of another, more contemporary, legislation, but the Bible shows knowledge of Plato's philosophy and laws, and thus must be dated by its most recent aspects. The so-called Covenant Code is a selection of platonic laws mixed with laws of another provenance. These laws do not contain a different theology than that of Leviticus or Deuteronomy; some of them will be repeated, but that does not involve several layers of redaction—it is all a deliberate writing technique.

The Acceptance of the Laws: **The Critias**

Then he said to Moses, 'Come up to the Lord, you and Aaron, Nadab, and Abihu, and seventy of the elders of Israel, and worship at a distance. Moses alone shall come near the Lord; but the others shall not come near, and the people shall not come up with him.' Moses came and told the people all the words of the Lord and all the ordinances; and all the people answered with one voice, and said, 'All the words that the Lord has spoken we will do'. And Moses wrote down all the words of the Lord. He rose early in the morning, and built an altar at the foot of the mountain, and set up twelve pillars, corresponding to the twelve tribes of Israel. *He sent young men of the people of Israel, who offered burnt-offerings and sacrificed oxen as offerings of well-being to the Lord.* Moses took half of the blood and put it in basins, and half of the blood he dashed against the altar. Then he took the book of the covenant, and read it in the hearing of the people; and they said, 'All that the Lord has spoken we will do, and we will be obedient'. *Moses took the blood and dashed it on the people*, and said, 'See the blood of the covenant that the Lord has made with you in accordance with all these words'. Then Moses and Aaron, Nadab, and Abihu, and seventy of the elders of Israel went up, and they saw the God of Israel. Under his feet there was something like a pavement of sapphire stone, like the very heaven for clearness. God did not lay his hand on the chief men of the people of Israel; also they beheld God, and they ate and drank. (Exod 24:1-11)

There were bulls who had the range of the temple of Poseidon; and the ten kings, being left alone in the temple, after they had offered prayers to the god that they might capture the victim which was acceptable to him, hunted the bulls, without weapons but with staves and nooses; and the bull which they caught they led up to the pillar and cut its throat over the top of it so that the blood fell upon the sacred inscription. Now on the pillar, besides the laws, there was inscribed an oath invoking mighty curses on the disobedient. *When therefore, after slaying the bull in the accustomed manner, they had burnt its limbs, they filled a bowl of wine and cast in a clot of blood for each of them*; the rest of the victim they put in the fire, after having purified the column all round. Then they drew from the bowl in golden cups and pouring a libation on the fire, they swore that they would judge according to the laws on the pillar, and would punish him who in any point had already transgressed them, and that for the future they would not, if they could help, offend against the writing on the pillar, and would neither command others, nor obey any ruler who commanded them, to act otherwise than according to the laws of their father Poseidon. This was the prayer which each of them offered up for himself and for his descendants, at the same time drinking and dedicating the cup out of which he drank in the temple of the god; and after they had supped and satisfied their needs, when darkness came on, and the fire about the sacrifice was cool, all of them put on most beautiful

azure robes, and, sitting on the ground, at night, over the embers of the
sacrifices by which they had sworn, and extinguishing all the fire about
the temple, they received and gave judgment, if any of them had an accusation to bring against any one; and when they given judgment, at day-
break they wrote down their sentences on a golden tablet, and dedicated it
together with their robes to be a memorial. (Plato, *Critias* 119 d-20 c)

Each generation, the kings of Atlantis gave up more and more laws that
their ancestors had sworn to respect forever, which eventually prompted
Zeus to destroy the entire Atlantean kingdom. We see similarities with
the Bible: after the laws have been accepted, oxen or bulls are sacrificed
and burnt as offerings, and sacrificial blood is spattered upon the kings or
the Israelites (Exod 24:8). Plato's Atlantis is closely tied to his other
political dialogues, namely the *Republic* and the *Laws*; they all represent
his attempts to create utopia. This biblical scene of the acceptance of the
first laws must be linked with the future disobedience of Israel's kings,
described in the book of Kings. In it, each generation of kings is said to
have been increasingly unfaithful to God's laws. This continues until
King Manasseh, who is the catalyst for God's decision to destroy Judah
(2 Kgs 21). The framework of the Ideal State, given perfect laws in order
to live eternally in harmony, is found in Plato's *Critias*, a clear reference
to which the biblical writer left in Exodus 24. The tale of the Israelite
slaves liberated by Moses, a man who encountered God in the solitude
of the desert; this is the allegory of the cave from the *Republic*. Exodus
21–22 contain strikingly similar laws to those in Plato, and the oath of
acceptance of these laws is taken from the *Critias*. The writer foretells
the end of his book—the destruction of Israel and Judah—with bitter
irony, both in this allusive reference to Plato's Atlantis, and explicitly in
the episode of the golden calf (Exod 32). Herodotus was a source for
many biblical narratives, but he was a source of inspiration for Plato
himself. To conjure the myth of Atlantis, Plato used the exotic descriptions of Egypt, and Asian cities such as Babylon and Agbatana in the
first three books of Herodotus. For instance, Plato imagined the ten kings
of Atlantis swearing to help each other, based on Herodotus II, 147, to be
compared with Plato, *Crit.* 120 c.[10] That passage from Plato follows the
lines quoted previously about the oath. As explained in the Introduction,
the biblical writer mixed several Greek sources by taking advantage of
the existing links between them. The second book of Herodotus, about
Egypt, appears to be a source for both Exodus and the book of Kings.

10.   Brisson and Pradeau, *Timée—Critias*, 322.

Bezalel, a Craftsman 'in the Shadow of God'

God gives abundant instructions to Moses for the creation of the divine sanctuary (Exod 25–31), which is to be executed by Bezalel, a craftsman from the tribe of Judah (Exod 35–40). It is noteworthy that chs. 35 to 40 repeat chs. 25 to 31 almost word for word, switching from the second person imperative to the third person indicative. The list of details given to Moses breaks the narrative tone familiar so far, and is quite boring to read. Why then would the writer decide to inflict upon his reader an almost identical repetition of these long verses? Professor Lambros Couloubaritsis has shown the importance of the use of catalogues in ancient (and even modern) literature, catalogues that interpretation must 'redress'.[11] For instance, Hesiod's genealogy of the gods in the *Theogony*, or Homer's list of the Acheans ships in *Iliad* II, are catalogues. The Bible uses genealogical catalogues extensively, especially in Genesis, and here in Exodus we are confronted with a doubled catalogue of ritual objects. This repetition catches the attention of the reader, for the writer could have been spared some effort by saying that Bezalel did everything according to Moses' plan, then passing directly on to Leviticus. But the very name of that craftsman, Bezalel, which could be translated as 'in the shadow of God', leads us to the shadow of Plato behind the biblical narrative.

The reader may see one example of how the writer repeats God's prescriptions and Bezalel's execution of them in comparing Exod 25:8-16 with Exod 37:1-5; as for the building of the ark. The reader should observe how closely chs. 35 to 40 mirror chs. 25 to 31. The divine model is perfectly imitated by the craftsman. This concept of imitation is borrowed from Plato's *Republic*. In book X, Socrates continues a discussion started in books II and III about imitation (*mimesis* in Greek). We saw in the Introduction how he proposed to censor poets like Homer and Hesiod, as what they wrote about the gods and the heroes was not suitable. In book X Socrates speaks of a craftsman that imitates a divine model of furniture. A painter representing the craftsman's work would only imitate the imitation, and therefore be three degrees removed from the divinity of the original idea. Socrates explains that there exists a divine model for any piece of furniture, as beds and tables. The craftsman who has invented these unique models has also invented the model of the whole world: he is the only god. Therefore, human craftsmen only imitate a model of divine furniture (Plato, *Rep.* 595 a-97 e).

11. Lambros Couloubaritsis, *Aux origines de la philosophie européenne: de la pensée archaïque au néoplatonisme*, Brussels: De Boeck University.

This very rich passage establishes the platonic conception of the world of ideas. The discussion in the *Timaeus*, analysed briefly in the first chapter, is supposed to take place the day after the discussion of the *Republic*. Thus, in continuation of these considerations, the world was created according God's own design. Book X of the *Republic* ends with the story of Er, and I have shown how this character discretely appears in Genesis as his homonym, the grandson of Jacob. Returning to Bezalel the craftsman, he does exactly what Socrates speaks about and faithfully imitates a model of furniture designed by God. However, the episode of the golden calf appears right between the gift of the model to Moses and its execution by the craftsman. Because it did not seem that Moses was coming back, the Israelites asked Aaron to give them a god; thus, from the melted gold they gave him, a golden calf was erected, which they worshiped. Upon seeing this, Moses breaks the two tables of the law and has those responsible killed. Israel showed itself to be unworthy of God's election, and while God proposes to make a new chosen people from Moses' offspring, Moses pleads for God's forgiveness on Israel's behalf (Exod 32:10-14). Only after that terrible episode of wrath and death do the people, turning back to God, offer Bezalel material to create the sanctuary. Between the gift of the sanctuary plan and its execution, the dramatic episode of the golden calf illustrates the evil kind of imitation that is despised by Plato—that of the sculptors, painters and poets who create images, vulgar representations of things of a divine nature that cannot be captured. That which God reveals of the divine essence is expressed in God's sanctuary, which can be rightly seen as a microcosm (as per Philo Judaeus, *De Vita Moses* II, 15-16). That is probably why the biblical author thought he should include the doubled catalogue of the sanctuary's furniture—for it, as a perfect imitation of a divine model, is meant to reflect God's presence in the human world. The author gives an interpretation of Plato's theory of ideas in a narrative and 'catalogical' form. The forbidding of divine images in the Bible is formulated in accordance with Plato:

> You shall not make for yourself an idol, whether in the form of anything that is in heaven above, or that is on the earth beneath, or that is in the water under the earth. (Exod 20:4)

> For this is he who is able to make not only vessels of every kind, but plants and animals, himself and all other things—the earth and heaven, and the things which are in heaven or under the earth; he makes the gods also. (Plato, *Rep.* 596 c)

The nameless god is the divine craftsman—the Demiurge—that created all that is on Earth, in heaven and beneath the ground, and even the gods. But did the biblical writer not find himself in a paradoxical situation, in his imitation of Greek poets that were banned from the *Republic*, Homer and Hesiod? On the contrary, by establishing this mimetic frame he extracts himself from that paradox, becoming a craftsman imitating a platonic model. By imitating the texts of Plato on imitation, the biblical writer negates the paradox and founds the legitimacy of his writing. The astuteness of the technique is supreme. If the platonic theory of ideas is still regarded as the summit of philosophy, then we can now understand *Plato's works as the Idea of the Bible*, as Professor Kupitz sums it up. We will verify this by analysing the foundation of the Ideal State, where the same duplicity is reproduced. First God has Moses take a census of the twelve tribes of Israel in order that the land may be shared (Num 1 and 26). Then the author gives two different catalogues of the tribes, divided into paternal clans, one generation having passed during the forty years of wandering. The book of Joshua narrates the foundation of the State after the conquest, and of the distribution of the land by lots to the tribes. This uses the same catalogues as in Numbers 26, detailing which lot was received by each tribe and family (Josh 14–19). This biblical cadastre is modelled after Plato's State in the *Laws* (745 b-c). In the same manner that Bezalel fashions the sanctuary's furniture according to the divine model, Joshua gives life to the Ideal State—the plan for which was given to Moses. The author uses catalogues in each case in order to give to his narrative some consistency and legitimacy; ritual objects are catalogued in the first case, tribes and paternal clans in the second. The interpretation of these doubled catalogues allows one to understand how in fact the biblical writer imitates a platonic model. The degrees of imitation explained by Socrates allow the biblical writer to play on a skilful double dialectic of imitation: one is internal to the biblical text, between the divine model and its execution in the sensible world, and the other external to the Bible, between the platonic model and its imitation by the biblical writer.

The use of the incriminated poets Homer and Hesiod as literary sources is not done in contradiction to Plato, who in modern culture is too often regarded as the opponent of poetry. We saw in the Introduction that there is a transition in the role given to the poet from the *Republic* to the *Laws*. In *Republic* X the poets are chased from the State, but on the other hand Plato tells the myth of Er, which is his version of Ulysses' descent into Hades in the *Odyssey*. For Letitia Mouze, the only Ideal State that Plato conceived of is that of the *Laws*. The *Republic* is an abstraction meant to define justice through the City. As the *Laws* aims to be more realistic,

Plato moderates his position on poetry to the extent that Socrates does not speak in this dialogue. Poetry is permitted, under the condition that it is employed to chant the laws. Moreover, in a speech given by the Athenian Stranger to some hypothetical poets who wished to dwell in the State of the *Laws*, that Ideal State is defined as 'the truest tragedy'—only an imitation of what is best in life (*Laws* 817 a-b). In the words of Plato himself, the Ideal State is called a tragedy, better than any poetry, which may have inspired the biblical writer to turn it into the tragic narrative of the Bible. The genius of the biblical writer was that he was able to render the philosophical transition from the *Republic* to the *Laws* by taking his characters out of the 'Egyptian Cave' to bring them to the Promised Land of the *Laws*, and by his adaptation of Homeric poetry through a platonic filter.

The Bacchantes / *Moses Hidden in the Cleft of a Rock*

Lo! I am come to this land of Thebes, Dionysus' the son of Zeus, of whom on a day Semele, the daughter of Cadmus, was delivered by a flash of lightning. Dionysus, whom on a day his mother in her sore travail brought forth untimely, yielding up her life beneath the lightning stroke of Zeus' winged bolt; but forthwith Zeus, the son of Cronos, found for him another womb wherein to rest, for he hid him in his thigh and fastened it with golden pins to conceal him from Hera. (*Bacchantes* 1-5, 89-110)

But Zeus loved Semele and bedded with her unknown to Hera. Now Zeus had agreed to do for her whatever she asked, and deceived by Hera she asked that he would come to her as he came when he was wooing Hera. Unable to refuse, Zeus came to her bridal chamber in a chariot, with lightnings and thunderings, and launched a thunderbolt. But Semele expired of fright, and Zeus, snatching the sixth-month abortive child from the fire, sewed it in his thigh. On the death of Semele the other daughters of Cadmus spread a report that Semele had bedded with a mortal man, and had falsely accused Zeus, and that therefore she had been blasted by thunder. But at the proper time Zeus undid the stitches and gave birth to Dionysus, and entrusted him to Hermes. And he conveyed him to Ino and Athamas, and persuaded them to rear him as a girl. But Hera indignantly drove them mad, and Athamas hunted his elder son Learchus as a deer and killed him, and Ino threw Melicertes into a boiling cauldron, then carrying it with the dead child she sprang into the deep. (Apollodorus, *Library* 3, 4, 3)

Moses said, 'Show me your glory, I pray'. And he said, 'I will make all my goodness pass before you, and will proclaim before you the name, 'The Lord'; and I will be gracious to whom I will be gracious, and will show mercy on whom I will show mercy. 'But', he said, 'you cannot see my face; for no one shall see me and live'. And the Lord continued, 'See,

> there is a place by me where you shall stand on the rock; and while my glory passes by I will put you in a cleft of the rock, and I will cover you with my hand until I have passed by; then I will take away my hand, and you shall see my back; but my face shall not be seen'. (Exod 33:18-23)

Here again in the biblical version we can see a trace of the demythologisation of Greek stories. Semele was Zeus' lover and she asked to see him in his full glory, but the shock killed her; Zeus saved her unborn child Dionysus by removing him and sewing him into his thigh. Dionysus was thus born from a male 'womb'—a narrative element that could not appear in the Bible, and something that Plato would have condemned. In the Bible, Moses wanted to see God's glory, which would also have been fatal, so once Moses was hidden in a cleft of rock, God's back is revealed. Moreover, the *Bacchantes* show some poetic elements that are also found in Exodus:

> With milk and wine and streams of luscious honey flows the earth, and Syrian incense smokes. (*Bacchantes* 140)

> 'Go up to a land flowing with milk and honey; but I will not go up among you, or I would consume you on the way, for you are a stiff-necked people.' (Exod 33:3; see Exod 3:8)

> And one took her thyrsus and struck it into the earth, and forth there gushed a limpid spring; and another plunged her wand into the lap of earth and there the god sent up a fount of wine; and all who wished for draughts of milk had but to scratch the soil with their finger-tips and there they had it in abundance, while from every ivy-wreathed staff sweet rills of honey trickled. (*Bacchantes* 700-710)

> The Lord said to Moses, 'Go on ahead of the people, and take some of the elders of Israel with you; take in your hand the staff with which you struck the Nile, and go. I will be standing there in front of you on the rock at Horeb. Strike the rock, and water will come out of it, so that the people may drink.' Moses did so, in the sight of the elders of Israel. (Exod 17:5-6)

> ...and on their hair they carried fire and it burnt them not. (*Bacchantes* 760)

> There the angel of the Lord appeared to him in a flame of fire out of a bush; he looked, and the bush was blazing, yet it was not consumed. Then Moses said, 'I must turn aside and look at this great sight, and see why the bush is not burned up'. (Exod 3:2-3)

The *Bacchantes* and Exodus have many themes in common: the rivers of milk and honey, the flame that does not burn, the staff that creates a spring of water. All of these are not mere coincidence. We saw previously how Euripides' *Helen* is the probable source of the Exodus story—here, another famous play of Euripides is used. This is another trace of a very coherent and scholarly work, as we can see how the general plot of the *Bacchantes* is related to Exodus. Pentheus, King of Thebes and Cadmus' grandson, refuses to worship Dionysus for he does not believe that he is a god. Dionysus tricks Pentheus and makes him look like a fool, at which point his female relatives dismember him horribly in a bacchanalian frenzy. This drama reminds us of the stubborn Pharaoh of Exodus who refuses to recognise Yahweh's godhood, until Yahweh kills his firstborn son. In both stories, a god uses a king, whose stubbornness in the end gives the god cause to reveal his might. At last, the so-called Song of the Sea, which scholars consider to be an ancient piece of poetry included in the Bible, seems a lot like the choir of the *Bacchantes* chanting the glory of Dionysus with tambourines:

> On, on, ye Bacchanals, pride of Tmolus with its rills of gold I to the sound of the booming drum, chanting in joyous strains the praises of your joyous god with Phrygian accents lifted high, what time the holy lute with sweet complaining note invites you to your hallowed sport, according well with feet that hurry wildly to the hills; like a colt that gambols at its mother's side in the pasture, with gladsome heart each Bacchante bounds along. (*Bacchantes* 55-65)

> Then the prophet Miriam, Aaron's sister, took a tambourine in her hand; and all the women went out after her with tambourines and with dancing. And Miriam sang to them: 'Sing to the Lord, for he has triumphed gloriously; horse and rider he has thrown into the sea'. (Exod 15:20-21)

3.

Leviticus

This third biblical book has fewer parallels with Greek literature and Plato's *Laws*. Some laws are found in Plato too, but most of those regarding purity seem to be found in the Bible alone. Leviticus is a particular case in the Bible, containing almost no narratives; it appears as the heart of biblical law. Narratives will appear again in Numbers, embedded with laws as in Exodus.

Sexuality

The Athenian stranger of *Laws* thinks that most of his laws can be accepted willingly, but that laws on sexuality (especially on homosexuality) will require more persuasion. The Spartans and the Cretans accepted homosexuality, but the Athenian wants to forbid it, by using the example of Laius (Plato, *Laws* 836 b-d). Laius was known as the instigator of pederasty, the reason for which he was fated to die at the hands of his son Oedipus. The Athenian Stranger wishes virtue to stem from the law. He believes that a seducer will not achieve the virtue of temperance if the law allows these practices, that any man who would imitate a woman will become effeminate, and that no law should support this behaviour. For the Athenian, there are three types of love: friendship (*philia*), desire (*epithumein*) and love per se (*eros*), which is a just mixture of the first two. The balance between friendly feelings and carnal desires is where the only true form of love resides. This is reminiscent of previous platonic dialogues in which the soul is described as being guided by two horses: a black one symbolising the desires of the body, and a white one symbolising the rational part (*Phaedro*). Plato encourages love without sex, '*a soul loving another soul*' (*Laws* 837 c). The Athenian says that there is an easy way to prevent deviant sexual practices—shame. In fact, most people refrain from sexual intercourse with relatives because shame forbids incest. The Athenian proposes to have the same shame proclaimed concerning homosexuality:

> I had a way to make men use natural love and abstain from unnatural relations with males, not intentionally destroying the seeds of human increase, or sowing them in stony places, in which they will take no root; and that I would command them to abstain too from any female field of increase in which that which is sown is not likely to grow? Now if a law to this effect could only be made perpetual, and gain an authority such as already prevents intercourse of parents and children—such a law, extending to other sensual desires, and conquering them, would be the source of ten thousand blessings. For, in the first place, moderation is the appointment of nature, and deters men from all frenzy and madness of love, and from all adulteries and immoderate use of meats and drinks, and makes them good friends to their own wives. (*Laws* 838 d-e)

The Athenian explains how athletes refrain from sex before competition, and how birds live in faithful heterosexual couples. Should men be worse than birds? They have to limit their sexual activity to the sole purpose of procreation, and remain in a state of holiness the rest of the time (*Laws* 840). If homosexuality cannot be avoided, then the Athenian suggests imposing heavy physical exercise in order to distract oneself from one's sexual appetites. Furthermore, he says that these laws can be presented in a fable (*Laws* 841 c-42 a).

Plato condemns free sexuality (outside of marriage) and homosexuality. Homosexuality was associated with incest, which was also considered shameful. Plato cites myths as reference: Laius instigated pederasty (*Laws* 836 c) and was duly cursed to die at the hands of his own son, Oedipus, who ended up marrying his mother Jocasta. Plato seems to suggest that one practice causally leads to the other; the same conception appears in the Bible. Mythical stories are used to illustrate the sexual depravation of earlier human generations that could only be healed by divine law, in order to avoid the catastrophes of the flood and of Sodom and Gomorrah. Noah cursed his son Ham for having seen him naked (Gen 9). Ham's descendants through his son Canaan, the Sodomites, had tried to rape the messengers of God. The daughters of Lot, survivor of Sodom, seduced him as the city was destroyed (Gen 19). These two stories reflect each other symmetrically. In Noah's story, the sons of God take the human women for wives, God floods the earth with water, and the survivor becomes drunk with wine and is sexually humiliated by one of his sons. In Lot's story the sons of God (the angels visiting Sodom) were nearly raped by the Sodomites, who then were destroyed by divine fire (as opposed to water), and here too the survivor's daughters abused him when he was drunk. Both stories illustrate the perverted nature of the Canaanites, dispossessed of their land. But the ancestors of Israel also committed incest.

Abraham confessed that he had married his own half-sister (Gen 20:12); Jacob married two sisters (Gen 29); Reuben raped his father's concubine (Gen 35:22); Judah slept with his daughter-in-law (Gen 38); and Moses' father Amram married his aunt Jocabed (Exod 6:20). Leviticus 18 lists the prohibitions against incest. A man is prohibited from having sex with relatives; the phrase used is 'to uncover their nakedness'. It is forbidden to uncover the nakedness of one's mother, or of the concubine of one's father (as Reuben did, as well as Absalom, son of David) because it equates to the father's nakedness. The same applies to uncovering the nakedness of one's sister or half-sister, from either one's father (as Abraham did) or mother, of one's father's sister (as Amram did), or one's daughter-in-law (as Judah did). Additionally, this holds for the wife of one's brother, one's granddaughter, for a woman and her daughter at the same time, or in the case of two living sisters (as Jacob did). A man shall not come to a woman while she is menstruating, nor shall he go with his kinsman's wife. A man is not to sacrifice his children to Moloch. A man must not sleep with another man (Lev 18:22), and humans must not lie with animals. God claims that those who were dispossessed of the land of Canaan practiced all of these sins, which is why the land 'vomited them out' (Lev 18:24-25). Israel should beware not to make the same mistakes, or else the land would be defiled and would 'vomit them out'. This is a paradoxical explanation, because the ancestors of Israel are described as practicing incest in Genesis and Exodus. However, Israel is ultimately expelled from the land. Second Kings 21:9 specifies that King Manasseh made Judah do everything that had caused the previous peoples to be chased from the land. In Leviticus, we encounter the conception called 'second type incest' by Françoise Héritier regarding the kin of a sexual partner or the sexual partners of a relative (such as one's daughter-in-law or sister-in-law).[1] Two sisters must not marry the same man while both remain alive, as it too is considered incest.

It is most likely that rules prohibiting incest existed in Judean society before the Bible, as they exist in different forms in all societies; yet the formulation of these laws in Leviticus shows similarities with Plato's reasoning—for example, homosexuality being associated with incest. This could seem obvious from our Judeo-Christian point of view, since these biblical laws have governed our conception of sexuality until very recently. But in antiquity, such a prohibition against homosexuality was not so obvious. Plato's earlier dialogues are the best example. In the

---

1. Françoise Héritier, *Les deux soeurs et leur mère—anthropologie de l'inceste*, Paris: Odile Jacob, 1995.

Symposium, friends gather to deliver an apology for love between men, and only Socrates explains that they should refrain from physical love. In Athens and Greece in general, pederasty was an institutional form of love between a grown man and an adolescent boy. In the *Laws*, the Athenian is seen to be more radical than Socrates and forbids any form of male homosexuality in his Ideal State. Plato even says that such practices would not be abandoned easily, which is why he proposes a second law. Moreover, Plato's law explains how it is forbidden to have relations with a woman without the intention to procreate, as in the story of Onan, son of Judah (Gen 38:9). We saw that Judah's elder son was named Er, a homonym of Plato's hero of *Republic* X. The platonic riddle will unfold in the story of Ruth, explaining the full genealogy of David. There, we will find Socrates' definition of love in the *Symposium*.

So far, one can still doubt that these laws of Plato have anything to do with the Bible. I invite the reader to open Plato's *Laws* and see how, right after these prescriptions on sexuality, Plato speaks on agricultural laws such as boundary stones and the gathering of fruits, laws that are found in Deuteronomy. And further on in Plato is the legislation on murder, which we encountered partly in Exodus. Quite simply, Plato's *Laws* were dismantled and assembled in a different order in the Bible.

Haircut

You shall not round off the hair on your temples or mar the edges of your beard. (Lev 19:27)

Egypt, Judah, Edom, the Ammonites, Moab, and all those with shaven temples who live in the desert. For all these nations are uncircumcised, and all the house of Israel is uncircumcised in heart. (Jer 9:26; see 25:23-24; 49:32)

Of gods (the Arabs) believe in Dionysus and Urania alone: moreover they say that the cutting of their hair is done after the same fashion as that of Dionysus himself; and they cut their hair in a circle round, shaving away the hair of the temples. Now they call Dionysus Orotalt and Urania they call Alilat. (Herodotus III, 8)

Here, the author seems to have wanted to distinguish Jews from the Arab populations of Edom, Ammon and Moab. Or maybe he desired newly converted proselytes from these populations to give up these haircuts, which Herodotus refers to as being in imitation of their god.

Status of the Stranger

When an alien resides with you in your land, you shall not oppress the alien. The alien who resides with you shall be to you as the citizen among you; you shall love the alien as yourself, for you were aliens in the land of Egypt: I am the Lord your God. (Lev 19:33-34)

Any one who likes may come and be a metic on certain conditions; a foreigner, if he likes, and is able to settle, may dwell in the land, but he must practise an art, and not abide more than twenty years from the time at which he has registered himself; and he shall pay no sojourner's tax, however small, except good conduct, nor any other tax for buying and selling. But when the twenty years have expired, he shall take his property with him and depart. (*Laws* 850 a-b)

Priesthood

Those who have the care of the temples shall be called priests. Those who hold hereditary offices as priests or priestesses shall not be disturbed; but if there be few or none such, as is probable at the foundation of a new city, priests and priestesses shall be appointed to be servants of the Gods who have no servants. Some of our officers shall be elected, and others appointed by lot, those who are of the people and those who are not of the people mingling in a friendly manner in every place and city, that the state may be as far as possible of one mind. The officers of the temples shall be appointed by lot; in this way their election will be committed to God, that He may do what is agreeable to Him. And he who obtains a lot shall undergo a scrutiny, first, as to whether he is sound of body and of legitimate birth; and in the second place, in order to show that he is of a perfectly pure family, not stained with homicide or any similar impiety in his own person, and also that his father and mother have led a similar unstained life. Now the laws about all divine things should be brought from Delphi, and interpreters appointed, under whose direction they should be used. The tenure of the priesthood should always be for a year and no longer; and he who will duly execute the sacred office, according to the laws of religion, must be not less than sixty years of age—the laws shall be the same about priestesses. (*Laws* 759 a-d)

This passage by Plato echoes the rules for priesthood in Lev 21:1-24. Purity of physical integrity (vv. 18-20) as well as purity of bloodline (v. 7) were necessary in the Bible, as in Plato's *Laws*. Priesthood is only hereditary in the Bible, which explains how the descendants of Aaron inherit it. However, Plato explains that a newly founded colony will not have a bloodline of priests, which will thus have to be created.

The Land Cannot be Sold

Leviticus instigates the Jubilee, wherein every fifty years all land returns to the family of its original owner. An owner may lease out land for several years until the Jubilee, when everybody returns to one's own property. That concept, based on the sabbatical economy, is not found in Plato, but the very idea that the lots of land cannot be sold is:

> The land shall not be sold in perpetuity, for the land is mine; with me you are but aliens and tenants. Throughout the land that you hold, you shall provide for the redemption of the land. If anyone of your kin falls into difficulty and sells a piece of property, then the next-of-kin shall come and redeem what the relative has sold. (Lev 25:23)

> Best of men, cease not to honour according to nature similarity and equality and sameness and agreement, as regards number and every good and noble quality. And, above all, observe the aforesaid number 5040 throughout life; in the second place, do not disparage the small and modest proportions of the inheritances which you received in the distribution, by buying and selling them to one another. For then neither will the God who gave you the lot be your friend, nor will the legislator; and indeed the law declares to the disobedient that these are the terms upon which he may or may not take the lot. In the first place, the earth as he is informed is sacred to the Gods; and in the next place, priests and priestesses will offer up prayers over a first, and second, and even a third sacrifice, that he who buys or sells the houses or lands which he has received, may suffer the punishment which he deserves; and these their prayers they shall write down in the temples, on tablets of cypress-wood, for the instruction of posterity. (*Laws* 741 b-c)

Foreign Slaves[2]

> The slave is a troublesome piece of goods, as has been often shown by the frequent revolts of the Messenians, and the great mischiefs which happen in states having many slaves who speak the same language, and the numerous robberies and lawless life of the Italian banditti, as they are called. A man who considers all this is fairly at a loss. Two remedies alone remain to us, —not to have the slaves of the same country, nor if possible, speaking the same language; in this way they will more easily be held in subjection: secondly, we should tend them carefully, not only out of regard to them, but yet more out of respect to ourselves. And the right treatment of slaves is to behave properly to them, and to do to them, if possible, even more justice than to those who are our equals; for he who naturally and genuinely reverences justice, and hates injustice, is discovered in his dealings with any class of men to whom he can easily

2. See Eusebius, *P.E.* XII, 37.

be unjust. And he who in regard to the natures and actions of his slaves is undefiled by impiety and injustice, will best sow the seeds of virtue in them; and this may be truly said of every master, and tyrant, and of every other having authority in relation to his inferiors. Slaves ought to be punished as they deserve, and not admonished as if they were freemen, which will only make them conceited. (*Laws* 777 b-d)

In Lev 25:39-47, it is said that an impoverished Israelite man may sell himself as a slave; but he will only do so for not more than seven years. He shall not be treated with harshness (Lev 25:43 and 47). Permanent slaves shall be taken among the nations living in Canaan (Lev 25:44). In both the Bible and Plato, slaves were to be taken from foreign populations, and were not to be treated with harshness. However, a master was allowed to kill a slave without being charged with murder (Exod 21:20-21 // *Laws* 865 c-d). One may think that, because Exodus and Leviticus contradict each other on slavery, they are therefore by different authors, but an identical 'contradiction' is also found in Plato.

Most of the laws governing religion and purity from Leviticus do not appear in Plato's *Laws*. Still, the last chapters (from Lev 18 to 25) to some extent show similarities regarding sexuality, priesthood, strangers, possession of land and slavery.

4.

Numbers

The whole book of Numbers emphasises one particular number: twelve. In the first chapter, God tells Moses to take a census of the twelve tribes of Israel, and the author gives us a catalogue of every paternal clan of each tribe. In ch. 2, their marching order is detailed. The sanctuary remains at the centre with the tribe of Levi; to the east—Judah, Issachar and Zebulun, to the south—Reuben, Simeon and Gad, to the west—Ephraim, Manasseh and Benjamin (all descendants of Rachel), and to the north—Dan, Asher and Naphthali. In ch. 7, the sanctuary is inaugurated and the tribal princes make similar offerings to God. The details of every prince's offering are all the same and each is repeated twelve times, making that chapter one of the longest in the Bible. In this first part of Numbers, the perfect balance of Israel's twelve tribes, which are all equal in the eyes of God, connotes a state of harmony. But in ch. 11, God's patience is exceeded by the dramatic episode of the quails, as are the reader's expectations. In ch. 13, Moses sends twelve spies—one per tribe—to explore the land of Canaan. They come back with terrible news, claiming that the country is filled with giants and will be impossible to conquer. The Israelite people are disappointed and wish that they had stayed in Egypt. God, in anger, decides that as the spies took forty days to visit the land, Israel will remain in the desert for forty years. More-over, none of those who fled Egypt will enter the Promised Land because they doubted God's word (except Joshua and Caleb). Out of the six hundred thousand Israelites that left Egypt, only two of them entered Canaan: Joshua and Caleb—the spies from the tribes of Joseph and Judah that believed that the land could be conquered. Everyone else perished in the desert—it was only their descendants under Joshua's rule that eventually conquered Canaan. It is from this drama, often forgotten by modern criticism, that Jacques Cazeaux understands the Bible to be an anti-epic that undermines any form of national exaltation. Israel failed in the desert to realize God's plan, and each new generation received a chance to redeem their fathers' faults, but in vain.

The Spies

While they were in this state of mind, the Indians that Cyrus had sent as spies to the enemy's camp returned with the report that Croesus had been chosen field-marshal and commander-in-chief of all the enemy's hosts, that all the allied kings had decided to join him with their entire forces, to contribute vast sums of money, and to expend them in hiring what soldiers they could and in giving presents to those whom they were under obligations to reward. They reported also that many Thracian swordsmen had already been hired and that Egyptians were under sail to join them, and they gave the number as one hundred and twenty thousand men armed with shields that came to their feet, with huge spears, such as they carry even to this day, and with sabres. Besides these, there was also the Cyprian army. The Cilicians were all present already, they said, as were also the contingents from both Phrygias, Lycaonia, Paphlagonia, Cappadocia, Arabia, and Phoenicia; the Assyrians were there under the king of Babylon; the Ionians also and the Aeolians and almost all the Greek colonists in Asia had been compelled to join Croesus, and Croesus had even sent to Lacedaemon to negotiate an alliance. This army, they said, was being mustered at the River Pactolus, but it was their intention to advance to Thymbrara, where even today is the rendezvous of the king's barbarians from the interior. And a general call had been issued to bring provisions to market there. The prisoners also told practically the same story as the Indian spies; for this was another thing that Cyrus always looked out for—that prisoners should be taken, from whom he was likely to gain some intelligence. And he used also to send out spies disguised as slaves to pretend that they were deserters from him. When Cyrus' army heard this report, they were disturbed, as was natural; they went about more subdued than had been their wont, they gathered in groups, and every corner was full of people discussing the situation and asking one another's opinion. When Cyrus perceived that a panic was spreading through his army, he called together the officers of the different divisions and all others whose despondency he thought might cause injury and whose enthusiasm would be a help. And he sent word to his aides-de-camp that if any one else of the armed soldiers wished to attend the meeting and listen to the speeches, they should not hinder him. And when they had come together, he addressed them as follows: 'Friends and allies, I have called you together because I observed that when this news came from the enemy, some of you looked as if you were frightened. Now it seems strange to me that any of you should really be afraid because the enemy are mustering; but when you see that we are mustered in much larger numbers than we had when we defeated them and that we are now,

thank heaven, much better equipped than we were then—it is strange that
when you see this you are not filled with courage! (Xenophon, *Cyropaedia*
VI, 2, 9-13)

This passage echoes Num 13:26-33, as the spies sent by Moses come
back with terrible news that discourages the people. Xenophon's
Cyropaedia appears to be a minor source for biblical narratives. It ends
with the scene of Cyrus on his deathbed, which was used for the scene of
Jacob in Genesis 49. Here, Cyrus sends spies into Syria and Lydia. They
come back with news that scares the soldiers, but Cyrus and one of his
generals convince them not to be afraid. The use of Xenophon as a
source is not due to chance, as he, like Plato, was a disciple of Socrates.
Cyrus is called a great king (*Laws* 695 e), and Xenophon portrays him as
the portrait of the philosopher king that Socrates had imagined. It is
likely, then, that the biblical writer used this portrayal as inspiration for
Jacob and Moses, who, though not kings, were leaders of the people.
Plato's *Laws* remain the blueprint that runs through the book of Numbers. For Jacques Cazeaux, the Israel of twelve tribes is better than the
Israel of the royal period. The first chapters of Numbers emphasise
Israel's unity, realised through the twelve tribes that act as one, each
prince making the same offering.[1]

Cazeaux calls attention to the slowness of the text and the minutiae of
apparently gratuitous details that try the reader's patience. My analysis is
in accordance with Cazeaux's, as I believe that the strong political
thinking behind these chapters is the teaching of Plato. The best form of
government is not kingship, but the Ideal State. One must also keep in
mind that Cyrus will become a character of the Bible, freeing Jerusalem
from its Babylonian occupiers. Finally, we saw in Genesis how Joseph
accused his brothers of being spies searching for Egypt's weaknesses
(Gen 42:9). Joseph foretold the inverse of the events of Numbers, when
twelve actual spies were sent to explore Canaan—each a descendant of
the twelve sons of Israel that fled Egypt. Because of the pessimistic
reports of the ten spies, the people planned to go back to Egypt; this final
catastrophe will eventually happen in 2 Kings 25. The synchronic reading that Lévi-Strauss proposed for the myths is quite applicable to the
Bible; there is a diachronic order, but at any time one either recalls the
beginning or anticipates the end.

1. Jacques Cazeaux, 'Le dieu d'Israël, gardien de la fraternité', in *La Cité biblique*, ed. Shmuel Trigano, Pardès 40-41, Paris: In Press Editions, 2006, 40-69 (57).

The Sedition of Korah

After these events, a Levite named Korah whips up support to become the new leader of Israel. Moses proposes to test whether he has been sent by God to be their leader or not:

> As soon as he finished speaking all these words, the ground under them was split apart. The earth opened its mouth and swallowed them up, along with their households—everyone who belonged to Korah and all their goods. So they with all that belonged to them went down alive into Sheol; the earth closed over them, and they perished from the midst of the assembly. All Israel around them fled at their outcry, for they said, 'The earth will swallow us too!' And fire came out from the Lord and consumed the two hundred and fifty men offering the incense. (Num 16:31-33)

> Amphiaraus fled beside the river Ismenus, and before Periclymenus could wound him in the back, Zeus cleft the earth by throwing a thunderbolt, and Amphiaraus vanished with his chariot and his charioteer Baton, or, as some say, Elato; and Zeus made him immortal. (Apollodorus, *Library* 3, 6, 8; see also Euripides, *Suppliants* 927; Sophocles, *Electra* 865; Pindar, *Nemean* IX, 24-26)

> Next, after what relates to the Gods, follows what relates to the dissolution of the state: Whoever by permitting a man to power enslaves the laws, and subjects the city to factions, using violence and stirring up sedition contrary to law, him we will deem the greatest enemy of the whole state... Every man who is worth anything will inform the magistrates, and bring the conspirator to trial for making a violent and illegal attempt to change the government. The judges of such cases shall be the same as of the robbers of temples; and let the whole proceeding be carried on in the same way, and the vote of the majority condemn to death. But let there be a general rule, that the disgrace and punishment of the father is not to be visited on the children, except in the case of some one whose father, grandfather, and great-grandfather have successively undergone the penalty of death. (Plato, *Laws* 856 b-c)

Here, the biblical writer combined the story of Amphiaraus' live descent into the netherworld with Plato's law against sedition. We will find the last sentence of this law further on in Deuteronomy.

Moses and Edom / Cambyses and the Arabs

> Moses sent messengers from Kadesh to the king of Edom, 'Thus says your brother Israel: ...let us pass through your land. We will not pass through field or vineyard, or drink water from any well; we will go along the King's Highway, not turning aside to the right hand or to the left until

we have passed through your territory'. But Edom said to him, 'You shall not pass through, or we will come out with the sword against you'. The Israelites said to him, 'We will stay on the highway; and if we drink of your water, we and our livestock, then we will pay for it. It is only a small matter; just let us pass through on foot'. But he said, 'You shall not pass through'. And Edom came out against them with a large force, heavily armed. Thus Edom refused to give Israel passage through their territory; so Israel turned away from them. (Num 20:14-21)

So when Cambyses had made his resolve to march upon Egypt, and was in difficulty about the march, as to how he should get safely through the waterless region, this man came to him and besides informing of the other matters of Amasis, he instructed him also as to the march, advising him to send to the king of the Arabians and ask that he would give him safety of passage through this region. (Herodotus III, 4)

It was the Persians who thus prepared this approach to Egypt, furnishing it with water in the manner which has been said, from the time when they first took possession of Egypt: but at the time of which I speak, seeing that water was not yet provided, Cambyses, in accordance with what he was told by his Halicarnassian guest, sent envoys to the Arabian king and from him asked and obtained the safe passage, having given him pledges of friendship and received them from him in return. (Herodotus III, 7)

The next lines of Herodotus speak about the hairstyle of the Arabs, which is forbidden in Leviticus, as seen above. Here, the sequence is reversed: as Cambyses' army marches from 'Syria of Palestine' to Egypt, the Arabs grant him passage and access to water; in contrast, the Edomites refused access to Moses and his people, on their way from Egypt to Palestine. The process of borrowing is coherent—the story of the spies is taken from Cyrus' campaign in Xenophon, while here the theme is applied to the campaign of Cyrus' son Cambyses in Herodotus. These borrowings obey a simple logic—Israel is now an army marching to conquer a land. In these same chapters of Herodotus, Wesselius[2] noticed a very accurate 'fingerprint', the detail of the three-day journey:

Now by this way only is there a known entrance to Egypt: for from Phoenicia to the borders of the city of Cadytis belongs to the Syrians who are called of Palestine, and from Cadytis, which is a city I suppose not much less than Sardis, from this city the trading stations on the sea-coast as far as the city of Ienysos belong to the king of Arabia, and then from Ienysos again the country belongs to the Syrians as far as the Serbonian lake, along the side of which Mount Casion extends towards the Sea. After that, from the Serbonian lake, in which the story goes that Typhon

2. Wesselius, *The Origin of the History of Israel*, 93.

is concealed, from this point onwards the land is Egypt. Now the region which lies between the city of Ienysos on the one hand and Mount Casion and the Serbonian lake on the other, which is of no small extent but as much as a three days' journey, is grievously destitute of water. (Herodotus III, 5)

Then Moses ordered Israel to set out from the Red Sea, and they went into the wilderness of Shur. They went for three days in the wilderness and found no water. (Exod 15:22)

Nehoushtan

As the Israelites complained again in the wilderness, God sent them poisonous serpents that bit the people (Num 21:4-6). Such a theme is also found in the *Argonautica*. The Argonauts are lost in the desert of Libya, where Mopsos treads upon a poisonous snake and dies (Apollonius of Rhodes, *Argonautica* IV 1518-28).

Note Num 21:8-9, which reads:

And the Lord said to Moses, 'Make a poisonous serpent, and set it on a pole; and everyone who is bitten shall look at it and live'. So Moses made a serpent of bronze, and put it upon a pole; and whenever a serpent bit someone, that person would look at the serpent of bronze and live.

Ovid tells of the metamorphosis of Aesculapus, the son of Apollo, god of medicine. The Romans were infested by a plague and sought Apollo's aid, but instead Aesculapus addressed the Roman king in his dreams:

Forget your fears; for I will come to you, and leave my altar. But now look well at the serpent with its binding folds entwined around this staff, and accurately mark it with your eyes that you may recognize it. I will transform myself into this shape but of a greater size, I will appear enlarged and of a magnitude to which a heavenly being ought to be transformed. (Ovid, *Metam.* XV, 650-60)

Aesculapus' staff still remains the symbol of modern pharmacies and is often confused with Hermes' Caduceus—which features two intertwined snakes. It seems that Ovid followed a tradition that the mere sight of Aesculapus' staff could heal.

Balaam's Donkey / Achilles' Horses

The Moabite King Balak, son of Zippor, is afraid of the damage that Israel wrought upon the Canaanites by defeating King Og of Bashan. Balak asks the great prophet Balaam to curse Israel. Balaam is a character also known from the Deir 'Alla inscription dated to the eighth century B.C.E.[3] Though this shows that the biblical writer used a famous character from the Near Eastern tradition, he portrayed Balaam as a fool using techniques borrowed from Greek literature:

> God's anger was kindled because he was going, and the angel of the Lord took his stand in the road as his adversary. Now he was riding on the donkey, and his two servants were with him. The donkey saw the angel of the Lord standing in the road, with a drawn sword in his hand; so the donkey turned off the road, and went into the field; and Balaam struck the donkey, to turn it back on to the road. Then the angel of the Lord stood in a narrow path between the vineyards, with a wall on either side. When the donkey saw the angel of the Lord, it scraped against the wall, and scraped Balaam's foot against the wall; so he struck it again. Then the angel of the Lord went ahead, and stood in a narrow place, where there was no way to turn either to the right or to the left. When the donkey saw the angel of the Lord, it lay down under Balaam; and Balaam's anger was kindled, and he struck the donkey with his staff. Then the Lord opened the mouth of the donkey, and it said to Balaam, 'What have I done to you, that you have struck me these three times?' Balaam said to the donkey, 'Because you have made a fool of me! I wish I had a sword in my hand! I would kill you right now!' But the donkey said to Balaam, 'Am I not your donkey, which you have ridden all your life to this day? Have I been in the habit of treating you in this way?' And he said, 'No'. (Num 22:22-30)

In the *Iliad*, Achilles withdrew his men from the war against Troy as a result of his quarrel with Agamemnon. But when his best friend Patroclus is killed, Achilles decides to avenge him and harnesses his horses. Patroclus had borrowed Achilles' horses and weapons, yet never came back alive. In his anger and sorrow, Achilles talks to his horses:

> Then with a loud voice he chided with his father's horses saying, 'Xanthus and Balius, famed offspring of Podarge—this time when we have done fighting be sure and bring your driver safely back to the host of the Achaeans, and do not leave him dead on the plain as you did Patroclus.' Then fleet Xanthus answered under the yoke—for white-armed Hera had endowed him with human speech—and he bowed his head till his mane touched the ground as it hung down from under the yoke-band. 'Dread Achilles', said he, 'we will indeed save you now, but the day of your death is near, and the blame will not be ours, for it will be heaven and stern fate that will destroy you. Neither was it through any sloth or slackness on our part that the Trojans stripped Patroclus of his armour; it was the mighty god whom lovely Leto bore that slew him as he fought among the foremost, and vouchsafed a triumph to Hector. We two can fly as swiftly as Zephyrus who they say is fleetest of all winds; nevertheless it is your doom to fall by the hand of a man and of a god.' When he had thus said the Erinyes stayed his speech. (Homer, *Il.* XIX, 400-20)

---

3. Thompson, *The Mythic Past*, 11.

Book XIX of the *Iliad* tells the story of the birth of Heracles and Eurystheus, which we analysed earlier from Genesis. Many scholars have noticed the parallel with Balaam's donkey,[4] and I believe that there are some other passages from the *Iliad* that demonstrate that this is not due to chance:

> Or as some lazy ass that has had many a cudgel broken about his back, when he into a field begins eating the corn—boys beat him but he is too many for them, and though they lay about with their sticks they cannot hurt him; still when he has had his fill they at last drive him from the field—even so did the Trojans and their allies pursue great Ajax, ever smiting the middle of his shield with their darts. (*Il.* XI, 560-65)

In the *Odyssey*, Athena appears to Ulysses and some dogs, but not to Telemachus; by comparison, the angel is not seen by Balaam, but rather by his donkey.

> Athena watched him well off the station, and then came up to it in the form of a woman—fair, stately, and wise. She stood against the side of the entry, and revealed herself to Ulysses, but Telemachus could not see her, and knew not that she was there, for the gods do not let themselves be seen by everybody. Ulysses saw her, and so did the dogs, for they did not bark, but went scared and whining off to the other side of the yards. (*Od.* XVI, 162)

Also, note the description of Achilles' shield wrought by Hephaestus (as per Kupitz):

> He wrought also a vineyard, golden and fair to see, and the vines were loaded with grapes. The bunches overhead were black, but the vines were trained on poles of silver. He ran a ditch of dark metal all round it, and fenced it with a fence of tin; there was only one path to it, and by this the vintagers went when they would gather the vintage. (*Il.* XVIII, 560-70)

> Then the angel of the Lord stood in a narrow path between the vineyards, with a wall on either side. (Num 22:24)

The scene of Balaam's donkey seems to be a crafty mixture of certain Homeric passages: that of Achilles' horses answering him, the stubborn donkey, Athena being seen by the dogs, and an alley with a fence in the vineyard. Balaam is asked by King Balak to curse Israel, but contrary to Balak's wishes, Balaam is instead inspired by God and blesses Israel (Num 23–24). These scenes (as well as the one with the donkey) are rather comical. They are reminiscent of Aristophanes' *The Peace*, in

---

4. Krenkel, *Biblische Parallelen zu Homeros*, 1888, reported by M.L. West, *The East Face of Helicon*, 428.

which Trygeus asks the son of Lamachos to sing odes to peace, but every time he instead sings Homeric war scenes, irritating Trygeus. After his third blessing upon Israel, Balaam foretells the distant future about a star that is to arise from Jacob, destined to smash Moab and Edom:

> But ships shall come from Kittim and shall afflict Asshur and Eber; and he also shall perish for ever. (Num 24:24)

Eber is a descendant of Shem and the ancestor of the Hebrews (Gen 10:21). Note that in the Bible, 'Hebrews' is a word used by the Egyptians and the Philistines to speak of the Israelites, but according to Genesis, the word encompasses more than just Israelites and is perhaps better equated with the Semites. Balaam's prophecy is clear: a fleet will invade the Near East that comes from Kittim, the capital of Cyprus. In 1 Macc 1:1, Alexander the Great was said to have departed from Kittim. Of course, this later book may have wanted to reference Balaam's prophecy, but how would the writer of Numbers have known such a thing? Was he, like his character Balaam, able to see the future? Noah's prophecy foretells that the descendants of Japhet will dwell in the country of the Semites (Gen 9:27).

Balaam's prophecy completes Noah's and makes it more accurate: by 'Japhet', the biblical writer meant the Greek branch through his son Ion (Yavan) and Ion's son, Kittim. If one does not believe in the possibility of prophecy, then it must be admitted that these books were written after the events they describe, exactly like the book of Daniel. From these prophecies in Genesis and Numbers we can determine a *terminus a quo* for the writing of the Bible—the beginning of the Hellenistic era—the *terminus ad quem* being the first Dead Sea scrolls. The Bible does not conceal when it was written, nor does it hide the fact that it was inspired by Greek sources, as it leaves allusions everywhere pointing to them.

Phineus and the Lemnian Women

In the epic of the Argonauts there is a blind seer named Phineus who tells the Argonauts the future. In book I of the *Argonautica*, the Argonauts arrive on the island of Lemnos where the women had killed their husbands and male children because their husbands cheated on them with captive women. Seeing the Argonauts, the women decided to seduce them in order that Lemnos may be repopulated. Almost all of them were seduced, and after a feast dedicated to Aphrodite, they slept with the Lemnian women. Heracles and a few other men stayed on the Argo, and he became angry with his companions who were seduced. Heracles made a speech to the Argonauts to shame them, as their goal was to seek out a

treasure—the Golden Fleece. They left the Lemnian women behind and
set sail towards their goal. Offspring were born of this union, including
Battos, descendant of Euphemos, our 'Greek Moses':

> The son of Aison set off for the palace of Hypsipyle and all the others
> went where chance led them, with the exception of Heracles. From his
> own choice he remained by the ship, together with a few comrades who
> stayed away from the merry-making. Soon the city was full of joyful
> dancing and the rich smoke of feasting; in their hymns and sacrifices they
> paid honour above all other immortals to the glorious son of Hera and to
> Cypris herself. The sailing was now continually deferred from one day to
> the next. They would have wasted a great deal of time remaining there,
> had not Heracles summoned his comrades together, without the women,
> and reproached them as follows: 'Poor fools, does the shedding of kin-
> dred blood prevent us from returning home? Have we left our homes to
> come here in search of brides, scorning the women of our cities? Do we
> want to live here and cut up the rich ploughland of Lemnos? We will not
> win glory shut up here interminably with foreign women. No god is going
> to hand over the fleece to us in answer to our prayers; we will have to
> work for it. Let us all return to our own countries and leave him to
> wallow all day in Hypsipyle's bed until he has won great renown by fill-
> ing Lemnos with his sons!' So did Heracles upbraid the crew. None dared
> look up to meet his gaze or say anything in answer to him, but without
> discussion the meeting broke up and speedily they made preparations for
> departure. (Apollonius of Rhodes, *Argonautica* I, 845-75)

This passage from the *Argonautica* can be likened to the episode of the
Israelites in Shittim. The men slept with Moabite women and worshipped
their god Baal-Peor. Moses received the order by God to kill the guilty
ones. As an Israelite came before the tent with his Midianite lover,
Phineas, son of Eleazaz, son of Aaron, pierced them both with a spear.
For his zeal, Phineas was granted priesthood for him and his offspring
(Num 25:1-13). Here it seems that we are confronted with a more
dramatic version of the Argonauts' Lemnos episode, as both Israel and
the Argonauts are on a quest—either for the law and the Promised Land,
or for the Golden Fleece. Since we saw the importance of the descendants of Euphemos and his Lemnian lover, it can be concluded here that
Phineas takes on the role of Heracles. He refuses to participate in what is
allusively referred to as an orgy and kills a couple to make an example of
them, for which he receives the promise of perpetual priesthood (Num
25:13). Moreover, his name—although from an Egyptian root—can be
associated with the name of the seer Phineus, appearing in the *Argonautica*. The theme of the slaying of lovers does not appear after the
Lemnian women slept with the Argonauts, but before, when they killed
their husbands who lay sleeping with captive lovers:

They destroyed not only their husbands together with their slave-girls in their beds, but also the entire male population with them, so that there could be no requital in the future of the awful murder. (*Argonautica* I, 613-14)

The Cadastre of the Twelve Tribes[5]

Finally in Numbers we come to the most significant parallel with Plato's Ideal State of the *Laws*: the twelve tribes. Moses took a census of them for the first time in ch. 1, and again in ch. 26, after a generation has passed:

This was the number of the Israelites enrolled: six hundred and one thousand seven hundred and thirty. The Lord spoke to Moses, saying: To these the land shall be apportioned for inheritance according to the number of names. To a large tribe you shall give a large inheritance, and to a small tribe you shall give a small inheritance; every tribe shall be given its inheritance according to its enrollment. But the land shall be apportioned by lot; according to the names of their ancestral tribes they shall inherit. Their inheritance shall be apportioned according to lot between the larger and the smaller. (Num 26:51-56)

Then we will divide the city into twelve portions, first founding temples to Hestia, to Zeus and to Athena, in a spot which we will call the Acropolis, and surround with a circular wall, making the division of the entire city and country radiate from this point. The twelve portions shall be equalized by the provision that those which are of good land shall be smaller, while those of inferior quality shall be larger. The number of the lots shall be 5040, and each of them shall be divided into two, and every allotment shall be composed of two such sections; one of land near the city, the other of land which is at a distance. This arrangement shall be carried out in the following manner: The section which is near the city shall be added to that which is on the borders, and form one lot, and the portion which is next nearest shall be added to the portion which is next farthest; and so of the rest. Moreover, in the two sections of the lots the same principle of equalization of the soil ought to be maintained; the badness and goodness shall be compensated by more and less. And the legislator shall divide the citizens into twelve parts, and arrange the rest of their property, as far as possible, so as to form twelve equal parts; and there shall be a registration of all. After this they shall assign twelve lots to twelve Gods, and call them by their names, and dedicate to each God their several portions, and call the tribes after them. And they shall distribute the twelve divisions of the city in the same way in which they divided the country; and every man shall have two habitations, one in the centre of the country, and the other at the extremity. (*Laws* 745 b-c)

5.   Eusebius, *P.E.* XII, 47.

Right after these lines, the Athenian says that double residence is quite impossible to achieve, and the legislator will only have to adapt the law at its best (*Laws* 746 a-d). The cadastre of biblical Israel is the simplified version of Plato's unrealistic utopia (see Ezek 47–48, however, for a 'vision' of such a plan). The biblical writer only retained the idea of the lots of land that were distributed amongst the twelve tribes by lottery. We saw in Leviticus, as in Plato, that these lots cannot be sold. The number of 5040 lots is not found in the Bible, and in fact the number of lots that were drawn is unknown. In the same manner that the catalogue of the sanctuary's furniture was duplicated in order to show a crafts-man's imitation of a divine model, here the doubled catalogue of Israel's tribes and paternal families is meant to give consistency to the Ideal State that will eventually be achieved by Joshua. Joshua will execute the plan that God gave to Moses, as Bezalel did. In both cases, this dialectic of imitation reflects the literary technique of the biblical writer, who himself imitates a platonic model. According to Kupitz, the Hebrew word *goral*, meaning 'lot', derives from the Greek word used by Plato, *kleros*. The Greek letter *kappa* becomes the Hebrew letter *gimel*, while the 'r' and the 'l' switch by common metathesis.[6] In both texts, the word 'lot' not only means 'a piece of land' but refers as well to the operation of choosing by chance. Plato refers to the distribution of land by lottery as a typical Spartan practice (*Laws* 648 d-e). He did not innovate, but fixed the number of tribes at twelve. In the Bible, the twelve tribes have the most important role. From Genesis to Kings, Israel changes form from one man with twelve sons to a kingdom divided into twelve tribes.

The Daughters of Zelophehad / The Epiclerate

In Numbers 27, the daughters of Zelopehad, from the tribe of Manasseh, son of Joseph, complain to Moses about the patrilinear law of inheritance from Numbers 26. As their father died leaving only five daughters, their part of the land of Israel shall be lost. Moses pleads the daughters' cause to God, and God answers through Moses that a daughter will be allowed to inherit from her father only if he had no sons (Num 27:1-11). But at the end of Numbers, the men of the tribe of Manasseh complain in turn that the lots of land of the daughters of Zelophehad will be lost to the tribe as the women will marry men from other tribes of Israel. Moses changes the law again and allows daughters to inherit from their sonless fathers only if they marry men from their paternal tribe (Num 36:1-12).

6. Kupitz, 'La Bible est-elle un plagiat?'.

This story is meant to draw attention to the inheritance of a clan of the tribe of Joseph. Cazeaux notices that it is very coherent with the end of Genesis because as Joseph's brothers meant to kill him, he may have been excluded from this partition. Moreover, it is mentioned that the sons of Makir (son of Manasseh), Zelophehad's ancestor, were born on Joseph's knees (Gen 50:23). Here, the end of Numbers also shows concern with Joseph's inheritance. This is an interesting case of how a law of Plato is introduced using characters. Plato explained that laws should be accompanied by preambles (*Laws* 738 b-c), so the biblical writer, rather than just giving us the law, added the story of the daughters of Zelophehad to illustrate it.

Note *Laws* 924 c-e, which reads:

> And if a man dying by some unexpected fate leaves daughters behind him, let him pardon the legislator if when he gives them in marriage, he have a regard only to two out of three conditions—nearness of kin and the preservation of the lot, and omits the third condition, which a father would naturally consider, for he would choose out of all the citizens a son for himself, and a husband for his daughter, with a view to his character and disposition—the father, I say, shall forgive the legislator if he disregards this, which to him is an impossible consideration. Let the law about these matters where practicable be as follows: If a man dies without making a will, and leaves behind him daughters, let his brother, being the son of the same father or of the same mother, having no lot, marry the daughter and have the lot of the dead man. And if he have no brother, but only a brother's son, in like manner let them marry, if they be of a suitable age; and if there be not even a brother's son, but only the son of a sister, let them do likewise, and so in the fourth degree, if there be only the testator's father's brother, or in the fifth degree, his father's brother's son, or in the sixth degree, the child of his father's sister. Let kindred be always reckoned in this way: if a person leaves daughters the relationship shall proceed upwards through brothers and sisters, and brothers' and sisters' children, and first the males shall come, and after them the females in the same family.

Plato's law favours the paternal side but permits a daughter to marry a man from the maternal side, whereas the biblical law does not. This law of inheritance was widespread in Greece and was called epiclerate in Athenian legislation (the daughter being *epikleros*, meaning 'on the lot'). It is in fact a general law in patriarchal societies.

However, only in Plato and the Bible is this law associated explicitly with a system of twelve lots given to twelve tribes by lottery, a cadastre that is meant to remain the same eternally. Moreover, there seem to have been differences between Spartan, Cretan and Athenian legislation. In Sparta the daughter was not called *epikleros* but *patroukhos*, meaning that she owned the land of her father, while in Gortyne a daughter was known as *patroiokos*. Biblical law seems to follow Athenian law more closely than the others, insofar as a daughter may only transmit the rights to her land—she may never possess land.[7]

7. Françoise Ruzé, 'Lycurgue de Sparte et ses collègues', in Sineux, ed., *Le législateur et la loi dans l'Antiquité*, 151-60; Claude Brixhe and Monique Bile, 'La circulation des biens dans les Lois de Gortyne', in Dobias-Lalou, ed., *Des dialectes grecs*, 75-116.

5.

Deuteronomy

Biblical scholarship calls chs. 12 to 26 'the Deuteronomic Code'; supposedly written under Josiah's reign,[1] this part was meant to replace the supposedly older 'Covenant Code' from Exodus 20–23. I believe this paradigm to be completely obsolete, especially when comparing the Bible to Plato's *Laws*.

Centralisation of the Cult

These are the statutes and ordinances that you must diligently observe in the land that the Lord, the God of your ancestors, has given you to occupy all the days that you live on the earth. You must demolish completely all the places where the nations whom you are about to dispossess served their gods, on the mountain heights, on the hills, and under every leafy tree. Break down their altars, smash their pillars, burn their sacred poles with fire, and hew down the idols of their gods, and thus blot out their name from their places. You shall not worship the Lord your God in such ways. But you shall seek the place that the Lord your God will choose out of all your tribes as his habitation to put his name there. You shall go there, bringing there your burnt offerings and your sacrifices, your tithes and your donations, your votive gifts, your freewill-offerings, and the firstlings of your herds and flocks. And you shall eat there in the presence of the Lord your God, you and your households together, rejoicing in all the undertakings in which the Lord your God has blessed you. You shall not act as we are acting here today, all of us according to our own desires, for you have not yet come into the rest and the possession that the Lord your God is giving you. When you cross over the Jordan and live in the land that the Lord your God is allotting to you, and when he gives you rest from your enemies all around so that you live in safety, then you shall bring everything that I command you to the place that the Lord your God will choose as a dwelling for his name: your burnt-offerings and your sacrifices, your tithes and your donations, and all your choice votive

1. Noth, *The Deuteronomistic History*.

gifts that you vow to the Lord. And you shall rejoice before the Lord your God, you together with your sons and your daughters, your male and female slaves, and the Levites who reside in your towns (since they have no allotment or inheritance with you). Take care that you do not offer your burnt offerings at any place you happen to see. But only at the place that the Lord will choose in one of your tribes—there you shall offer your burnt-offerings and there you shall do everything I command you. (Deut 12:1-14)

In all these cases there should be one law, which will make men in general less liable to transgress in word or deed, and less foolish, because they will not be allowed to practise religious rites contrary to law. And let this be the simple form of the law: No man shall have sacred rites in a private house. When he would sacrifice, let him go to the temples and hand over his offerings to the priests and priestesses, who see to the sanctity of such things, and let him pray himself, and let any one who pleases join with him in prayer. The reason of this is as follows: Gods and temples are not easily instituted, and to establish them rightly is the work of a mighty intellect. And women especially, and men too, when they are sick or in danger, or in any sort of difficulty, or again on their receiving any good fortune, have a way of consecrating the occasion, vowing sacrifices, and promising shrines to Gods, demigods, and sons of Gods; and when they are awakened by terrible apparitions and dreams or remember visions, they find in altars and temples the remedies of them, and will fill every house and village with them, placing them in the open air, or wherever they may have had such visions; and with a view to all these cases we should obey the law. (*Laws* 909 d-10 a)

If there is found among you, in one of your towns that the Lord your God is giving you, a man or woman who does what is evil in the sight of the Lord your God, and transgresses his covenant by going to serve other gods and worshipping them—whether the sun or the moon or any of the host of heaven, which I have forbidden—and if it is reported to you or you hear of it, and you make a thorough inquiry, and the charge is proved true that such an abhorrent thing has occurred in Israel, then you shall bring out to your gates that man or that woman who has committed this crime and you shall stone the man or woman to death. On the evidence of two or three witnesses the death sentence shall be executed; a person must not be put to death on the evidence of only one witness. The hands of the witnesses shall be the first raised against the person to execute the death penalty, and afterwards the hands of all the people. So you shall purge the evil from your midst. (Deut 17:2-7)

No one shall possess shrines of the Gods in private houses, and he who is found to possess them, and perform any sacred rites not publicly authorised—supposing the offender to be some man or woman who is not guilty of any other great and impious crime—shall be informed against by him who is acquainted with the fact, which shall be announced by him to the guardians of the law; and let them issue orders that he or she shall carry away their private rites to the public temples, and if they do not persuade them, let them inflict a penalty on them until they comply. And if a person be proven guilty of impiety, not merely from childish levity, but such as grown-up men may be guilty of, whether he have sacrificed publicly or privately to any Gods, let him be punished with death, for his sacrifice is impure. Whether the deed has been done in earnest, or only from childish levity, let the guardians of the law determine, before they bring the matter into court and prosecute the offender for impiety. (*Laws* 910 b-c)

Both texts are very forthright about the centralisation of the cult. In Kings, it appears as a recurrent theme: although Solomon built the temple, he and the kings of Israel and Judah allowed the high places to remain, so that people offered sacrifices wherever they wished. Both documents maintain that an inquiry shall be raised if people are caught participating in an illegal cult, and they shall be put to death. Plato's law is similar to the story of Jacob erecting an altar in Bethel after he had the vision of the ladder (Gen 28:18). The place that God will choose is not yet named in Deuteronomy, but it is understood as Jerusalem.

The Moderate King

When you have come into the land that the Lord your God is giving you, and have taken possession of it and settled in it, and you say, 'I will set a king over me, like all the nations that are around me', you may indeed set over you a king whom the Lord your God will choose. One of your own community you may set as king over you; you are not permitted to put a foreigner over you, who is not of your own community. Even so, he must not acquire many horses for himself, or return the people to Egypt in order to acquire more horses, since the Lord has said to you, 'You must never return that way again'. And he must not acquire many wives for himself, or else his heart will turn away; also silver and gold he must not acquire in great quantity for himself. When he has taken the throne of his kingdom, he shall have a copy of this law written for him in the presence of the levitical priests. It shall remain with him and he shall read in it all the days of his life, so that he may learn to fear the Lord his God, diligently observing all the words of this law and these statutes, neither exalting himself above other members of the community nor turning aside from the commandment, either to the right or to the left, so that he and his descendants may reign long over his kingdom in Israel. (Deut 17:14-20)

'Come, legislator', we will say to him; 'what are the conditions which you require in a state before you can organize it?' How ought he to answer this question? Shall I give his answer? Cleinias: Yes. Athenian: He will say—'Give me a state which is governed by a tyrant, and let the tyrant be young and have a good memory; let him be quick at learning, and of a courageous and noble nature; let him have that quality which, as I said before, is the inseparable companion of all the other parts of virtue, if there is to be any good in them'. Cleinias: I suppose, Megillus, that this companion virtue of which the Stranger speaks, must be temperance? Athenian: Yes, Cleinias, temperance in the vulgar sense; not that which in the forced and exaggerated language of some philosophers is called prudence, but that which is the natural gift of children and animals, of whom some live continently and others incontinently, but when isolated, was, as we said, hardly worth reckoning in the catalogue of goods. I think that you must understand my meaning... Then our tyrant must have this as well as the other qualities, if the state is to acquire in the best manner and in the shortest time the form of government which is most conducive to happiness; for there neither is nor ever will be a better or speedier way of establishing a polity than by a tyranny. (*Laws* 709 e-10 b)

Tyranny may be the best way to force law's acceptance as a tyrant's power is total over his people—though temperance must be a tyrant's main quality. The constitution of Plato's State does not involve a king, but rather a person who is wise enough to abdicate in favour of the laws. Plato refers to his own experience in Sicily, where he had tried to sway both King Dionysius I and II in favour of his political ideas, without success. In the Bible, King Josiah portrays the wise king that helps promote the law (2 Kgs 22–23). All the qualities of the future king mentioned in Deuteronomy 17 refer to him, as he did find a copy of the law in the temple and made the people return to God. But unfortunately this was too late, as God had already decided to destroy Judah during the reign of Manasseh (2 Kgs 21). In the 'reproaches' to the future king we recognise King Solomon, whose excesses (including wives, riches and horses from Egypt, in 1 Kgs 11) were the cause of Israel's schism into two separate kingdoms. If scholars have deduced correctly that the same person who wrote Kings wrote Deuteronomy and the books in between, then I assert that the same author wrote all books from Genesis to Kings. It is circular reasoning to believe that Josiah himself had Deuteronomy written under his authority. Josiah is a biblical character, even though he existed, and he is meant to represent Plato's moderate tyrant. So was Solomon, but he failed to respect these biblical commandments. Had this perfect king come earlier, then Israel would have prevailed, but the author wanted to explain the reasons of its downfall, using Plato's *Critias*: the kings themselves were the cause of Israel's downfall for they gave up God's sacred laws.

Prohibition of Magic

When you come into the land that the Lord your God is giving you, you must not learn to imitate the abhorrent practices of those nations. No one shall be found among you who makes a son or daughter pass through fire, or who practises divination, or is a soothsayer, or an augur, or a sorcerer, or one who casts spells, or who consults ghosts or spirits, or who seeks oracles from the dead. For whoever does these things is abhorrent to the Lord; it is because of such abhorrent practices that the Lord your God is driving them out before you. You must remain completely loyal to the Lord your God. Although these nations that you are about to dispossess do give heed to soothsayers and diviners, as for you, the Lord your God does not permit you to do so. (Deut 18:9-14)

Let the law, then, run as follows about poisoning or witchcraft: He who employs poison to do any injury, not fatal, to a man himself, or to his servants, or any injury, whether fatal or not, to his cattle or his bees, if he be a physician, and be convicted of poisoning, shall be punished with death; or if he be a private person, the court shall determine what he is to pay or suffer. But he who seems to be the sort of man who injures others by magic knots, or enchantments, or incantations, or any of the like practices, if he be a prophet or diviner, let him die; and if, not being a prophet, he be convicted of witchcraft, as in the previous case, let the court fix what he ought to pay or suffer. (*Laws* 933 c-e)

Plato's law concerning magic is introduced by a long preamble. Both Plato and the Bible do not think of magic as a superstition; rather, they hold that it does work and must be prohibited. King Saul will transgress this law by asking the witch of En-Dor to invoke the spirit of Samuel (1 Sam 28). In book X, Plato offers a refutation of atheism. In Athens, some people did not believe in gods. This dialectic does not appear at all in the Bible, which only opposes worshippers of false gods to the worshippers of Yahweh.

A Judge Cannot Accept Gifts

You shall appoint judges and officials throughout your tribes, in all your towns that the Lord your God is giving you, and they shall render just decisions for the people. You must not distort justice; you must not show partiality; and you must not accept bribes, for a bribe blinds the eyes of the wise and subverts the cause of those who are in the right. Justice, and only justice, you shall pursue, so that you may live and occupy the land that the Lord your God is giving you. (Deut 16:18-20)

Those who serve their country ought to serve without receiving gifts, and there ought to be no excusing or approving the saying, 'Men should receive gifts as the reward of good, but not of evil deeds'; for to know which we are doing, and to stand fast by our knowledge, is no easy matter. The safest course is to obey the law which says, 'Do no service for a bribe', and let him who disobeys, if he be convicted, simply die. (*Laws* 955 c-d)

Involuntary Homicide

Now this is the case of a homicide who might flee there and live, that is, someone who has killed another person unintentionally when the two had not been at enmity before: Suppose someone goes into the forest with another to cut wood, and when one of them swings the axe to cut down a tree, the head slips from the handle and strikes the other person who then dies; the killer may flee to one of these cities and live. But if the distance is too great, the avenger of blood in hot anger might pursue and overtake and put the killer to death, although a death sentence was not deserved, since the two had not been at enmity before. (Deut 19:4-6)

Having begun to speak of homicide, let us endeavour to lay down laws concerning every different kind of homicide; and, first of all, concerning violent and involuntary homicides. If any one in an athletic contest, and at the public games, involuntarily kills a friend, and he dies either at the time or afterwards of the blows which he has received; or if the like misfortune happens to any one in war, or military exercises, or mimic contests of which the magistrates enjoin the practice, whether with or without arms, when he has been purified according to the law brought from Delphi relating to these matters, he shall be innocent. And so in the case of physicians: if their patient dies against their will, they shall be held guiltless by the law. And if one slay another with his own hand, but unintentionally, whether he be unarmed or have some instrument or dart in his hand; or if he kill him by administering food or drink, or by the application of fire or cold, or by suffocating him, whether he do the deed by his own hand, or by the agency of others, he shall be deemed the agent, and shall suffer one of the following penalties. (*Laws* 865 a-c)

In the Bible, exile for homicide does not result in exclusion from the land, but instead confinement in one of the six given cities of refuge—until the death of the high-priest in charge. In Num 35:22-28, these cities are meant to be a haven for an involuntary murderer to escape an avenger of blood (most likely the closest kinsman of the deceased). The cities of refuge seem to be an adaptation of the usual Greek exile as discussed in Plato. Book IX of Plato's *Laws* offers a coherent discussion about homicide, from involuntary to voluntary. The Bible chose to dismantle this progression of the laws on homicide by dispersing them throughout the biblical books:

If any one voluntarily obeys this law, the next of kin to the deceased, seeing all that has happened, shall take pity on him, and make peace with him, and show him all gentleness. But if any one is disobedient, and either ventures to go to any of the temples and sacrifice un-purified, or will not continue in exile during the appointed time, the next of kin to the deceased shall proceed against him for murder; and if he be convicted, every part of his punishment shall be doubled. (*Laws* 866 a-b)

Proportionality of Punishments

When a man does another any injury by theft or violence, for the greater injury let him pay greater damages to the injured man, and less for the smaller injury; but in all cases, whatever the injury may have been, as much as will compensate the loss. And besides the compensation of the wrong, let a man pay a further penalty for the chastisement of his offence: he who has done the wrong instigated by the folly of another, through the light-heartedness of youth or the like, shall pay a lighter penalty; but he who has injured another through his own folly, when overcome by pleasure or pain, in cowardly fear, or lust, or envy, or implacable anger, shall endure a heavier punishment. (*Laws* 933 e-34 a)

This can be related to the famous *lex talionis* which has its roots in the *Code of Hammurabi*. The biblical law (Exod 21:22-25; Lev 24:17-21; Deut 19:21) seems more violent than Plato's, but the Talmud (*Baba Kama* 83 b) explains that the *lex talionis* always referred to financial compensation.

Boundary Stones

Let us first of all, then, have a class of laws which shall be called the laws of husbandmen. And let the first of them be the law of Zeus, the God of boundaries. Let no one shift the boundary line either of a fellow-citizen who is a neighbour, or, if he dwells at the extremity of the land, of any stranger who is conterminous with him, considering that this is truly 'to move the immovable', and every one should be more willing to move the largest rock which is not a landmark, than the least stone which is the sworn mark of friendship and hatred between neighbours; for Zeus, the god of kindred, is the witness of the citizen, and Zeus, the god of strangers, of the stranger, and when aroused, terrible are the wars which they stir up. He who obeys the law will never know the fatal consequences of disobedience, but he who despises the law shall be liable to a double penalty, the first coming from the Gods, and the second from the law. For let no one wilfully remove the boundaries of his neighbour's land, and if any one does, let him who will inform the landowners, and let them bring him into court, and if he be convicted of re-dividing the land by stealth or by force, let the court determine what he ought to suffer or pay. (*Laws* 843 a-b)

You must not move your neighbour's boundary marker, set up by former generations, on the property that will be allotted to you in the land that the Lord your God is giving you to possess. (Deut 19:14)

That law comes immediately after the discussion on sexuality in book VIII of Plato's *Laws*, which I believe is the source for Leviticus 18. Deuteronomy seems to follow books X to XII of the *Laws*, but sometimes harkens back to previous books. In Deut 20:8 it is ordered that cowards shall not go to war; book XII of the *Laws* has a long speech about cowards who abandon their weapons on the battlefield.

False Witnesses

If a malicious witness comes forward to accuse someone of wrongdoing, then both parties to the dispute shall appear before the Lord, before the priests and the judges who are in office in those days, and the judges shall make a thorough inquiry. If the witness is a false witness, having testified falsely against another, then you shall do to the false witness just as the false witness had meant to do to the other. (Deut 19:16-19)

And either of the parties in a cause may bring an accusation of perjury against witnesses, touching their evidence in whole or in part, if he asserts that such evidence has been given; but the accusation must be brought previous to the final decision of the cause. The magistrates shall preserve the accusations of false witness, and have them kept under the seal of both parties, and produce them on the day when the trial for false witness takes place. If a man be twice convicted of false witness, he shall not be required, and if thrice, he shall not be allowed to bear witness; and if he dare to witness after he has been convicted three times, let any one who pleases inform against him to the magistrates, and let the magistrates hand him over to the court, and if he be convicted he shall be punished with death. (*Laws* 937 b-c)

Honesty of Merchants

You shall not have in your bag two kinds of weights, large and small. You shall not have in your house two kinds of measures, large and small. You shall have only a full and honest weight; you shall have only a full and honest measure, so that your days may be long in the land that the Lord your God is giving you. For all who do such things, all who act dishonestly, are abhorrent to the Lord your God. (Deut 25:13-16)

If a man exchanges either money for money, or anything whatever for anything else, either with or without life, let him give and receive them genuine and unadulterated, in accordance with the law... No one shall call the Gods to witness, when he says or does anything false or deceitful or dishonest, unless he would be the most hateful of mankind to them. And he is most hateful to them who takes a false oath, and pays no heed to the Gods; and in the next degree, he who tells a falsehood in the presence of his superiors… He who sells anything in the agora shall not ask two prices for that which he sells, but he shall ask one price, and if he do not obtain this, he shall take away his goods; and on that day he shall not value them either at more or less; and there shall be no praising of any goods, or oath taken about them. (*Laws* 916 d)

Discovery of a Corpse and an Unknown Murderer

If, in the land that the Lord your God is giving you to possess, a body is found lying in open country, and it is not known who struck the person down, then your elders and your judges shall come out to measure the distances to the towns that are near the body. The elders of the town nearest the body shall take a heifer that has never been worked, one that has not pulled in the yoke; the elders of that town shall bring the heifer down to a wadi with running water, which is neither ploughed nor sown, and shall break the heifer's neck there in the wadi. Then the priests, the sons of Levi, shall come forward, for the Lord your God has chosen them to minister to him and to pronounce blessings in the name of the Lord, and by their decision all cases of dispute and assault shall be settled. All the elders of that town nearest the body shall wash their hands over the heifer whose neck was broken in the wadi, and they shall declare: 'Our hands did not shed this blood, nor were we witnesses to it. Absolve, O Lord, your people Israel, whom you redeemed; do not let the guilt of innocent blood remain in the midst of your people Israel.' Then they will be absolved of bloodguilt. So you shall purge the guilt of innocent blood from your midst, because you must do what is right in the sight of the Lord. (Deut 21:1-9)

If a man is found dead, and his murderer be unknown, and after a diligent search cannot be detected, there shall be the same proclamation as in the previous cases, and the same interdict on the murderer; and having proceeded against him, they shall proclaim in the agora by a herald, that he who has slain such and such a person, and has been convicted of murder, shall not set his foot in the temples, nor at all in the country of the murdered man, and if he appears and is discovered, he shall die, and be cast forth unburied beyond the border. Let this one law then be laid down by us about murder; and let cases of this sort be so regarded. (*Laws*, 874 b)

The laws are different, but both are meant to purify the city of the impurity brought about by a dead body. This law of Plato is located between that of the murderous animal (*Laws* 873 e) and the nocturnal thief (*Laws* 874 c-d), two laws that appeared in Exodus 21–22. This is one of the finest examples of how the author rearranged the order of the laws.

Protection of Orphans

You shall not abuse any widow or orphan. If you do abuse them, when they cry out to me, I will surely heed their cry; my wrath will burn, and I will kill you with the sword, and your wives shall become widows and your children orphans. (Exod 22:22-24; see Deut 24:17)

Men should also fear the souls of the living who are aged and high in honour; wherever a city is well ordered and prosperous, their descendants cherish them, and so live happily; old persons are quick to see and hear all that relates to them, and are propitious to those who are just in the fulfilment of such duties, and they punish those who wrong the orphan and the desolate, considering that they are the greatest and most sacred of trusts. To all which matters the guardian and magistrate ought to apply his mind, if he has any, and take heed of the nurture and education of the orphans, seeking in every possible way to do them good, for he is making a contribution to his own good and that of his children. He who obeys the tale which precedes the law, and does no wrong to an orphan, will never experience the wrath of the legislator. But he who is disobedient, and wrongs any one who is bereft of father or mother, shall pay twice the penalty which he would have paid if he had wronged one whose parents had been alive. (*Laws* 927 b-e)

The Disowned Son

If someone has a stubborn and rebellious son who will not obey his father and mother, who does not heed them when they discipline him, then his father and his mother shall take hold of him and bring him out to the elders of his town at the gate of that place. They shall say to the elders of his town, 'This son of ours is stubborn and rebellious. He will not obey us. He is a glutton and a drunkard.' Then all the men of the town shall stone him to death. So you shall purge the evil from your midst; and all Israel will hear, and be afraid. (Deut 21:18-21)

He who in the sad disorder of his soul has a mind, justly or unjustly, to expel from his family a son whom he has begotten and brought up, shall not lightly or at once execute his purpose; but first of all he shall collect together his own kinsmen, extending to cousins, and in like manner his son's kinsmen by the mother's side, and in their presence he shall accuse his son, setting forth that he deserves at the hands of them all to be dismissed from the family; and the son shall be allowed to address them in a similar manner, and show that he does not deserve to suffer any of these things. And if the father persuades them, and obtains the suffrages of more than half of his kindred, exclusive of the father and mother and the offender himself—I say, if he obtains more than half the suffrages of all the other grown-up members of the family, of both sexes, the father shall be permitted to put away his son, but not otherwise. And if any other citizen is willing to adopt the son who is put away, no law shall hinder him; for the characters of young men are subject to many changes in the course of their lives. And if he has been put away, and in a period of ten years no one is willing to adopt him, let those who have the care of the superabundant population which is sent out into colonies, see to him, in order that he may be suitably provided for in the colony. (*Laws* 929 a-d)

Plato's law shows much more clemency than its biblical counterpart, as the son will only be sent to a colony, not put to death.

No Lending with Interest

If you lend money to my people, to the poor among you, you shall not deal with them as a creditor; you shall not exact interest from them. (Exod 22:25)

You shall not charge interest on loans to another Israelite, interest on money, interest on provisions, interest on anything that is lent. On loans to a foreigner you may charge interest, but on loans to another Israelite you may not charge interest, so that the Lord your God may bless you in all your undertakings in the land that you are about to enter and possess. (Deut 23:19-20)

And no one shall deposit money with another whom he does not trust as a friend, nor shall he lend money upon interest; and the borrower should be under no obligation to repay either capital or interest. (*Laws* 742 b)

Free Gathering of Fruits

If you go into your neighbour's vineyard, you may eat your fill of grapes, as many as you wish, but you shall not put any in a container. If you go into your neighbour's standing grain, you may pluck the ears with your hand, but you shall not put a sickle to your neighbour's standing grain. (Deut 23:24-25)

When you reap your harvest in your field and forget a sheaf in the field, you shall not go back to get it; it shall be left for the alien, the orphan, and the widow, so that the Lord your God may bless you in all your undertakings. When you beat your olive trees, do not strip what is left; it shall be for the alien, the orphan, and the widow. When you gather the grapes of your vineyard, do not glean what is left; it shall be for the alien, the orphan, and the widow. Remember that you were a slave in the land of Egypt; therefore I am commanding you to do this. (Deut 24:19-22)

The goddess of Autumn has two gracious gifts: one the joy of Dionysus which is not treasured up; the other, which nature intends to be stored. Let this be the law, then, concerning the fruits of autumn: He who tastes the common or storing fruits of autumn, whether grapes or figs, before the season of vintage which coincides with Arcturus, either on his own land or on that of others—let him pay fifty drachmae, which shall be sacred to

Dionysus, if he pluck them from his own land; and if from his neighbour's land, a mina, and if from any others', two-thirds of a mina. And he who would gather the 'choice' grapes or the 'choice' figs, as they are now termed, if he take them off his own land, let him pluck them how and when he likes; but if he take them from the ground of others without their leave, let him in that case be always punished in accordance with the law which ordains that he should not move what he has not laid down. And if a slave touches any fruit of this sort, without the consent of the owner of the land, he shall be beaten with as many blows as there are grapes on the bunch, or figs on the fig tree. Let a metic purchase the 'choice' autumnal fruit, and then, if he pleases, he may gather it; but if a stranger is passing along the road, and desires to eat, let him take of the 'choice' grape for himself and a single follower without payment, as a tribute of hospitality. The law however forbids strangers from sharing in the sort which is not used for eating; and if any one, whether he be master or slave, takes of them in ignorance, let the slave be beaten, and the freeman dismissed with admonitions, and instructed to take of the other autumnal fruits which are unfit for making raisins and wine, or for laying by as dried figs. As to pears, and apples, and pomegranates, and similar fruits, there shall be no disgrace in taking them secretly; but he who is caught, if he be of less than thirty years of age, shall be struck and beaten off, but not wounded; and no freeman shall have any right of satisfaction for such blows. Of these fruits the stranger may partake, just as he may of the fruits of autumn. And if an elder, who is more than thirty years of age, eat of them on the spot, let him, like the stranger, be allowed to partake of all such fruits, but he must carry away nothing. If, however, he will not obey the law, let him run the risk of failing in the competition of virtue, in case any one takes notice of his actions before the judges at the time. (*Laws* 844 d-45 d)

The biblical law has two sides—one that pertains to those who may gather freely, and another that pertains to the owner of a field. Both laws suggest that anyone is allowed to claim a small quantity from another's field, but of course that person must not take complete provision. This law appears in Plato soon after the law concerning boundary stones.

The Sins of the Fathers Will Not Befall their Children

Parents shall not be put to death for their children, nor shall children be put to death for their parents; only for their own crimes may persons be put to death. (Deut 24:16; see 2 Kgs 14:5-6)

The judges of such cases shall be the same as of the robbers of temples; and let the whole proceeding be carried on in the same way, and the vote of the majority condemn to death. But let there be a general rule, that the disgrace and punishment of the father is not to be visited on the children, except in the case of someone whose father, grandfather, and great-grandfather have successively undergone the penalty of death. (*Laws* 856 c-d)

Levirate / Adoption of an Inheritor

When brothers reside together, and one of them dies and has no son, the wife of the deceased shall not be married outside the family to a stranger. Her husband's brother shall go in to her, taking her in marriage, and performing the duty of a husband's brother to her, and the firstborn whom she bears shall succeed to the name of the deceased brother, so that his name may not be blotted out of Israel. But if the man has no desire to marry his brother's widow, then his brother's widow shall go up to the elders at the gate and say, 'My husband's brother refuses to perpetuate his brother's name in Israel; he will not perform the duty of a husband's brother to me'. Then the elders of his town shall summon him and speak to him. If he persists, saying, 'I have no desire to marry her', then his brother's wife shall go up to him in the presence of the elders, pull his sandal off his foot, spit in his face, and declare, 'This is what is done to the man who does not build up his brother's house'. Throughout Israel his family shall be known as 'the house of him whose sandal was pulled off'. (Deut 25:5-10)

And if any one of the houses be unfortunate, and stained with impiety, and the owner leave no posterity, but dies unmarried, or married and childless, having suffered death as the penalty of murder or some other crime committed against the Gods or against his fellow-citizens, of which death is the penalty distinctly laid down in the law; or if any of the citizens be in perpetual exile, and also childless, that house shall first of all be purified and undergo expiation according to law; and then let the kinsmen of the house, as we were just now saying, and the guardians of the law, meet and consider what family there is in the state which is of the highest repute for virtue and also for good fortune, in which there are a number of sons; from that family let them take one and introduce him to the father and forefathers of the dead man as their son, and, for the sake of the omen, let him be called so, that he may be the continuer of their family, the keeper of their hearth, and the minister of their sacred rites with better fortune than his father had; and when they have made this supplication, they shall make him heir according to law, and the offending person they shall leave nameless and childless and portionless when calamities such as these overtake him. (*Laws* 877 e-78 b)

Here the law is different, though it has the same aim: the land must not be left without a male owner. As we will see further on, the story of Ruth illustrates such a concern, although Ruth's marriage to Boaz is not a levirate but in fact a juridical arrangement to reassign an abandoned lot to a male possessor. Genesis 38 speaks of the levirate, in which there appears a name from Plato's *Republic*, Er. Plato says that one can refuse a marriage arranged by the legislator, but will be shunned (*Laws* 926 b-d).

A Strange Curse

She who is the most refined and gentle among you, so gentle and refined that she does not venture to set the sole of her foot on the ground, will begrudge food to the husband whom she embraces, to her own son, and to her own daughter, begrudging even the afterbirth that comes out from between her thighs, and the children that she bears, because she is eating them in secret for lack of anything else, in the desperate straits to which the enemy siege will reduce you in your towns. (Deut 28:56-57)

Love is young and also tender; he ought to have a poet like Homer to describe his tenderness, as Homer says of Ate, that she is a goddess and tender: 'Her feet are tender, for she sets her steps, not on the ground but on the heads of men': herein is an excellent proof of her tenderness,—that she walks not upon the hard but upon the soft. (Plato, *Sym.* 195 d)

The citation comes from Homer, *Il.* XIX, 92. We saw that the story of Ate, which led Hera to cause Eurystheus to be born before Heracles, was a source for the rivalry between Jacob and Esau. In regarding this strange and horrible curse in Deuteronomy, one may ask how a woman might walk without ever setting her feet on the ground. Does she always walk with shoes on, or is she carried on a litter? Rather, the goddess Ate never sets foot on the ground, but walks on the heads of men—such a murderous goddess may well be the source of this verse.

6.

Joshua

The previous chapters complete the analysis of what religious tradition calls the Pentateuch. My aim, however, is to show that this caesura does not reflect the intentions of the author, who also wrote the so-called books of the Prophets from Joshua to Kings (as maintained by Spinoza, and more recently, Wesselius). Joshua is the direct continuation of Deuteronomy, and there is no break in style, language or content whatsoever. Moses is now dead, outside of the Promised Land, and his successor Joshua takes up the mantle of leadership. The conquest of the land of Canaan seems to have been inspired by the Trojan War, as the story of the fall of Jericho recycles a minor episode of the fall of Troy. The second part of the book describes the distribution of the lots of land by lottery—thus the platonic Ideal State is achieved. The author uses lists of actual cities to add an appearance of authenticity to his narrative, but we know now that his main model was Plato.

Rahab / Theano

Joshua sends two spies to the city of Jericho. There, they are hidden in the house of a prostitute named Rahab (Josh 2:1-24). They sneak out of her house (adjacent to the walls) via a rope lowered from a window. The spies promise that they will spare her house when the attack on the city begins, and she is to leave a crimson rope tied to her window as a sign for the soldiers. Joshua and his army surround the city in ch. 6, and when the trumpets are sounded, the walls of Jericho collapse. Rahab's home is evacuated, and all of her family survives (Josh 6:22-23). Right after the battle, a man from the tribe of Judah, called Achan, son of Zabdi, son of Zerah, son of Judah, is put to death for taking some spoils from Jericho (Josh 7). The rabbinic sources have commented upon these chapters, claiming that the two spies hidden by Rahab were actually the twin sons of Judah—Perez and Zerah—born to Judah and his daughter-in-law

Tamar.[1] This does not seem to make much sense, as these characters should have been long dead; but let us understand how this rabbinic comment has in fact captured the spirit of that story. If we go back to the story of Judah and Tamar, we see that she dressed herself as a prostitute (Hebrew *zonah*, Gen 38:15 and Josh 2:1):

> When the time of her delivery came, there were twins in her womb. While she was in labour, one put out a hand; and the midwife took and bound on his hand a crimson thread, saying, 'This one came out first'. But just then he drew back his hand, and out came his brother; and she said, 'What a breach you have made for yourself!' Therefore he was named Perez. Afterwards his brother came out with the crimson thread on his hand; and he was named Zerah. (Gen 38:27-30)

The crimson thread appears in both the stories of Tamar and Rahab. In Genesis, the midwife put a crimson thread on the arm of Zerah as he was being born, but his brother pulled him back in utero and was born first. The violent birth of the twins tears their mother's vulva. In Joshua, two grown men come out of the wall of Jericho via a window, to which a crimson rope is tied as a sign for the soldiers to spare that house. And right after the battle, a descendant of Zerah is sentenced to death. Moreover, the city of Jericho is sometimes called the City of Tamar, which means 'palm tree' (Deut 34:3 and Judg 3:13). In a sense, this violent birth scene is figuratively replicated on a larger scale when the two spies breech the wall of Jericho hanging from a crimson rope, as if the city itself was a pregnant woman. In Genesis, Tamar is a pregnant woman giving birth to twins, whereas in Joshua, 'Tamar' is a city surrounded by a wall from which two men escape. A crimson thread was first attached to Zerah's arm, now a crimson rope is attached to a wall of the city itself. We could relate Rahab to Tamar for she is a prostitute (albeit, unlike Tamar, a real one), but as she helps the men escape, Rahab rather seems to play the role of midwife. Thus, if Rahab is the midwife then Jericho itself fulfils the role of the pregnant woman. With a metonymic game, the city is compared to a pregnant woman.[2] This would explain why the rabbis identified the two spies as Perez and Zerah:

> The two of them, Perez and Zerah, were sent by Joshua as spies. The thread that Rahab tied to her window as a sign for Israel's army, she received it from Zerah. It was the crimson thread that the midwife had tied on his wrist to point him as the first-born, before he was pulled back.[3]

1. Louis Ginzberg, *Les légendes des Juifs*, V, Paris: Cerf, 2004, 131.
2. In French there is a double entendre that makes this very clear, as the word *enceinte* means both the 'walls around a city' and 'pregnant'.
3. Louis Ginzberg, *Les légendes des Juifs*, III, Paris: Cerf, 2001, 30.

The biblical writer created a diptych: while the first story is found in Genesis and its counterpart in Joshua, clues were left for the reader to solve the riddle. This fits with Lévi-Strauss' synchronic reading of a myth. It does not matter if Perez and Zerah were supposed to be dead at the time as the author deliberately wanted the reader to identify them with the spies; proof of this is in the involvement of a descendant of Zerah in ch. 7. Moreover, this literary technique of turning a pregnant woman into a city fits perfectly with the character of Jacob—in Genesis, he is portrayed as a man with twelve sons, yet in the book of Joshua he is in the process of becoming a country composed of twelve tribes. All of this brings us back to the platonic conception of the Ideal State, which is a soul on a wider scale. The collapse of Jericho, the Canaanite city *par excellence*, announces the birth of Israel; in a similar vein, Tamar gives birth via a painful delivery to the offspring of Judah, who is meant to inherit kingship. Matthew's Gospel adds Rahab as an ancestor of David, as she would have been Boaz' mother (Matt 1:5). Several Greek sources explain how Antenor and his wife Theano hid Menelaus and Ulysses, who had come to Troy as spies (*Il.* III, 200-25), and with them negotiated for their survival. For the Acheans to recognise their house, a leopard skin had to be attached to the window (Pausanias, *Description of Greece* 10, 27, 2).[4] The original source for this story is likely Sophocles' play *Antenorides*, known only through fragments. The biblical writer used this episode, and in replacing the leopard skin with the crimson rope, he thus entered this metonymic dialectic between the city and the pregnant woman—the prostitute and the midwife. We may understand this crimson rope itself as a metaphor for the umbilical cord, tying the infant to his mother.

The Stopping of the Sun

There are more clues that point to the Trojan War as being a source for the book of Joshua. Both Joshua and King Agamemnon pray for the sun to stop before they have defeated their enemies.[5]

> On the day when the Lord gave the Amorites over to the Israelites, Joshua spoke to the Lord; and he said in the sight of Israel, 'Sun, stand still at Gibeon, and Moon, in the valley of Aijalon'. And the sun stood still, and the moon stopped, until the nation took vengeance on their enemies. Is this not written in the Book of Jashar? The sun stopped in mid-heaven,

4. West, *The East Face of Helicon*, 488-89.
5. Ibid., 357.

and did not hurry to set for about a whole day. There has been no day like it before or since, when the Lord heeded a human voice; for the Lord fought for Israel. (Josh 10:12-14)

Agamemnon prayed, saying, 'Zeus, most glorious, supreme, that dwellest in heaven, and ridest upon the storm-cloud, grant that the sun may not go down, nor the night fall, till the palace of Priam is laid low, and its gates are consumed with fire. Grant that my sword may pierce the shirt of Hector about his heart, and that full many of his comrades may bite the dust as they fall dying round him. (*Il.* II, 410-20)

Homer writes that Zeus did not fulfil the wish of Agamemnon, whereas the book of Joshua tells that God stopped the sun. The biblical writer quotes his source—the Book of the Just (or Jashar)—but its existence is in doubt.[6] Rather, the *Iliad* appears to be the actual source. Further on, Athena hastens the setting of the sun to spare the Greeks from their losing battle (*Il.* XVIII, 239-42). In this same chapter (Josh 10:3), one of the five Amorite kings is named Piram, which could be a reference to King Priam of Troy.

Joshua / Ulysses

We have seen how the story of Joseph is inspired by the story that Ulysses tells his servant Eumeus in *Odyssey* XIV. The previous book tells of how Ulysses landed on his home island of Ithaca after twenty long years of war and wandering, bearing a treasure offered by the Phaecians. There he met Athena, but did not recognise her immediately. Several passages of *Odyssey* XIII seem to be the source for certain parts of the book of Joshua. This is no coincidence, as Joshua's conquest of Canaan is the 'return' of Israel to the Promised Land, after Jacob and his sons had left it for Egypt:

Once when Joshua was near Jericho, he looked up and saw a man standing before him with a drawn sword in his hand. Joshua went to him and said to him, 'Are you one of us, or one of our adversaries?' He replied, 'Neither; but as commander of the army of the Lord I have now come'. And Joshua fell on his face to the earth and worshipped, and he said to him, 'What do you command your servant, my lord?' The commander of the army of the Lord said to Joshua, 'Remove the sandals from your feet, for the place where you stand is holy'. And Joshua did so. (Josh 5:13-15)

Then Athena came up to him disguised as a young shepherd of delicate and princely mien, with a good cloak folded double about her shoulders: she had sandals on her comely feet and held a javelin in her hand. Ulysses

6. See Stott, *Why Did They Write This Way?*

was glad when he saw her, and went straight up to her. 'My friend,' said he, 'you are the first person whom I have met with in this country; I salute you, therefore, and beg you to be will disposed towards me. Protect these my goods, and myself too, for I embrace your knees and pray to you as though you were a god. (*Od.* XIII, 220-30)

Joshua said, 'Ah, Lord God! Why have you brought this people across the Jordan at all, to hand us over to the Amorites so as to destroy us? Would that we had been content to settle beyond the Jordan! (Josh 7:7)

Alas,' he exclaimed, 'among what manner of people am I fallen? Are they savage and uncivilized or hospitable and humane? Where shall I put all this treasure, and which way shall I go? I wish I had stayed over there with the Phaeacians; or I could have gone to some other great chief who would have been good to me and given me an escort. As it is I do not know where to put my treasure, and I cannot leave it here for fear somebody else should get hold of it. (*Od.* XIII, 200-205)

But when the inhabitants of Gibeon heard what Joshua had done to Jericho and to Ai, they on their part acted with cunning: they went and prepared provisions, and took worn-out sacks for their donkeys, and wineskins, worn-out and torn and mended, with worn-out, patched sandals on their feet, and worn-out clothes; and all their provisions were dry and mouldy. (Josh 9:3-5)

As she spoke Athena touched him with her wand and covered him with wrinkles, took away all his yellow hair, and withered the flesh over his whole body; she bleared his eyes, which were naturally very fine ones; she changed his clothes and threw an old rag of a wrap about him, and a tunic, tattered, filthy, and begrimed with smoke; she also gave him an undressed deer skin as an outer garment, and furnished him with a staff and a wallet all in holes, with a twisted thong for him to sling it over his shoulder. (*Od.* XIII, 430-40)

Meanwhile, these five kings fled and hid themselves in the cave at Makkedah. And it was told Joshua, 'The five kings have been found, hidden in the cave at Makkedah'. Joshua said, 'Roll large stones against the mouth of the cave, and set men by it to guard them. (Josh 10:16-18)

'Take heart, and do not trouble yourself about that,' rejoined Athena, 'let us rather set about stowing your things at once in the cave, where they will be quite safe. Let us see how we can best manage it all.' Therewith she went down into the cave to look for the safest hiding places, while Ulysses brought up all the treasure of gold, bronze, and good clothing which the Phaecians had given him. They stowed everything carefully away, and Athena set a stone against the door of the cave. (*Od.* XIII, 360-70)

And Achan answered Joshua, 'It is true; I am the one who sinned against the Lord God of Israel. This is what I did: when I saw among the spoil a beautiful mantle from Shinar, and two hundred shekels of silver, and a

> bar of gold weighing fifty shekels, then I coveted them and took them. They now lie hidden in the ground inside my tent, with the silver underneath. (Josh 7:20-21)

All these parallels are clustered in *Odyssey* XIII; when compared to several similar chapters of Joshua, there is little room left for coincidence.

The Division of the Land

Chapters 14 to 19 of Joshua describe the division of the land to each tribe. Reuben, Gad and half of Manasseh had already settled on the eastern side of the Jordan (Num 30), though they did participate in the conquest. Judah receives the first piece of land and the author gives a long list of cities—though mentioning that Jerusalem itself was not conquered (Josh 15:36). Joseph receives a large share, but the men of that tribe complain it is not enough, for they are very numerous. Next is Benjamin, whose territory is between Joseph and Judah. The seven remaining tribes are allotted their parts, and the State of Israel is formed. However, the author specifies that some Canaanite cities did retain their indigenous populations. Chapter 20 tells of the cities of refuge, according to the laws set out in Numbers 35. Chapter 21 describes the cities given to the Levites (they had no lots of land). Chapter 22 repeats the story of the Trans-Jordanian tribes. Chapter by chapter, the reader sees the State— the plan for which had been given by God to Moses—come to life.

Through the use of long catalogues, this correspondence between the model and its realisation recalls the craftsman's realisation of the sanctuary in imitating a divine model; this actually reflects the biblical writer's mimetic technique towards his platonic model. Here in Joshua, the cadastre of the twelve tribes of Plato's *Laws* (745 b-c) is achieved. The Levites did not receive a portion of the land, but Joseph received a double part, so that the land is still divided into twelve parts. From a literary standpoint, the tradition that holds the Pentateuch to be independent from the books that follow is based on no other grounds than religious ones. The books from Genesis to 2 Kings show a perfect literary unity, a testament to their continuity being in the underlying Greek sources that bind them.

Joseph's Burial

At the end of his life, Joshua gathers all of Israel to an assembly in Shechem and reminds them of their history. They pledge once more to observe God's laws. Special attention is paid to Joseph's corpse, which had been taken from Egypt by Moses (Exod 13:19)—Joseph had prophesied it before dying (Gen 50:25-26)—and carried in the desert throughout the entire forty years of wandering. Joseph is eventually buried in Shechem (Josh 24:32), in the piece of land bought by Jacob for a hundred pieces of money.[7] I believe that this thread of Joseph's corpse being brought back to Canaan has something to do with the epic of the Argonauts, who had to bring the Golden Fleece back to Greece to ease the spirit of Phrixos who did not receive a proper funeral (Pindar, *Pythian* IV). Genesis ends with the words of Joseph, and Joshua ends one line further. The end of Numbers is also concerned with Joseph's offspring, as the daughters of Zelophehad are of his tribe. Joseph's return to Canaan somehow refers to Ulysses' return to his homeland of Ithaca, as, even though Joseph did not come home alive, Ulysses was the inspiration for his character. Joseph's direct descendant Joshua is also inspired by Ulysses, and fulfils his ancestor's prophecy. Proof that Joseph and Joshua are linked can be seen in that both their lives end at one hundred and ten years (Gen 50:26 and Josh 24:29). We saw how the anonymous spies sent by Joshua mirrored the twin sons of Judah, and we will see how David repeats the stories of his ancestor Jacob. All the threads of the Bible, including the epics and the platonic motifs, are blended into a single fine, seamless garment.

7. As per Gen 33:19, the coins (in Hebrew *kesitah*) can be identified with the Lydian currency *cistophorus*.

7.

Judges

The book of Judges relates how the people of Israel lived in the land alongside the Canaanite populations that God allowed to remain there. The program is explained in ch. 2: every time Israel started to worship the local gods, God sent an enemy to afflict them; they would repent, and a 'judge' would free them. Jacques Cazeaux has shown how this biblical book, although seemingly made of heroic tales from various origins, was in fact a fine literary piece of work. Cazeaux believes that the aim of Judges was to show—through the portraits of the judges—that the fraternal unity of Israel is better than kingship.[1] Indeed, with the exception of Abimelech, the Judges do not pretend to be kings of Israel. The book ends with a civil war in which Benjamin is almost exterminated. This story, often considered by scholars to be an addition because no 'judge' seems to emerge from it, in fact makes perfect sense. The next book, Samuel, explains why Israel will make itself a king, moreover one that comes from the very tribe of Benjamin, Saul. 'In those days there was no king in Israel; all the people did what was right in their own eyes' (Judg 21:25). That sentence which closes the book of Judges is perhaps the final word of the whole Bible itself, since Judges is the 'beginning of the end'—the reason why Israel will abandon its tribal organisation and replace it with a tyrant. The book of Joshua is the acme of the Bible, and one gets a feeling of disappointment from reading the following books. As it does not respect the laws, Israel becomes unworthy of God's favour. Here, I believe that the perfect platonic State, created according to the model of the *Laws*, is becoming Plato's Atlantis, slowly sinking towards its demise. Cazeaux demonstrated the unity of the book of Judges brilliantly. I will focus on showing the Greek sources behind the stories, most of which come from Herodotus (except for Samson, who is modelled after Heracles). Stories related to Benjamin are similar to Roman myths—notably the first of them, that of Ehud.

1. Cazeaux, *Le refus de la guerre sainte*.

Ehud / Mucius Scaevola

Scholars have noticed that the story of Ehud shares a theme with the Roman myth of Mucius Scaevola.[2] A Roman soldier named Mucius decided to assassinate the Etruscan king Porsenna, who was besieging Rome. Mucius hid a dagger under his cloak and entered the enemy's camp, but ended up killing Porsenna's secretary by mistake. When brought before the king, he put his right hand in the flame of a brazier and let it burn, saying that three hundred men with the same determination would come after him. Impressed, the king decided to make peace with Rome. Back in Rome, Mucius was welcomed as a hero and received the nickname 'Scaevola'—meaning 'left-handed' (Titus Livius, II:12, Plutarch, *Publicola* 17, 4). This is similar in a way to the story of Ehud from the tribe of Benjamin, who decided to kill King Eglon of Moab, in Judges 3. Ehud was said to be left-handed (Judg 3:15), and he hid his sword next to his right thigh, so that the men of Eglon did not find it. He pretended to have a special message to deliver to Eglon, and murdered him. The resemblance is vague, and is only due to the fact that Ehud is said to be left-handed. But this seems to be a play on words because the best warriors of Benjamin are said to have all been left-handed (Judg 20:16); also, in Hebrew 'Benjamin' means 'son of the right'. This parallel will only become apparent once we analyse the other story involving Benjamin in Judges (19–21).

Shamgar / Lycurgus

After him came Shamgar son of Anath, who killed six hundred of the Philistines with an ox-goad. He too delivered Israel. (Judg 3:31)

Lycurgus, son of Dryas, did not live long when he took to fighting with the gods. He it was that drove the nursing women who were in charge of frenzied Dionysus through the land of Nysa, and they flung their thyrsi on the ground as murderous *Lycurgus beat them with his ox-goad*. Dionysus himself plunged terror-stricken into the sea, and Thetis took him to her bosom to comfort him, for he was scared by the fury with which the man reviled him. Thereon the gods who live at ease were angry with Lycurgus and the son of Cronos struck him blind, nor did he live much longer after he had become hateful to the immortals. (Homer, *Iliad*, VI, 135-40; see also Apollodorus, *Library* 3, 5, 1)

Even though the story of Shamgar is contained in a single verse, a reference to Homer is made.

---

2. Bordreuil and Briquel-Chatonnet, *Le temps de la Bible*, 165-66; Dumézil, *Mythe et épopée, I, II, III*.

Deborah / Melissa

Katel Berthelot and Yaakov Kupitz wrote an article comparing the prophetess and judge Deborah to the Delphic Pythia.[3] Deborah used to sit under a palm tree (Judg 4:5). Israel was threatened by Jabin, king of Hazor. Barak from the tribe Ephraim asked for Deborah's help in order to defeat Sisera, Jabin's general. She accepted, but told Barak that a woman would have victory over Sisera (Judg 4:4-10). Sisera was defeated, fled from the battlefield and hid in the tent of Yael, wife of Heber. He fell asleep, and she killed him with a tent-peg that she stuck in his temple (Judg 4:21), thus fulfilling Deborah's prophecy: Barak's ultimate victory eluded him since it was a woman who killed Sisera. For Kupitz and Berthelot, an oracle given by the Delphic Pythia was the inspiration for this scene. Cleomenes, king of Sparta (we saw the story of his birth above), tries to take the city of Argos. But the oracle had told the Argians:

> But when the female at length shall conquer the male in the battle, conquer and drive him forth, and glory shall gain among Argives, then many wives of the Argives shall tear both cheeks in their mourning; so that a man shall say some time, of the men that came after, 'Quelled by the spear it perished, the three-coiled terrible serpent. (Herodotus VI, 77)

The name of Deborah means 'bee'. The Pythia of Delphi is called Melissa (*Pythian* IV, 6), which bears the same meaning. Like the Pythia, Deborah sits under a palm-tree. Thus, in predicting the victory of a woman, Deborah resembles the Pythia's obscure oracle that remains unexplained by Herodotus. Pausanias later commented that it points to a poetess, Telessila. Whatever the original meaning of the oracle, it seems that the biblical writer used it to create the scene of the death of Sisera—he is like the snake quelled by the spear. We will see further on how Cleomenes was the source for the character Abimelech—evidence that Kupitz and Berthelot are right. Kupitz sees a resemblance between Sisera fleeing from the battlefield and Xerxes himself. In Judges 5, the so-called Song of Deborah, supposedly older than the book of Judges itself, recounts how the mother of Sisera and her servants expect his glorious return:

> Out of the window she peered, the mother of Sisera gazed through the lattice: 'Why is his chariot so long in coming? Why tarry the hoofbeats of his chariots?' Her wisest ladies make answer, indeed, she answers the

---

3. Katell Berthelot and Yaakov Kupitz, 'Deborah and the Delphic Pythia: A New Interpretation of Judges 4, 4-5', communicated in person by Professor Kupitz.

question herself: 'Are they not finding and dividing the spoil?—A girl or two for every man; spoil of dyed stuffs for Sisera, spoil of dyed stuffs embroidered, two pieces of dyed work embroidered for my neck as spoil?' (Judg 5:28-30)

The Persian dames, with many a tender fear, in grief's sad vigils keep the midnight hour; Shed on the widowed couch the streaming tear, and the long absence of their loves deplore. (Aeschylus, *The Persians* 60)[4]

Although two women stood before my eyes gorgeously vested, one in Persian robes adorned, the other in the Doric garb. With more than mortal majesty they moved, of peerless beauty; sisters too they seemed. (*The Persians* 180-83)

And thou, whose age the miseries of thy Xerxes sink with sorrow, go to thy house, thence choose the richest robe, and meet thy son; for through the rage of grief his gorgeous vestments from his royal limbs are foully. rent (*The Persians* 832-33)

The song of Deborah mocks Sisera's mother for expecting her son's return, while Aeschylus' *The Persians* tells how Queen Atossa, Xerxes' mother, anxiously awaits her son's return from Greece. Xerxes is fleeing, as the ghost of Darius tells her. In fact, the war of Greece against Persia is the main source for the narratives from Judges 4 to 12.

Gideon / Leonidas

Leonidas was the brother of King Cleomenes of Sparta, who inherited his throne after he died. Leonidas fought the Persian army at Thermopylae with his three hundred men, and lost his life. The courage and resistance they showed, however, caused Xerxes to doubt his ability to conquer Greece. This is very similar to the story of Gideon, who faced the army of the Midianites, the Amalekites and all the people of the east (Judg 6:33). Gideon, from the tribe of Manasseh, called for allies throughout Israel. But God told him that his army was too numerous and that he was to reduce it, for Israel should not believe that it could defeat its enemy by itself: only God's power would save them. Thus, God made Gideon choose the best warriors, among those who lapped water while drinking from the river, excluding those who kneeled. From this operation, only three hundred men were retained (Judg 7:1-8). This specific number recalls of Leonidas' three hundred elite warriors. Leonidas himself had many allies, but Herodotus relates how he sent away those who were scared:

4. Translated by Robert Potter.

He then at this time went to Thermopylai, having chosen the three hundred who were appointed by law and men who chanced to have sons. (Herodotus VII, 205)

These, I say, had intended to do thus: and meanwhile the Hellenes at Thermopylai, when the Persian had come near to the pass, were in dread, and deliberated about making retreat from their position. To the rest of the Peloponnesians then it seemed best that they should go to the Peloponnesus and hold the Isthmus in guard; but Leonidas, when the Phokians and Locrians were indignant at this opinion, gave his vote for remaining there, and for sending at the same time messengers to the several States bidding them to come up to help them, since they were but few to repel the army of the Medes. (Herodotus VII, 207)

Leonidas perceived that the allies were out of heart and did not desire to face the danger with him to the end, he ordered them to depart, but held that for himself to go away was not honourable, whereas if he remained, a great fame of him would be left behind, and the prosperity of Sparta would not be blotted out... I am of opinion that Leonidas considering these things and desiring to lay up for himself glory above all the other Spartans, dismissed the allies, rather than that those who departed did so in such disorderly fashion, because they were divided in opinion. (Herodotus VII, 220)

So the three companies blew the trumpets and broke the jars, holding in their left hands the torches, and in their right hands the trumpets to blow; and they cried, 'A sword for the Lord and for Gideon!' Every man stood in his place all around the camp, and all the men in the camp ran; they cried out and fled. When they blew the three hundred trumpets, the Lord set every man's sword against his fellow and against all the army; and the army fled as far as Beth-shittah towards Zererah, as far as the border of Abel-meholah, by Tabbath. (Judg 7:20-22)

The soldiers, then, in accordance with the orders given them, forming in a compact body fell by night upon the encampment of the Persians, Leonidas leading the attack; and the barbarians, because of the unex-pectedness of the attack and their ignorance of the reason for it, ran together from their tents with great tumult and in disorder, and thinking that the soldiers who had set out with the Trachinian had perished and that the entire force of the Greeks was upon them, they were struck with terror. Consequently many of them were slain by the troops of Leonidas, and even more perished at the hands of their comrades, who in their ignorance took them for enemies. For the night prevented any under-standing of the true state of affairs, and the confusion, extending as it did throughout the entire encampment, occasioned, we may well believe, great slaughter; since they kept killing one another, the conditions not allowing of a close scrutiny, because there was no order from a general nor any demanding of a password nor, in general, any recovery of reason. (Diodorus Siculus, *Library* XI, 10)

The night-time attack found in Diodorus is extremely similar to that of Judges 7, where the enemies are so frightened that they kill each other. The main difference is that Leonidas and his men eventually perish, whereas Gideon wins his battle. The tribes of Israel ask Gideon to reign over them as king after this military success, but he refuses.

Abimelech

Gideon had seventy legitimate sons, and one named Abimelech from his Shechemite concubine. Abimelech convinced his maternal uncles to make him king over them (the Shechemites at the time were Canaanites). Abimelech massacred his seventy brothers, but the youngest of them, Jotham, escaped. When Abimelech was proclaimed king, Jotham stood facing Shechem on Mount Gerizim, and shouted the following:

> The trees once went out to anoint a king over themselves. So they said to the olive tree, 'Reign over us'. The olive tree answered them, 'Shall I stop producing my rich oil by which gods and mortals are honoured, and go to sway over the trees?' Then the trees said to the fig tree, 'You come and reign over us'. But the fig tree answered them, 'Shall I stop producing my sweetness and my delicious fruit, and go to sway over the trees?' Then the trees said to the vine, 'You come and reign over us'. But the vine said to them, 'Shall I stop producing my wine that cheers gods and mortals, and go to sway over the trees?' So all the trees said to the bramble, 'You come and reign over us'. And the bramble said to the trees, 'If in good faith you are anointing me king over you, then come and take refuge in my shade; but if not, let fire come out of the bramble and devour the cedars of Lebanon. (Judg 9:8-15)

These verses are also known from a fable of Aesop, the legendary fable teller from the sixth century B.C.E. There is no need to quote this for they are word for word identical, with the exception that the fable of Aesop does not mention the vine—though this could be due to the omission of a copyist.[5] It is possible that some Byzantine Christian copyist added this fable to Aesop's corpus by taking it from the Septuagint (likely from the Alexandrinus version), but it could also be that it was first a document from the Greek tradition that the biblical writer took and translated into Hebrew, word for word. By retroversion, the Septuagint and the original fable would have thus ended up similar. In reading the rest of Aesop's fables, one can easily see that the fable of the trees is of the same genre as the others; animals or trees discuss together, often criticising kingship and politics. Indeed, Jotham's speech is meant to mock the assembly of

---

5. Aesop, *Fables*, Paris: Les Belles Lettres, 1960.

Shechem—those making Abimelech king. Two other fables of Aesop appear in the Bible (in Judges and 2 Kings) but those are adapted from their original versions.

The Shechemites soon revolted against Abimelech. He put an ambush in the fields. He divided his troops in three companies, waited for the Shechemite troops to come out, and took the city back. The lords of Shechem hid in a tower. Abimelech told his men to cut some wood and set fire to the tower. The lords of Shechem perished. The inhabitants of the next city Thebez also hid in a tower, and Abimelech planned to kill them the same way, but a woman threw a millstone on his head, and crushed his skull. He asked his armour-bearer to kill him (Judg 9:34-57). This story is echoed by two stories found in Herodotus:

> So Cleomenes thereupon ordered all the Helots to pile up brushwood round the sacred grove; and they obeying, he set fire to the grove. And when it was now burning, he asked one of the deserters to what god the grove was sacred, and the man replied that it was sacred to Argos. When he heard that, he groaned aloud and said, 'Apollo who utterest oracles, surely thou hast greatly deceived me, saying that I should conquer Argos: I conjecture that the oracle has had its fulfilment for me already. (Herodotus VI, 80)

> Some others however of the Kyrenians fled to a great tower belonging to Aglomachos a private citizen, and Arkesilaos burnt them by piling up brushwood round. Then after he had done the deed he perceived that the Oracle meant this, in that the Pythian prophetess forbade him, if he found the jars in the furnace, to heat them fiercely. (Herodotus IV, 164)

Abimelech is the son of Gideon. We have seen how Gideon was mostly inspired by the character of Leonidas. Cleomenes, Leonidas' brother, was used as a source for Abimelech. Two stories in Herodotus tell of a king who burned people alive either in the woods, or in a tower. Abimelech's story seems to be a mixture of both of these. In Herodotus' stories, the king fulfils an oracle that will cause his own death. Abimelech fulfilled the oracle of his younger brother Jotham in becoming the bramble from which came a fire that devoured the Shechemites. The biblical writer did not pick his sources randomly; he used the conflicts between Greek cities found in Herodotus. These chapters of Judges also contain a reference to Genesis 34, in which the Prince of Shechem raped Dinah and Simeon and Levi massacred the Shechemites in retaliation. The bloodbath is repeated by Abimelech, and again shows the difficulty Israelites and Canaanites have in living together.

Jephthah / Gelon / Idomeneus

The first verses describing Jephthah find an accurate echo in the speech Ulysses tells his servant Eumeus, which we saw in analysing the story of Joseph:

> Now Jephthah the Gileadite, the son of a prostitute, was a mighty warrior. Gilead was the father of Jephthah. Gilead's wife also bore him sons; and when his wife's sons grew up, they drove Jephthah away, saying to him, 'You shall not inherit anything in our father's house; for you are the son of another woman'. Then Jephthah fled from his brothers and lived in the land of Tob. Outlaws collected around Jephthah and went raiding with him. (Judg 11:1-3)

> I am by birth a Cretan; my father was a well-to-do man, who had many sons born in marriage, whereas I was the son of a slave whom he had purchased for a concubine; nevertheless, my father Castor son of Hylax (whose lineage I claim, and who was held in the highest honour among the Cretans for his wealth, prosperity, and the valour of his sons) put me on the same level with my brothers who had been born in wedlock. When, however, death took him to the house of Hades, his sons divided his estate and cast lots for their shares, but to me they gave a holding and little else...when I had picked my men to surprise the enemy with an ambuscade I never gave death so much as a thought, but was the first to leap forward and spear all whom I could overtake. (*Od.* XIV, 200-210)

The Ammonites waged a war against Israel; and the elders asked Jephthah for his help. First, he pretended to be offended, for he had been rejected. Then he accepted to offer his help, on the condition that he would be the head and commander over them (Judg 11:4-11).

Note Herodotus VII, 157-58, which reads:

> In the manner then which has been described Gelon had become a powerful despot; and at this time when the envoys of the Hellenes had arrived at Syracuse, they came to speak with him and said as follows: 'The Lacedemonians and their allies sent us to get thee to be on our side against the Barbarian; for we suppose that thou art certainly informed of him who is about to invade Hellas, namely that a Persian is designing to bridge over the Hellespont, and to make an expedition against Hellas, leading against us out of Asia all the armies of the East, under colour of marching upon Athens, but in fact meaning to bring all Hellas to subjection under him. Do thou therefore, seeing that thou hast attained to a great power and hast no small portion of Hellas for thy share, being the ruler of Sicily, come to the assistance of those who are endeavouring to free Hellas, and join in making her free... The envoys spoke thus; and Gelon was very vehement with them, speaking to them as follows: 'Hellenes, a selfish speech is this, with which ye have ventured to come

and invite me to be your ally against the Barbarian... However, though I have met with contempt at your hands, I will not act like you; but I am prepared to come to your assistance, supplying two hundred triremes and twenty thousand hoplites, with two thousand horsemen, two thousand bowmen, two thousand slingers and two thousand light-armed men to run beside the horsemen; and moreover I will undertake to supply corn for the whole army of the Hellenes, until we have finished the war. These things I engage to supply on this condition, namely that I shall be commander and leader of the Hellenes against the Barbarian; but on any other condition I will neither come myself nor will I send others.

Gelon says he had wanted to avenge the death of Dorieus, son of Anaxandrides, the brother of Cleomenes and Leonidas. Again, the biblical writer found his sources in the same books of Herodotus—the sixth and seventh—and carefully mixed the story of Ulysses (which was used mostly for Joseph) with that of Gelon. Moreover, Herodotus says that when Cleomenes ascended to the throne of Sparta, Dorieus refused to be his subject and left Greece with some men to found a colony (Herodotus V, 42). The theme of Jephthah as a vagabond was inspired both by Homer and Herodotus. Gideon, Abimelech and Jephthah are all from the half-tribe of Manasseh (part of the tribe of Joseph) whereas the brothers Leonidas, Cleomenes and Dorieus are all sons of Anaxandrides, king of Sparta—whose story about his two wives inspired Genesis 16. Jephthah made the vow that if he came home victorious from the war, he would sacrifice to God the first person to welcome him. It was his only daughter who welcomed him; and as he could not undo his vow, Jephthah did sacrifice his own daughter (Judg 11:30-35). King Idomeneus of Crete is said to have fled his own kingdom (Virgil, *Aeneid* III, 400). Later commentaries explained that during his journey back from Troy his ship was lost in a storm, and so he promised that if he ever reached his homeland he would sacrifice to Poseidon the first living being he met. His son the prince welcomed him, and like Jephthah, Idomeneus could not take back his vow. He sacrificed his son, and was cast out by the Cretans for committing such a horrible deed. The story is very similar to that of Jephthah yet it is known only through late, minor sources. On the other hand, the story of King Agamemnon's sacrifice of his daughter Iphigenia before the Trojan War is well attested. The Greek fleet was stuck in Aulis because there were no winds. In his *Iphigenia in Aulis* Euripides told of how she was brought there under the pretext that she was to marry Achilles, but instead her father tried to sacrifice her. In Euripides' play, she escaped and was replaced by a doe, thanks to Artemis—which reminds us of the story of Phrixos, who was replaced by a ram (also in a play by Euripides).

However, other sources make it clear that Iphigenia was killed; that is the reason why Clytemnestra, Agamemnon's wife, killed him upon his return from Troy. I believe that the biblical author combined the story of Agamemnon killing his daughter and that of Idomeneus killing his son.

Samson / Heracles / Aristeus

We will here summarize the well-known similarities between Samson and Heracles. We will also look at Aristeus, the first bee-keeper of the Greek tradition. The wife of Manoah, a man of the tribe of Dan, was visited by God's angel. She was told that her child to come would be a Nazirite, that he would refrain from alcoholic beverages. He would eventually free Israel from the hands Philistines (Judg 13:2-7). Such a story may remind us of Aristeus:

> Hypseus raised his lovely-armed daughter Cyrene... Once the god of the broad quiver, Apollo who works from afar, came upon her wrestling alone and without spears with a terrible lion. Immediately he called Cheiron from out of his halls and spoke to him: 'Leave your sacred cave, son of Philyra, and marvel at the spirit and great strength of this woman; look at what a struggle she is engaged in, with a fearless head, this young girl with a heart more than equal to any toil; her mind is not shaken with the cold wind of fear. From what mortal was she born? From what stock has this cutting been taken, that she should be living in the hollows of the shady mountains and putting to the test her boundless valor? Is it lawful to lay my renowned hand on her? And to cut the honey-sweet grass of her bed?'... You came to this glen to be her husband, and you will bear her over the sea to the choicest garden of Zeus, where you will make her the ruler of a city, when you have gathered the island-people to the hill encircled by plains. And now Queen Libya of the broad meadows will gladly welcome your glorious bride in her golden halls. There she will right away give her a portion of land to flourish with her as her lawful possession, not without tribute of all kinds of fruit, nor unfamiliar with wild animals. There she will bear a child, whom famous Hermes will take from beneath his own dear mother and carry to the Seasons on their lovely thrones and to Gaia. They will admire the baby on their knees and drop nectar and ambrosia on his lips, and they will make him immortal, to be called Zeus and holy Apollo, a delight to men he loves, an ever-present guardian of flocks, Agreus and Nomius, and others will call him Aristaeus. (Pindar, *Pythian* IX, 20-65)

A few verses later Pindar mentions the birth of Heracles. In the *Ninth Pythian Ode*, Aristeus and Heracles are closely linked. Note the importance of honey, as Aristeus was known as the first keeper of bees. His mother Cyrene once fought a lion with her bare hands. The centaur

Chiron tells Apollo that Aristeus will be fed with nectar and ambrosia—in comparison, Samson will be raised as a Nazirite and will abstain from wine. Thomas L. Thompson has pointed out that the story of Manoah's wife is full of ironic humour.[6] It is reminiscent of the promise of Isaac's birth in Genesis 18, a story inspired seemingly by the birth of Orion. In this case, we can see a link to the birth of Heracles himself:

> When Amphitryon was away subduing Oechalia, Alcimena, thinking Jove was her husband, received him in her chamber. When he had entered her room, and told her what he had done in Oechalia, she lay with him, thinking he was her husband. He lay with her with so much pleasure that he spent one day and doubled two nights, so that Alcimena wondered at such a long night. Later when the word came to her that her husband was at hand, a victor, she showed no concern, because she thought she had already seen her husband. When Amphitryon came into the palace, and saw her carelessly unconcerned, he began to wonder and to complain that she did not welcome him when he appeared. Alcimena replied: You already came and lay with me, and told me what you had done in Oechalia. When she had given him all the evidence, Amphitryon realized that some divinity had assumed his form, and from that day did not lie with her. But she, from the embrace of Jove, bore Hercules. (Hyginus, *Fables* XXIX)

Upon reading Judges 13 closely, one can infer that the angel of God is in fact the father of Samson. Contrary to Genesis 18, we are not told that Manoah 'knew' his wife after the angel's coming; Thompson suggests that Manoah may be a cuckold, much like Amphitryon. Samson's first heroic deed was slaying a lion with his bare hands (Judg 14:5-6), much like Heracles:

> First he (Heracles) cleared the grove of Zeus of a lion, and put its skin upon his back, hiding his auburn hair in its fearful gaping jaws. (Euripides, *Heracles* 360-64)

This parallel is, of course, greatly renowned and commented upon, and many have identified Samson with Heracles. Recall that certain episodes of the stories of Jacob and Moses were also inspired by the cycle of Heracles, and that these stories do not appear again. This embodies the result of a conscious work, not of an oral tradition. Samson later passed by the carcass of the lion; it was rotten, and a swarm of bees lived in it. He ate some honey from it (Judg 14:8-11).

6. Thompson, *The Mythic Past*, 323-52.

Note Virgil, *Georgics* IV, 540-60, which reads:

> The self-same hour he hies him forth to do his mother's bidding: to the
> shrine he came, the appointed altars reared, and thither led four chosen
> bulls of peerless form and bulk, with kine to match, that never yoke had
> known. Then, when the ninth dawn had led in the day, to Orpheus sent
> his funeral dues, and sought the grove once more. But suddenly, strange
> to tell a portent they espy: through the oxen's flesh, waxed soft in
> dissolution, hark! there hum bees from the belly; the rent ribs overboil in
> endless clouds they spread them, till at last on yon tree-top together fused
> they cling, and drop their cluster from the bending boughs.[7]

Aristeus, the first keeper of bees, asked old Proteus the reason why all
his bees had perished. Proteus told him that Eurydice, Orpheus' wife,
died because of him. Orpheus descended to the Underworld to reclaim
her, and Hades agreed to let her return to the world of the living on the
sole condition that they not look back as they left (which Orpheus did).

We saw that this theme was used in Genesis 19, as Lot's wife was lost
in the same way as Eurydice. Orpheus then died of sadness after losing
his wife for the second time. Aristeus' mother Cyrene suggested that he
offer a sacrifice (as mentioned above), and as Aristeus had appeased
Orpheus' spirit, he recovered his bees. The theme of bees born out of the
rotten flesh of an animal seems to derive from a reflection on the nature
of honey.[8] Honey is a natural food, but one made by insects—produced
(or 'cooked') in the bees' stomachs and excreted from their mouths.
Honey was considered to be a divine food that could not rot in ancient
Greece, similar to nectar and ambrosia. Rotting food can be thought of as
having been 'cooked' by nature, and thus the concept of bees coming
forth from rotten meat seems a logical reasoning on the essence of food.
In the Latin version the bees come out of a rotten ox, but in the Bible
they come from a lion. This can be explained, as Samson is mixture of
both Heracles, who slew a lion, and Aristeus, who kept bees. The definite
proof of this is in Pindar's *Ninth Pythian Ode*, in which both Aristeus
and Heracles are found; the two themes were mixed into one, the lion
giving birth to bees. Samson will later use that story to invent a riddle,
and will have an argument with his Philistine comrades. He kills thirty
men in Ashkelon, and his new wife is given to another man (Judg 14:13-
20). A similar theme is also found in the cycle of Heracles.

Note the following citations:

7. Translated by John Dryden.
8. Gilles Tétart, *Le sang des fleurs*, Paris: Odile Jacob, 2004; Claude Lévi-
Strauss, *Mythologiques*. II. *Du miel aux cendres*, Paris: Plon, 1966.

After a while, at the time of the wheat harvest, Samson went to visit his wife, bringing along a kid. He said, 'I want to go into my wife's room'. But her father would not allow him to go in. Her father said, 'I was sure that you had rejected her; so I gave her to your companion. Is not her younger sister prettier than she? Why not take her instead?' Samson said to them, 'This time, when I do mischief to the Philistines, I will be without blame'. So Samson went and caught three hundred foxes, and took some torches; and he turned the foxes tail to tail, and put a torch between each pair of tails. When he had set fire to the torches, he let the foxes go into the standing grain of the Philistines, and burned up the shocks and the standing grain, as well as the vineyards and olive groves. (Judg 15:1-3)

After his labours Hercules went to Thebes and gave Megara to Iolaus, and, wishing himself to wed, he ascertained that Eurytus, prince of Oechalia, had proposed the hand of his daughter Iole as a prize to him who should vanquish himself and his sons in archery. So he came to Oechalia, and though he proved himself better than them at archery, yet he did not get the bride; for while Iphitus, the elder of Eurytus' sons, said that Iole should be given to Hercules, Eurytus and the others refused, and said they feared that, if he got children, he would again kill his offspring. (Apollodorus, *Library* 2, 6, 1; see Sophocles, *Trachinians*, 266)

A Farmer, who bore a grudge against a Fox for robbing his poultry yard, caught him at last, and being determined to take an ample revenge, tied some rope well soaked in oil to his tail, and set it on fire. The Fox by a strange fatality rushed to the fields of the Farmer who had captured him. *It was the time of the wheat harvest*; but the Farmer reaped nothing that year and returned home grieving sorely. (Aesop, *Fables*, 'The Farmer and the Fox')

We saw earlier that Jotham's speech uses the exact same wording as a fable of Aesop. Here, it seems as though the fable was adapted to the character of Samson. The 'fingerprint' is that in both texts it happens during the time of the wheat harvest.

Note the following quote from Herodotus:

When (Heracles) came to Egypt, the Egyptians put on him wreaths and led him forth in procession to sacrifice him to Zeus; and he for some time kept quiet, but when they were beginning the sacrifice of him at the altar, he betook himself to prowess and slew them all. (Herodotus II, 45; see Apollodorus, *Library* 2, 5, 11)

Similarly, Samson let himself be captured by the men of Judah, who delivered him to the Philistines, but then he got easily rid of his bounds. He massacred a thousand men with the jawbone of a donkey (Judg 15:11-16). As suggested by Prof. Kupitz, the jawbone may well be the equivalent of Heracles' famous club, which was full of pins, like teeth embedded in a jaw. Then Samson was very thirsty, and God slipt a rock open, and water come from it. Samson drank and was revived (Judg 15:18-19).

> He (Heracles) too came with a raging thirst, as you would expect from someone travelling the land on foot. He dashed about all over here looking for water, which he was unlikely to see! But there is a certain rock near Lake Triton and, whether he had the idea himself or was inspired by a god, he kicked it violently at the bottom, and a great steam of water flowed out. Pressing both arms and his breast to the ground, he drank a vast quantity from the cleft of the rock, until, flat on the ground, he had filled the pit of his belly like a grazing beast. (Apollonius of Rhodes, *Argonautica*, IV, 1440-50)

> Once Samson went to Gaza, where he saw a prostitute and went in to her. The Gazites were told, 'Samson has come here'. So they encircled the place and lay in wait for him all night at the city gate. They kept quiet all night, thinking, 'Let us wait until the light of the morning; then we will kill him'. But Samson lay only until midnight. Then at midnight he rose up, took hold of the doors of the city gate and the two posts, pulled them up, bar and all, put them on his shoulders, and carried them to the top of the hill that is in front of Hebron. (Judg 16:1-3)

> To famed Mycenae will I go; crow-bars and pick-axes must I take, for I will heave from their very base with iron levers those city-walls which the Cyclopes squared with red plumb-line and mason's tools.' 'But before he could, the poor mother caught up her babe and carried him within the house and shut the doors; forthwith the madman, as though he really were at the Cyclopean walls, prizes open the doors with levers, and, hurling down their posts, with one fell shaft laid low his wife and child... To the ground he fell, smiting his back against a column that had fallen on the floor in twain when the roof fell in. (Euripides, *Heracles* 990-1010)

> She let him fall asleep on her lap; and she called a man, and had him shave off the seven locks of his head. He began to weaken, and his strength left him. Then she said, 'The Philistines are upon you, Samson!' When he awoke from his sleep, he thought, 'I will go out as at other times, and shake myself free'. But he did not know that the Lord had left him. (Judg 16:19-20)

> Now, so long as Pterelaus lived, he could not take Taphos; but when Comaetho, daughter of Pterelaus, falling in love with Amphitryon, pulled out the golden hair from her father's head, Pterelaus died, and Amphitryon subjugated all the islands. He slew Comaetho, and sailed with the booty to Thebes, and gave the islands to Heleus and Cephalus; and they founded cities named after themselves and dwelt in them. (Apollodorus, *Library* 2, 4, 7)

The theme of a treacherous woman cutting another's hair (which gives life or strength to that character) is also found in the story of Heracles' father. These events happened at the same time Zeus visited Alcmene. The biblical writer simply took that idea and adapted it to Samson himself.

Note the following quotations:

> So the Philistines seized him and gouged out his eyes. They brought him down to Gaza and bound him with bronze shackles; and he ground at the mill in the prison. (Judg 16:21)

> Parents are too prone to sternness with their children… Recently, not far away, the violent Echetos pierced his daughter's eyes with bronze pins and her life wastes away in grief-filled doom as she grinds bronze in a dark hut. (Apollonius of Rhodes, *Argonautica* IV 1090-1105)

> And Samson said to the attendant who held him by the hand, 'Let me feel the pillars on which the house rests, so that I may lean against them. (Judg 16:26)

> Afterwards he (Orion) went to Chios and wooed Merope, daughter of Oenopion. But Oenopion made him drunk, put out his eyes as he slept, and cast him on the beach. But he went to the smithy of Hephaestus, and snatching up a lad set him on his shoulders and bade him lead him to the sunrise. (Apollodorus, *Library* 1, 4, 3)

Here, two different themes are blended: Orion's eyes were gouged out as he slept, as Samson's were right after he woke up, and Echetos gouged out his daughter's eyes, leaving her to spend her days grinding bronze in the dark. The accuracy of this detail, plus that of the spring of water coming forth from rock seen above, lends credence to the idea that Apollonius was among the direct sources of the Bible. At last, Samson grasping the pillars of the temple of Dagon and having it collapsing over himself and the Philistines recalls of Heracles' frenzy:

> I call the sun-god to witness that herein I am acting against my will; but if indeed I must forthwith serve thee and Hera and follow you in full cry as hounds follow the huntsman, why go I will; nor shall the ocean with its moaning waves, nor the earthquake, nor the thunderbolt with blast of agony be half so furious as the headlong rush I will make into the breast of Heracles; through his roof will I burst my way and swoop upon his house, after first slaying his children. (Euripides, *Heracles* 860-65)

Samson's dramatic death may have been inspired by Heracles' madness in Euripides' tragic play of the same name. Note the myriad Greek sources that relate the story of Heracles, while only four chapters of the Bible speak of Samson. Samson is only known through one text, yet

Heracles is known from works ranging from Homer and Hesiod to such Roman-era handbooks as Apollodorus' *Library*, as well as an immense number of iconographic representations. Heracles is often associated with the sun, primarily due to his twelve labours, which can be interpreted as the progression of the sun across the twelve constellations of the Zodiac. Another famous episode is Heracles' journey on the ocean aboard the vessel of the sun god Helios (*Library* 2, 5, 11).

This may explain the root of Samson's name, *shimshon*, meaning 'small sun'. Also noteworthy is the fact that Heracles is a descendant of Danaea, Perseus' mother, herself a descendant of *Danaos*; Samson is a descendant of *Dan*, one of Jacob's twelve sons. We have seen how the births of Heracles and his ancestors inspired the episodes from Jacob's story of the fighting twins and the elder robbed of his right, as well as the hero who unknowingly sleeps with different sisters. Heracles' birth was the inspiration for Moses' abandonment and his return to his natural mother (thanks to his sister). These themes were not used again here in the cycle of Samson. It seems almost certain that the biblical writer knew the complete Heraclean cycle, as found in Apollodorus or Diodorus Siculus' *Libraries*, and dismantled it to create several characters. A random diffusion of oral tales could never have reached such a perfect balance between the Greek and biblical episodes. The main theme of Heracles' twelve labours does not appear in Samson's story, but the very framework of the whole biblical narrative is built on the story of Jacob becoming Israel through the creation of twelve tribes from his twelve sons. Twelve labours of Samson do not appear in Judges, but through each tribe the twelve 'labours' of Israel do.

Dan / Massalia

Massalia, founded by the Phocæans, is built in a stony region. Its harbour lies beneath a rock, which is shaped like a theatre, and looks towards the south. It is well surrounded with walls, as well as the whole city, which is of considerable size. Within the citadel are placed the Ephesium and the temple of the Delphian Apollo. This latter temple is common to all the Ionians; the Ephesium is the temple consecrated to Artemis of Ephesus. They say that when the Phocæans were about to quit their country, an oracle commanded them to take from Artemis of Ephesus a conductor for their voyage. On arriving at Ephesus they therefore inquired how they might be able to obtain from the goddess what was enjoined them. The goddess appeared in a dream to Aristarcha, one of the most honourable women of the city, and commanded her to accompany the Phocæans, and to take with her a plan of the temple and statues. These things being performed, and the colony being settled, the Phocæans built a temple, and evinced their great respect for Aristarcha by making her priestess. All the colonies [sent out from Massalia] hold this goddess in peculiar reverence, preserving both the shape of the image [of the goddess], and also every rite observed in the metropolis. (Strabo, *Geography* IV, 1, 4)[9]

The Danites, having taken what Micah had made, and the priest who belonged to him, came to Laish, to a people quiet and unsuspecting, put them to the sword, and burned down the city. There was no deliverer, because it was far from Sidon and they had no dealings with Aram. It was in the valley that belongs to Beth-rehob. They rebuilt the city, and lived in it. They named the city Dan, after their ancestor Dan, who was born to Israel; but the name of the city was formerly Laish. Then the Danites set up the idol for themselves. Jonathan son of Gershom, son of Moses, and his sons were priests to the tribe of the Danites until the time the land went into captivity. So they maintained as their own Micah's idol that he had made, as long as the house of God was at Shiloh. (Judg 18:27-31)

This parallel has been discussed by Nadav Na'aman, who believes that the Deuteronomist, working in the late sixth century B.C.E., may have heard of this Greek tradition and incorporated it into Judges. Na'aman admits that the foundation of Massalia (today's Marseilles) has a historical background while the story of the Danites is a political satire meant to point out the idolatrous cult of Jeroboam's calf (located in the city of Dan, as in 1 Kgs 13).[10] The scholarly theory of the Deuteronomist supposes that every book from Deuteronomy to Kings is by the same author; in contrast, I believe that every book from Genesis to Kings is from the same hand. However, it seems quite clear that this story from Judges was meant to be a criticism of idolatry, as it ends with the mention of the captivity that was to take place centuries later. Whereas the older manuscripts of the Septuagint and the Vulgate clearly mention the 'son of Moses', the Masoretic Bible corrected it to read the 'son of Manasseh' by adding the Hebrew letter *nun*—apparently because the Masoretes would not admit that the grandson of Moses could be the priest of an idolatrous cult. However, this final revelation of the Levite's identity is seemingly intended to disappoint the reader. This detail fits with the next story of the Benjaminites, as we are told that Phineas, son of Eleazar, son of Aaron, was the High Priest of Israel at the time (Judg 20:28). The last two stories of Judges give a role to the tribe of Levi through its two main branches: the descendants of Moses, who were not entitled to be priests, and the descendants of Aaron, who did receive that privilege. These

9. Translated by H.L. Jones.
10. Nadav Na'aman, 'The Danite Campaign Northward', *Vetus Testamentum* 55 (2005): 47-60.

stories are not late additions, but rather they contribute to the portrayal of Israel's inability to live according to the rules of God. Chapter 18 starts with the same sentence that the book of Judges ends with: 'In those days, there was no king in Israel' (Judg 18:1; 19:1; 21:25). The reader is thus prepared to read about the rise of kingship in Samuel, the next book.

Benjamin / Rome

Two stories in Judges can be linked to Roman myths: that of Ehud (loosely) and that of the war against Benjamin in Judges 19–21. The Roman authors that we will consider are thought to have post-dated the Bible. Yet, as in the case of the parallels that Genesis shares with the works of Ovid, the accuracy of the similarities is puzzling. Judges 19 tells how a Levite and his unfaithful concubine spent a night in Gibeah, a town of Benjamin, where they received hospitality from an old man.

At night, some inhabitants of Gibeah came to his door and asked to 'know' his guest. The old man implored them not to commit such a sin, and proposed to give them his virgin daughter and the Levite's concubine (reminiscent of Lot and the angels in Sodom in Gen 19). But the Levite threw his concubine out, and the men of Benjamin raped her to death. The Levite found her body in the morning, placed her on his donkey and went back to Ephraim. There he cut her into twelve parts and sent one to each tribe of Israel (Judg 19). All of the people of Israel were shocked, and though they summoned Benjamin to deliver the guilty men of Gibeah, they were refused. Since such a heinous crime had never been seen, a war broke out between Benjamin and the eleven other tribes of Israel. They rose up against the small tribe of Benjamin, but the eleven were defeated during the two first attacks. On their third attempt, they successfully ambushed the Benjaminites away from their city; Israel won the battle and the tribe of Benjamin was almost annihilated (Judg 20)— only six hundred men survived, hidden in the desert. Then, as one of its tribes was nearly driven to extinction, Israel felt regret. Though they would like to help the survivors of Benjamin find new wives, they promised themselves not to give their daughters to Benjamin. When it was revealed that the town of Jabesh-Gilead did not participate in the war against Benjamin, everyone in that city was murdered except for the virgin women, and they were given as spouses to some of the survivors of Benjamin. But as these women were not enough, Israel decided to allow Benjamin to abduct women at the festival of Shiloh (Judg 21:20-25).

This story is full of paradoxes. Israel decides to destroy Benjamin because some of its men have raped a woman to death, but in the end, the survivors are authorised to abduct young women. A tribe cannot be missing, even if it has committed a great sin. This concern for the unity of Israel was already present in Genesis, when Joseph was almost killed by his brothers and only their peaceful reunion guaranteed Israel's harmony. The same pattern is reproduced here in Judges, except the twelve brothers have become tribes. The concubine raped to death and cut into twelve pieces is a shocking metaphor for Israel bursting into civil war. This episode is far from being a late addition, for every previous book has prepared the reader to understand that Israel is only complete through its twelve tribes. At the end of Numbers a part of the tribe of Joseph was also threatened with extinction, and a solution had to be found. The first verse of Judges 19 and the last verse of Judges 21 repeat that in those days there was no king in Israel. We are now approaching the royal period of Israel; these sentences act like stone markers, insisting upon the reasons why Israel will slowly abandon the system of the tribes. Ultimately, they were not able to respect it, as shown throughout the whole book of Judges. Not all the tribes joined the war against Sisera (Judg 5). Abimelech decided to become king of Israel without consulting the other tribes, and his brief reign ended in a bloodbath (Judg 9–10). This initial attempt at kingship, right in the middle of Judges, is a shifting moment in the narration. Ephraim declared war upon Manasseh after Jephthah defeated Ammon (Judg 12). The men of Judah made Samson of Dan a prisoner and delivered him to the Philistines (Judg 14). Joshua established the Ideal State of Israel, the plan for which had been given to Moses—but the law was forgotten as the generations passed, and in the following book of Samuel, Israel anoints a king. Very gradually, through the details of these 'judges', the author introduces the reasons for the fall of his platonic Israel.

The story of the abduction of the women is very similar to the abduction of the Sabine women in the myth of Rome's foundation (Titus Livius, I, 9-13). Romulus founded Rome, and though all kinds of men were accepted to inhabit it, there was a dearth of women; all the surrounding peoples had explicitly refused to give them their daughters for matrimonial alliances. Romulus invited these peoples to a festival in Rome, and the Romans captured the Sabine women, whose families protested and soon waged war against Rome. During the war, the newly wedded wives begged their fathers, brothers and new husbands to make peace. This parallel of the abduction of women has been long known and is often considered to be a 'common mythical theme from antiquity'. A similar story is also found in the Pelasgian abduction of Athenian women during a festival (Herodotus VI, 138), which I believe to be a direct literary source for Judges 21. A more important parallel is found at the end of the first book of Livy. Tarquin the Proud, a tyrant hated by his people, had a son, Sextus, who raped a noble woman, Lucretia, by coming to her at night and threatening her with his sword. The next day she asked her father and her husband to visit her, told them what Sextus had done to her, and made them promise to avenge her. She then withdrew a dagger and stabbed herself in the heart:

> They carried the body of Lucretia from her home down to the Forum, where, owing to the unheard-of atrocity of the crime, they at once collected a crowd. Each had his own complaint to make of the wickedness and violence of the royal house. Whilst all were moved by the father's deep distress, Brutus bade them stop their tears and idle laments, and urged them to act as men and Romans and take up arms against their insolent foes... He made a speech quite out of keeping with the character and temper he had up to that day assumed. He dwelt upon the brutality and licentiousness of Sextus Tarquin, the infamous outrage on Lucretia and her pitiful death, the bereavement sustained by her father, Tricipitinus, to whom the cause of his daughter's death was more shameful and distressing than the actual death itself... By enumerating these and, I believe, other still more atrocious incidents which his keen sense of the present injustice suggested, but which it is not easy to give in detail, he goaded on the incensed multitude to strip the king of his sovereignty and pronounce a sentence of banishment against Tarquin with his wife and children. (Titus Livius, I, 59)[11]

The first book of Livy ends with the rape and the suicide of Lucretia, which explains how Roman monarchy came to its end. Tarquin the Proud had already aroused his subjects' anger for he enslaved them to build Roman temples and palaces (much like Solomon would do to the people of Israel). After that incident Tarquin and his family were banished from Rome, and the Republic was installed. This is the opposite of the biblical narrative. Soon after the rape and murder of the Levite's concubine and the war that followed it, Israel gave itself a king—Saul—a man from the very same tribe of Benjamin and city of Gibeah. Livy obviously worked with older sources that have been lost to us, like Quintus Fabius Pictor, an author from the third century B.C.E. who wrote in Greek. It seems as though the biblical writer had knowledge of Roman myths relating to the foundation of Rome and the end of kingship, and applied them isomorphically to the tribe of Benjamin. With this in mind, Judge Ehud of Benjamin is likely linked to Mucius Scaevola, the 'left-

11. Translated by the Reverend Canon Roberts.

handed' hero who saved Rome. It must be mentioned that rabbinic sources were well aware of these similarities. Judges 20:47 says that the survivors of Benjamin fled to a village called Rimon, which the rabbis interpreted as Rome.[12] What if the author indeed intended 'Rimon', in Hebrew meaning 'pomegranate', to be a cryptic reference to Rome? We can also look back at Jacob's blessing of Benjamin: 'Benjamin is a ravenous wolf, in the morning devouring the prey, and at evening dividing the spoil' (Gen 49:27). This too could be a reference, perhaps, to Rome's symbol of the she-wolf, which nourished Romulus and Remus (Titus Livius, I, 5).

The story in Judges 19 of the Levite in Gibeah reminds the reader of the angels that visited Sodom in Genesis 19. We saw how the story in Joshua 2 of Rahab helping Joshua's two spies out of Jericho's walls was an echo of the tale of the birth of Tamar's twins in Genesis 38; here, the biblical author creates another diptych. His aim is quite clear, and he shows that Israel now behaves like the Sodomites—but the Levite now replaces God's angels. As God destroyed Sodom for its sins, Israel destroys Benjamin. But in both stories the survivors find a way to have children by transgressing the normal laws: Lot sleeps with his two daughters, and the survivors of Benjamin abduct women. Whenever a bloodline is in danger of disappearing, the transgression of sexual rules is permitted. This is the very logic of the levirate, for in normal times a man must not sleep with his brother's wife or ex-wife as it is considered incestuous. But if a man's brother died childless, then that man is forced to marry his brother's widow, in effect providing the deceased's family with offspring. The other example of that logic is the story of Ruth.

Ruth's Symposium

The small book of Ruth can be considered as an addition to the book of Judges, placed among the Five Scrolls in the Hebrew and Protestant canons of the Bible, and between Judges and 1 Samuel in the Catholic canon. As per Spinoza, I believe that Ruth was authored by the same person who wrote Genesis–Kings. It tells how a man from the tribe of Judah named Elimelech left his native Bethlehem to dwell in the land of Moab. His two sons married Moabite women, and the three of them eventually died in Moab. Naomi, Elimelech's widow, was left with her two daughters-in-law, Ruth and Orpah. Naomi decided to go back to Bethlehem, and though Ruth accompanied her, Orpah stayed. Naomi was

.

12. Ginzberg, *Les légendes des Juifs*, V, 44 and 168 n. 135.

too poor and old to take care of her late husband's plot of land. She suggested that Ruth work for Boaz, a rich man who happened to be Elimelech's kin. Boaz noticed Ruth, and Naomi suggested that she seduce him, for he had the dual right to both buy the plot and to marry her. Ruth obeyed her mother-in-law and Boaz accepted the proposition—but only on the condition that another relative of Elimelech's, closer than Boaz in the order of succession, were to decline his right. The other relative did not want to marry Ruth as she was a Moabite woman, so instead Boaz obtained the piece of land and they were wed (Ruth 4:9-10). A son is born to Boaz and Ruth:

> The women of the neighbourhood gave him a name, saying, 'A son has been born to Naomi'. They named him Obed; he became the father of Jesse, the father of David. Now these are the descendants of Perez: Perez became the father of Hezron, Hezron of Ram, Ram of Amminadab, Amminadab of Nahshon, Nahshon of Salmon, Salmon of Boaz, Boaz of Obed, Obed of Jesse, and Jesse of David (Ruth 4:17-22).

The ultimate aim of this book is to introduce the full genealogy of David. We saw how Perez was born to Judah and his daughter-in-law Tamar by means of a levirate that was not carried out according to the law. Here, the union of Ruth and Boaz resembles a levirate, but this is not the case as Boaz is a relative and not a brother of the deceased. This story is a good example of how biblical Israel was meant to function. Boaz buys the abandoned piece of land and gives it to a male inheritor, who is then adopted by Naomi. This is a perfect illustration of Plato's concerns and the equivalent laws in Leviticus and Deuteronomy discussed above. Contrary to the book of Judges, we are shown here how Israel is supposed to work. We also see the same reasoning as in the story of Benjamin: Moabites cannot enter God's assembly (Deut 23:4), which is the likely reason for the deaths of Elimelech's sons. Boaz may marry Ruth, however, because a lineage is in danger of disappearing.

As the story of Benjamin gives the origin of Saul of Benjamin, the first king of Israel, the story of Ruth explains the origin of his rival, David. The genealogy from Perez, son of Judah, to David reminds the reader of the union of Tamar and Judah. Judah's first son, Tamar's first husband, was named Er, a name that appears at the end of Plato's *Republic*. This might seem like a mere coincidence, but we have shown how biblical Israel was modelled after the platonic State of the *Laws*. The story of Ruth and Boaz can be seen as a romance, a love story. There is a platonic dialogue about love, the *Symposium*, in which each actor gives his own definition of love. We saw how Aristophanes' speech was used as a source for Adam and Eve, in that they were portrayed as a single being divided in two. The best definition of love in the *Symposium*—according to its narrator—comes from the wise Socrates. He recalls a lesson he had learnt from Diotima, a priestess:

> On the birthday of Aphrodite there was a feast of the gods, at which the god Poros or Plenty, who is the son of Metis or Discretion, was one of the guests. When the feast was over, Penia or Poverty, as the manner is on such occasions, came about the doors to beg. Now Plenty who was the worse for nectar (there was no wine in those days), went into the garden of Zeus and fell into a heavy sleep, and Poverty considering her own straitened circumstances, plotted to have a child by him, and accordingly she lay down at his side and conceived Love, who partly because he is naturally a lover of the beautiful, and because Aphrodite is herself beautiful, and also because he was born on her birthday, is her follower and attendant. And as his parentage is, so also are his fortunes. (Plato, *Sym.* 203 b-c)

> So she went down to the threshing-floor and did just as her mother-in-law had instructed her. When Boaz had eaten and drunk, and he was in a contented mood, he went to lie down at the end of the heap of grain. Then she came quietly and uncovered his feet, and lay down. At midnight the man was startled and turned over, and there, lying at his feet, was a woman! He said, 'Who are you?' And she answered, 'I am Ruth, your servant; spread your cloak over your servant, for you are next-of-kin'. He said, 'May you be blessed by the Lord, my daughter; this last instance of your loyalty is better than the first; you have not gone after young men, whether poor or rich. And now, my daughter, do not be afraid; I will do for you all that you ask, for all the assembly of my people know that you are a worthy woman. (Ruth 3:6-11)

Here, at last, the platonic riddle of David's genealogy is unfolded. We discussed how biblical actors enacted the Allegory of the Cave in Exodus and then gave life to the platonic State; in this case Ruth, who is poor, and Boaz, who is rich, represent the union of the allegorical deities Penia and Poros (Poverty and Plenty)—together giving birth to Eros (Love). They are the great-grandparents of David, whose name means 'lover'. The same process can be seen in the book of Ruth as in the books from Genesis to Kings: a platonic allegory involving minor gods is recreated using human characters. From Adam to Jacob, from the deceased Er to Perez and from Boaz to David, platonic references are spread throughout David's entire genealogy.

The 'platonic' love scene between Ruth and Boaz did not involve sexual intercourse, though they slept together under the same cloak (Ruth 3:9 and 14). There is a parallel scene at the end of Plato's *Symposium*: Alcibiades arrives at the banquet and explains how he failed to seduce Socrates. They slept together under the same cloak but did not have sexual intercourse. In this final speech, Plato implicitly compares Socrates himself to Love (*Sym.* 219 b-d). Of course, the homosexual aspect of that story was changed into a heterosexual one, for male homosexuality was forbidden in both Plato's *Laws* and biblical law.

We must remember that Ruth is of Moabite descent; she is the result of Lot's incest with his elder daughter (Gen 19). Boaz himself is a descendant of the 'second-type' incest between Judah and his daughter-in-law (Gen 38), and moreover, Deuteronomy forbids his marriage to Ruth. Tamar, being of Canaanite descent, bears the curse of Noah for Ham's indecent act (Gen 9). It is as if David is the culmination of these multiple sexual stories, all of which go against biblical law. This will become more understandable as we see that David is a new incarnation of Jacob, and hence of Israel; but he will commit a sin of a sexual nature that will be the downfall of the whole nation. Following the postulation that biblical Israel can be considered a soul on a wider scale, biblical characters can be seen as allegories of philosophical principles such as Eros. This approaches Philo of Alexandria's allegorical interpretation of the Bible (later enhanced by Origen), or even the Jewish Kabbalah of the Middle Ages, which holds biblical characters to be emanations of the deity, the *sephirot*. According to Jacques Cazeaux, Ruth's story was not solely meant to show how a pious foreign woman was added to the genealogy of David (and hence of Jesus); rather, its first aim was to emphasise the importance of maintaining a male inheritor for every piece of land in Israel.[13] It is Israel's kings who will be the ones to destroy it, as in the story of King Ahab stealing Naboth's vineyard (1 Kgs 21). The power of the king is supreme and arbitrary. Even if Ruth's story seems exempt from violence, as opposed to the terrible book of Judges, it also contributes to the 'prophecy' against royal power.

13. Cazeaux, *Le refus de la guerre sainte*.

8.

Samuel

Samuel / Ion

Once again, I am indebted to Professor Kupitz for this parallel. After the troubled period in Judges comes the story of Samuel. We are told that of his two wives, the one that Elkanah loved, Hannah, was barren. Every year they would offer a sacrifice at the sanctuary of Shiloh, and one day, she prayed to God for a son. God granted her wish, and after her husband knew her she became pregnant. In gratitude, she promised to dedicate the child to God's service (see especially 1 Sam 1:11-28; 2:18-20). A similar story is told of Ion in Euripides' eponymous play: Creusa, an Athenian woman, had been seduced by Apollo and became pregnant. She abandoned the child (Ion) as she was not married, and Apollo had him brought to the temple of Delphi where the priestess adopted him. Creusa later married Xuthus and, as they had no children, they went to Delphi to pray for the birth of a son. Apollo induced Xuthus to adopt Ion as his legitimate child:

> All his youthful years sportive he wandered round the shrine, and there was fed: but when his firmer age advanced to manhood, over the treasures of the god the Delphians placed him, to his faithful care consigning all; and in this royal dome his hallowed life he to this hour hath passed. Meantime Creusa, mother of the child, to Xuthus was espoused, the occasion this:—On Athens from Euboean Chalcis rolled the waves of war; be joined their martial toil, and with his spear repelled the foe; for this to the proud honour of Creusa's bed advanced; no native, in Achaea sprung from Aeolus, the son of Zeus. Long time unblessed with children, to the oracular shrine of Phoebus are they come, through fond desire of progeny: to this the god hath brought the fortune of his son, nor, as was deemed, forgets him; but to Xuthus, when he stands this sacred seat consulting, will he give that son, declared his offspring; that the child, when to Creusa's house brought back, by her may be recognized; the bridal rites of Phoebus kept secret, that the youth may claim the state due to his birth, through all the states of Greece named Ion, founder of the colonies on the Asiatic coast. (Euripides, *Ion* 40-80)

The sequence of the story is inverted in the story of Samuel: Hannah, barren, prays for a child, who is then consecrated to the shrine of Shiloh. Creusa prays for a son in Delphi, not knowing that her son is still alive and has been raised, like Samuel, as an attendant of the temple. Ion and Creusa meet in front of the temple, and when she weeps at the memory of abandoning her child, Ion asks her why she cries (*Ion* 240-50). This scene of tears echoes the scene where Eli encounters Hannah praying silently. He first thinks her drunk (1 Sam 1:12-17). Further, Samuel lives in the sanctuary of Shiloh (1 Sam 3:2), while Ion in the temple of Delphi (*Ion* 315). As Ion's body is hallowed to Apollo (*Ion* 1280), Samuel's is dedicated to Yahweh (1 Sam 1:22). The story of Creusa and Ion closes in a scene of recognition:

> CREUSA: Silence is mine no more; instruct not me; For I behold the ark, wherein of old I laid thee, O my son, an infant babe; and in the caves of Cecrops, with the rocks of Macrai roofed, exposed thee: I will quit this altar, though I run on certain death. ION: Is this vase empty, or contains it aught? CREUSA: Thy infant vests, in which I once exposed thee. ION: And wilt thou name them to me, ere thou see them? CREUSA: If I recount them not, be death my meed. ION: Speak then: thy confidence hath something strange. CREUSA: A tissue, look, which when a child I wrought... ION: Such is the woof, and such the vest I find. CREUSA: Thou old embroidery of my virgin bands!... ION: O my dear mother! I with joy behold thee. With transport against thy cheek my cheek recline. (They embrace.) (*Ion* 1410-40)

From this moving scene, the objects Creusa had made for her child find an echo in the story of Samuel in the account of how every year Hanna sewed a robe for her son, living at the sanctuary in Shiloh (1 Sam 2:19). That Ion is presented as the ancestor of the Ionian Greeks in Gen 10:2 clearly shows that this particular Greek tradition is known to the biblical writer.

Eli / Phineus

In Apollonius, the Argonauts passed by the place where the seer Phineus dwelt:

> There Phineus, son of Agenor, had his home by the sea, Phineus who above all men endured most bitter woes because of the gift of prophecy which Leto's son had granted him aforetime. And he reverenced not a whit even Zeus himself, for he foretold unerringly to men his sacred will. Wherefore Zeus sent upon him a lingering old age, and took from his eyes the pleasant light, and suffered him not to have joy of the dainties untold that the dwellers around ever brought to his house, when they came to enquire the

will of heaven. But on a sudden, swooping through the clouds, the Harpies with their crooked beaks incessantly snatched the food away from his mouth and hands... But straightway when he heard the voice and the tramp of the band he knew that they were the men passing by, at whose coming Zeus' oracle had declared to him that he should have joy of his food. And he rose from his couch, like a lifeless dream, bowed over his staff, and crept to the door on his withered feet, feeling the walls; and as he moved, his limbs trembled for weakness and age; and his parched skin was caked with dirt, and naught but the skill held his bones together. And he came forth from the hall with wearied knees and sat on the threshold of the court-yard; and a dark stupor covered him, and it seemed that the earth reeled round beneath his feet, and he lay in a strengthless trance, speechless. (Apollonius of Rhodes, *Argonautica* II 180-205)

In 1 Samuel, the high priest Eli has two sons: Pinehas (comparable to the Greek Phineus) and Hophni, who were evil and abused their priestly office (1 Sam 2:12-17). Like Phineus, Eli ends up losing his sight, and his two sons are killed at war (1 Sam 4:13-18). This scene of Eli waiting for news of his sons is similar to the fate of the blind seer Phineus, who collapsed while waiting on his seat for the Argonauts to arrive. Both Eli and Phineus are cursed because they abused a divine privilege—Eli his priesthood and Phineus his divination.

The Ark / Cadmus and the Cow

The Philistines have stolen the Ark and God afflicts them with plagues. Their priests are consulted and they warn that the Ark must be brought back on a chariot pulled by two cows that have never been yoked. This recalls the very first verses of the *Iliad*, as Apollo smites the Acheans with a plague for they have kidnapped the daughter of Chryses, Apollo's priest:

The ark of the Lord was in the country of the Philistines for seven months. *Then the Philistines called for the priests and the diviners* and said, 'What shall we do with the ark of the Lord? Tell us what we should send with it to its place'. They said, 'If you send away the ark of the God of Israel, do not send it empty, but by all means return him a guilt-offering. (1 Sam 6:1-3)

'Son of Atreus', said he, 'I deem that we should now turn roving home if we would escape destruction, for we are being cut down by war and pesti-lence at once. *Let us ask some priest or prophet*, or some reader of dreams (for dreams, too, are of Zeus) who can tell us why Phoebus Apollo is so angry, and say whether it is for some vow that we have broken, or heca-tomb that we have not offered, and whether he will accept the savour of lambs and goats without blemish, so as to take away the plague from us.' (*Il.* I, 60-70)

The thematic element of following a cow that has never been yoked occurs also in the story of Cadmus, who had received such an oracle while searching for his sister Europa:

> Now then, get ready a new cart and two milk-cows that have never borne a yoke, and yoke the cows to the cart, but take their calves home, away from them. Take the ark of the Lord and place it on the cart, and put in a box at its side the figures of gold, which you are returning to him as a guilt-offering. Then send it off, and let it go on its way. And watch; if it goes up on the way to its own land, to Beth-shemesh, then it is he who has done us this great harm; but if not, then we shall know that it is not his hand that struck us; it happened to us by chance. (1 Sam 6:7-9)

> To this land came Cadmus of Tyre, at whose feet an unyoked heifer threw itself down, giving effect to an oracle on the spot where the god's response bade him take up his abode in Aonia's rich cornlands, where gushing Dirce's fair rivers of water pour over verdant fruitful fields. (Euripides, *Phoenissae* 640-50)

> When…Cadmus…came to Delphi to inquire about Europa, the god told him not to trouble about Europa, but to be guided by a cow, and to found a city wherever she should fall down for weariness. After receiving such an oracle he journeyed through Phocis; then falling in with a cow among the herds of Pelagon, he followed it behind. And after traversing Boeotia, it sank down where is now the city of Thebes. (Apollodorus, *Library* 3, 4, 1)

Samuel's Prophecy / The Tyrant in Euripides' Suppliants

After the Philistines attacked Israel, the people ask Samuel to give them a king like other nations. But Samuel passes on a divine warning to them about the despotic tendency of kings, clearly echoing Euripides' praise of democracy:

> These will be the ways of the king who will reign over you: he will take your sons and appoint them to his chariots and to be his horsemen, and to run before his chariots; and he will appoint for himself commanders of thousands and commanders of fifties, and some to plough his ground and to reap his harvest, and to make his implements of war and the equipment of his chariots. He will take your daughters to be perfumers and cooks and bakers. He will take the best of your fields and vineyards and olive orchards and give them to his courtiers. He will take one-tenth of your grain and of your vineyards and give it to his officers and his courtiers. He will take your male and female slaves, and the best of your cattle and donkeys, and put them to his work. He will take one-tenth of your flocks, and you shall be his slaves. And in that day you will cry out because of your king, whom you have chosen for yourselves; but the Lord will not answer you in that day. (1 Sam 8:11-18)

Naught is more hostile to a city than a despot; where he is, there are first no laws common to all, but one man is tyrant, in whose keeping and in his alone the law resides, and in that case equality is at an end. But when the laws are written down, rich and poor alike have equal justice, and it is open to the weaker to use the same language to the prosperous when he is reviled by him, and the weaker prevails over the stronger if he have justice on his side. Freedom's mark is also seen in this: 'Who hath wholesome counsel to declare unto the state?' And he who chooses to do so gains renown, while he, who hath no wish, remains silent. What greater equality can there be in a city? Again, where the people are absolute rulers of the land, they rejoice in having reserve of youthful citizens, while a king counts this a hostile element, and strives to slay the leading men, all such as he deems discreet, for he fears for his power. How then can a city remain stable, where one cuts short all enterprise and mows down the young like meadow-flowers in spring-time? What boots it to acquire wealth and livelihood for children, merely to add to the tyrant's substance by one's toil? Why train up virgin daughters virtuously in our homes to gratify a tyrant's whim, whenever he will, and cause tears to those who rear them? May my life end if ever my children are to be wedded by violence! (Euripides, *The Suppliants* 430-60)

According to Jacques Cazeaux, this prophecy of Samuel is at the centre of the greater narrative.[1] The prophecy predicts the story's future; for the demented Saul will disobey God's order, David will have his own faithful servant murdered to appropriate his wife, and Solomon, the apostate, will rouse the anger of the northern tribes and permanently divide the kingdom. The Ideal State of the twelve tribes under Yahweh cannot be maintained by a king—that is the main plot line of Samuel–Kings. The criticism of tyranny is well present in Plato's *Statesman*, the *Republic* and the *Laws*, but a literal parallel to the biblical narrative is clearest in this speech of Theseus of Athens, responding to the Theban herald. Euripides offers an apology for Athenian democracy, while the biblical author opposes the tyranny of the platonic state.

Jonathan

Then Jonathan said, 'Now we will cross over to those men and will show ourselves to them. If they say to us, 'Wait until we come to you', then we will stand still in our place, and we will not go up to them. But if they say, 'Come up to us', then we will go up; for the Lord has given them into our hand. That will be the sign for us.' So both of them showed themselves to the garrison of the Philistines; and the Philistines said,

---

1.   Cazeaux, *Saül, David et Salomon*, and *Le partage de minuit*, 286.

'Look, Hebrews are coming out of the holes where they have hidden themselves'. The men of the garrison hailed Jonathan and his armour-bearer, saying, 'Come up to us, and we will show you something'. Jonathan said to his armour-bearer, 'Come up after me; for the Lord has given them into the hand of Israel'. (1 Sam 14:8-12)

This scene of Jonathan's attack on the Philistines, in accordance to the sign Yahweh gives them, finds an amusing parallel in Herodotus' etiological tale of the *paion:*

The Paionians from the Strymon had been commanded by an oracle of their god to march against the Perinthians; and if the Perinthians, when encamped opposite to them, should shout aloud and call to them by their name, they were to attack them; but if they should not shout to them, they were not to attack them: and thus the Paionians proceeded to do. Now when the Perinthians were encamped opposite to them in the suburb of their city, a challenge was made and a single combat took place in three different forms; for they matched a man against a man, and a horse against a horse, and a dog against a dog. Then, as the Perinthians were getting the better in two of the three, in their exultation they raised a shout of paion, and the Paionians conjectured that this was the very thing which was spoken of in the oracle, and said doubtless to one another, 'Now surely the oracle is being accomplished for us, now it is time for us to act'. So the Paionians attacked the Perinthians when they had raised the shout of paion, and they had much the better in the fight, and left but few of them alive. (Herodotus V, 1)

As the *paion* is a song dedicated to Apollo, the *Paionians* understood this to be the meaning of the oracle. In the Bible, the play on words is, of course, lost, although the theme of the story remains: if the enemy calls out, God will grant victory.

Note 1 Sam 14:13-15, which reads:

Then Jonathan climbed up on his hands and feet, with his armour-bearer following after him. *The Philistines fell before Jonathan, and his armour-bearer, coming after him, killed them.* In that first slaughter Jonathan and his armour-bearer killed about twenty men within an area about half a furrow long in an acre of land. *There was a panic in the camp*, in the field, and among all the people; the garrison and even the raiders trembled; the earth quaked; and it became a very great panic.

This scene of Jonathan and his armour-bearer seems similarly inspired by the *Iliad*—specifically the scenes of Ulysses and Diomedes' attack on a Trojan camp at night and of the panic that followed:

The two then went onwards amid the fallen armour and the blood, and came presently to the company of Thracian soldiers, who were sleeping, tired out with their day's toil; their goodly armour was lying on the ground beside them all orderly in three rows, and each man had his yoke of horses beside him. Rhesus was sleeping in the middle, and hard by him his horses were made fast to the topmost rim of his chariot. Ulysses from some way off saw him and said, 'This, Diomed, is the man, and these are the horses about which Dolon whom we killed told us. Do your very utmost; dally not about your armour, but loose the horses at once—or else kill the men yourself, while I see to the horses.' Thereon Athena put courage into the heart of Diomed, and he smote them right and left. They made a hideous groaning as they were being hacked about, and the earth was red with their blood. As a lion springs furiously upon a flock of sheep or goats when he finds without their shepherd, so did the son of Tydeus set upon the Thracian soldiers till he had killed twelve. *As he killed them Ulysses came and drew them aside by their feet one by one*, that the horses might go forward freely without being frightened as they passed over the dead bodies, for they were not yet used to them... (Hipocoon) started up out of his sleep and saw that the horses were no longer in their place, and that the men were gasping in their death-agony; on this he groaned aloud, and called upon his friend by name. *Then the whole Trojan camp was in an uproar* as the people kept hurrying together, and they marvelled at the deeds of the heroes who had now got away towards the ships. (*Il.* X, 470-505, 520-25)

In both stories, two warriors attack an enemy camp; one fights while the other drags back the bodies, and tumult is raised in both camps. Kupitz suggests a fingerprint to support these passages' connection:

Jonathan and his armour-bearer killed about twenty men *within an area about half a furrow long in an acre of land.* (1 Sam 14:14)

Dolon suspected nothing and soon passed them, but when he had got about as far *as the distance by which a mule-ploughed furrow exceeds one that has been ploughed by oxen* (for mules can plough fallow land quicker than oxen) they ran after him. (*Il.* X, 350-55)

Goliath

The Philistines stood on the mountain on one side, and Israel stood on the mountain on the other side, with a valley between them. And there came out from the camp of the Philistines a champion named Goliath, of Gath, whose height was six cubits and a span. He had a helmet of bronze on his head, and he was armoured with a coat of mail; the weight of the coat was five thousand shekels of bronze. He had greaves of bronze on his legs and a javelin of bronze slung between his shoulders. The shaft of his spear was like a weaver's beam, and his spear's head weighed six hundred shekels of iron; and his shield-bearer went before him… Saul clothed David with his armour; he put a bronze helmet on his head and clothed him with a coat of mail. David strapped Saul's sword over the armour, and he tried in vain to walk, for he was not used to them. Then David said to Saul, 'I cannot walk with these; for I am not used to them'. So David removed them. (1 Sam 17:3-7, 37-38)

The comic scene of great Saul lending his armour to the small shepherd boy, David, carries an echo of the story of Achilles, lending his weapons to Patroclus:

As he spoke Patroclus put on his armour. First he greaved his legs with greaves of good make, and fitted with ankle-clasps of silver; after this he donned the cuirass of the son of Aeacus, richly inlaid and studded. He hung his silver-studded sword of bronze about his shoulders, and then his mighty shield. On his comely head he set his helmet, well wrought, with a crest of horse-hair that nodded menacingly above it. He grasped two redoubtable spears that suited his hands, but he did not take the spear of noble Achilles, so stout and strong, for none other of the Achaeans could wield it, though Achilles could do so easily. This was the ashen spear from Mount Pelion, which Chiron had cut upon a mountain top and had given to Peleus, wherewith to deal out death among heroes. (*Il.* XVI, 130-40)

Metaphors comparing warriors to wild animals are a typical Homeric form. This recalls David's description of himself fighting animals:

But David said to Saul, 'Your servant used to keep sheep for his father; and whenever a lion or a bear came, and took a lamb from the flock, I went after it and struck it down, rescuing the lamb from its mouth; and if it turned against me, I would catch it by the jaw, strike it down, and kill it. Your servant has killed both lions and bears; and this uncircumcised Philistine shall be like one of them, since he has defied the armies of the living God.' David said, 'The Lord, who saved me from the paw of the lion and from the paw of the bear, will save me from the hand of this Philistine'. So Saul said to David, 'Go, and may the Lord be with you!' (1 Sam 17:34-37)

As two lions whom their dam has reared in the depths of some mountain forest to plunder homesteads and carry off sheep and cattle till they get killed by the hand of man, so were these two vanquished by Aeneas, and fell like high pine-trees to the ground. (*Il.* V, 550-55)

In the following passages, duelling warriors, about to fight, insult each other and proclaim that the other's corpse will feed the wild animals:

The Philistine said to David, 'Am I a dog, that you come to me with sticks?' And the Philistine cursed David by his gods. The Philistine said to David, '*Come to me, and I will give your flesh to the birds of the air and to the wild animals of the field*'. But David said to the Philistine,

'You come to me with sword and spear and javelin; but I come to you in the name of the Lord of hosts, the God of the armies of Israel, whom you have defied. This very day the Lord will deliver you into my hand, and I will strike you down and cut off your head; and *I will give the dead bodies of the Philistine army this very day to the birds of the air and to the wild animals of the earth*, so that all the earth may know that there is a God in Israel, and that all this assembly may know that the Lord does not save by sword and spear; for the battle is the Lord's and he will give you into our hand.' (1 Sam 17:43-47)

But Hector answered, 'Ajax, braggart and false of tongue, would that I were as sure of being son for evermore to aegis-bearing Zeus, with Queen Hera for my mother, and of being held in like honour with Athena and Apollo, as I am that this day is big with the destruction of the Achaeans; and *you shall fall among them if you dare abide my spear; it shall rend your fair body and bid you glut our hounds and birds of prey with your fat and your flesh*, as you fall by the ships of the Achaeans'. (*Il.* XIII, 825-30)

Let us look at the recurring concept of the lethal stone throw:

When the Philistine drew nearer, David ran quickly towards the battle line to meet the Philistine. David put his hand in his bag, took out a stone, slung it, and struck the Philistine on his forehead; the stone sank into his forehead, and he fell face down on the ground. (1 Sam 17:48-49)

Hector now struck him on the head with a stone just as he had caught hold of the body, and his brains inside his helmet were all battered in, so that he fell face foremost upon the body of Sarpedon, and there died. (*Il.* XVI, 570-75)

Patroclus then sprang from his chariot to the ground, with a spear in his left hand, and in his right a jagged stone as large as his hand could hold. He stood still and threw it, nor did it go far without hitting some one; the cast was not in vain, for the stone struck Cebriones, Hector's charioteer, a bastard son of Priam, as he held the reins in his hands. The stone hit him on the forehead and drove his brows into his head for the bone was smashed, and his eyes fell to the ground at his feet. (*Il.* XVI, 735-45)

The fight between two champions (where one uses a sling) is found in another Greek myth, about the Epeians versus the Etolians:

(Aetolus) collected an army and returned from Aetolia to attack the Epeians who were in possession of Elis; but when the Epeians met them with arms, and it was found that the two forces were evenly matched, Pyraechmes the Aetolian and Degmenus the Epeian, in accordance with an ancient custom of the Greeks, advanced to single combat. Degmenus was lightly armed with a bow, thinking that he would easily overcome a heavy-armed opponent at long range, but Pyraechmes armed himself with a sling and a bag of stones, after he had noticed his opponent's ruse (as it happened, the sling had only recently been invented by the Aetolians); and since the sling had longer range, Degmenus fell, and the Aetolians drove out the Epeians and took possession of the land. (Strabo, *Geog.* VIII, 3:33)

Oxylus was anxious to get the kingdom of Elis without a battle, but Dius would not give way; he proposed that, instead of their fighting a pitched battle with all their forces, a single soldier should be chosen from each army to fight as its champion. This proposal chanced to find favour with both sides, and the champions chosen were the Elean Degmenus, an archer, and Pyraechmes, a slinger, to represent the Aetolians. Pyraechmes won and Oxylus got the kingdom. (Pausanias, *Description of Greece* V, 4, 1-2)[2]

Saul's Madness / Cambyses

Saul becomes jealous of David's success and popularity. Twice he tries to kill him with his spear, but David avoids the attacks, then flees (1 Sam 18:10-11; see also 19:4-6, 9-10). Saul's divinely sent madness can be compared to that of the Persian Cambyses who had killed the sacred Egyptian ox of Apis:

These were the acts of madness done by Cambyses towards those of his own family, whether the madness was produced really on account of Apis or from some other cause, as many ills are wont to seize upon men; for it is said moreover that Cambyses had from his birth a certain grievous malady, that which is called by some the 'sacred' disease: and it was certainly nothing strange that when the body was suffering from a grievous malady, the mind should not be sound either. (Herodotus III, 33)

Like Jonathan, Croesus, the advisor to Cambyses' father Cyrus, tries to reason with Cambyses:

'O king, do not thou indulge the heat of thy youth and passion in all things, but retain and hold thyself back: it is a good thing to be prudent, and forethought is wise. Thou however are putting to death men who are of thy own people, condemning them on charges of no moment, and thou art putting to death men's sons also. If thou do many such things, beware lest the Persians make revolt from thee. As for me, thy father Cyrus gave me charge, earnestly bidding me to admonish thee, and suggest to thee that which I should find to be good.' Thus he counselled him, manifesting goodwill towards him; but Cambyses answered: 'Dost thou venture to counsel me, who excellently well didst rule thy own country, and well didst counsel my father, bidding him pass over the river Araxes and go

2.   Translated by W.H.S. Jones and H.A. Ormerod.

against the Massagetai, when they were willing to pass over into our land, and so didst utterly ruin thyself by ill government of thy own land, and didst utterly ruin Cyrus, who followed thy counsel. However thou shall not escape punishment now, for know that before this I had very long been desiring to find some occasion against thee.' *Thus having said he took his bow meaning to shoot him, but Crœsus started up and ran out: and so since he could not shoot him, he gave orders to his attendants to take and slay him. The attendants however, knowing his moods, con- cealed Crœsus, with the intention that if Cambyses should change his mind and seek to have Crœsus again, they might produce him and receive gifts as the price of saving his life*; but if he did not change his mind nor feel desire to have him back, then they might kill him. Not long after- wards Cambyses did in fact desire to have Crœsus again, and the attendants perceiving this reported to him that he was still alive: and Cambyses said that he rejoiced with Crœsus that he was still alive, but that they who had preserved him should not get off free, but he would put them to death: and thus he did. (Herodotus III, 36)

Like Cambyses in his murderous rage, at first Saul wants to kill David, yet Jonathan persuaded him not to; and the king changes his mind. In the days that follow, Saul wonders why David is not present at his table, as if he had forgotten about trying to kill him (1 Sam 20). Saul pursues David and commits a religious crime by killing the priests of Nob who had welcomed David, not knowing that Saul wanted him dead (1 Sam 22). Cambyses also had committed such a crime when he entered an Egyptian temple and burnt its statues (Herodotus III, 37-38). Saul's inquiry concerning David's identity (1 Sam 17:55-58) also finds its signifying precedent in Herodotus:

For whenever Xerxes (sitting just under the mountain opposite Salamis, which is called Aigaleos) saw any one of his own side display a deed of valour in the sea-fight, he inquired about him who had done it, and the scribes recorded the name of the ship's captain with that of his father and the city from whence he came. (Herodotus VIII, 90)

Ulysses' Madness

When Agamemnon and Menelaus, son of Atreus, were assembling the leaders who had pledged themselves to attack Troy, they came to the island of Ithaca to Ulysses, son of Laertes. He had been warned by an oracle that if he went to Troy he would return home alone and in need, with his comrades lost, after twenty years. And so when he learned that spokesmen would come to him, he put on a cap, pretending madness, and yoked a horse and an ox to the plow. Palamedes felt he was pretending when he saw this, and taking his son Telemachus from the cradle, put him in front of the plow with the words: 'Give up your pretense and come and join the allies'. Then Ulysses promised that he would come; from that time he was hostile to Palamedes. (Hyginus, *Fables* 95; see also the variant in Apollodorus, *Epitome* 3, 6, 7)

David rose and fled that day from Saul; he went to King Achish of Gath. The servants of Achish said to him, 'Is this not David the king of the land? Did they not sing to one another of him in dances, "Saul has killed his thousands, and David his tens of thousands"?' David took these words to heart and was very much afraid of King Achish of Gath. So he changed his behaviour before them; he pretended to be mad when in their presence. He scratched marks on the doors of the gate, and let his spittle run down his beard. Achish said to his servants, *'Look, you see the man is mad; why then have you brought him to me? Do I lack madmen, that you have brought this fellow to play the madman in my presence? Shall this fellow come into my house?'* (1 Sam 21:10-15)

Another parallel confirms the association with Ulysses:[3]

On this Antinous began to abuse the swineherd. 'You precious idiot', he cried, *'what have you brought this man to town for? Have we not tramps and beggars enough already to pester us as we sit at meat*? Do you think it a small thing that such people gather here to waste your master's property and must you bring this man as well?' (*Od.* XVII, 375-80)

Night Incursion

During the story of David's flight from Saul, at night as everyone is sleeping, David sneaks inside Saul's camp to steal his spear. This scene reiterates that of Priam entering the Achean camp in the *Iliad*:

David and Abishai went to the army by night; there Saul lay sleeping within the encampment, with his spear stuck in the ground at his head; and Abner and the army lay around him. Abishai said to David, 'God has given your enemy into your hand today; now therefore let me pin him to the ground with one stroke of the spear; I will not strike him twice'. But David said to Abishai, 'Do not destroy him; for who can raise his hand against the Lord's anointed, and be guiltless?' David said, 'As the Lord lives, the Lord will strike him down; or his day will come to die; or he will go down into battle and perish. The Lord forbid that I should raise my hand against the Lord's anointed; but now take the spear that is at his head, and the water-jar, and let us go.' So David took the spear that was at Saul's head and the water-jar, and they went away. No one saw it, or knew it, nor did anyone awake; for they were all asleep, because a deep sleep from the Lord had fallen upon them. (1 Sam 26:5-12)

---

3.   West, *The East Face of Helicon*, 429.

David climbs the hill next to the encampment and rouses everyone; he tells Saul that he would never hurt him, Saul weeps and asks David to forgive him. In the *Iliad*, Achilles rejoined the fighting at Troy because Hector had killed Patroclus. After killing Hector, Achilles returns to the Greek camp dragging the corpse in tow. At night, Priam enters the camp and begs Achilles to give back his son's body. Hermes brings sleep upon the Greeks:

> When they reached the trench and the wall that was before the ships, those who were on guard had just been getting their suppers, and *the slayer of Argus threw them all into a deep sleep*. Then he drew back the bolts to open the gates, and took Priam inside with the treasure he had upon his wagon. (*Il.* XXIV, 440-45)

As they speak of the friendship that had bound Priam and Achilles' father, Peleus, both Achilles and Priam weep (*Il.* XXIV, 485-505). Kupitz points out that the theme of Saul sleeping, surrounded by his men with his spear stuck in the ground is also in the *Iliad*:

> First they went to Diomed son of Tydeus, and found him outside his tent clad in his armour with *his comrades sleeping round him and using their shields as pillows; as for their spears, they stood upright on the spikes* of their butts that were driven into the ground, and the burnished bronze flashed afar like the lightning of father Zeus. (*Il.* X, 150-55)

The Witch of Endor / Circe

Saul is constantly defeated by the Philistines. Since God does not respond to him, decides to consult a witch, even though biblical law forbids it:

> So Saul disguised himself and put on other clothes and went there, he and two men with him. They came to the woman by night. And he said, 'Consult a spirit for me, and bring up for me the one whom I name to you'. The woman said to him, 'Surely you know what Saul has done, how he has cut off the mediums and the wizards from the land. *Why then are you laying a snare for my life to bring about my death?'* But Saul swore to her by the Lord, 'As the Lord lives, no punishment shall come upon you for this thing'. Then the woman said, 'Whom shall I bring up for you?' He answered, 'Bring up Samuel for me'. *When the woman saw Samuel, she cried out with a loud voice; and the woman said to Saul, 'Why have you deceived me? You are Saul!'* The king said to her, 'Have no fear; what do you see?' The woman said to Saul, 'I see a divine being coming up out of the ground'. He said to her, 'What is his appearance?' She said, 'An old man is coming up; he is wrapped in a robe'. So Saul knew that it was Samuel, and he bowed with his face to the ground, and did obeisance. (1 Sam 28:8-14)

Samuel's ghost tells Saul that God has abandoned him, and that he will die in battle with his three sons:

> The woman came to Saul, and when she saw that he was terrified, she said to him, 'Your servant has listened to you; I have taken my life in my hand, and have listened to what you have said to me. Now therefore, you also listen to your servant; let me set a morsel of bread before you. *Eat, that you may have strength when you go on your way'. He refused, and said, 'I will not eat'.* But his servants, together with the woman, urged him; and he listened to their words. So he got up from the ground and sat on the bed. Now the woman had a fatted calf in the house. She quickly slaughtered it, and she took flour, kneaded it, and baked unleavened cakes. She put them before Saul and his servants, and they ate. Then they rose and went away that night. (1 Sam 28:21-25)

This scene closely echoes Ulysses' encounter with the witch Circe, who tells him to consult the spirit of Teiresias, a dead seer that can tell Ulysses the way back to Ithaca:

> I rushed at her with my sword drawn as though I would kill her, whereon *she fell with a loud scream,* clasped my knees, and spoke piteously, saying, 'Who and whence are you? From what place and people have you come?... *Surely you can be none other than the bold hero Ulysses,* who Hermes always said would come here some day with his ship while on his way home form Troy; so be it then; sheathe your sword and let us go to bed, that we may make friends and learn to trust each other.' And I answered, 'Circe, how can you expect me to be friendly with you when you have just been turning all my men into pigs? And now that you have got me here myself, you mean me mischief when you ask me to go to bed with you, and will unman me and make me fit for nothing. *I shall certainly not consent to go to bed with you unless you will first take your solemn oath to plot no further harm against me'.* So she swore at once as I had told her, and when she had completed her oath then I went to bed with her... *(A servant) drew a clean table beside me; an upper servant brought me bread and offered me many things of what there was in the house, and then Circe bade me eat, but I would not, and sat without heeding what was before me, still moody and suspicious.* When Circe saw me sitting there without eating, and in great grief, she came to me and said, 'Ulysses, why do you sit like that as though you were dumb, gnawing at your own heart, and refusing both meat and drink? Is it that you are still suspicious? You ought not to be, for I have already sworn solemnly that I will not hurt you.' And I said, 'Circe, no man with any sense of what is right can think of either eating or drinking in your house until you have set his friends free and let him see them. If you want me to eat and drink, you must free my men and bring them to me that I may see them with my own eyes.' (*Od.* X, 315-380)

We see here an inversion of sequence. When Circe realizes that she is facing Ulysses, she screams loudly, exactly as the witch does when she becomes aware that the man in front of her is Saul. Ulysses asks Circe to swear not to hurt him, whereas, in the biblical story, the witch entreats Saul (before she recognises him) to swear not to hurt her. In both texts, the hero declines any food, yet the witch (or her servant) prepares a meal. Ulysses goes on to meet Teiresias as per Circe's advice, and Teiresias tells Ulysses how he is eventually to get home (*Od.* XI). This famous part of the *Odyssey* describes the dead souls living in Hades. The biblical episode suggests that magic does work (although it is prohibited in Deut 18:9-14 as in Plato's *Laws* 933 e). Neither Plato nor the biblical author dared call magic a vain superstition, lest they deny the existence of God.

Saul / Ajax

Samuel's prediction will be fulfilled:

> The battle pressed hard upon Saul; the archers found him, and he was badly wounded by them. Then Saul said to his armour-bearer, 'Draw your sword and thrust me through with it, so that these uncircumcised may not come and thrust me through, and make sport of me'. But his armour-bearer was unwilling; for he was terrified. So Saul took his own sword and fell upon it. When his armour-bearer saw that Saul was dead, he also fell upon his sword and died with him. So Saul and his three sons and his armour-bearer and all his men died together on the same day. (1 Sam 31:3-6)

A similar theme occurs in Sophocles' *Ajax* when Ajax is unwilling to die at the hands of his enemies and throws himself on his sword (Sophocles, *Ajax* 815-60).

Asahel of the Swift Feet

After Saul's death, the house of Saul, held by his cousin Abner, fights with the house of David for the kingship of Israel:

> The three sons of Zeruiah were there, Joab, Abishai, and Asahel. Now *Asahel was as swift of foot as a wild gazelle.* Asahel pursued Abner, turning neither to the right nor to the left as he followed him. Then Abner looked back and said, 'Is it you, Asahel?' He answered, 'Yes, it is'. Abner said to him, 'Turn to your right or to your left, and seize one of the young men, and take his spoil'. But Asahel would not turn away from following him. Abner said again to Asahel, 'Turn away from following me; why should I strike you to the ground? How then could I show my face to your brother Joab?' But he refused to turn away. So Abner struck him in the

stomach with the butt of his spear, so that the spear came out at his back. He fell there, and died where he lay. And all those who came to the place where Asahel had fallen and died, stood still. (2 Sam 2:18-23)

This scene, like that of the fight of David against Goliath, is full of typical Homeric themes. First, the swift feet of Asahel are an obvious reference to the 'swift-footed Achilles', (see *Il*. I, 55). When Abner tells Asahel that for Joab's sake he does not want to kill him, and suggests that Asahel attack another warrior, this is reminiscent of the meeting of Glaucus and Diomedes:

Henceforth, however, I must be your host in middle Argos, and you mine in Lycia, if I should ever go there; let us avoid one another's spears even during a general engagement; there are many noble Trojans and allies whom I can kill, if I overtake them and heaven delivers them into my hand; so again with yourself, there are many Achaeans whose lives you may take if you can; we two, then, will exchange armour, that all present may know of the old ties that subsist between us. (*Il*. VI, 220-30)

But as Asahel pursues Abner, who turns back and strikes him, the same Glaucus turns back to kill Bathycles:

Glaucus, captain of the Lycians, was the first to rally them, by killing Bathycles son of Chalcon who lived in Hellas and was the richest man among the Myrmidons. Glaucus turned round suddenly, just as Bathycles who was pursuing him was about to lay hold of him, and drove his spear right into the middle of his chest, whereon he fell heavily to the ground. (*Il*. XVI, 595-99; cf. *Il*. XVI, 818-22)

Asahel has some affinity with Patroclus, Achilles' cousin and best friend. The scene of Joab blowing his horn at the end of the battle at sundown (2 Sam 2:28) is similar to Achilles' approach to the battlefield, shouting to make the battle stop (*Il*. XVIII, 230-40). As the Acheans mourned Patroclus, so Joab's men mourn Asahel.

The Wrath of Abner

Ishbaal accuses Abner of sleeping with Saul's concubine, which angers Abner as he had supported Ishbaal against David, as Achilles did Agamemnon. Abner forges an alliance with David, who accepts on the condition that he get his wife Michal back, mentioning that he gained her for the price of the foreskins of one hundred Philistines (2 Sam 3:6-16). In comparison, the *Iliad* commences with this argument between Agamemnon and Achilles (*Il*. I, 110-80). Both Abner and Achilles are so vexed that they threaten to withdraw their precious support. That same scene was already used in 1 Samuel 6, when the Philistines asked their priests and prophets what should be done with the ark (in the same manner as the Greeks asked why Apollo was striking them). In his anger and frustration, Abner asks if he is 'a dog's head for Judah' (2 Sam 3:8) and in his own rage, Achilles calls Agamemnon a 'dog face':

> 'Wine-bibber', he cried, 'with the face of a dog and the heart of a hind, you never dare to go out with the host in fight, nor yet with our chosen men in ambuscade. (*Il*. I, 220-25)

Michal is taken from her new husband Paltiel and brought to David; Paltiel weeps, as Achilles did when Agamemnon's men came to take Briseis from him (*Il*. I, 345-50).

Abner's Funerals

To avenge Asahel's death, Joab murders Abner. David regrets this, as he himself had made an alliance with Abner to become the legitimate king of Israel, even though Saul had left Ishbaal as his successor. David organises national funeral rites and shows how sorry he is so that the people may know that this assassination was not at his order. David walks behind the bier, pronounces a moving speech, and everybody weeps:

> Then David said to Joab and to all the people who were with him, 'Tear your clothes, and put on sackcloth, and mourn over Abner'. And King David followed the bier. They buried Abner at Hebron. The king lifted up his voice and wept at the grave of Abner, and all the people wept. The king lamented for Abner, saying, 'Should Abner die as a fool dies? Your hands were not bound, your feet were not fettered; as one falls before the wicked you have fallen'. And all the people wept over him again. *Then all the people came to persuade David to eat something while it was still day; but David swore, saying, 'So may God do to me, and more, if I taste bread or anything else before the sun goes down!'* All the people took notice of it, and it pleased them; just as everything the king did pleased all the people. So all the people and all Israel understood that day that the king had no part in the killing of Abner son of Ner. (2 Sam 3:31-36)

> When they had thrown down their great logs of wood over the whole ground, they stayed all of them where they were, but Achilles ordered his brave Myrmidons to gird on their armour, and to yoke each man his horses; they therefore rose, girded on their armour and mounted each his chariot—they and their charioteers with them. The chariots went before, and they that were on foot followed as a cloud in their tens of thousands after. In the midst of them his comrades bore Patroclus and covered him with the locks of their hair which they cut off and threw upon his body.

> Last came Achilles with his head bowed for sorrow, so noble a comrade was he taking to the house of Hades. When they came to the place of which Achilles had told them they laid the body down and built up the wood. Achilles then bethought him of another matter. He went a space away from the pyre, and cut off the yellow lock which he had let grow for the River Spercheius. He looked all sorrowfully out upon the dark sea, and said, 'Spercheius, in vain did my father Peleus vow to you that when I returned home to my loved native land I should cut off this lock and offer you a holy hecatomb; fifty she-goats was I to sacrifice to you there at your springs, where is your grove and your altar fragrant with burnt-offerings. Thus did my father vow, but you have not fulfilled his prayer; now, therefore, that I shall see my home no more, I give this lock as a keepsake to the hero Patroclus.' As he spoke he placed the lock in the hands of his dear comrade, and all who stood by were filled with yearning and lamentation. (*Il.* XXIII, 120-50)

Again, we see a 'fingerprint', as both David and Achilles refuse to eat until sunset:

> The elders of the Achaeans gathered round Achilles and prayed him to take food, but he groaned and would not do so. 'I pray you', said he, 'if any comrade will hear me, bid me neither eat nor drink, for I am in great heaviness, and will stay fasting even to the going down of the sun'. (*Il.* XIX, 315-20)

The process of drawing on these chapters is very coherent. The biblical author reiterates the most important themes and scenes of the *Iliad*, such as the argument between Agamemnon and Achilles that opens book I, and Patroclus' death in book XVI. The death of Achilles' dearest comrade is the reason why in book XIX he decides to reconcile with Agamemnon and rejoin the battle. This same book is also the source of the story of Ate, a story told by Agamemnon, bearing some echo in the dispute between Jacob and Esau in Genesis, as well as for the curse of the woman whose feet never touch the ground in Deuteronomy.

Mephi-Bosheth and David: The Lame and the Red-haired

David reigns over all Israel thanks to his alliance with Abner. David conquers Jerusalem, still inhabited by Jebusites and makes it his capital. He defeats the peoples of many lands around Israel, such as the Philistines, Moab, and Edom (2 Sam 8:13-14). After these victories, David wants to know if Saul has left an heir. He is told that Jonathan left a son, named Mephi-Bosheth in the Masoretic text, who is lame. David seeks reconciliation with Saul's house through Mephi-Bosheth (2 Sam 9:1-13). Outwardly, David shows generosity towards his best friend's son. But David knows better than anyone that eating at the king's table everyday implies a client's indebtedness (1 Sam 20).

The reader is not fooled though, for David obviously wants to keep an eye on Saul's only legitimate heir, with the right to Israel's throne. Ziba, his jealous servant, will later accuse Mephi-Bosheth of having wanted to wrest the kingship from David when he was in a weakened state (2 Sam 16). Mephi-Bosheth is lame in both legs, reminiscent of the lame Hephaistos:

> Saul's son Jonathan had a son who was crippled in his feet. He was five years old when the news about Saul and Jonathan came from Jezreel. His nurse picked him up and fled; and, in her haste to flee, it happened that he fell and became lame. His name was Mephi-Bosheth. (2 Sam 4:4)

> Then she called Hephaistos and said, 'Hephaistos, come here, Thetis wants you'; and the far-famed lame god answered, 'Then it is indeed an august and honoured goddess who has come here; she it was that took care of me when I was suffering from the heavy fall which I had through my cruel mother's anger—for she would have got rid of me because I was lame. It would have gone hardly with me had not Eurynome, daughter of the ever-encircling waters of Oceanus, and Thetis, taken me to their bosom. (*Il.* XVIII, 395-400)

Both Mephi-Bosheth and Hephaistos fell when they were children and became lame. In differing versions of the Greek myth, Hera hurled Hephaistos from Mount Olympus, either because he was ugly (and thus became lame from the impact of landing) or because he was already lame. There is also a scene in the epic of the Argonauts that is similar to the story of David and Mephi-Bosheth. King Pelias had put Aison under house arrest in the king's palace, where he secretly begat a son, Jason. Pretending that the baby died at birth, Aison sent him to be raised by the centaur Chiron (Apollonius, *Argonautica* I, 5-15; for a longer account see Pindar, *Pythian* IV). Jason, the legitimate heir to the throne of Iolchos, arrives before the usurper Pelias with but a single shoe, as if he walked with a limp. This scene shows the same pattern as the one in which David pretends to welcome the lame Mephi-Bosheth, the deserved inheritor to the throne of Israel. He was, like Hephaistos, lame due to an accident in his childhood. He arrives at David's court as Jason did— representing his rival's offspring. It seems the biblical writer again mixes two different Greek themes into one.

With echoes of Jacob/Israel's brother Esau, David, the red-haired king of Israel, conquers Edom and in so doing, fulfils Isaac's blessing. In the next episode of the chain narrative, David rids himself of Mephi-Bosheth, the lame, the last of Saul's offspring (and the last threat to his throne). In Genesis, it is Jacob/Israel who is lame and his rival Esau red-haired; Jacob robbed Esau of his birthright and their father's blessing. Jacob's two wives, Leah and Rachel, are also rivals. Leah gives birth to Judah, ancestor of David, and Rachel to Benjamin, ancestor of Saul. Now, the story is reversed and the red-headed David robs his lame rival from the house of Saul of his inheritance, the throne of Israel.

This inversion is significant: Jacob, in the scene of Isaac's deception, covered his arms with goat hair (a motif which recurs in Michal's bed, 1 Sam 19:16). Though Isaac had heard Jacob's voice, he felt Esau's hairy arms (Gen 27:22). Jacob tried to impersonate his twin brother, but failed; he still feared him, fled from him, and when he returned, prostrated himself before him seven times (Gen 33:3). In Samuel, David's victory—Israel's victory—over Edom is total and David has achieved his ancestor Jacob's desire to overpower and to become Edom. David is Jacob's literary twin—the new Jacob, having Esau's strength. Lévi-Strauss' method aims to find 'packs of relations' in the different episodes of a myth. I believe that the relationship between Jacob and David matches Lévi-Strauss' method and demonstrates its relevance.

David and Uriah / Proetus and Bellerophon

Soon after, David embroiled Israel in a war against Ammon, though he himself stayed in the safety of his palace. One night, he saw from his terrace a beautiful woman bathing, and ordered that she be brought before him. Her name was Bathsheba, daughter of Eliam and wife of Uriah the Hittite. David seduced her, and she became pregnant. Later, David asked his general Joab to summon Uriah. David treated him well, and suggested that he rest and sleep with his wife. But, since Israel was at war, Uriah refused and slept outside the palace. David realised that as he could not force Uriah upon Bathsheba, she would be accused of adultery when her pregnancy was noticed. Thus, he decided to get rid of Uriah (2 Sam 11:1-27).

David is the supreme king of Israel, and, as Samuel had prophesied, takes to himself a woman of his own choice. David's crime marks the beginning of the end for Israel; his first child will die after a week, while his second child with Bathsheba is Solomon. In 1 Samuel, David seemed to be portrayed as the perfect hero. But in 2 Samuel, his hypocrisy and enmity towards the house of Saul culminates in murder. David loses God's trust, and the reader's as well as kingship proves to be fatal for Israel. Saul had disobeyed God's orders and David transgressed three commandments of the ten: 'You shall not murder' (Exod 20:13), 'You shall not commit adultery' (Exod 20:14) and 'You shall not covet thy neighbour's wife' (Exod 20:17). The kings abandoned the divine law given to Moses and Israel; this reflects the platonic framework of Atlantis sinking to its demise. The thematic element of the letter, which David has sent with the order to kill its bearer (2 Sam 11:15) appears already in the epic of Sargon of Akkad. But it is also in the *Iliad*, in the speech of Glaucus to Diomedes:

> For Antea, wife of Proetus, lusted after him, and would have had him lie with her in secret; but Bellerophon was an honourable man and would not, so she told lies about him to Proteus. 'Proetus', said she, 'kill Bellerophon or die, for he would have had converse with me against my will'. The king was angered, but shrank from killing Bellerophon, so he sent him to Lycia with lying letters of introduction, written on a folded tablet, and containing much ill against the bearer. He bade Bellerophon show these letters to his father-in-law, to the end that he might thus perish; Bellerophon therefore went to Lycia, and the gods conveyed him safely. (*Il.* VI, 150-60)

The Revolt of Absalom

The prophet Nathan warns David that God has cursed him; his neighbour will take his wives in the light of the sun (2 Sam 12:12). The following chapter tells of how David's daughter Tamar (who bears the same name as their ancestor, Judah's daughter-in-law) is raped by her half-brother Amnon, David's elder son. David, however, does not punish him, but Tamar's full brother Absalom avenges her by killing Amnon. Absalom goes into exile, fleeing to his grandfather Talmai, king of Geshour. Absalom returns to Jerusalem after three years and pretends to reconcile with his father, slowly fomenting the people to rise up against him. David is forced to flee Jerusalem. Claiming the throne and bringing humiliation on David, Absalom rapes David's ten concubines in front of all of Israel, fulfilling Nathan's prophecy. David, however, eventually raises an army and defeats Absalom, who is killed by Joab. David retakes his palace a broken man, knowing that his son has paid the price for his sin.

Tamar / Nitocris

> So his servant put her out, and bolted the door after her. But Tamar put ashes on her head, and tore the long robe that she was wearing; she put her hand on her head, and went away, crying aloud as she went. After two full years Absalom had sheepshearers at Baal-hazor, which is near

Ephraim, and Absalom invited all the king's sons... But Absalom pressed him until he let Amnon and all the king's sons go with him. Absalom made a feast like a king's feast. Then Absalom commanded his servants, 'Watch when Amnon's heart is merry with wine, and when I say to you, "Strike Amnon", then kill him. Do not be afraid; have I not myself commanded you? Be courageous and valiant.' So the servants of Absalom did to Amnon as Absalom had commanded. Then all the king's sons rose, and each mounted his mule and fled. (2 Sam 13:18-19, 23-29)

In Herodotus' second book we find the story of Queen Nitocris. Herodotus tells of the Egyptian kings, a chronicle that finds some reiteration in both the end of Samuel and Kings:

Of (*Nitocris*) they said that desiring to take vengeance for her brother, whom the Egyptians had slain when he was their king and then, after having slain him, had given his kingdom to her—desiring, I say, to take vengeance for him, she destroyed by craft many of the Egyptians. For she caused to be constructed a very large chamber under ground, and making as though she would handsel it but in her mind devising other things, she invited those of the Egyptians whom she knew to have had most part in the murder, and gave a great banquet. Then while they were feasting, she let in the river upon them by a secret conduit of large size. Of her they told no more than this, except that, when this had been accomplished, she threw herself into a room full of ashes, in order that she might escape vengeance. (Herodotus II, 100)

The parallel is inverted: the Queen avenges her brother by inviting his murderers to a banquet and killing them, whereas Absalom avenges his sister by killing Amnon at a banquet.

Three Years of Exile

It is not a coincidence that Absalom goes into exile for three years. Even though the requirement of such a banishment does not appear in biblical law, it is found in Plato:

But Absalom fled, and went to Talmai son of Ammihud, king of Geshur. David mourned for his son day after day. Absalom, having fled to Geshur, stayed there for three years. And the heart of the king went out, yearning for Absalom; for he was now consoled over the death of Amnon. (2 Sam 13:37-39)

If in a fit of anger a husband kills his wedded wife, or the wife her husband, the slayer shall undergo the same purification, and the term of exile shall be three years. And when he who has committed any such crime returns, let him have no communication in sacred rites with his children, neither let him sit at the same table with them, and the father or son who disobeys shall be liable to be brought to trial for impiety by any one who pleases. If a brother or a sister in a fit of passion kills a brother or a sister, they shall undergo purification and exile, as was the case with parents who killed their offspring: they shall not come under the same roof, or share in the sacred rites of those whom they have deprived of their brethren, or of their children. (Plato, *Laws* 868 d-e)

The Half-shaven Beards

So Hanun seized David's envoys, shaved off half the beard of each, cut off their garments in the middle at their hips, and sent them away. When David was told, he sent to meet them, for the men were greatly ashamed. The king said, 'Remain at Jericho until your beards have grown, and then return'. (2 Sam 10:4-5)

He then, as it was now far on in the night, first took down the body of his brother, and then in mockery shaved the right cheeks of all the guards; and after that he put the dead body upon the asses and drove them away home, having accomplished that which was enjoined him by his mother. (Herodotus II, 121 d)

The Rape of the Concubines: Absalom / Phoenix

Ahithophel said to Absalom, 'Go in to your father's concubines, the ones he has left to look after the house; and all Israel will hear that you have made yourself odious to your father, and the hands of all who are with you will be strengthened'. So they pitched a tent for Absalom upon the roof; and Absalom went in to his father's concubines in the sight of all Israel. (2 Sam 16:20-22)

While Israel lived in that land, Reuben went and lay with Bilhah his father's concubine; and Israel heard of it. (Gen 35:22)

We have linked Jacob's accusation of Reuben to the story of Hippolytus, in the homonymous play by Euripides. In the *Iliad*, Achilles' tutor Phoenix tells his story:

I was then flying the anger of my father Amyntor, son of Ormenus, who was furious with me in the matter of his concubine, of whom he was enamoured to the wronging of his wife my mother. My mother, therefore, prayed me without ceasing to lie with the woman myself, that so she hated my father, and in the course of time I yielded. But my father soon came to know, and cursed me bitterly, calling the dread Erinyes to witness. He prayed that no son of mine might ever sit upon his knees—and the gods, Zeus of the world below and awful Persephone, fulfilled his curse. I took counsel to kill him, but some god stayed my rashness and bade me think on men's evil tongues and how I should be branded as the

> murderer of my father: nevertheless I could not bear to stay in my father's
> house with him so bitter against me... I then fled through Hellas till I
> came to fertile Phthia, mother of sheep, and to King Peleus, who made
> me welcome and treated me as a father treats an only son who will be heir
> to all his wealth. He made me rich and set me over much people,
> establishing me on the borders of Phthia where I was chief ruler over the
> Dolopians. (*Il.* IX, 440-80)

This theme—a son sleeping with his father's concubine and then fleeing—resembles the story of Reuben, who raped his father's concubine
after the death of Rachel and is played out most famously in the figure of
Oedipus:

> Oedipus, as tradition says, when dishonoured by his sons, invoked on
> them curses which every one declares to have been heard and ratified by
> the Gods, and Amyntor in his wrath invoked curses on his son Phoenix,
> and Theseus upon Hippolytus, and innumerable others have also called
> down wrath upon their children, whence it is clear that the Gods listen to
> the imprecations of parents; for the curses of parents are, as they ought to
> be, mighty against their children as no others are. (Plato, *Laws* 931 b-c)

Plato commented on these Greek stories shortly after the laws on inheritance and immediately before the law prohibiting magic. It seems very
likely that Phoenix and Hippolytus were sources of inspiration for both
the stories of Absalom and Reuben. Jacob dismissed Ruben of his birthright because Reuben 'went up to his father's bed' (Gen 49:4). It is the
same thematic element which is used in the story of Absalom. Absalom
eventually died, caught up in tree by his long hair; and Joab pierced him
with three javelins (2 Sam 18).

On Mourning and Atonement

In the final chapters of 2 Samuel, Joab forces David to stop mourning for
Absalom (2 Sam 19). When David returns to Jerusalem, a man of
Benjamin named Sheba, son of Bikri, starts another revolt, declaring
David to be a usurper of Saul's throne (2 Sam 20).

When a three-year-long famine strikes the country because Saul had
killed the people of Gibeon, who had made an alliance with Joshua (Josh
9), David executes seven descendants of Saul in atonement (2 Sam 21).
Saul's concubine tends to their corpses, hung outside, until David allows
their burial. This echoes Euripides' *Suppliants*, in which the Seven
against Thebes are dead, and their mothers beg King Theseus (whose
speech against tyranny was used in 1 Sam 8) to claim their bodies from
the Thebans for proper burial.

Synthesis of the Book of Samuel: Jacob, Israel, David

In many ways, David is presented in 1–2 Samuel as a new Jacob, a new Israel. As king, David *is* Israel. This reflects Plato in the *Republic*, who describes the State as a soul on a wider scale. David and Saul's rivalry for the throne echoes both the rivalry of Jacob and his elder brother, Esau, and that between Leah and Rachel (the maternal ancestors of David and Saul, respectively). From this, we might infer that the stories in Samuel were first based on the *Iliad* and on Heracles' ancestry, and the story of Jacob was composed to mirror them. Jacob and Esau fought in their mother's womb (Gen 25:21-23), as did the twins Acrisius and Proetus. That same Proetus later dispatched Bellerophon, bearing a letter containing orders to have him killed (*Il.* VI, 150-160), much as David had sent Uriah (2 Sam 11). Acrisius' descendant Eurystheus succeeded to power in place of his cousin Heracles because of the treachery of Hera (*Il.* XIX), much as Jacob had obtained Isaac's blessing instead of Esau, because of Rebecca's treachery (Gen 27). Jacob fled from his brother Edom ('red') and found refuge with his maternal uncle Laban ('white'). He slept with Leah on his wedding night, believing that she was Rachel (Gen 29:23), a scene comparable to that of Heracles with the daughters of Thespios. Saul promised his elder daughter to David but instead gave her his youngest, Michal (1 Sam 18), with a bride price of two hundred Philistines, as opposed to the hundred that had been requested initially. In the same vein, Jacob worked for fourteen years rather than seven to gain Rachel's hand in marriage. Leah is the mother of Judah, Rachel of Benjamin. When fleeing from Laban, Rachel hid the teraphim in her luggage and pretended to have her period (Gen 31:35), whereas Michal hid the teraphim in her bed and covered them with a pillow of goat hair (1 Sam 19:16) to create the illusion that David was ill in bed (in the same way that Jacob had covered his arms with goat hair to disguise himself as his brother). Laban gave up the search for his teraphim, and made a covenant with Jacob in Mizpah (Gen 31:49). Rachel died while delivering Benjamin on the way to Bethlehem (Gen 35:18-19).

Generations later, Saul hides in the baggage before he is proclaimed king of Israel, in a place called Mizpah (1 Sam 10:17-22). He was the descendant of Rachel through Benjamin, the tribe that had almost been annihilated in Judges (Judg 19–21) for committing a crime similar to that of the Sodomites in Genesis 19. Rachel, metaphorically brooding with the teraphim, gave birth to Benjamin, while Michal, who remained barren (2 Sam 6:23), hid the teraphim in her bed in lieu of her new husband. As Laban gave up the search for his teraphim, hidden under

Rachel's saddle, Saul resurfaces from the luggage generations later, in a city bearing the same name, Mizpah. Through this complex play of reflecting narratives, the author presents the role of the king as that of an empty idol.

On his return from Haran after twenty years, Jacob awoke at night to fight a divine messenger who broke his hip and made him lame (Gen 32:31). Thereafter, he became reconciled with Esau and, sharing their father's 'promised land', Esau took Seir for his part, the land of Edom, and Jacob took Canaan, the future land of Israel (Gen 33). This story reflects that of the twins Acrisius and Proetus, who shared their father's land after years of war. In his story, David, who had red hair like Esau (Gen 25:25; 1 Sam 16:12), defeated and submitted Edom (2 Sam 8:14) as Isaac had prophesied. David put Saul's legitimate inheritor, who—like Jacob—was lame, under house arrest under the pretence that he was being honoured. Mephi-Bosheth's limp literarily combines Hephaistos' crippling fall (*Il.* XVIII // 2 Sam 4:4) with Jason's apparent lameness (he had lost a sandal on his way to confront Pelias and thus walked with a limp). David, who had Uriah killed with a treacherous letter (*Il.* VI // 2 Sam 11), is cursed for it. Absalom slew Amnon for raping his sister Tamar, the equivalent of Simeon and Levi avenging Dinah's rape (2 Sam 13 // Gen 34—which in turn can be compared with Theseus' abduction of Helen). Absalom chased David out of Jerusalem and raped his concubines (2 Sam 16:22), much like Reuben raped Jacob's concubine (Gen 35:22). Both narratives could be described as a mixture of the stories of Phoenix (*Il.* IX) and Euripides' Hippolytus. In Genesis, the birthrights of Reuben, Simeon and Levi are dismissed, and the fourth son of Jacob, Judah, inherits the promise of kingship.

Some biblical critics have proposed that the double accounts of stories in the biblical narratives are evidence of multiple redactions, failing to understand that the reiteration of narrative is a common and deliberate technique of biblical composition.[4] The main biblical theme is that the king of Israel is the people's worst enemy. Jacob was the first figure for Israel, as Israel was his divinely given name. He was to become a united kingdom of twelve tribes through his twelve sons, inspired both by the plan of Plato's *Laws* and by the dialectic of the soul and the state in the *Republic*. The installation of kingship was a fatal mistake. Through David, Bathsheba gave birth to Solomon, who became an apostate tyrant, the cause that Israel was decisively divided after his death. The immuta-

---

4. Jan-Wim Wesselius, *God's Election and Rejection: The Literary Strategy of the Historical Books at the Beginning of the Bible* (forthcoming; see online: http://www.jwwesselius.nl/).

ble cadastre of the twelve tribes was forever destroyed by the faults of these two kings, who are still revered as heroes by popular tradition. The kingship of Judah over the other tribes as prophesied by Jacob on his deathbed held the risk of the State's demise implicit; hence the portrayal of the wise Joseph as being 'a king who is not king'.[5] Book IX of Plato's *Republic* reveals the mind of the tyrant, who oppresses his people because his own erotic instincts rule him. As we saw earlier, David's ancestors, Ruth and Boaz, re-enact Plato's allegory of the birth of Eros (Love) in the *Symposium*. David's crime was that he had had his faithful servant killed to gain his wife. In this, he fulfils Plato's definition of the erotic tyrant.

> But now that he is under the dominion of love, he becomes always and in waking reality what he was then very rarely and in a dream only; he will commit the foulest murder, or eat forbidden food, or be guilty of any other horrid act. Love is his tyrant, and lives lordly in him and lawlessly, and being himself a king, leads him on, as a tyrant leads a State, to the performance of any reckless deed by which he can maintain himself and the rabble of his associates, whether those whom evil communications have brought in from without, or those whom he himself has allowed to break loose within him by reason of a similar evil nature in himself. Have we not here a picture of his way of life? (Plato, *Rep.* 575 a)

David matches this definition. He is the tyrant of Israel, and as he himself is tyrannised by Love he commits a murder for love's sake. This constant parallel between the state and the individual is a central motif in the *Republic*. The soul of the tyrant is a slave to Love, and the State thus becomes the slave of the tyrant (*Rep.* 578 e). The end of Plato's discussion about the tyrant concludes with pity for him. Even if the tyrant appears to be the master, he has no friends, only enemies, and can never leave his palace (the same concept can be seen in Xenophon's *Hieron*):

> He who is the real tyrant, whatever men may think, is the real slave, and is obliged to practise the greatest adulation and servility, and to be the flatterer of the vilest of mankind. He has desires which he is utterly unable to satisfy, and has more wants than any one, and is truly poor, if you know how to inspect the whole soul of him: all his life long he is beset with fear and is full of convulsions, and distractions, even as the State which he resembles: and surely the resemblance holds? (*Rep.* 580 e)

The figure of David in 1–2 Samuel both governs and resembles the state of Israel. At the end of Samuel, the reader simultaneously hates David for the crimes he committed and pities him. He pays a heavy price for

---

5.   Cazeaux, *Le partage de minuit*.

the deaths he orchestrated. Three of his sons die during his lifetime (Bathsheba's first child, Amnon and Absalom). His general Joab manipulated him, helped him to gain the throne and killed Abner. As David failed to punish him for that crime, Joab allowed Uriah to die on the battlefield without asking any questions. Joab also killed Absalom, disobeying David's orders. Perhaps, David knew that Joab would do what he, David, could not: kill his own son. David, once a young shepherd and musician, who defeated Goliath, ends his days an impotent old man, a helpless tyrant, at the mercy of the general, who knew his secrets. The passions of a single man thus caused the ruin of the whole state. One could well point to Xenophon's Cyrus as an inspiration for Jacob on his deathbed in Genesis. On his deathbed, David gives the kingship to Solomon, and a series of assassinations immediately follow. The message of the Bible is that the observance of the Law is greater than kingship. It is illustrated by Israel's most famous kings. In the book of Samuel, we first encountered the figure of Samuel, inspired by Euripides' *Ion*. When the people ask Samuel to install a king, he is inspired by Euripides' *Suppliants* to speak against kingship. With Cazeaux, one might describe these words as being at the core of the biblical narrative: kingship was a catastrophe for Israel.

9.

Kings

At the opening of the book of Kings, David is old, and must choose a successor. However, his son Adonijah decides that he will be the new king and gains the support of Joab and the priest Abiathar. The priest Zadok and the prophet Nathan do not support him and Bathsheba, Solomon's mother, pleads for her son to become David's successor and encourages David to order Solomon to be anointed as the new king of Israel and Judah. When Adonijah hears of Solomon's anointment he fears for his life and hides in the sanctuary, grabbing the horns of the altar. Solomon promises to spare his life and Adonijah submits and recognizes Solomon as his patron (1 Kgs 1). On his deathbed, David wishes Solomon success and advises him to murder Joab, for it was he who had murdered both Abner and Shimei, a Benjaminite, who had once cursed David. David dies, after a reign of forty years—seven years in Hebron and thirty-three in Jerusalem (1 Kgs 2:10), thirty-three reiterating the number of generations that had separated David from Adam. David's life ends with the young girl, Abishag, 'the Shunammite', keeping the once-great king warm in his bed. When Adonijah, after David dies, asked the queen Bathsheba for Abishag as a wife, Solomon understood the request as evidence for disloyalty: that Adonijah planned to usurp David's throne. When Solomon sent Benaiah to kill his brother (1 Kgs 2:25) and Joab heard of it, he too 'grasped the horns of the altar'. Solomon, nevertheless, ordered Benaiah to kill Joab at the altar. Taking the role of another Cain, Solomon began his reign with the murder of a brother. Solomon then kills Joab, following David's order. Did David have Joab killed to avenge Abner or was he aware that Joab had killed Absalom? In either case, Solomon (whose name signifies 'peace') begins his reign with terror, fratricide and assassination.

The motif of seeking refuge by grasping the horns of an altar is also common in Greek literature, especially in the tragedies. Exodus 21:14 states that a murderer who attacks with treachery shall be taken from the altar for execution. In, for instance, Apollodorus, we are told concerning the mother of Pelias:

> Now Tyro, daughter of Salmoneus and Alcidice, was brought up by Cretheus, brother of Salmoneus, and conceived a passion for the River Enipeus, and often would she hie to its running waters and utter her plaint to them. But Poseidon in the likeness of Enipeus lay with her, and she secretly gave birth to twin sons, whom she exposed... When they were grown up, they discovered their mother and killed their stepmother Sidero. For knowing that their mother was ill-used by her, they attacked her, but before they could catch her she had taken refuge in the precinct of Hera. However, Pelias cut her down on the very altars, and ever after he continued to treat Hera with contumely. (Apollodorus, *Library* 1, 9, 7-8; also *Od.* XI, 235-60)

Tyro later married her uncle Cretheus and bore Aison, father of Jason. Apparently, the common thread of these stories is of a person taking refuge in a sanctuary, only to be murdered on the altar. The very name of Salmoneus echoes that of Solomon (Salomon in the LXX). Among the ancestors of David and Solomon, is the father of Boaz, Salmon (Ruth 4:20-21)—the more typical Greek form of this name. This is not likely to be a coincidence if the epic of the Argonauts was indeed a source for biblical narrative as we have argued. Salmoneus and Tyro are surely of Semitic origin; yet, they appear in Homer, long before the Bible. Even if this myth once had a Semitic variation, it reached the Bible via its Greek prism. Salmoneus was a mad king full of hubris, and therefore Zeus struck him down with lightning. In the biblical narrative, God also punished Solomon for hubris. Moreover, in that story, Solomon became the close ally of Hiram of Tyre (1 Kgs 5:12-17). Do the characters of Solomon and Hiram of Tyre reflect a Hebrew deformation of Salmoneus and his daughter Tyro?

Solomon as Pharaoh

As part of his alliance with Tyre, Solomon begins construction of the temple—480 years after Israel came out of Egypt (1 Kgs 6:1). This specific chronological detail is a hallmark of the unitary redaction of these books. Moreover, 480 equals twelve generations of forty, both figures bearing significance in the biblical narrative. According to Cazeaux, by reminding the reader of the Exodus at this point, the biblical writer wants to associate the forced labour that Solomon imposed upon Israel with the former slavery in Egypt; this can be supported by pointing out the Greek sources. If David appeared as a new Jacob, Solomon was a new Pharaoh.

He too conscripted forced labour (1 Kgs 5:13). Work on the temple lasted seven years, yet it took thirty years to complete the building of Solomon's palace (1 Kgs 7:1). He also had another palace built exclusively for his wife, the daughter of the Egyptian king. After twenty years of work, Solomon offered the king of Tyre twenty cities of Israel in payment for the cedars and stones for the work, but Hiram refused them (1 Kgs 9:10-13), which forced Solomon to raise a tax to pay him. Solomon had a collection of horses from Egypt (1 Kgs 10:26). He collected foreign wives and concubines who lured him into worshipping foreign idols, such as Kemosh of the Moabites, Milkom and Moloch of the Ammonites and Astarte of the Sidonian. He built temples for these gods, around the temple of Yahweh (1 Kgs 11)—the very fact of which was to bring about Israel's downfall.

Solomon is widely understood in the Judeo-Christian tradition as a wise and peaceful king who built the temple during Israel's golden age. However, in the biblical story, his reign brought political murder, the forced labour of the population to satisfy his thirst for monuments as well as for the accumulation of gold, wives and horses—precisely what the future king of Israel in Deuteronomy was not to do (1 Kgs 10:26-29; 11:1-13):

> He must not acquire many horses for himself, or return the people to Egypt in order to acquire more horses, since the Lord has said to you, 'You must never return that way again'. And he must not acquire many wives for himself, or else his heart will turn away; also silver and gold he must not acquire in great quantity for himself. (Deut. 17:16-17)

> Solomon gathered together chariots and horses; he had fourteen hundred chariots and twelve thousand horses, which he stationed in the chariot cities and with the king in Jerusalem. The king made silver as common in Jerusalem as stones, and he made cedars as numerous as the sycamores of the Shephelah. Solomon's import of horses was from Egypt and Kue, and the king's traders received them from Kue at a price. A chariot could be imported from Egypt for six hundred shekels of silver, and a horse for one hundred and fifty; so through the king's traders they were exported to all the kings of the Hittites and the kings of Aram. (1 Kgs 10:26-29)

Israel's unity is destroyed forever because of the sins of its king. Scholars usually explain the prophecies of Deuteronomy and their realisation in Kings as indicating a 'Deuteronomistic redaction'; however, these internal references are of the same nature as the parallels between Jacob and David. Genesis–Kings is a single book. Cazeaux sees Solomon as a tyrant who behaved like Pharaoh, causing Israel to revert to slavery:

The naïve temptation that leads some to transform biblical heroes into pharaohs or Egyptian characters, does not understand the context: Egypt is present everywhere in the Bible, but from the inside, the great Egyptian being Solomon.[1]

Cazeaux's analysis can be supported by textual links between Solomon and Cheops in Herodotus:

Down to the time when Rhampsinitos was king, they told me there was in Egypt nothing but orderly rule, and Egypt prospered greatly; but after him Cheops became king over them and brought them to every kind of evil: for he shut up all the temples, and having first kept them from sacrificing there, he then bade all the Egyptians work for him. So some were appointed to draw stones from the stone-quarries in the Arabian mountains to the Nile, and others he ordered to receive the stones after they had been carried over the river in boats, and to draw them to those which are called the Libyan mountains; and they worked by a hundred thousand men at a time, for each three months continually. Of this oppression there passed ten years while the causeway was made by which they drew the stones, which causeway they built, and it is a work not much less, as it appears to me, than the pyramid; for the length of it is five furlongs and the breadth ten fathoms and the height, where it is highest, eight fathoms, and it is made of stone smoothed and with figures carved upon it. For this, they said, the ten years were spent, and for the underground chambers on the hill upon which the pyramids stand, which he caused to be made as sepulchral chambers for himself in an island, having conducted thither a channel from the Nile. For the making of the pyramid itself there passed a period of twenty years; and the pyramid is square, each side measuring eight hundred feet, and the height of it is the same. It is built of stone smoothed and fitted together in the most perfect manner, not one of the stones being less than thirty feet in length. (Herodotus II, 124; cf. Exod 1:8-14; 1 Kgs 5:13-18; 6:7; 9:10-22)

Exodus and Kings are linked by internal references, either explicitly (the significance of 480 years) or implicitly (Solomon behaving like a Pharaoh), but also through their common source: Herodotus. Additionally, the latter specifies the quality of the stones and the total duration of the work—twenty years, as in the case of Solomon—and the working shift of three months (1 Kgs 5:14), that is found in the story about the building of the temple. On the other hand, the evil Pharaoh Cheops is similar to the Pharaoh in Exodus, who was successor to the Joseph story's benevolent king. The biblical writer claims that though Solomon did not force any of the Israelites into slavery they were put to hard labour, and

---

1. Cazeaux, *Saül, David et Salomon*, 382, my translation from the French; see also 384, 386.

the tribes of the North revolted against Rehoboam. Herodotus' chronicle of the Egyptian kings is very similar to the structure of Kings, in which good kings alternate with bad kings; some of them were pious, some were not:

> This Cheops, the Egyptians said, reigned fifty years; and after he was dead his brother Chephren succeeded to the kingdom. This king followed the same manner as the other, both in all the rest and also in that he made a pyramid (Herodotus II, 127). After him, they said, Mykerinos became king over Egypt, who was the son of Cheops; and to him his father's deeds were displeasing, and he both opened the temples and gave liberty to the people, who were ground down to the last extremity of evil, to return to their own business and to their sacrifices; also he gave decisions of their causes juster than those of all the other kings besides. (Herodotus II, 129; cf. the very close parallel in 2 Kgs 21:1-3, 19-22)

The kings of Israel and Judah are portrayed and judged according to the model of the Egyptian kings of Herodotus. Even if the late kings existed historically, the biblical writer still used Herodotus' stories to portray them. Similarly, in creating the character of Solomon, he drew on the king from Herodotus' first book, namely, Croesus.

Solomon / Croesus

I am also indebted to Professor Kupitz for this parallel. We have already pointed out how Solomon murdered his brother Adonijah for attempting to claim the throne for himself. In Herodotus, we find the following story:

> Now those which he sent to Delphi and to the temple of Amphiaraos he dedicated of his own goods and as first-fruits of the wealth inherited from his father; but the other offerings were made of the substance of a man who was his foe, who before Croesus became king had been factious against him and had joined in endeavouring to make Pantaleon ruler of the Lydians. Now Pantaleon was a son of Alyattes and a brother of Croesus, but not by the same mother, for Croesus was born to Alyattes of a Carian woman, but Pantaleon of an Ionian. And when Croesus had gained possession of the kingdom by the gift of his father, he put to death the man who opposed him, drawing him upon the carding-comb; and his property, which even before that time he had vowed to dedicate, he then offered in the manner mentioned to those shrines which have been named. About his votive offerings let it suffice to have said so much. (Herodotus I, 92)

This demonstrates the very same pattern we saw in Solomon's dispute with Adonijah (his half-brother of a different mother) and Joab, who supported Adonijah before Solomon became king (1 Kgs 1–2). The first book of Herodotus seems to be the source for Solomon's grandiose kingship:

> Then when the Hellenes in Asia had been conquered and forced to pay tribute, he designed next to build for himself ships and to lay hands upon those who dwelt in the islands... As time went on, nearly all those dwelling on the side of the River Halys had been subdued. Except the Cilicians and the Lycians, Croesus subdued and kept under his rule all the nations, that is to say Lydians, Phrygians, Mysians, Mariandynoi, Chalybians, Paphlagonians, Thracians both Thynian and Bithynian, Carians, Ionians, Dorians, Aiolians, and Pamphylians. (Herodotus I, 27-28; cf. 1 Kgs 4:29-34; 5:1)

The biblical writer follows Herodotus: after Croesus had built a strong empire and subdued his neighbours, he received a visit from Solon, a wise Greek legislator (he who was supposed to have brought back from Egypt the narrative of Atlantis in Plato's *Critias*):

> (Continued from Herodotus I:28) when these, I say, had been subdued, and while he was still adding to his Lydian dominions, there came to Sardis, then at the height of its wealth, all the wise men of the Hellas who chanced to be alive at that time, brought thither severally by various occasions; and of them one was Solon the Athenian, who after he had made laws for the Athenians at their bidding, left his native country for ten years and sailed away saying that he desired to visit various lands, in order that he might not be compelled to repeal any of the laws which he had proposed. For of themselves the Athenians were not competent to do this, having bound themselves by solemn oaths to submit for ten years to the laws which Solon should propose for them... So Solon, having left his native country for this reason and for the sake of seeing various lands, came to Amasis in Egypt, and also to Crœsus at Sardis. Having there arrived he was entertained as a guest by Crœsus in the king's palace; and afterwards, on the third or fourth day, at the bidding of Crœsus his servants led Solon round to see his treasuries; and they showed him all things, how great and magnificent they were: and after he had looked upon them all and examined them as he had occasion, Crœsus asked him as follows: 'Athenian guest, much report of thee has come to us, both in regard to thy wisdom and thy wanderings, how that in thy search for wisdom thou hast traversed many lands to see them; now therefore a desire has come upon me to ask thee whether thou hast seen any whom thou deemest to be of all men the most happy'. This he asked supposing that he himself was the happiest of men; but Solon, using no flattery but the truth only, said: 'Yes, O king, Tellos the Athenian'. (Herodotus I, 29-30; cf. 1 Kgs 10:1-13)

The passages are very alike, except that Solon is presented as being cleverer than his host, while Solomon is presented as having been more than what the queen of Sheba had expected. The 'fingerprint' marking the association is found in Croesus' saying that he had heard of Solon's reputation for wisdom, precisely as the queen of Sheba describes Solomon (1 Kgs 10:6). Ironically, Solomon is the happier man, like Tellos the Athenian. Nevertheless, in the very next chapter, we are presented with Solomon's fall from grace because of apostasy. Solon's lesson, found in the lines of Herodotus that followed, was that a man may only be judged happy when his life is over. Thus, even if Solomon's reign seemed magnificent, his fall is like that of Croesus, who lost his country to Cyrus the Persian. (Compare Herodotus I, 47 with 1 Kgs 4:29 for the metaphor of knowledge of the grains of sand in the sea.)

The treasure offered by Croesus in chs. 50 to 52 of Herodotus' first book can be compared with the great quantity of gold used by Solomon for the temple (1 Kgs 6 and 7). For instance, the description of the vessels in 1 Kgs 7:48-51 can be well compared with Herodotus:

> And when he had finished the sacrifice, he melted down a vast quantity of gold, and of it he wrought half-plinths making them six palms in length and three in breadth, and in height one palm; and their number was one hundred and seventeen. Of these four were of pure gold weighing two talents and a half each, and others of gold alloyed with silver weighing two talents. And he caused to be made also an image of a lion of pure gold weighing ten talents; which lion, when the temple of Delphi was being burnt down, fell from off the half-plinths, for upon these it was set, and is placed now in the treasury of the Corinthians, weighing six talents and a half, for three talents and a half were melted away from it. So Crœsus having finished all these things sent them to Delphi, and with them these besides:—two mixing bowls of great size, one of gold and the other of silver, of which the golden bowl was placed on the right hand as one enters the temple, and the silver on the left, but the places of these also were changed after the temple was burnt down, and the golden bowl is now placed in the treasury of the people of Clazomenai, weighing eight and a half talents and twelve pounds over, while the silver one is placed in the corner of the vestibule and holds six hundred amphors (being filled with wine by the Delphians on the feast of the Theophania): this the people of Delphi say is the work of Theodoros the Samian, and, as I think, rightly, for it is evident to me that the workmanship is of no common kind: moreover Crœsus sent four silver wine-jars, which stand in the treasury of the Corinthians, and two vessels for lustral water, one of gold and the other of silver, of which the gold one is inscribed 'from the Lacedemonians'... And many other votive offerings Crœsus sent with these, not specially distinguished, among which are certain castings of silver of a round shape, and also a golden figure of a woman three cubits high, which the Delphians say is a statue of the baker of Crœsus. More

over Crœsus dedicated the ornaments from his wife's neck and her girdles. These are the things which he sent to Delphi. (Herodotus I, 50-52; cf. 1 Kgs 10:14-20)

Both Croesus and Solomon offer hecatombs:

King Solomon and all the congregation of Israel, who had assembled before him, were with him before the ark, sacrificing so many sheep and oxen that they could not be counted or numbered. (1 Kgs 8:5)

After this with great sacrifices he endeavoured to win the favour of the god at Delphi: for of all the animals that are fit for sacrifice he offered three thousand of each kind, and he heaped up couches overlaid with gold and overlaid with silver, and cups of gold, and robes of purple, and tunics, making of them a great pyre, and this he burnt up, hoping by these means the more to win over the god to the side of the Lydians: and he proclaimed to all the Lydians that every one of them should make sacrifice with that which each man had. (Herodotus I, 50)

Eventually, the Babylonians plunder Solomon's great treasure (2 Kgs 24:12-13; 25:8-9); indeed, it is said that in the aftermath of several wars the treasure offered by Croesus was also stolen. Solomon married Pharaoh's daughter in a political alliance (1 Kgs 3:3); Allyates, Croesus' father, similarly gave his daughter to Astyages, king of the Medes (Herodotus I, 74). Croesus thought that he would defeat Cyrus; for the oracle of Delphi had told him that he would destroy a great country if he went to war. Little did he know that he would in fact destroy his own country. The oracle explains the reason for this disaster:

When the Lydians came and repeated that which they were enjoined to say, it is related that the Pythian prophetess spoke as follows: 'The fated destiny it is impossible even for a god to escape. And Crœsus paid the debt due for the sin of his fifth ancestor, who being one of the spearmen of the Heracleidai followed the treacherous device of a woman, and having slain his master took possession of his royal dignity, which belonged not to him of right. And although Loxias eagerly desired that the calamity of Sardis might come upon the sons of Crœsus and not upon Crœsus himself, it was not possible for him to draw the Destinies aside from their course; but so much as these granted he brought to pass, and gave it as a gift to Crœsus: for he put off the taking of Sardis by three years; and let Crœsus be assured that he was taken prisoner later by these years than the fated time: moreover secondly, he assisted him when he was about to be burnt. (Herodotus I, 91)

Loxias' desire to delay the curse until a future generation is echoed in the biblical story, which reflects a similar story pattern. Here, however, the narrator, after informing the reader of Yahweh's anger and the divine curse, speaks of the curse being both mitigated and delayed until the next generation (1 Kgs 11:9-13). Solomon is thus responsible for the splitting of Israel that occurs under his son Rehoboam's reign. Samuel's prophecy continues to be fulfilled. While Saul had disobeyed and while David had murdered his loyal captain for his wife, Solomon betrayed God with idolatry. The borrowing is clever: Croesus will be defeated by Cyrus, who defeats Babylon (in the second part of Herodotus' book I)—the very same Babylon which will defeat Judah at the end of 2 Kings. Babylon also is presented in the very beginning of Genesis in the story of the tower of Babel, the description of which can be compared with Herodotus' description of the temple of Bel-Marduk. The biblical narrative reflects back upon itself, for the tower of Babel functions also as a figure for Solomon's temple—a monument too big and too ambitious, which will be destroyed by God himself.

Solomon's Kingdom as Babylon and Plato's Atlantis

> And as to the resources of the Babylonians how great they are, I shall show by many other proofs and among them also by this: For the support of the great king and his army, apart from the regular tribute the whole land of which he is ruler has been distributed into portions. Now whereas twelve months go to make up the year, for four of these he has his support from the territory of Babylon, and for the remaining eight months from the whole of the rest of Asia… And of horses he had in this province as his private property, apart from the horses for use in war, eight hundred stallions and sixteen thousand mares, for each of these stallions served twenty mares: of Indian hounds moreover such a vast number were kept that four large villages in the plain, being free from other contributions, had been appointed to provide food for the hounds. (Herodotus I, 192; cf. 1 Kgs 4:7, 26-28)

Like the Babylonian king, who had divided the necessary tribute of provisions according to the calendar, in twelve months, Solomon had twelve officials, one from each tribe of Israel, contributing a twelfth of the food. This is also an implicit reference to the book of Numbers (ch. 7), in which each of the twelve tribal princes gave identical offerings to God. Now that a king has taken God's place, Israel's harmony reaches its end.

We can understand so far how the biblical writer read both Plato and Herodotus, and was well aware of textual links between them, taking advantage of them to create his own narrative. We saw already that in Exodus 24 the oath taken by Israel was very similar to the oath of the Atlantean kings; bulls were sacrificed, and their blood was spread on the people. Solomon's wealth and luxuriousness appear to fit Plato's description of Atlantis, deserving of destruction (see Plato, *Crit.* 115b-17a). The books from Genesis to Joshua show textual parallels with Plato's writings. Judges, however reflects none, except that the unity of the twelve-tribe State seemed impossible to maintain. The book of Ruth showed how David's ancestors Ruth and Boaz were meant to reflect Poverty and Plenty, parents of Love, according to Socrates' definition in the *Symposium*. The book of Samuel does not seem to have any textual parallel with Plato, yet David can be identified with the erotic tyrant of the *Republic*. Solomon's magnificent kingdom and the narrative of 1–2 Kings as a whole reflects Plato's Atlantis—the myth of the would-be Ideal State, which was destroyed by Zeus because its kings disobeyed the laws that their ancestors had forever promised to follow. The *Critias* was a satirical poem meant to reflect Athens' downfall after the war of the Peloponnesus.

In Kings, Rehoboam sat on the throne of Judah after Solomon's death, while the ten tribes of the north took Jeroboam for their king. Therefore, two kingdoms existed separately: Israel of the North (with Samaria for its capital) and Judah (including the tribe of Benjamin), with its capital in Jerusalem. Jeroboam received God's promise that his descendants would have kingship forever, but he built golden calves and installed them as the new gods of Israel in Dan and Bethel. God therefore decided that the dynasty must instead pass to another lineage. King Ahab, son of Omri, married a Sidonian princess named Jezebel. After her impulse, Israel began to worship the 'Canaanite' gods Baal, Astarte and others. Then follows the long narrative of Ahab's conflict with the prophet Elijah.

Elijah / Aeacus

> Now Elijah the Tishbite, of Tishbe in Gilead, said to Ahab, 'As the Lord the God of Israel lives, before whom I stand, there shall be neither dew nor rain these years, except by my word'. (1 Kgs 17:1)

> After many days the word of the Lord came to Elijah, in the third year of the drought, saying, 'Go, present yourself to Ahab; I will send rain on the earth'. So Elijah went to present himself to Ahab. The famine was severe in Samaria. (1 Kgs 18:1-2)

Elijah engages in a contest with the priests of Baal, to see who is the one true god—Baal or Yahweh. Each is to build a separate altar, and wait for fire to descend from the sky. The priests of Baal dance in circles, limping and cutting themselves, while Elijah mocks them, suggesting that perhaps their god sleeps. When Elijah's turn comes, he builds an altar of twelve stones:

At the time of the offering of the oblation, the prophet Elijah came near and said, 'O Lord, God of Abraham, Isaac, and Israel, let it be known this day that you are God in Israel, that I am your servant, and that I have done all these things at your bidding. Answer me, O Lord, answer me, so that this people may know that you, O Lord, are God, and that you have turned their hearts back.' *Then the fire of the Lord fell and consumed the burnt-offering,* the wood, the stones, and the dust, and even licked up the water that was in the trench. When all the people saw it, they fell on their faces and said, 'The Lord indeed is God; the Lord indeed is God'. Elijah said to them, 'Seize the prophets of Baal; do not let one of them escape'. Then they seized them; and Elijah brought them down to the Wadi Kishon, and killed them there. (1 Kgs 18:36-40)

In Apollodorus, we find the following story:

Now Aeacus was the most pious of men. Therefore, when Greece suffered from infertility on account of Pelops, because in a war with Stymphalus, king of the Arcadians, being unable to conquer Arcadia, he slew the king under a pretence of friendship, and scattered his mangled limbs, oracles of the gods declared that Greece would be rid of its present calamities if Aeacus would offer prayers on its behalf. So Aeacus did offer prayers, and Greece was delivered from the dearth. Even after his death Aeacus is honored in the abode of Pluto, and keeps the keys of Hades. (Apollodorus, *Library* 3, 12, 6; cf. Isocrates, *Evagoras* 9, 14; Pausanias, *Description of Greece* 2, 29, 7-8)

Elijah is the only surviving prophet of Yahweh, after Jezebel had all the others killed. Like Aeacus, he and only he can bring the rain again. The building of the altar could be linked to Patroclus' funerals, as M.L. West[2] has shown:

When King Agamemnon heard this he dismissed the people to their ships, but those who were about the dead heaped up wood and built a pyre a hundred feet this way and that; then they laid the dead all sorrowfully upon the top of it... He also put twelve brave sons of noble Trojans to the sword and laid them with the rest, for he was full of bitterness and fury. Then he committed all to the resistless and devouring might of the fire; he groaned aloud and called on his dead comrade by name. 'Fare well', he cried, 'Patroclus, even in the house of Hades; I am now doing all that I have promised you. Twelve brave sons of noble Trojans shall the flames consume along with yourself, but dogs, not fire, shall devour the flesh of Hector son of Priam'... Now the pyre about dead Patroclus would not kindle. Achilles therefore bethought him of another matter; he went apart and prayed to the two winds Boreas and Zephyrus vowing them goodly offerings. He made them many drink-offerings from the golden cup and besought them to come and help him that the wood might make haste to

---

2. West, *The East Face of Helicon*, 399.

kindle and the dead bodies be consumed. Fleet Iris heard him praying and started off to fetch the winds. They were holding high feast in the house of boisterous Zephyrus when Iris came running up to the stone threshold of the house and stood there, but as soon as they set eyes on her they all came towards her and each of them called her to him, but Iris would not sit down. 'I cannot stay', she said, 'I must go back to the streams of Oceanus and the land of the Ethiopians who are offering hecatombs to the immortals, and I would have my share; but Achilles prays that Boreas and shrill Zephyrus will come to him, and he vows them goodly offerings; he would have you blow upon the pyre of Patroclus for whom all the Achaeans are lamenting.' With this she left them, and the two winds rose with a cry that rent the air and swept the clouds before them. They blew on and on until they came to the sea, and the waves rose high beneath them, but when they reached Troy *they fell upon the pyre till the mighty flames roared under the blast that they blew.* (*Il.* XXIII, 190-220)

The divine fire falls upon the pyre, as it does when Elijah praises God. We understand that the biblical writer wanted to match his description of the only god to Plato's, who himself wished to censure Homer. The subject of Elijah's mockery of Greek/Canaanite cults (and thus, the mockery of the author too) is seen in Iris meeting the gods at a banquet, or Zeus sleeping (*Il.* XIV, 290-350), or Poseidon on a journey (*Od.* I, 20-25).

Note 1 Kgs 18:27, which reads:

At noon Elijah mocked them, saying, 'Cry aloud! Surely he is a god; either he is meditating, or he has wandered away, or he is on a journey, or perhaps he is asleep and must be awakened.'

Moreover, Achilles sacrificed twelve Trojan warriors, while Elijah built an altar of twelve stones and then killed all the priests of Baal. Achilles' wish that dogs devour Hector's body is itself echoed in the same biblical chapters—Jezebel too will be eaten by dogs when Jehu kills her (1 Kgs 21:23-24 and 2 Kgs 9:36).

Elijah Comes Out of the Cave

After the priests of Baal have been killed, Elijah flees to the desert, fearing for his life. Elijah wishes to die, but God's angel comforts and feeds him. He then walks forty days in the wilderness and finally reaches Mount Horeb:

At that place he came to a cave, and spent the night there. Then the word of the Lord came to him, saying, 'What are you doing here, Elijah?' He answered, 'I have been very zealous for the Lord, the God of hosts; for the Israelites have forsaken your covenant, thrown down your altars, and killed your prophets with the sword. I alone am left, and they are seeking my life, to take it away'. He said, 'Go out and stand on the mountain before the Lord, for the Lord is about to pass by'. Now there was a great wind, so strong that it was splitting mountains and breaking rocks in pieces before the Lord, but the Lord was not in the wind; and after the wind an earthquake, but the Lord was not in the earthquake; and after the earthquake a fire, but the Lord was not in the fire; and after the fire a sound of sheer silence. When Elijah heard it, he wrapped his face in his mantle and went out and stood at the entrance of the cave. Then there came a voice to him that said, 'What are you doing here, Elijah?' He answered, 'I have been very zealous for the Lord, the God of hosts; for the Israelites have forsaken your covenant, thrown down your altars, and killed your prophets with the sword. I alone am left, and they are seeking my life, to take it away'. (1 Kgs 19:9-14)

Exodus and Kings are linked; everything is set for the reader to recall the events of Israel coming out of Egypt. Elijah appears as a new Moses, alone in the wilderness for forty days. He hides in a cave and meets God when he emerges, who gives him a mission. We have seen how the Exodus story could be interpreted as a staging of the Allegory of the Cave from Plato's *Republic*. A wise man is forced to leave the cave of ignorance where people worship illusions as gods so that he may contemplate the Idea of the Good (the only god) and return to free his comrades from their slavery. Elijah must do the same, as he is the only prophet to remain. In Exodus, the period of slavery in Egypt was a metaphor for the Cave, but here in Kings, Elijah comes out of a real cave and departs to try to bring Israel back to the cult of Yahweh. Elijah is like a new Moses, however, it is already too late—Israel has abandoned the law.

In ch. 21, Ahab steals the vineyard of Naboth. The latter had refused to sell it to the king, since the lots of land are transmitted from fathers to sons and can never be sold. The king bribed false witnesses that accused Naboth, who was executed. Here is another example of how the kings of Israel transgress the laws given by God.

The Lying Spirit / The Dream of Agamemnon

In 1 Kgs 22:1-23, Ahab is at war with Aram, and makes an alliance with the king of Judah, Jehoshaphat. They consult the prophets of Israel, who all say that they will defeat Aram. Jehoshaphat still wants to consult the prophet Micaiah. Micaiah reveals that he saw the 'army of heavens' seated around Yahweh. Yahweh sent a lying spirit, that inspired the other prophets, to tell Ahab that he would be victorious over Aram; but in fact he was to die in the battle. This story has a close parallel in the beginning of the *Iliad*:

But Jehoshaphat said, 'Is there no other prophet of the Lord here of whom we may inquire?' The king of Israel said to Jehoshaphat, 'There is still one other by whom we may inquire of the Lord, Micaiah son of Imlah; *but I hate him, for he never prophesies anything favourable about me, but only disaster.*' (1 Kgs 22:7-8)

With these words he sat down, and Agamemnon rose in anger. His heart was black with rage, and his eyes flashed fire as he scowled on Calchas and said, '*Seer of evil, you never yet prophesied smooth things concerning me, but have ever loved to foretell that which was evil.* You have brought me neither comfort nor performance; and now you come seeing among Danaans, and saying that Apollo has plagued us because I would not take a ransom for this girl, the daughter of Chryses.' (*Il.* I, 100-110)

Then Micaiah said, 'Therefore hear the word of the Lord: I saw the Lord sitting on his throne, with all the host of heaven standing beside him to the right and to the left of him. And the Lord said, 'Who will entice Ahab, so that he may go up and fall at Ramoth-gilead?' Then one said one thing, and another said another, until a spirit came forward and stood before the Lord, saying, 'I will entice him.' 'How?' the Lord asked him. He replied, 'I will go out and be a lying spirit in the mouth of all his prophets'. Then the Lord said, 'You are to entice him, and you shall succeed; go out and do it'. So you see, the Lord has put a lying spirit in the mouth of all these your prophets; the Lord has decreed disaster for you. (1 Kgs 22:19-23)

Now the other gods and the armed warriors on the plain slept soundly, but Zeus was wakeful, for he was thinking how to do honour to Achilles, and destroyed much people at the ships of the Achaeans. In the end he deemed it would be best to send a lying dream to King Agamemnon; so he called one to him and said to it, 'Lying Dream, go to the ships of the Achaeans, into the tent of Agamemnon, and say to him word to word as I now bid you. Tell him to get the Achaeans instantly under arms, for he shall take Troy. There are no longer divided counsels among the gods; Hera has brought them to her own mind, and woe betides the Trojans.' The dream went when it had heard its message, and soon reached the ships of the Achaeans. It sought Agamemnon son of Atreus and found him in his tent, wrapped in a profound slumber. It hovered over his head in the likeness of Nestor, son of Neleus, whom Agamemnon honoured above all his councillors, and said:- 'You are sleeping, son of Atreus; one who has the welfare of his host and so much other care upon his shoulders should dock his sleep. Hear me at once, for I come as a messenger from Zeus, who, though he be not near, yet takes thought for you and pities you. He bids you get the Achaeans instantly under arms, for you shall take Troy. There are no longer divided counsels among the gods; Hera has brought them over to her own mind, and woe betides the Trojans at the hands of Zeus. Remember this, and when you wake see that it does not escape you.' The dream then left him, and he thought of things that were, surely not to be accomplished. He thought that on that same day he was to take the city of

Priam, but he little knew what was in the mind of Zeus, who had many another hard-fought fight in store alike for Danaans and Trojans. Then presently he woke, with the divine message still ringing in his ears; so he sat upright, and put on his soft shirt so fair and new, and over this his heavy cloak. He bound his sandals on to his comely feet, and slung his silver-studded sword about his shoulders; then he took the imperishable staff of his father, and sallied forth to the ships of the Achaeans. (*Il.* II, 1-50)

In the *Republic*, Plato condemns the misrepresentations of the gods, which are found in Homer:

Then no motive can be imagined why God should lie?—None whatever.— Then the superhuman and divine is absolutely incapable of falsehood?— Yes.—Then is God perfectly simple and true both in word and deed; he changes not; he deceives not, either by sign or word, by dream or waking vision.—Your thoughts, he said, are the reflection of my own.—You agree with me then, I said, that this is the second type or form in which we should write and speak about divine things. The gods are not magicians who transform themselves, neither do they deceive mankind in any way.— I grant that.—Then, although we are admirers of Homer, we do not admire the lying dream which Zeus sends to Agamemnon. (Plato, *Rep.* 382 e-83 b)

This parallel is of crucial importance. Genesis–Kings re-writes Greek mythology through a platonic filter. The lying spirit sent to Ahab in 1 Kings 22 is a variant reiteration of the lying dream sent to Agamemnon, excepting the difference that Micaiah reveals God's intention of lying. As God's true prophet, he cancels this intention to deceive. Ahab deserves for God to treat him like Zeus treated Agamemnon. The 'fingerprint' marking the thematic citation is that Ahab hates Micaiah for never saying anything good—only evil (1 Kgs 22:8)—exactly like Agamemnon and the seer Calchas in the first lines of the *Iliad* (a passage that is also used for Abner's wrath in 2 Sam 3). The biblical writer chose this episode of the *Iliad* because Plato had criticised it and he corrected it according to the principles of the *Republic*. Moreover, Ahab's death recalls of Agamemnon wounded on the battlefield and dragged on his chariot:

But a certain man drew his bow and unknowingly struck the king of Israel between the scale-armour and the breastplate; *so he said to the driver of his chariot, 'Turn around, and carry me out of the battle, for I am wounded'*. The battle grew hot that day, and the king was propped up in his chariot facing the Arameans, until at evening he died; the blood from the wound had flowed into the bottom of the chariot. Then about sunset a shout went through the army, 'Every man to his city, and every man to his country!' (1 Kgs 22:34-36)

Eilithuiae, goddesses of childbirth, daughters of Hera and dispensers of cruel pain, send upon a woman when she is in labour—even so sharp were the pangs of the son of Atreus. *He sprang on to his chariot, and bade his charioteer drive to the ships, for he was in great agony.* With a loud clear voice he shouted to the Danaans, 'My friends, princes and counsellors of the Argives, defend the ships yourselves, for Zeus has not suffered me to fight the whole day through against the Trojans'. With this the charioteer turned his horses towards the ships, and they flew forward nothing loth. Their chests were white with foam and their bellies with dust, as they drew the wounded king out of the battle. (*Il.* XI 270-80)

Elijah / Romulus and Heaven's Fiery Chariot

As they (i.e., Elijah and Elisha) continued walking and talking, a chariot of fire and horses of fire separated the two of them, and Elijah ascended in a whirlwind into heaven. Elisha kept watching and crying out, 'Father, father! The chariots of Israel and its horsemen!' (2 Kgs 2:11-12)

But Tatius by Lavinian fury slain; great Romulus continued long to reign. Now warrior Mars his burnished helm puts on, and thus addresses Heaven's imperial throne. Since the inferior world is now become one vassal globe, and colony to Rome, this grace, O Jove, for Romulus I claim, admit him to the skies, from whence he came. Long hast thou promised an aetherial state to Mars's lineage; and thy word is Fate. The sire, that rules the thunder, with a nod, declared the Fiat, and dismissed the God. Soon as the Power armipotent surveyed the flashing skies, the signal he obeyed; and leaning on his lance, he mounts his car, his fiery coursers lashing through the air. Mount Palatine he gains, and finds his son good laws enacting on a peaceful throne; the scales of heavenly justice holding high, with steady hand, and a discerning eye. Then vaults upon his car, and to the spheres, swift, as a flying shaft, Rome's founder bears. The parts more pure, in rising are refined, the gross, and perishable lag behind. His shrine in purple vestments stands in view; He looks a God, and is Quirinus now. (Ovid, *Metam.* XIV, 805-30; see also Titus Livius 1:16; Plutarch, *Life of Romulus* 27; 28:1-4)

Elisha, Hermes and the Axe

Now the company of prophets said to Elisha, 'As you see, the place where we live under your charge is too small for us. Let us go to the Jordan, and let us collect logs there, one for each of us, and build a place there for us to live.' He answered, 'Do so'. Then one of them said, 'Please come with your servants'. And he answered, 'I will'. So he went with them. When they came to the Jordan, they cut down trees. But as one was felling a log, his axehead fell into the water; he cried out, 'Alas,

master! It was borrowed'. Then the man of God said, 'Where did it fall?'
When he showed him the place, he cut off a stick, and threw it in there,
and made the iron float. He said, 'Pick it up'. So he reached out his hand
and took it. (2 Kgs 6:1-7)

A workman, felling wood by the side of a river, let his axe drop—by
accident into a deep pool. Being thus deprived of the means of his
livelihood, he sat down on the bank and lamented his hard fate. Hermes
appeared and demanded the cause of his tears. After he told him his
misfortune, Hermes plunged into the stream, and, bringing up a golden
axe, inquired if that were the one he had lost. On his saying that it was not
his, Hermes disappeared beneath the water a second time, returned with a
silver axe in his hand, and again asked the workman if it were his. When
the workman said it was not, he dived into the pool for the third time
and brought up the axe that had been lost. The workman claimed it and
expressed his joy at its recovery. Hermes, pleased with his honesty, gave
him the golden and silver axes in addition to his own. The workman, on
his return to his house, related to his companions all that had happened.
One of them at once resolved to try and secure the same good fortune for
himself. He ran to the river and threw his axe on purpose into the pool at
the same place, and sat down on the bank to weep. Hermes appeared to
him just as he hoped he would; and having learned the cause of his grief,
plunged into the stream and brought up a golden axe, inquiring if he had
lost it. The workman seized it greedily, and declared that truly it was the
very same axe that he had lost. Hermes, displeased at his knavery, not
only took away the golden axe, but refused to recover for him the axe he
had thrown into the pool. (Aesop, *Fables*, 'Hermes and the Workmen')[3]

Joas / Darius

Now when Elisha had fallen sick with the illness of which he was to die,
King Joash of Israel went down to him, and wept before him, crying, 'My
father, my father! The chariots of Israel and its horsemen!' Elisha said to
him, 'Take a bow and arrows'; so he took a bow and arrows. Then he said
to the king of Israel, 'Draw the bow'; and he drew it. Elisha laid his hands
on the king's hands. Then he said, 'Open the window to the east'; and he
opened it. Elisha said, 'Shoot'; and he shot. Then he said, 'The Lord's
arrow of victory, the arrow of victory over Aram! For you shall fight the
Arameans in Aphek until you have made an end of them.' He continued,
'Take the arrows'; and he took them. He said to the king of Israel, 'Strike
the ground with them'; he struck three times, and stopped. Then the man
of God was angry with him, and said, 'You should have struck five or six
times; then you would have struck down Aram until you had made an
end of it, but now you will strike down Aram only three times'. (2 Kgs
13:14-19)

3. See Kupitz, 'La Bible est-elle un plagiat?'

The Elisha story follows Herodotus, where victory is sought against the Athenians by shooting an arrow heavenward. In Kings, Herodotus' threefold chant is transposed to measure Israel's victory over Aram.

Note Herodotus V, 105, which reads:

> Onesilos then was besieging Amathus; and meanwhile, when it was reported to King Dareios that Sardis had been captured and burnt by the Athenians and the Ionians together, and that the leader of the league for being about these things was the Milesian Aristagoras, it is said that at first being informed of this he made no account of the Ionians, because he knew that they at all events would not escape unpunished for their revolt, but he inquired into who the Athenians were; and when he had been informed, he asked for his bow, and having received it and placed an arrow upon the string, he discharged it upwards towards heaven, and as he shot into the air he said: 'Zeus, that it may be granted me to take vengeance upon the Athenians!' Having so said he charged one of his attendants, that when dinner was set before the king he should say always three times: 'Master, remember the Athenians'.

Hezekiah / Sethos

Hezekiah went up to the house of the Lord and spread it before the Lord. And Hezekiah prayed before the Lord, and said: 'O Lord the God of Israel, who are enthroned above the cherubim, you are God, you alone, of all the kingdoms of the earth; you have made heaven and earth. Incline your ear, O Lord, and hear; open your eyes, O Lord, and see; hear the words of Sennacherib, which he has sent to mock the living God. Truly, O Lord, the kings of Assyria have laid waste the nations and their lands, and have hurled their gods into the fire, though they were no gods but the work of human hands—wood and stone—and so they were destroyed. So now, O Lord our God, save us, I pray you, from his hand, so that all the kingdoms of the earth may know that you, O Lord, are God alone... That very night the angel of the Lord set out and struck down one hundred and eighty-five thousand in the camp of the Assyrians; when morning dawned, they were all dead bodies. Then King Sennacherib of Assyria left, went home, and lived at Nineveh. (2 Kgs 19:14-36)

After him there came to the throne the priest of Hephaistos, whose name was Sethos. This man, they said, neglected and held in no regard the warrior class of the Egyptians, considering that he would have no need of them; and besides other slights which he put upon them, he also took from them the yokes of corn-land which had been given to them as a special gift in the reigns of the former kings, twelve yokes to each man. After this, Sanacharib king of the Arabians and of the Assyrians marched a great host against Egypt. Then the warriors of the Egyptians refused to come to the rescue, and the priest, being driven into a strait, entered into

the sanctuary of the temple and bewailed to the image of the god the
danger which was impending over him; and as he was thus lamenting,
sleep came upon him, and it seemed to him in his vision that the god
came and stood by him and encouraged him, saying that he should suffer
no evil if he went forth to meet the army of the Arabians; for he himself
would send him helpers. Trusting in these things seen in sleep, he took
with him, they said, those of the Egyptians who were willing to follow
him, and encamped in Pelusion, for by this way the invasion came: and
not one of the warrior class followed him, but shop-keepers and artisans
and men of the market. Then after they came, there swarmed by night
upon their enemies mice of the fields, and ate up their quivers and their
bows, and moreover the handles of their shields, so that on the next day
they fled, and being without defence of arms great numbers fell. And at
the present time this king stands in the temple of Hephaistos in stone,
holding upon his hand a mouse, and by letters inscribed he says these
words: 'Let him who looks upon me learn to fear the gods'. (Herodotus
II, 141)

In this case, the parallel concerns both the mythical aspect and the historical. The Assyrian king did besiege Jerusalem. The biblical narrator
claims the annals of the kings of Israel and Judah as his source.[4] He
apparently took advantage of the mention of Sennacherib's campaign in
Herodotus and craftily mixed the real event with the mythical story of
the king praying in his temple, whose enemy withdrew the very next day
thanks to divine influence. Wesselius commented on this parallel,[5] and I
found more links between Hezekiah and Herodotus' pharaohs. In 2 Kgs
20:1-7, Hezekiah laments his mortal illness because he has always been
pious, and his lifespan is then extended of fifteen more years. Mykerinos
complains for the same reasons, and by turning nights into days he
stretches his lifespan by six more years (Herodotus II, 133). God does
not behave with irony in the Bible, as do the gods in the works of
Herodotus. Mykerinos was the son of Cheops, who was a source for
Solomon. On the other hand, the report of Sennacherib's campaign is
only eight paragraphs further on in Herodotus.

Note the following examples:

4. On the use of cited books within the biblical narrative, see Stott, *Why Did
They Write This Way?*. It is likely that the author possessed a list of kings with some
accurate historical details; however, it remains uncertain whether the annals of the
kings of Israel and Judah existed at all. On the historical background, see L.L.
Grabbe, ed., *Like a Bird in a Cage: The Invasion of Sennacherib in 701 BCE*,
London: T&T Clark, 2003.
   5. Wesselius, *The Origin of the History of Israel*, 94-95.

Hezekiah said to Isaiah, 'What shall be the sign that the Lord will heal me, and that I shall go up to the house of the Lord on the third day?' Isaiah said, 'This is the sign to you from the Lord, that the Lord will do the thing that he has promised: the shadow has now advanced ten intervals; shall it retreat ten intervals?' Hezekiah answered, 'It is normal for the shadow to lengthen ten intervals; rather let the shadow retreat ten intervals'. The prophet Isaiah cried to the Lord; and he brought the shadow back the ten intervals, by which the sun had declined on the dial of Ahaz. (2 Kgs 20:8-11)

In this time they said that the sun had moved four times from his accustomed place of rising, and where he now sets he had thence twice had his rising, and in the place from whence he now rises he had twice had his setting; and in the meantime nothing in Egypt had been changed from its usual state, neither that which comes from the earth nor that which comes to them from the river nor that which concerns diseases or deaths. (Herodotus II, 142)

Josiah

Sargon destroyed the kingdom of Israel in accordance with the will of God, because of its idolatry (2 Kgs 17). The immediate reason that God finally decided to destroy Judah (2 Kgs 21) was because of Manasseh's sin of worshipping the Canaanite gods, which had transformed Judah into a nation worse than those whom God had displaced for their sake. The last good king of Judah was Josiah, who was compared to David (2 Kgs 22:2). The biblical writer presented him as a pious king, whose reign had been foretold to Jeroboam by a prophet in 1 Kgs 13:2. He decided to repair the temple, and during the works a discovery was made of a scroll of the Law (2 Kgs 22:8). 2 Kings 23 describes the 'reformation' furthered by Josiah. He gave a public reading of the 'book of the covenant' and brought everything that was related to the cults of Asherah, Baal, and Astarte out of the temple. He suppressed their priests and forbade the sacrifice of children to Moloch. He destroyed those places around the temple that had been raised by Solomon, those of Jeroboam in Bethel, and those of Samaria built by the kings of Israel. Then he celebrated Passover, as in the times of the Judges. Josiah's reformation corresponds to some precepts of Deuteronomy. Moreover, the portrait of the wise king reading the law (Deut 17) matches Josiah, while Solomon did what the king could not do. We saw how Plato had portrayed such a wise and moderate king—a king who would promote the law—in the *Laws*. Second Kings' Josiah takes on this role, while his ancestors, the former kings of Jerusalem, take the role of evil tyrants described in the *Republic*.

Since M. Noth, much of biblical scholarship has assumed that this 'Josianic' reformation was historical and that the law presented as having been 'discovered' in the temple was to be identified with Deuteronomy, written during his reign. Archaeologist Israel Finkelstein tried unsuccessfully to confirm this theory by showing how, in the seventh century B.C.E., cults outside of Jerusalem had been suddenly abandoned.[6] I do not believe that these data are sufficient to confirm that either the Bible or the 'Deuteronomistic History' was written during Josiah's reign. On the contrary, the story of the finding of the law should not be read within a 'rationalizing paraphrase', but it is rather a decisive part of the biblical myth of the divine gift of the law. Josiah is the last pious king. His piety came too late, after God had already determined the fate of Judah. Josiah's story is meant to show the reader how for centuries the law of God had been forgotten by Israel, yet was found again in the temple. Israel constantly disobeyed God and his Law, even forgetting it for centuries. This had brought about the disasters of the Assyrian and Babylonian invasions. Like Josiah, and even more so like Ezra, the reader of the Bible is invited to 'come back' to God's law, 'with all his heart'. There is nothing historical in this reformation; that is to say that there is probably nothing that concerns the Bible as we know it, since at least four centuries separate its writer from the real Josiah. Even if there had been an historical king with the name Josiah, his role in the Bible is no more historical than that of Moses, who wrote the law. This 'book within a book' hides the writer's source of inspiration—Plato's *Laws*.[7]

Note the following citations:

> Now the rest of the acts of Josiah, and all that he did, are they not written in the Book of the Annals of the Kings of Judah? In his days Pharaoh Neco king of Egypt went up to the king of Assyria to the river Euphrates. King Josiah went to meet him; but when Pharaoh Neco met him at Megiddo, he killed him. His servants carried him dead in a chariot from Megiddo, brought him to Jerusalem, and buried him in his own tomb. The people of the land took Jehoahaz son of Josiah, anointed him, and made him king in place of his father. (2 Kgs 23:28-30)

6. Finkelstein and Silberman, *The Bible Unearthed*, 292.

7. Stott, *Why Did They Write This Way?*, 99-100, shows that the discovery of the book of the law is echoed notably in Livy (40, 29) and Plutarch (*Numa* 22:4-5). The books of the laws of King Numa of Rome were said to have been discovered in his grave, centuries after his death. For Stott, the use of the motif of lost and found books of laws may have been a literary technique meant to bolster the credibility of the narrative, which sometimes served to hide the actual sources of the writer.

Thus having ceased from the work of the channel, Necos betook himself to waging wars, and triremes were built by him, some for the Northern Sea and others in the Arabian gulf for the Erythraian Sea; and of these the sheds are still to be seen. These ships he used when he needed them; and also on land Necos engaged battle at Magdolos with the Syrians, and conquered them; and after this he took Cadytis, which is a great city of Syria: and the dress which he wore when he made these conquests he dedicated to Apollo, sending it to Branchidai of the Milesians. After this, having reigned in all sixteen years, he brought his life to an end, and handed on the kingdom to Psammis his son. (Herodotus II, 159)

Again, the biblical writer disguises his sources: Herodotus mentioned a battle pitting Pharaoh Neco against the 'Syrians', and engaged them in the battle of Magdolos, while 2 Kings suggests that it was the 'Annals of the kings of Judah' which recounted how Pharaoh Neco killed Josiah at Meggido. Apparently, 'Magdolos' stands for the biblical narrative's 'Meggido'. 'Cadytis' is 'Gaza'. For Wesselius, the biblical writer had intended for the reader of Herodotus to identify the 'Syrians of Palestine' with the Judeans of the Bible.[8]

The Fall of Jerusalem / Sestos

Wesselius[9] also noted that both Herodotus' *Histories* and 2 Kings end abruptly with the fall of a great city:

To this town of Sestos, since it was the greatest stronghold of those in that region, men had come together from the cities which lay round it, when they heard that the Hellenes had arrived at the Hellespont, and especially there had come from the city of Cardia Oiobazos a Persian, who had brought to Sestos the ropes of the bridges. The inhabitants of the city were Aiolians, natives of the country, but there were living with them a great number of Persians and also of their allies… Those however who were within the walls had now come to the greatest misery, so that they boiled down the girths of their beds and used them for food; and when they no longer had even these, then the Persians and with them Artaÿctes and Oiobazos ran away and departed in the night, climbing down by the back part of the wall, where the place was left most unguarded by the enemy; and when day came, the men of the Chersonese signified to the Athenians from the towers concerning that which had happened, and opened the gates to them. So the greater number of them went in pursuit, and the rest occupied the city. Now Oiobazos, as he was escaping into Thrace, was caught by the Apsinthian Thracians and sacrificed to their native god Pleistoros with their rites, and the rest who were with him they slaughtered

8.　Wesselius, *The Origin of the History of Israel*, 96.
9.　Ibid., 45.

in another manner: but Artaÿctes with his companions, who started on their flight later and were overtaken at a little distance above Aigospota-moi, defended themselves for a considerable time and were some of them killed and others taken alive: and the Hellenes had bound these and were bringing them to Sestos, and among them Artaÿctes also in bonds together with his son... They brought him therefore to that headland to which Xerxes made the passage across, or as some say to the hill which is over the town of Madytos, and there they nailed him to boards and hung him up; and they stoned his son to death before the eyes of Artaÿctes himself. (Herodotus IX, 115, 118-20; cf. 2 Kgs 24:20–25:7)

Herodotus' *Histories* end with the fall of Sestos. Exactly as in the fall of Jerusalem, the city is besieged, its leaders leave by night; they are caught, the king is chained and his son killed in front of him. There are two other paragraphs that recall Cyrus, wiser than his grandson Xerxes (who tried and failed to invade Greece). Wesselius understands that the conquest of Joshua failed similarly, as Israel had proven itself to be unworthy of its election and was chased from the Promised Land (God had threatened this already in Leviticus and Deuteronomy). According to Wesselius, the biblical writer deliberately chose the fall of Sestos as a model for the fall of Jerusalem—a last homage to his main source of inspiration. The nine books of the 'Primary History' end the same as the nine books of Herodo-tus do. Moreover, soon after the biblical events, the historical Cyrus rose to conquer Babylon, thus closing the 'chronological loop' joining 2 Kings to Herodotus I. After Jerusalem is destroyed, the people of Judah flee to Egypt, while the elite are deported to Babylon. Of those deported, some will dwell in the Persian Empire—as in the book of Esther.

'Estherodotus'

It has been long noticed that the two heroes of the book of Esther bear the names of Babylonian deities, Marduk and Ishtar in their Hebrew form, Mordecai and Esther. The book of Esther tells of intrigues at the court of Susa, the southern capital of the Persian Empire. Herodotus' third book appears as its main source, and Xenophon is featured as well:

This happened in the days of Ahasuerus, the same Ahasuerus who ruled over one hundred and twenty-seven provinces from India to Ethiopia. (Est. 1:1)

That Cyrus' empire was the greatest and most glorious of all the kingdoms in Asia—of that it may be its own witness. For it was bounded on the east by the Indian Ocean, on the north by the Black Sea, on the west by Cyprus and Egypt, and on the south by Ethiopia. (Xenophon, *Cyropaedia* VIII, 8, 1)

A few lines later, Xenophon criticises how the Persians drank too much at banquets:

> They had also the custom of not bringing pots into their banquets, evidently because they thought that if one did not drink to excess, both mind and body would be less uncertain. So even now the custom of not bringing in the pots still obtains, but they drink so much that, instead of carrying anything in, they are themselves carried out when they are no longer able to stand straight enough to walk out... But since Artaxerxes and his court became the victims of wine, they have neither gone out themselves in the old way nor taken the others out hunting. (Xenophon, *Cyropaedia* VIII, 8, 10-12)

> Drinks were served in golden goblets, goblets of different kinds, and the royal wine was lavished in accordance with the bounty of the king. Drinking was by flagons, without restraint; for the king had given orders to all the officials of his palace to do as each one desired. Furthermore, Queen Vashti gave a banquet for the women in the palace of King Ahasuerus. (Est. 1:7-9)

During that banquet Ahasuerus gets too drunk, and wants to show his wife Vashti to his subjects wearing the royal crown—but she refuses. The name of Queen Vashti reiterates that of Queen Atossa (considering that the Hebrew *waw* corresponds to the Greek *o*), the daughter of Cyrus, wife of Darius and mother of Xerxes:

> Moreover Dareios made the most noble marriages possible in the estimation of the Persians; for he married two daughters of Cyrus: Atossa and Artystone, of whom the one, Atossa, had before been the wife of Cambyses her brother and then afterwards of the Magian, while Artystone was a virgin. (Herodotus III, 88)

When Vashti refuses to show herself, Ahasuerus rejects Vashti and decides to look for a new queen. Rabbinic exegesis understood that Ahasuerus' request for the queen to appear 'wearing the royal crown' meant that she must wear nothing else; therefore she refused to appear naked. The first story told by Herodotus is that of King Candaules of Lydia, who wanted to show off his wife naked to his counsellor Gyges:

> This Candaules then of whom I speak had become passionately in love with his own wife; and having become so, he deemed that his wife was fairer by far than all other women; and thus deeming, to Gyges the son of Daskylos (for he of all his spearmen was the most pleasing to him), to this Gyges, I say, he used to impart as well the more weighty of his affairs as also the beauty of his wife, praising it above measure: and after no long time, since it was destined that evil should happen to Candaules,

he said to Gyges as follows: 'Gyges, I think that thou dost not believe me
when I tell thee of the beauty of my wife, for it happens that men's ears
are less apt of belief than their eyes: contrive therefore means by which
thou may look upon her naked'. (Herodotus I, 8)

Candaules, when he considered that it was time to rest, led Gyges to the
chamber; and straightway after this the woman also appeared: and Gyges
looked upon her after she came in and as she laid down her garments; and
when she had her back turned towards him, as she went to the bed, then
he slipped away from his hiding-place and was going forth. And as he
went out, the woman caught sight of him, and perceiving that which had
been done by her husband she did not cry out, though struck with shame,
but she made as though she had not perceived the matter, meaning to
avenge herself upon Candaules: for among the Lydians as also among
most other Barbarians it is a shame even for a man to be seen naked.
(Herodotus I, 8, 10)

The queen then plots with Gyges to overthrow Candaules. Both the first
book of Herodotus and the first chapter of Esther open with the story of a
king wanting to show off the beauty of his wife to his subject(s), leaving
her feeling humiliated. In the book of Esther, Mordecai, the cousin and
tutor of Hadassah, suggests that she try to become the new queen. The
king chooses Esther (her new name), thanks to her great beauty. Through
Esther, Mordecai tries to influence the king in order to avoid the
massacre of the Jews planned by Haman, Ahasuerus' hateful counsellor.
In Herodotus, a story of conspiracy is recounted in book III. A Magian
has killed King Smerdis, brother of Cambyses, and has taken his place
on the throne of Persia. None have seen his face, and even the women of
his harem are not allowed to talk to each other. Seven Persian nobles
suspect the impostor, and start to investigate. One of them, Otanes, has a
daughter among the king's wives:

This Otanes was the first who had had suspicion of the Magian, that he
was not Smerdis the son of Cyrus but the person that he really was,
drawing his inference from these facts, namely that he never went abroad
out of the fortress, and that he did not summon into his presence any of
the honourable men among the Persians: and having formed a suspicion
of him, he proceeded to do as follows: Cambyses had taken to wife his
daughter, whose name was Phaidyme; and this same daughter the Magian
at that time was keeping as his wife and living with her as with all the rest
also of the wives of Cambyses. Otanes therefore sent a message to this
daughter and asked her who the man was by whose side she slept,
whether Smerdis the son of Cyrus or some other. She sent back word to
him saying that she did not know, for she had never seen Smerdis the son
of Cyrus, nor did she know otherwise who he was who lived with her.
Otanes then sent a second time and said: 'If thou dost not thyself know

Smerdis the son of Cyrus, then do thou ask of Atossa who this man is, with whom both she and thou live as wives; for assuredly it must be that she knows her own brother'. To this the daughter sent back word: 'I am not able either to come to speak with Atossa or to see any other of the women who live here with me; for as soon as this man, whosoever he may be, succeeded to the kingdom, he separated us and placed us in different apartments by ourselves'. When Otanes heard this, the matter became more and more clear to him. (Herodotus III, 68-69)

Now Esther had not revealed her kindred or her people, as Mordecai had charged her; for Esther obeyed Mordecai just as when she was brought up by him. In those days, while Mordecai was sitting at the king's gate, Bigthan and Teresh, two of the king's eunuchs, who guarded the threshold, became angry and conspired to assassinate King Ahasuerus. But the matter came to the knowledge of Mordecai, and he told it to Queen Esther, and Esther told the king in the name of Mordecai. When the affair was investigated and found to be so, both the men were hanged on the gallows. It was recorded in the book of the annals in the presence of the king. (Est. 2:20-23)

In both texts, conspiracies are hatched to overthrow the king. Smerdis' impostor will be killed by the seven—led by Darius, who will become the new king and marry Atossa:

After these things King Ahasuerus promoted Haman son of Hammedatha the Agagite, and advanced him and set his seat above all the officials who were with him. And all the king's servants who were at the king's gate bowed down and did obeisance to Haman; for the king had so commanded concerning him. But Mordecai did not bow down or do obeisance. Then the king's servants who were at the king's gate said to Mordecai, 'Why do you disobey the king's command?' When they spoke to him day after day and he would not listen to them, they told Haman, in order to see whether Mordecai's words would avail; for he had told them that he was a Jew. When Haman saw that Mordecai did not bow down or do obeisance to him, Haman was infuriated. But he thought it beneath him to lay hands on Mordecai alone. So, having been told who Mordecai's people were, Haman plotted to destroy all the Jews, the people of Mordecai, throughout the whole kingdom of Ahasuerus. (Est. 3:1-6)

Thus they answered Hydarnes; and then, after they had gone up to Susa and had come into the presence of the king, first when the spearmen of the guard commanded them and endeavoured to compel them by force to do obeisance to the king by falling down before him, they said that they would not do any such deed, though they should be pushed down by them head foremost; for it was not their custom to do obeisance to a man, and it was not for this that they had come. (Herodotus VII, 136)

These two men were Spartan heralds sent to meet Xerxes. Like Mordecai, they refused to make obedience to another man. After Haman decided to exterminate the Jews, Mordecai heard about the plot. He sent a message to Esther, asking her to speak to the king in favour of the Jews:

> Hathach went and told Esther what Mordecai had said. Then Esther spoke to Hathach and gave him a message for Mordecai, saying, 'All the king's servants and the people of the king's provinces know that if any man or woman goes to the king inside the inner court without being called, there is but one law—all alike are to be put to death. Only if the king holds out the golden sceptre to someone, may that person live. I myself have not been called to come in to the king for thirty days.' (Est. 4:9-11)

When the seven conspirators have overthrown the Magian, they bestow privileges upon themselves:

> These were special gifts for Otanes; and this they also determined for all in common, namely that any one of the seven who wished might pass in to the royal palaces without any to bear in a message, unless the king happened to be sleeping with his wife; and that it should not be lawful for the king to marry from any other family, but only from those of the men who had made insurrection with him. (Herodotus III, 84)

The model for the character of Mordecai appears in the Greek character Demokedes, a prisoner deported from Greece who became Darius' doctor and advisor:

> Then after this, when Dareios had committed the case to him, by using Hellenic drugs and applying mild remedies after the former violent means, he caused him to get sleep, and in a short time made him perfectly well, though he had never hoped to be sound of foot again. Upon this Dareios presented him with two pairs of golden fetters; and he asked him whether it was by design that he had given to him a double share of his suffering, because he had made him well. Being pleased by this saying, Dareios sent him to visit his wives, and the eunuchs in bringing him in said to the women that this was he who had restored to the king his life. Then each one of them plunged a cup into the gold-chest and presented Demokedes with so abundant a gift that his servant, whose name was Skiton, following and gathering up the coins which fell from the cups, collected for himself a very large sum of gold. (Herodotus III, 130)

> Then Demokedes having healed King Dareios had a very great house in Susa, and had been made a table-companion of the king; and except the one thing of returning to the land of the Hellenes, he had everything. And first as regards the Egyptian physicians who tried to heal the king before him, when they were about to be impaled because they had proved inferior to a physician who was a Hellene, he asked their lives of the king and rescued them from death: then secondly, he rescued an Eleian prophet,

who had accompanied Polycrates and had remained unnoticed among the
slaves. In short Demokedes was very great in the favour of the king.
(Herodotus III, 132)

This portrait not only is reminiscent of Mordecai but of Joseph, Daniel
and Zerubbabel as well. This Demokedes, like Mordecai, will try to
influence the king's politics through the queen. After Demokedes heals
Queen Atossa of a tumour, he then asks her to speak to the king:

So when after this by his treatment he had made her well, then Atossa
instructed by Demokedes uttered to Dareios in his bedchamber some such
words as these: 'O king, though thou hast such great power, thou dost sit
still, and dost not win in addition any nation or power for the Persians... I
pray thee, make an expedition against Hellas; for I am desirous to have
Lacedemonian women and Argive and Athenian and Corinthian, for attendants, because I hear of them by report: and thou hast the man who of all
men is most fitted to show thee all things which relate to Hellas and to be
thy guide, that man, I mean, who healed thy foot.' Dareios made answer:
'Woman, since it seems good to thee that we should first make trial of
Hellas, I think it better to send first to them men of the Persians together
with him of whom thou speak, to make investigation, that when these have
learnt and seen, they may report each several thing to us; and then I shall
go to attack them with full knowledge of all'. (Herodotus III, 134)

By this, Demokedes hopes to be able to gain his freedom upon reaching
Greece, but he has actually launched a war that will continue through
Xerxes' reign. Mordecai tells Queen Esther to speak to the king so that
the Jews will not be massacred:

On the third day Esther put on her royal robes and stood in the inner court
of the king's palace, opposite the king's hall. The king was sitting on his
royal throne inside the palace opposite the entrance to the palace. As soon
as the king saw Queen Esther standing in the court, she won his favour and
he held out to her the golden sceptre that was in his hand. Then Esther
approached and touched the top of the sceptre. The king said to her, 'What
is it, Queen Esther? What is your request? It shall be given you, even to
the half of my kingdom.' Then Esther said, 'If it pleases the king, let the
king and Haman come today to a banquet that I have prepared for the
king'. (Est. 5:1-4)

Esther organises a banquet for the king, and for Haman to be an honoured guest. After the first day of the banquet Haman goes home happy,
thinking that he has the favour of the queen:

Haman went out that day happy and in good spirits. But when Haman saw
Mordecai in the king's gate, and observed that he neither rose nor trembled before him, he was infuriated with Mordecai; nevertheless, Haman
restrained himself and went home. Then he sent and called for his friends

and his wife Zeresh, and Haman recounted to them the splendour of his riches, the number of his sons, all the promotions with which the king had honoured him, and how he had advanced him above the officials and the ministers of the king. Haman added, 'Even Queen Esther let no one but myself come with the king to the banquet that she prepared. Tomorrow also I am invited by her, together with the king. Yet all this does me no good so long as I see the Jew Mordecai sitting at the king's gate'. Then his wife Zeresh and all his friends said to him, 'Let a gallows fifty cubits high be made, and in the morning tell the king to have Mordecai hanged on it; then go with the king to the banquet in good spirits'. This advice pleased Haman, and he had the gallows made. (Est. 5:9-14)

When Harpagos heard this, he did reverence and thought it a great matter that his offence had turned out for his profit and moreover that he had been invited to dinner with happy augury; and so he went to his house. And having entered it straightway, he sent forth his son, for he had one only son of about thirteen years old, bidding him go to the palace of Astyages and do whatsoever the king should command; and he himself being overjoyed told his wife that which had befallen him. But Astyages, when the son of Harpagos arrived, cut his throat and divided him limb from limb, and having roasted some pieces of the flesh and boiled others he caused them to be dressed for eating and kept them ready. (Herodotus I, 119)

Harpagos, like Haman, is happy to have been invited by the king to a banquet. Harpagos does not know that he will be served his own son to eat (as in the myth of Atreus and Thyestes). Haman, however, will be executed instead of Mordecai, for in her revelation to the king that she is Jewish, Esther denounced Haman:

So the king and Haman went in to feast with Queen Esther. On the second day, as they were drinking wine, the king again said to Esther, 'What is your petition, Queen Esther? It shall be granted you. And what is your request? Even to the half of my kingdom, it shall be fulfilled.' Then Queen Esther answered, 'If I have won your favour, O king, and if it pleases the king, let my life be given me—that is my petition—and the lives of my people—that is my request. For we have been sold, I and my people, to be destroyed, to be killed, and to be annihilated. If we had been sold merely as slaves, men and women, I would have held my peace; but no enemy can compensate for this damage to the king.' Then King Ahasuerus said to Queen Esther, 'Who is he, and where is he, who has presumed to do this?' Esther said, 'A foe and enemy, this wicked Haman!' Then Haman was terrified before the king and the queen. (Est. 7:1-6)

The theme of a banquet organised by the queen, during which the king must not refuse anything she may ask, is also found at the very end of Herodotus' book IX:

She waited then until her husband Xerxes had a royal feast set before him: this feast is served up once in the year on the day on which the king was born, and the name of this feast is in Persian tycta, which in the tongue of the Hellenes means 'complete'; also on this occasion alone the king washes his head, and he makes gifts then to the Persians: Amestris, I say, waited for this day and then asked of Xerxes that the wife of Masistes might be given to her. And he considered it a strange and untoward thing to deliver over to her his brother's wife, especially since she was innocent of this matter; for he understood why she was making the request. At last however as she continued to entreat urgently and he was compelled by the rule, namely that it is impossible among them that he who makes request when a royal feast is laid before the king should fail to obtain it, at last very much against his will consented. (Herodotus IX, 110-11)

Haman will be hanged on the very gallows upon which he had prepared to hang Mordecai. The king agreed to revoke the orders to kill the Jews throughout the empire; instead, the Jews massacred their enemies that had planned to kill them. That day became the feast of Purim. Even that aetiology can be found in Herodotus, after the seven killed the Magians:

Now in the twelfth month, which is the month of Adar, on the thirteenth day, when the king's command and edict were about to be executed, on the very day when the enemies of the Jews hoped to gain power over them, but which had been changed to a day when the Jews would gain power over their foes, the Jews gathered in their cities throughout all the provinces of King Ahasuerus to lay hands on those who had sought their ruin; and no one could withstand them, because the fear of them had fallen upon all peoples. All the officials of the provinces, the satraps and the governors, and the royal officials were supporting the Jews, because the fear of Mordecai had fallen upon them. For Mordecai was powerful in the king's house, and his fame spread throughout all the provinces as the man Mordecai grew more and more powerful. So the Jews struck down all their enemies with the sword, slaughtering, and destroying them, and did as they pleased to those who hated them. In the citadel of Susa the Jews killed and destroyed five hundred people… Mordecai recorded these things, and sent letters to all the Jews who were in all the provinces of King Aha-suerus, both near and far, enjoining them that they should keep the fourteenth day of the month Adar and also the fifteenth day of the same month, year by year, as the days on which the Jews gained relief from their enemies, and as the month that had been turned for them from sorrow into gladness and from mourning into a holiday; that they should make them days of feasting and gladness, days for sending gifts of food to one another and presents to the poor. So the Jews adopted as a custom what they had begun to do, as Mordecai had written to them. (Est. 9:1-7, 20-23)

So when they had slain the Magians and cut off their heads, they left behind those of their number who were wounded, both because they were unable to go, and also in order that they might take charge of the fortress, and the five others taking with them the heads of the Magians ran with shouting and clashing of arms and called upon the other Persians to join them, telling them of that which had been done and showing the heads, and at the same time they proceeded to slay every one of the Magians who crossed their path. So the Persians when they heard of that which had been brought to pass by the seven and of the deceit of the Magians, thought good themselves also to do the same, and drawing their daggers they killed the Magians wherever they found one; so that if night had not come on and stopped them, they would not have left a single Magian alive. This day the Persians celebrate in common more than all other days, and upon it they keep a great festival which is called by the Persians the festival of the slaughter of the Magians, on which no Magian is permitted to appear abroad, but the Magians keep themselves within their houses throughout that day. (Herodotus III, 79)

In the face of these strikingly detailed parallels, some conclusions can be drawn: (1) the technique of borrowing and adapting story patterns from Herodotus is exactly the same as in Genesis–Kings, and the author borrowed primarily those stories concerning the Persians and Susa; (2) the themes from Herodotus found in Esther were not used in Genesis–Kings—this economy of the themes is significant, as such balance hardly results from chance; (3) the book of Esther tells a story that took place a few decades after the events narrated in 2 Kings, and Mordecai (who bears a Babylonian name) is a descendant of the people deported to Babylon; (4) Ahasuerus, Vashti and Esther do not correspond clearly to any particular Persian sovereigns because they are a composite of Persian characters found in Herodotus. If Ahasuerus were Xerxes, then Atossa/ Vashti should be his mother, not his wife. Darius' other wife Artystone can be identified with Esther, but the same problem arises. As in Genesis and Exodus, the pharaohs cannot be clearly identified, yet we saw that they were mostly inspired by Herodotus' second book. In the Septuagint, Ezra 4:6 translates 'Ahasuerus' as 'Xerxes'.

On the basis of these four correspondences, I believe it likely that the same person who wrote Genesis–Kings also wrote the book of Esther; the evidence being that all these books took their departure from Herodotus. The book of Esther, as well as those of Ezra and Nehemiah, in general, speak well of Persian rulers but remain completely silent about the main subject of Herodotus' *Histories*—the great campaigns of Darius and Xerxes to conquer Greece. This silence is very significant, as if the Jews of the Bible could not have known anything of the Greeks, even during the Persian era, the time during which classic literature arose in Greece. Herodotus, however, relates how all those peoples who submitted to the Persian Empire were engaged in the war against Greece, notably the 'Syrians of Palestine' (Herodotus VII, 79). Judeans were, therefore, likely a part of this contingent, but the biblical writer chose not to refer to this probable encounter between his people and the Greeks. Esther's author could have known Persian stories from the two centuries of Persian domination, yet I believe that this writer lived in the Hellenistic era and therefore would not have known of the Persian domination at first hand. He drew his work rather from Greek sources, such as Herodotus and Xenophon.

10.

Conclusions

I believe that I have successfully demonstrated that the point of departure for the biblical literature was in Greek classical literature. I am guided by Lévi-Strauss' important principle that any myth consists of all of its variants.[1] Accordingly, a myth is always foreign—always a 'translation' from another version coming from another culture; yet the believers of a myth are never eager to admit this—it is the work of the structural analyst to show it.[2] The case of the Bible indeed verifies this assumption. The strongest argument against the thesis of the present work would be that, if it were true, it would have been realised long ago. How could generations of scholars have missed the point? This question is important and needs to be answered. I wish to conclude by reviewing three authors outside of the field of biblical studies (other than Lévi-Strauss) who, in their respective fields of philosophy, psychology and sociology, have come close to my own conclusions. This may sound presumptuous, yet Nietzsche, Freud and Bourdieu all wrote that *something* in the functioning of our culture seemed both hidden and repressed.

Nietzsche

The Bible now appears to us as a platonic book and, in matters of philosophy, probably no one has written against Plato with such fierceness as has Nietzsche. Nietzsche opposed Christianity, which he held to be a 'Platonism for the people'.[3] On the other hand, he admired the literary style of the Old Testament, while accusing the priests of the Second Temple (who, according to him, wrote the Bible) of producing a gigantic literary falsification. Nietzsche's harshness toward the Jewish and Christian religions, combined with the fact that his works were upheld (and falsified) by the Nazi regime has raised a suspicion of anti-

1. Lévi-Strauss, '*La structure des mythes*'.
2. Lévi-Strauss, *L'homme nu*, 576.
3. F. Nietzsche, '*Par-delà Bien et Mal*', Paris, Gallimard, 1971, 18.

Semitism. However, his works are full of passages where he sincerely and strongly condemns the wave of anti-Semitism that was growing in Germany, together with its nationalism.[4]

In 'Untimely Meditations', in the section 'On use and abuse of history for life', Nietzsche denounces the problem of history. Throughout the nineteenth century, German society was all too fond of History, which, for Nietzsche, was unhealthy. For him, history needed to serve life in the immediate, not the reverse. Too much history is harmful to humans, to individuals, a people or even a civilisation. One must be able to forget. The great men of action, he thought, were always unhistorical. Historians look for the meaning of the present in the past. The metaphysical conception of history is what is criticised here, much as Lévi-Strauss later explains how history plays the role of a myth in the dominant philosophical system of modernism.[5]

How does the notion of good and evil arise? That is the question of the first treatise of 'On the Genealogy of Morals'. The answer is because a sacerdotal class, full of resentment against those in power, invent stories to gain all the rights. The priests have no power in the face of aristocratic warriors, so the priests take vengeance upon them. The strong will be considered evil and the weak will be seen as good. Nietzsche believed that Judaism was born from the resentment of the Jewish priests toward the great empires that dominated Judea throughout history: Assyria, Babylon, Persia and Greece. But when he speaks of Christianity, Nietzsche identifies the Roman Empire as the source of the Jews' grudge. His point is that the figure of Christ is a Jewish invention, even though the Jews did not follow him. Nietzsche was perhaps close to finding out that the Old Testament is in fact itself a platonic book, with Greek origins. The 'genealogy of morals' Nietzsche wished to discover has been reconstructed: Socrates taught Plato, the anonymous biblical writer learnt platonic philosophy and wrote the Bible, and the founder of Christianity, perhaps Paul, completed the picture and brought that new religion to the Roman Empire. In 'The Antichrist', Nietzsche believes that Christianity is not in opposition with Judaism, as held by theology, but is its perfect continuation.

Nietzsche's intuition has been confirmed by my analysis: the priests of the Second Temple rewrote the history of Israel in order to make it look like the divine law had been revealed long ago, but that the people had forgotten it. It was subsequently 'discovered' again and published. The

4. See F. Nietzsche *Humain, trop humain*, vol. I, Paris, Gallimard, 1988, or *Beyond Good and Evil* for explicit condemnations of anti-Semitism.

5. Lévi-Strauss, *La pensée sauvage*, Paris: Plon, 1962.

so-called reformation of Josiah, still believed to be historical by modern theologians and biblical scholars, is nothing more than a noble lie that was probably similar to the strategy used when the Bible itself was published. Christian priests and theologians relayed the role of the Jewish priests in that lie until this day.

Nietzsche's 'Antichrist' is much more than an atheist pamphlet against religion. He knew that historians of his time were allied with theology, and that they only meant to reproduce the initial falsification in the Bible. Nietzsche tried to understand how the Christian religion had succeeded in becoming so powerful, believing that its origins would be found in Judaism, but his harshness earned him the undue reputation of being anti-Semitic (the title of his last work, 'The Antichrist', says who he was really against). At the same time, though, he did understand well the platonic roots of Christianity. He could have managed to complete his genealogy of morals, had he not lost his mind after finishing *'The Antichrist'*. In the preface of *Beyond Good and Evil*, Nietzsche thought that Plato was a pre-Christian philosopher, and that Christianity is a 'Platonism for the people'.

If we compare the character of Jesus in the New Testament to Socrates in the platonic dialogues, many lines of similarity appear, for both taught new religious ideas to their disciples. Socrates criticised the traditional vision of the Greek gods, so much so that he was accused of denying their existence. His unjust trial led to his execution (Plato, *The Apology of Socrates*), yet he never complained and refused to escape (Plato, *Crito*). Death was not the end, as he explained to his friends and disciples, for the soul is eternal and will come back to life (Plato, *Phaedo*). It is likely that Socrates believed in a monotheistic form of god, and that his disciples Xenophon and Plato decided to spread the teachings of their master through writing. Plato carefully avoided denying the existence of the traditional Greek gods openly; instead, he made them the creatures of a nameless god that created the whole universe (Plato, *Republic*, *Timaeus*). The platonic dialogues are the philosophical source for the books of Genesis–Kings, the story of the life and death of Plato's Ideal State. Still, the Old Testament lacked the character of the philosopher that was put to death unjustly by the ignorant masses, who were not ready for his teaching. This is the role allotted to Jesus himself in the New Testament. Socrates' death is in a way the start of the platonic dialogues, while the death of Jesus, the Jewish son of God, appears at the 'end' of the Bible—the New Testament. Jesus plays the role of Socrates, dying in the ruins of the platonic Ideal State that is biblical Israel. Like Socrates, Jesus never wrote anything, and his disciples took it upon themselves to record the teachings of their master after his unjust death.

If the theory of the platonic roots of the Old Testament is correct, then it holds that a platonic movement existed in Jerusalem in the temple. This school probably continued its literary production after the publication of the 'Old Testament', until the figure of Jesus was invented—a perfect mixture of the philosopher Socrates with previous 'dying sons of gods' such as Dionysus, Heracles, Adonis and Romulus.

The Old Testament was never a 'Jewish' book in the first place; rather it is a platonic one that re-writes Greek mythology through a monotheistic filter. The Talmud, which can be seen as 'the Jews' New Testament', is the basis of rabbinic Judaism. Among the books of the Bible, only those that took place before the Hellenistic era were chosen by rabbinic Judaism to be held as sacred.[6] The 'complete' Old Testament (including the Deutero-canonical books, since they show Greek and platonic roots) now appears as a 'pre-Christian' book, and the Triumph of Christianity in the Roman Empire can be explained by the fact that both Testaments are essentially platonic philosophy turned into a religion. In 'Beyond Good and Evil', Nietzsche could not understand how the two Testaments had been joined, as if it were a mistake. Most Jews would agree with him; however, our deeply anchored understanding that the Christian religion was born from Jewish religion is itself a myth. Both religions arose during the first centuries C.E., as divergent interpretations of the Bible.

Freud

In *Moses and Monotheism*, Freud attempts to transpose his theory of repression to monotheistic religion.[7] The work met with little success in the fields of psychology and history of religion, especially since Freud himself admitted in the conclusions that his theory of an Egyptian Moses was not convincing. According to Freud, the real Moses was an Egyptian priest who had known of the monotheistic ideas of Pharaoh Akhenaton. Moses was to have brought these ideas to the first Israelites and freed them, after which they allegedly killed him; after his death they regretted his murder, and Moses' Law thus became sacred as a result of the Israelites' guilt. Freud took his myth of the murder of the father of the primitive horde that he developed twenty years earlier in *Totem and Taboo* and transposed it to the Bible.[8] Both of these essays received very skeptical

6. Lemche, 'The Old Testament: A Hellenistic Book?'
7. Sigmund Freud, *L'homme Moïse et la religion monothéiste*, Paris: Gallimard, 1939 (repr. 1986).
8. Sigmund Freud, *Totem et Tabou—Quelques concordances entre la vie psychique des sauvages et celle des névrosés*, Paris: Gallimard, 1913 (repr. 1993).

criticism, yet based on Freud's intellectual reputation they remain considered and are still published regularly. Frazer's *Golden Bough* was an influence on Freud when he was writing *Totem and Taboo*; *Moses and Monotheism* was a result of Freud having been caught up in the Egyptomania that swept through the first decades of the twentieth century.

However, when reading Freud's last book, written in the last year of his life, one is left with an *uncanny* feeling: the Uncanny (*Unheimlich*), as per Freud, being something that was repressed in one's unconscious, and that resurfaces, creating a feeling of strangeness—a feeling that we may experience when reading Greek myths in regards of their biblical counterparts. According to Freud, the founder of the Jewish religion came from a refined culture, an exogenic origin that was repressed by the people when the religion became a tradition. Freud missed his goal, yet I believe this intuition, in light of my work, was correct. The Austrian psychoanalyst had too much experience in revealing repressed elements in the words of his patients not to be intrigued by something in the Jewish religion. His portrait of an Egyptian Moses that had been raised in a high culture fits with my understanding of the biblical writer, who probably studied Greek philosophy and literature in Alexandria. The very existence of that person was completely lost from the sight of the Judeo-Christian tradition for Moses and the other prophets replaced him. In fact, Freud placed his Moses a millennium too early. By considering the great empires of the ancient Near East for too long, Freud and the biblical scholars failed to understand that the culture from which the Bible actually borrowed its main material did not appear explicitly in the biblical narrative. Egypt, Assyria, Babylon and Persia are actors on the front stage of the Bible, while Greece appears only through sibylline prophecies. We can now suggest a 'Greek Moses' to replace Freud's Egyptian Moses. Freud was conscious of the unlikelihood of his historical reconstruction, but remained convinced of the soundness of his psychological explanation, and we can indeed give him credit for the latter.

Bourdieu

The thesis defended here goes beyond mere structural analysis of myths. It is in some ways a criticism of the whole system of teaching, including that of universities and schools, responsible in the first place for ignoring the Greek roots of the Bible. The institutionalised separation of the involved disciplines—biblical scholarship (mostly confined within Christian theology), Greek studies and philosophy—has contributed to the prohibition against seeing the links between the Bible and Plato. However, no particular actor from the academic milieu can be pointed to as deliberately having 'hidden' that truth. The present work is not a 'conspiracy theory'; all scholars genuinely ignored that possibility, and that ignorance must be questioned.

It is as if repression functions not only on the individual level, but also on the social scale. To explain how these mechanisms of self-censorship take place, I will use sociologist Pierre Bourdieu's theory of teaching from his book *La reproduction*, published with Jean-Claude Passeron.[9] They explain how pedagogical action (PA) is a form of *symbolic violence*, non-physical violence exerted by communication that is at the core of force relations between the dominant and dominated classes. As the State holds the monopoly on legitimate physical violence, as in Weber's classical definition, the pedagogical authority (PAu) has the monopoly on legitimate symbolic violence, which is at least as powerful as physical violence:

> Any power of symbolic violence, i.e., any power that succeeds in impos-
> ing meanings upon others and in imposing them as legitimate by hiding
> the force relations that are at the foundation of its force, enhances its own
> force, i.e., properly symbolic, to these force relations.[10]

Any pedagogical action imposes a cultural arbitrariness that represents the interests of the dominant classes.[11] In the specific case of religious teaching, this arbitrariness appears to me in the tacit decree still taught in schools and universities that biblical narratives are totally distinct from Greek and Roman myths. I remember studying Latin in secondary school and being told that Orpheus looking back at Eurydice was a poetic myth, a remnant of the old civilisation; in Jewish religion class, however, the story of Lot's wife was told as true, the pillars of salt around the Dead Sea an ancient testament to her transformation. I remember noticing how 'Jove' sounded similar to 'Jehova', the latter name being forbidden to pronounce. From one class to another children are told the same stories, and the question of their possible links is put out of sight completely. Therein lies the ultimate arbitrary content of teaching: whereas the Greeks and Romans told 'myths', false stories that have some poetic and grammatical interest, the Bible is held to be a series of revealed stories that happened for real. Only very recent generations have been told that the earlier narratives from Genesis are probably 'myths' as well—the Bible remained history for centuries. The roots of that separation lie in the speeches of the Jewish and Christian apologetic writers of the first

9. Bourdieu and Passeron, *La reproduction*.
10. Ibid., 18. My translation from the French, as in the following quotations.
11. Ibid., 23.

four centuries of the Christian era. Philo, Josephus, Clement, Origen and Eusebius neutralised the critics from the Greco-Roman world that claimed that the Bible had plagiarised their tradition. That neutralisation was a success, and only the texts of the winners were transmitted down to us. Celsus' *True Word* was lost, and we have only Origen's refutation.

Since Christianity became the religion of the Roman Empire, any speech that went against the dominant vision of the Bible's anteriority to Greek literature was simply suppressed. That denial, whose fight against 'pagan' religion took several centuries to win, still prevails today in modern scholarship, as Christianity is still the dominant ideology of the Western world.

For Bourdieu, universities and schools form a system. The elitist schools provide universities with elite students; these future teachers will themselves reproduce the arbitrary culture that has produced them, so effectively that this arbitrary vision is maintained over the generations and presented as the common heritage of the whole society, when it is really just the privilege of the highest classes.[12] The entire truth of the cultural arbitrary never fully appears, for if it did the pedagogical action could not be exerted:

> Logically contradictory, the idea that a PA would be exerted without a PAu is sociologically impossible: a PA that would aim to unveil its objective truth of violence through its exercise, and to then destroy the fundaments of the PAu of the agent, would be self-destructive... As an arbitrary power of imposition which, by the sole fact that it is ignored as such, finds itself recognised as a legitimate authority, the PAu, power of symbolic violence that manifests itself in the form of a right of legitimate imposition, reinforces the arbitrary power that founds it and that it conceals.[13]

With Freud, Nietzsche and Bourdieu, we understand that what is deeply repressed is the relation between Greek literature and the Bible. The concealment of that relationship first was elaborated upon by the biblical writer himself, who found justifications of his own noble lie in Plato's texts, a lie that he was to address to the youth of his 'Ideal State'. This author was probably raised among the elite of the Hellenised Judean priestly class; he may have been instructed at the Library of Alexandria, and even at the platonic Academy of Athens—two institutions that were the ancestors of what eventually became our system of teaching. The Hasmonean State, I believe, is the most likely institution to have had the power to establish the Bible as the official national history of Israel and Judah. There we find a Hellenised princedom, a political power that was

12. Ibid., 25.
13. Ibid., 26, 28.

officially bound to Rome and forced the Edomites to convert (Josephus Flavius, *Ant.* XIII, 9, 1; see also Strabo, *Geog.* XVI, 2, 34). It is probable that 'conversion' to the new biblical religion even took place in Judea. The Hasmoneans may have been a political and religious party that was closely related to the person who wrote the Bible and his team.

The religious war between 'conservative' and 'Hellenised' Jews, as depicted in the books of Maccabees, probably hides a conflict between those who wished to promote the newly written Bible and other Judeans who did not hold that Bible to be sacred. This is a conjecture, but it is likely that the Bible was either written or published with strong political support, and the Hasmonean State is the most plausible candidate for that support. Even though the Bible strongly criticises kingship, its philosophical author may have reached a compromise with the Maccabees— corrupt men of war that were also priests; we can infer ties between the biblical writer, probably a priest himself, and that family. The priests of the Hasmonean State can be identified as the first 'pedagogical authority' that had the monopoly on symbolic violence needed in order to promote the Bible to its sacred status, as the example of forced conversion tells us.[14] Let us remember that during the reign of the Hasmoneans a man coming from Judea-Palestine, Antiochus of Ascalon, became the head of the platonic Academy of Athens—a solid lead that should be explored further in trying to identify the milieu of the biblical writer.

In the terms of Bourdieu, the authority of the Hasmonean priests gained legitimacy through the use of physical and symbolic violence, so that their vision of history and religion became dominant. The high class of the priests managed to obtain power over the lower classes. The latter did not have the intellectual means to refute the truth of the Bible, and while some of them probably did try, their voices were reduced to silence. In a few generations, the Bible was accepted as the official history of Israel. When the Romans destroyed the temple of Jerusalem, the priesthood lost its reason to remain, and the need to establish the pedagogical authority of the rabbis arose. Within early Judaism, the doctors of the Law soon became the only legitimate representatives of the Jewish religion, and they forbade the teaching of 'Greek wisdom'.[15] The con-

14. Lev 19:27 forbids a certain haircut that Herodotus III:8 describes as being that of the Arabs, who imitated their god. This little detail could be relevant as it may show the will of the Bible and its author in including Edomite populations and having them give up their old customs.

15. Talmud of Babylon, *Sota* 49b and *Baba Kama* 87a; where it is related that Gamaliel did study Greek wisdom. Interestingly, Paul claims to be Gamaliel's student (Acts 5:34-39 and 22:3).

frontation of the Bible with its Greek sources was prevented by a deliberate strategy of avoiding them.

Christianity itself developed from the same roots, marking an opening, which was more of a return, to the Greco-Roman world. There, Greco-Roman religion and Platonism took more time to disappear, since they were better rooted. Facing the Christians and the Old Testament, the text that provided them with their legitimacy, 'Pagans' replied that it was a copy of their own traditions. However, the Church Fathers turned that argument against them.

When Constantine converted to Christianity, the Church took its chance to become the new and soon only legitimate pedagogical authority in the Roman Empire. Two centuries later in 529 C.E., the Christian Emperor Justinian decided that the Platonic Academy of Athens, which had existed for a millennium, was to be closed. Thereafter, criticism from platonic philosophers about a possible 'plagiarism' was forever silenced. In both Judaism and Christianity, strategies to impose the truth of the Bible were adopted, and its comparison to other ancient texts was forbidden.

If we consider in this light the modern biblical criticism that saw the rise of the historical-critical method, we now understand it to be a perpetuation of the dogma rather than a true criticism. The paradox described by Bourdieu is playing out. Despite having weakened in the last decades, the theories that search for the sources of the Pentateuch, formulated by theologians, still prevail in biblical scholarship. Theologian is a title that grants one the legitimacy to speak of the Bible, a title that is conferred by the Church—by Christianity. The theologians do not deny the existence of the biblical god, and look for a rational version of the divine inspiration of the Bible. Between the believers, who submit to their authority, and the Church, which provides that authority, only these doctors of theology have the legitimacy to find and prove the origins of the Bible. According to Bourdieu, the pedagogical authority can never reveal the arbitrariness of its content, for it would destroy itself. Therefore, the game of confrontation between different paradigms during the nineteenth and twentieth centuries has only had the effect of diverting the quest for the sources of the Bible to within the Bible itself, a purely circular reasoning; Greek classical literature, although available in any university library, has remained confined to the fields of Greek studies and philosophy. As other humanities sciences were not allowed to enter the biblical field (recall the rejection of Freud's *Moses*, though it is not any more or less scientific than the authorised theories), the biblical discipline remained free to account for its method to these sciences by referring only to the supreme authority of the Church, which ended up admitting to and encouraging the documentary hypothesis. This is all but a minor detail, since what appeared at first to contest Moses' authorship of the Pentateuch has now become a religious dogma.

Thus, even if biblical studies took on an appearance of a scientific speech that challenged the religious dogma, it has not, until very recently, crossed the line of suggesting Greek sources as direct inspiration for the Old Testament, a most unthinkable idea. The ignorance of such a possibility, the reactions of surprise, doubt and sarcastic hostility to my even suggesting it, are the result of more than twenty centuries of symbolic violence, exerted partly on the tacit demand of the believers.

Indeed, for Bourdieu, the speech of the religious prophet is only welcomed because he is the mandated representative of an authority delegated beforehand. In conclusion, the maintaining of the Bible as a sacred text seems to a have little to do with spirituality or belief; rather, it has to do with relations of power between the sacerdotal and aristocratic classes:

> Therefore, the most hidden and most specific function of the teaching system consists of hiding its objective function, in other words to mask the objective truth of its relation to the structure of class relations.[16] If there is only a science of the hidden, the science of society is, by itself, critical. The hidden is, in this case, a secret, and a well-kept secret, even though nobody is appointed to its guard, because it contributes to the reproduction of a 'social order', founded on the concealment of the most efficient mechanisms of its reproduction, and serves the interests of those who have an interest in the conservation of that order.[17]

It is in no way forbidden to read the *Laws* of Plato, nor to read Eusebius' *Preaparatio Evangelica* nor the accurate comparison he had made between the *Laws* and the Bible. The 'secret' is indeed well kept since nobody guards it. In *Langage et pouvoir symbolique*, Bourdieu raises the question of censorship in an intellectual field, based on his own critique of a text by Martin Heidegger. Censorship does not necessarily come from an external authority, or even from the subject that would censor himself. The mechanism comes from symbolic violence, and the ignorance that it supposes:

> Censorship is never as perfect and invisible as when any agent (of the field) has nothing else to say than what he is authorised to say... By imposing the shaping, the censorship exerted by the structure of the field determines the

16. Ibid., 250.
17. Ibid., 250 n. 35.

form…and the content, indissociable of its adequate expression, thus unthinkable (literally) outside of known and recognised forms.[18]

In the case of the Bible, entire generations of scholars felt that they were allowed to speak only of the J, E, D and P sources. The imposition of a precise form in that field goes by a mandatory recognition of the theories produced by theologians, under the penalty of ejection:

> The legitimate works exert a violence which protects them from the vio-
> lence necessary to apprehend the expressive interests that they express only
> in a form that denies them.[19] The form through which symbolic productions
> participate the most directly to the social conditions of their production, is
> also the mean through which is exerted their most specific social effect, the
> properly symbolic violence, that can only be exerted by the one who exerts
> it and endured by those who endure it under such a form that it is not
> understood for what it is and thus recognised as legitimate.[20]

Bourdieu's theory is meant to be the most general possible, and targets all the educative and intellectual fields. However, I believe that the biblical question is paradigmatic of Bourdieu's theory of symbolic violence, as Christianity is the dominant ideology of the Western civilisation. The refusal to recognise the Western roots of that religion, presented as necessarily oriental and Semitic, is the source of the most unbearable and oppressive symbolic violence, exerted on every subject, from believers to atheists, who all ignore that which they should know. Let us underline how the speeches surrounding the Bible that are considered scientific do reproduce the initial denial that the biblical writer himself and his publishers wanted, they who came from the dominant Hellenised priestly and royal classes of Judea (most likely, the Hasmonean State itself). This denial was of the Greek sources; it was a denial of their anteriority, of the Hellenised and platonic character of the Bible. All of this happened together with the absolute paradox of a sophisticated teaching of philosophy that revered Plato as the forefather of Western thought, yet simultaneously dismissed his *Laws* and reduced the debates in which Church Fathers opposed the late platonic philosophers to vain ideological quarrels; denied was the simple possibility of a convergence between Plato's *Laws* and the Bible, even though for seventeen centuries the existence of Eusebius' comparative study had been pointing to a deeply anchored similarity. Christianity is a Platonism for the people—that is the main ideology of our civilisation that has yet to be expressed in its objective truth.

18. Pierre Bourdieu, *Langage et pouvoir symbolique*, Paris: Seuil, 2001, 345.
19. Ibid., 346.
20. Ibid., 347.

Bibliography

Aeschylus, *Tragédies complètes*, Paris: Folio Gallimard, 1982.

Aesop, *Fables*, Paris : Les Belles Lettres, 1960.

Apollodorus, *The Library*, trans. James George Frazer, Cambridge, Mass.: Harvard University Press, 1939.

Apollonius of Rhodes, *Jason and the Golden Fleece (The Argonautica)*, trans. Richard Hunter, Oxford: Oxford University Press, 1993.

—*Argonautiques*, Paris: Les Belles Lettres, 2002.

Astour, Michael, *Hellenosemitica*, Leiden: E.J. Brill, 1965.

Avalos, Hector, *The End of Biblical Studies*, New York: Prometheus Books, 2007.

Balaudé, Jean-François, *D'une cité possible: sur les Lois de Platon*, Nanterre: Université Paris X, 1995.

Bertrand, Jean-Marie, *De l'écriture à l'oralité: une lecture des Lois de Platon*, Paris: Publications de la Sorbonne, 1999.

Bordreuil, Pierre, and Briquel-Chatonnet, Françoise, *Le temps de la Bible*, Paris: Gallimard, 2000.

Bottéro, Jean, and Kramer, Samuel Noah, 'Lorsque les Dieux faisaient l'homme', Paris: Gallimard, 1989.

Bourdieu, Pierre, and Passeron, Jean-Claude, *La reproduction, essai pour une théorie générale de l'enseignement*, Paris: Editions de minuit, 1970.

Bourdieu, Pierre, *Langage et pouvoir symbolique*, Paris: Seuil, 2001.

Brisson, Luc, *Platon, les mots et les mythes, comment et pourquoi Platon nomma le mythe*, Paris: La Découverte, 1994.

Brisson, Luc, and Jean-François Pradeau, 'Introduction', in *Timée—Critias*, Paris: Flammarion, 2001, 321.

Brixhe, Claude, and Monique Bile. 'La circulation des biens dans les Lois de Gortyne', in Dobias-Lalou, ed., *Des dialectes grecs*.

Michèle Broze, Baudouin Decharneux, Philippe Jespers and Danielle Jonckers, *Oralité et Ecriture dans la Pratique du Mythe* (Civilisations 46.1-2; Brussels: Institut de Sociologie de l'Université Libre de Bruxelles, 1998).

Michèle Broze, and Françoise Labrique, 'Hélène, le cheval de bois et la peau de l'âne', in *Le mythe d'Hélène*, ed. Michèle Broze et al., Brussels: Ousia, 2003, 133-87.

Brun, Jean, *Platon et l'Académie*, Paris: P.U.F., 1960.

Calame, Claude, *Mythe et histoire dans l'Antiquité grecque: la création symbolique d'une colonie*, Lausanne: Payot, 1996.

Calame, Claude, and Chartier, Roger, eds, *Identités d'auteur dans l'Antiquité et la tradition européenne*, Grenoble: Jérôme Millon, 2004.

Calmet, Dom. 'Dictionnaire biblique', online: www.456-Bible.com.

Caquot, André, and Sznycer, Maurice, *Ugaritic Religion*, Leiden: Brill, 1980.

Cazeaux, Jacques, 'Le dieu d'Israël, gardien de la fraternité', in *La Cité biblique*, ed. Shmuel Trigano, Pardès 40-41, Paris: In Press Editions, 2006, 40-69.

Cazeaux, Jacques, *Le refus de la guerre sainte—Josué, les Juges et Ruth*, Lectio Divina 174, Paris: Cerf, 1998.

Cazeaux, Jacques, *Saül, David et Salomon*, Lectio Divina 174, Paris: Cerf, 2003.

Cazeaux, Jacques, *Le partage de minuit, essai sur la Genèse*, Lectio Divina 174, Paris: Cerf, 2006.

Cazeaux, Jacques, *La contre-épopée du désert—L'Exode, le Lévitique, es Nombres*, Lectio Divina 174, Paris: Cerf, 2007.

Chamonard, Joseph, 'Introduction', in *Ovide les Métamorphoses*, Paris: GF-Flammarion, 1966.

Clare, R.J., *The Path of the Argo*, Cambridge: Cambridge University Press, 2002.

Clement of Alexandria, *Stromate V*, Paris: Cerf, 1981.

Couloubaritsis, Lambros, *Aux origines de la philosophie européenne: de la pensée archaïque au néoplatonisme*, Brussels: De Boeck University.

Cross, Frank Moore, *The Themes of the Book of Kings and the Structure of the Deuteronomistic History*, Cambridge, Mass.: Harvard University Press, 1973.

Davies, Philip R., *In Search of 'Ancient Israel'*, Sheffield: Sheffield Academic Press, 1992.

Delcominette, Sylvain, *L'inventivité dialectique dans le Politique de Platon*, Brussels: Ousia, 2000.

Dever, William G., *Aux origines d'Israël*, Paris: Bayard, 2005.

Diodorus Sicilus, *Bibliothèque historique*, Paris: Les Belles Lettres, 1973, 1997.

Dobias-Lalou, Catherine, *Des dialectes grecs aux lois de Gortyne*, Nancy: A.D.R.A.; Paris: De Boccard, 1999.

Dumézil, Georges, *Mythe et épopée, I, II et III*, Paris: Gallimard, 1995.

Euripides, *Tragédies*. VIII. Deuxième partie: *Fragments de Bellérophon à Protésilas*, Paris: Les Belles Lettres, 2000.

—*Tragédies complètes*, Paris: Gallimard, 1962.

Eusebius of Caesarea, *La Préparation Evangélique*, Paris: Cerf, 9 vols., 1974–91.

Finkelstein, Israel, and Neil Asher Silberman, *The Bible Unearthed*, New York: Free Press, 2001.

Frazer, James George, *Le Rameau d'Or*, Paris: Robert Laffont, 1983.

Friedman, Richard Elliott, *Who Wrote the Bible?*, San Francisco: Harper One, 1997.

Freud, Sigmund, *L'homme Moïse et la religion monothéiste*, Paris: Gallimard, 1986 (repr. 1939).

—*Totem et Tabou—Quelques concordances entre la vie psychique des sauvages et celle des névrosés*, Paris: Gallimard, 1913 (repr. 1993).

Genette, Gérard, *Figures II*, Paris: Seuil, 1969.

—*Palimpseste, la littérature au second degré*, Paris: Seuil, 1982.

Ginzberg, Louis, *Les légendes des Juifs*, 5 vols., Paris: Cerf, 1996–2004.

Gmirkin, Russell E., *Berossus and Genesis, Manetho and Exodus: Hellenistic Histories and the Date of the Pentateuch*, Library of Hebrew Bible/Old Testament Studies, 433; Copenhagen International Series, 15; New York/London: T&T Clark International, 2006.

Gordon, Cyrus, *Before the Bible: The Common Background of Greek and Hebrew Civilisations*, London: Collins, 1962.

Grabbe, L.L., ed., 'Did Moses Speak Attic', Sheffield: Sheffield Academic Press, 1998.

Grabbe, L.L., ed., *Like a Bird in a Cage: The Invasion of Sennacherib in 701 BCE*, London: T&T Clark, 2003.

Hallo, William, ed., *The Context of Scripture*. I. *Canonical Compositions from the Biblical World*, Leiden/New York: Brill, 1997.

Héritier, Françoise, *Les deux soeurs et leur mère—anthropologie de l'inceste*, Paris: Odile Jacob, 1995.

Herodotus, *L'Enquête*, I and II, Paris: Gallimard, 1964–90.

—*Histoires*, Paris: Les Belles Lettres, 1948.

Homer, *Iliade—Odyssée*, Paris: Gallimard, Pléiade, 1955.

Hesiod, *Théogonie—Les travaux et les jours*, Paris: Arléa, 1998.

Hunter, Richard, *The Argonautica of Apollonius: Literary Studies*, Cambridge: Cambridge University Press, 1993.

Hyginus, *L'Astronomie*, Paris: Les Belles Lettres, 1983.

—*Fables*, Paris: Les Belles Lettres, 1997.

Inowlocki, Sabrina, *Eusebius and the Jewish Authors—His Citation Technique in an Apologetic Context*, Leiden/Boston: Brill, 2006.

Josephus, Flavius, *Les Antiquités Juives*, Paris: Cerf, 2005.

—*Contre Apion*, Paris: Les Belles Lettres, 1930.

Knight, Virginia, *The Renewal of Epic—Responses to Homer in the Argonautica of Apollonios,* Leiden: E.J. Brill, 1995.

Kupitz, Yaakov, 'La Bible est-elle un plagiat?', *Sciences et Avenir*, Hors-série, December 1997, 85-88.

Laks, André, 'Qu'importe qui parle: l'anonymat platonicien et ses antécédents', in *Identités d'auteur dans l'Antiquité et la tradition européenne*, ed. Claude Calame and Roger Chartier, Grenoble: Jérôme Millon, 2004, 99-119.

Lecoq, Pierre, *Les inscriptions de la Perse achéménide*, Paris: Gallimard, 1997.

Lemche, Niels Peter, 'How Does one Date an Expression of Mental History? The Old Testament and Hellenism', in Grabbe, ed., *Did Moses Speak Attic?*, 220-24.

—'The Old Testament: A Hellenistic Book?', in *Did Moses Speak Attic?*, ed. L.L. Grabbe, Sheffield: Sheffield Academic Press, 1998, 287-318.

—'On the Problems of Reconstructing pre-Hellenistic Israelite (Palestinian) History', contribution to the symposium of Aarhus University 1999. Online: http://www.pphf.hu/kat/bib/cikkek/prehellen.pdf.

Lévi-Strauss, Claude, *Anthropologie structurale*, Paris: Plon, Agora Pocket, 1998.

—'Exode sur Exode', *L'Homme* 106-107 (1988): 13-23.

—*Histoire de Lynx*, Paris: Plon, 1991.

—*Mythologiques I: Le Cru et le Cuit*, Paris: Plon, 1964.

—*Mythologiques II: Du miel aux cendres*, Paris: Plon, 1966.

—*Mythologiques III : L'origine des manières de table*, Paris: Plon, 1968.

—*Mythologiques IV: L'homme nu*, Paris: Plon, 1971.

—*La potière jalouse*, Paris: Plon, 1985.

—'La structure des mythes', in *Anthropologie structurale*, Paris: Plon, 1958, 235-65.

—*La voie des Masques*, Paris: Plon, 1979.

Margolies DeForest, Mary, *Apollonius' Argonautica: A Callimachean Epic*, Leiden: E.J. Brill, 1994.

Mauss, Marcel, *Essai sur le don*, Paris: Quadrige P.U.F., 2007.

Mélèze-Modrezejewski, Joseph, *Les Juifs d'Égypte, de Ramsès II à Hadrien*, Paris: Armand Collin, 1991.

Morrow, G.R., *Plato's Cretan City*, Princeton: Princeton University Press, 1960.

Mouze, Létitia, *Le législateur et le poète, une interprétation des Lois de Platon*, Lille: P.U. du Septentrion, 2005.

Na'aman, Nadav, 'The Danite Campaign Northward', *Vetus Testamentum* 55 (2005): 47-60.

Nielsen, Flemming A.J., *The Tragedy in History, Herodotus and the Deuteronomistic History*, Sheffield: Sheffield Academic Press, 1997.

Nietzsche, Friedrich, *L'Antéchrist*, Paris: Gallimard, 1974.

—*Le Cas Wagner–Crépuscule des idoles*, Paris: Flammarion, 2005.

—*Considérations inactuelles*, Paris: Gallimard, 2001.

—*Le Gai Savoir*, Paris: Le Livre de Poche, 1993.

—*La Généalogie de la morale*, Paris: Le Livre de Poche, 2000.

—*Humain, trop humain I*, Paris: Gallimard, 1988.

—*La Naissance de la tragédie*, Paris: Le Livre de Poche, 1994.

—*Par-delà Bien et Mal*, Paris: Gallimard, 1971.

Noth, Martin, *The Deuteronomistic History*, 2nd ed., Sheffield: Sheffield Academic Press, 1991.

Onfray, Michel, *Traité d'athéologie, physique de la métaphysique*, Paris: Grasset, 2005.

Origen, *Contre Celse*, 5 vols., Paris: Cerf, 1967–76.

Orrieux, Claude, and Edouard Will, *Ioudaïsmos—Hellenismos; essai sur le judaïsme judéen à l'époque hellénistique*, Nancy: P.U., 1986.

Ovid, *Les Métamorphoses*, Paris: Flammarion, 1966.

Patai, Raphael, *The Hebrew Goddess*, Detroit: Wayne State University Press, 1990.

Pausanias, *Description of Greece*, trans. James George Frazer, London: Macmillan, 1913.

Pindar, *Alcibiade*, Paris: GF Flammarion, 1999.

—*Critias—L'Atlantide*, Paris: Les Belles Lettres, 2002.

—*Gorgias, Ménon*, Paris: Gallimard, 1950–99.

—*Ion, Ménéxène, Euthydème, Cratyle*, Paris: Tel Gallimard, 1989.

—*Les Lois*, Paris: Les Belles Lettres, 1951.

—*Les Lois*, Paris: Flammarion, 2006.

—*Œuvres complètes, I et II*, Paris: Gallimard, Pléiade, 1950.

—*Œuvres complètes*, Paris: La Différence, 1990.

—*Phédon, Le Banquet, Phèdre*, Paris: Tel Gallimard, 1983, 1985, 1989.

—*Le Politique, Philèbe, Timée, Critias*, Paris: Les Belles Lettres, 1935, 1978, 1985.

—*La République*, Paris: Flammarion, 1966.

Popper, Karl, *La société ouverte et ses ennemis, Tome 1 : l'ascendant de Platon*, Paris: Seuil, 1979.

Pradeau, Jean-François, *Platon et la cité*, Paris: P.U.F., 1997.

Pucci, Pietro, *Ulysse Polutropos, lectures intertextuelles de l'Iliade et l'Odyssée*, Lille: Presses Universitaires du Septentrion, 1995.

Rad, Gerhard von, *Théologie de l'Ancien Testament*, Genève: Labor et Fidès, 1972.

Rendtorff, Rolf, 'The "Yahwist" as a Theologian? The Dilemma of Pentaeuchal Criticism', *JSOT* 3 (1976): 2-9.

Rogue, Christophe, *D'une cité l'autre—Essai sur la politique platonicienne, de la République aux Lois*, Paris: Armand Collin, 2005.

Römer, Thomas, 'L'exégèse et l'air du temps', *Théolib* 16 (2001): 26-39.
—'La formation du Pentateuque selon l'exégèse historico-critique', in *Introduction à l'Ancien Testament*, Geneva: Labor et Fidès, 2004, 67-84.
Ruzé, Françoise, 'Lycurgue de Sparte et ses collègues', in Sineux, ed., *Le législateur et la loi dans l'Antiquité*, 151-60.
Saïd, Edward, *L'Orientalisme—L'Orient créé par l'Occident*, Paris: Seuil, 1997.
Sineux, Pierre, ed., *Le législateur et la loi dans l'Antiquité: hommage à Françoise Ruzé*, Cæn: Presses Universitaires de Cæn, 2005.
Soler, Jean, *L'invention du monothéisme*, Paris: Fallois, 2002.
Sophocles, *Tragédies complètes*, Paris: Gallimard, 1973.
Spinoza, Bénédict, *Traité des autorités théologique et politique*, Paris: Gallimard, 1954.
Strauss, Léo, *La Cité et l'homme*, Paris: Librairie générale française, (1963) 2005.
—*Socrates and Aristophanes*, New York /London: Basic Books, 1966.
Stott, Katherin M. *Why Did They Write This Way? Reflections on References to Written Documents in the Hebrew Bible and Ancient Literature*, New York: T&T Clark, 2008.
Tétart, Gilles, *Le sang des fleurs*, Paris: Odile Jacob, 2004.
Thucydides, *La Guerre du Péloponnèse*, Paris: Gallimard, 1964–2000.
Thompson, Thomas L., *The Historicity of Patriarchal Narratives*, BZAW 133, Berlin/New York: W. de Gruyter, 1974.
—*The Mythic Past*, New York: Basic Books, 1999.
Trigano, Shmuel, ed., *La Cité biblique, une lecture politique de la Bible*, Paris: In Press Editions, 2006.
Van Seters, John, *Abraham in History and Tradition*, New Haven/London: Yale University Press, 1975.
—*The Edited Bible: The Curious History of the 'Editor' in Biblical Criticism*, Winona Lake, Ind.: Eisenbrauns, 2006.
Vidal-Naquet, Pierre, 'Athènes et l'Atlantide', in *Le chasseur noir*, Paris: Maspero, 1981, 335-60.
Virgil, *Les Géorgiques*, Paris: Editions Jules Talandier, 1931.
Voltaire, *Dictionnaire philosophique*, Paris: Gallimard, 1994.
Wellhausen, Julius, *Die Composition des Hexateuchs und der historichen Bücher des Alter Testaments*, 4th ed., Berlin, 1963.
Wesselius, Jan-Wim, *God's Election and Rejection: The Literary Strategy of the Historical Books at the Beginning of the Bible*. Forthcoming (see online http://www.jwwesselius. nl/).
—*The Origin of the History of Israel: Herodotus' Histories as Blueprint for the First Books of the Bible*, London/New York: Sheffield Academic Press, 2002.
West, Martin L., *The East Face of Helicon*, Oxford/New York: Clarendon Press, 1997.
Whitelam, Keith, *The Invention of Ancient Israel: The Silencing of Palestinian History*, Sheffield: Sheffield Academic Press, 1997.
Young, Ian, Robert Rezetko and Martin Ehrensvärd, *Linguistic Dating of Biblical Texts*, 2 vols., London: Equinox, 2008.
Xenophon, *République des Lacédémoniens*, Paris: Garnier, 1933.

Indexes

Index of References

Index of Authors